FOAL

BY DAVID PHILIPPS

Alpha: Eddie Gallagher and the War for the Soul of the Navy SEALs

Wild Horse Country: The History, Myth, and Future of the Mustang

Lethal Warriors: When the New Band of Brothers Came Home

ALPHA

ALPHA

EDDIE GALLAGHER
AND THE WAR FOR THE SOUL
OF THE NAVY SEALS

DAVID PHILIPPS

CROWN
NEW YORK

Published in the United States by Crown, an imprint of Random House, a division of Penguin Random House LLC, New York.

CROWN and the Crown colophon are registered trademarks of Penguin Random House LLC.

LIBRARY OF CONGRESS CATALOGING-IN-PUBLICATION DATA
Names: Philipps, David, author.
Title: Alpha / David Philipps.
Description: New York : Crown, [2021] | Includes index.
Identifiers: LCCN 2021012804 (print) | LCCN 2021012805 (ebook) |
ISBN 9780593238387 (hardcover) | ISBN 9780593238394 (ebook)
Subjects: LCSH: Gallagher, Eddie, 1979– —Trials, litigation, etc. |
Trials (Murder)—United States. | War crime trials—United States. |
Courts-martial and courts of inquiry—United States. |
Iraq War, 2003–2011—Campaigns—Iraq—Mosul. |
United States. Navy. SEALs—Military life. |
Military discipline—United States. | United States. Naval Special Warfare
Command. SEAL Team Seven. Alpha Platoon—Biography. |
IS (Organization)
Classification: LCC KF225.G35 P45 2021 (print) |
LCC KF225.G35 (ebook) | DDC 956.7044/34092 [B]—dc23
LC record available at https://lccn.loc.gov/2021012804
LC ebook record available at https://lccn.loc.gov/2021012805

Printed in the United States of America on acid-free paper

crownpublishing.com

2 4 6 8 9 7 5 3 1

First Edition

Book design by Edwin Vazquez

To Henry, James, Walter,
Wren, Harper, Charlie,
and all the others.

FOREWORD

In any war story, but especially a true one, it's difficult to separate what happened from what seemed to happen. What seems to happen becomes its own happening and has to be told that way.

—Tim O'Brien

T HIS IS A true war story, with all the contradiction that implies. It is the story of dangerous men in dangerous places who had known years of war but never victory, and certainly nothing like peace; a generation of elite fighters who in the absence of any clear end to conflict, had to decide what the hell they were fighting for.

Even in the best circumstances, the facts of any true war story are hard to track down. But through more than two years of research and reporting, I have worked to sift the facts from a pile of confusion, misinformation, and intentional lies. This account braids together interviews with more than two dozen current and former Navy SEALs and more than nine thousand pages of court transcripts and confidential Navy documents. The facts have also been assembled from service records, medical records, performance evaluations, interviews with Eddie Gallagher's family, and videos of law enforcement interrogations. The effort benefited from a trove of more than six thousand text messages sent by Gallagher to friends, his wife, and his superiors, and twenty-three hundred messages sent among the SEALs in Alpha platoon. Those texts gave special insight into the moment-to-moment, unfiltered thinking of Gallagher and his men without the benefit of hindsight. Through it all, Gallagher, who is the main presence in this book, never said a word for the project, despite my attempts to interview him. In public he has denied the darkest accusations made against him, and in court he was acquitted of nearly all wrongdoing. Like the Navy authorities that investigated the platoon, I ran into several SEALs who are included in this account but refused my interview requests. Some had reason to hide what happened, to say nothing, or to lie. What is missing is as telling as what is included.

Because the people I was able to interview inevitably had gaps in knowledge, the details included in this account are supported by multiple sources and, wherever possible, by photos, letters, journals, texts, and videos. The result is the most complete and accurate account ever compiled of the story of Alpha platoon, and perhaps the first book to offer an unvarnished look at life in the SEAL Teams.

I tried to tell the story the way it was told to me. Because of that, the language is often the raw, full-throttle talk of young warfighters, and the accounts of war and death are presented with the same grim, unfiltered details that the SEALs experienced. Despite no shortage of deceit and betrayal, what follows is ultimately a chronicle of hope. Even when hit and knocked down over and over, the SEALs at the core of this fight remained determined never to ring the bell. This is their war story.

CONTENTS

CAST OF CHARACTERS

ALPHA PLATOON, SEAL TEAM 7
(IN ORDER OF RANK AND SENIORITY)

Lieutenant Jake Portier, officer in charge

Lieutenant Junior Grade Tom MacNeil, assistant officer in charge

Lieutenant Junior Grade Alan James (A. J.) Hansen,
assistant officer in charge

Special Operations Chief Edward Gallagher, platoon chief

Special Operator First Class Craig Miller, lead petty officer

Special Operator First Class Dalton Tolbert, sniper

Special Operator First Class Corey Scott, medic

Special Operator First Class Christopher Shumake, sniper

Special Operator First Class Joe Arrington, sniper/Joint Terminal
Attack Controller

Special Operator First Class Dylan Dille, sniper

Special Operator First Class David Shaw, Joint Terminal Attack
Controller

Special Operator First Class Terence Charles (T. C.) Byrne III,
medic/Puma pilot

Special Operator First Class Josh Vriens, sniper

Special Operator Second Class Christian Mullan,
Switchblade pilot

Special Operator Second Class Michael Stoner, mortarman

Special Operator Second Class Joshua Graffam, spotter

Special Operator Second Class Ivan Villanueva, gopher

Special Operator Second Class John Ariens, medic

NAVY EXPLOSIVES ORDNANCE DISPOSAL TECHNICIANS

Chief Petty Officer Joshua Mainferme-McCandless, chief

Petty Officer First Class St. John Mondragon-Knapp, technician

OTHER PERSONNEL ATTACHED TO ALPHA PLATOON

Marine Corps Staff Sergeant Giorgio Kirylo, signals intelligence

Air Force Staff Sergeant Ryan Rynkowski, Joint Terminal Attack Controller

SEAL TEAM 7, TROOP 1 LEADERSHIP

Lieutenant Commander Robert Breisch, commanding officer

Master Chief Brian Alazzawi, senior enlisted advisor

NAVY LEADERSHIP (IN ORDER OF RANK)

Navy Secretary Richard Spencer, civilian executive officer appointed by the president to oversee the U.S. Navy

Chief of Naval Operations Admiral Michael Gilday, a four-star admiral and the active-duty military commander in charge of all U.S. Navy operations

Navy Special Warfare Commander Rear Admiral Collin Green, a two-star admiral in charge of the Navy's eight SEAL Teams and supporting units

Navy Special Warfare Group One Commodore Captain Matthew Rosenbloom, in charge of all SEALs on the West Coast

CHIEF GALLAGHER

THE RING OF vibrating brass Tibetan bowls filled the silent room. It flowed across sailors and Marines stretched out on their backs with their eyes closed. The ancient, wordless chorus of the bells played from a recording in the corner of the room, lapping at the present and washing away tension and nagging thoughts like waves on the shore of a clear, cold lake.

It was September 11, 2018. Special Operations Chief Edward R. Gallagher pulled in a breath as the bells rippled across the silence and his mind floated. The Navy SEAL let his breath go gently and drew in another. Three weeks into an intensive program at a military traumatic brain injury clinic near San Diego, he was finally easing into the rhythm.

The clinic was called the Intrepid Spirit Center, and it was made for guys just like Eddie. It had opened less than a year before to help all the troops who had spent the better part of their adult lives getting battered and blasted by repeated deployments to Iraq and Afghanistan. It was a haven where, finally, they could heal.

Eddie had joined the Navy at age nineteen in 1999, two years before the World Trade Center came down, and had been fighting the war on terror ever since under various official names: Operation Enduring Freedom, Operation Iraqi Freedom, Operation Inherent

Resolve. He'd gone up against Taliban warlords, Baathist insurgents, Shia militia, mujahideen, and crazed ISIS fanatics. For seventeen years Eddie had been in a constant cycle of training and combat. All told he had spent almost four years deployed overseas. Seven deployments, first as a medic in a Marine infantry platoon, then as a Navy SEAL shooter, then finally as a platoon chief. Different jobs, different countries, different years, different wars, same fight.

Eddie looked like a Navy SEAL poster boy. He had close-cropped blond hair, glacier-blue eyes, a strong, square jaw, the shoulders of a lion, and a lion's killer instinct. He was fast, agile, strong, and a dead shot. But a closer look revealed a face deeply lined from years in the desert sun. After so many deployments, the mileage was starting to show. He was thirty-nine years old. In the military, where the average age is twenty-seven, he was closing in on obsolescence. His back hurt. His neck hurt. His shoulders hurt. He had ringing in his ears from too many gunfights. Sometimes he had trouble remembering things. Not that he regretted any of it. For all the talk about post-traumatic stress disorder and the unfair burden the nation had put on its warfighters, Eddie never once saw combat as a hardship. He had chosen it. He was good at it. He thrived on it. Truth be told, it was cool as hell. He loved the heart-pounding exhilaration of gunfights. He loved the simple intensity of war. Sometimes he felt it was the only thing that made sense. If there were bad guys out there looking to take on the United States and become martyrs, he was happy to punch their ticket.

In the SEAL Teams, guys repeatedly described Eddie using one word—a word that in most places is a term of caution but in the Teams is the highest praise: *aggressive*. He was aggressive in training. He was aggressive as a leader. He was aggressive in battle. Now he was trying to bring the same intensity to meditation and healing.

A buffalo drum joined the timeless song of the Tibetan bowls. Eddie kept his eyes closed, oblivious to the patients around him, listening to the rhythmic thump, pulling in slow breaths as if pulling in a line from that deep, silent lake. A woman with wavy brown hair who was leading the therapy quietly urged the group to feel the presence of each joint and muscle fiber in every angle of their fingers, every curve of their spine and every crease in their brow, then let the tension drain away. Feel the weight of the body, the strain. Then relax, reflect, release.

Eddie pulled in a breath. The Intrepid Spirit program included a lot of granola bullshit, to be sure. Not exactly his style. He was an old-school guy. He didn't talk much about his feelings. He didn't complain. He pushed through whatever was coming and moved on. But his wife, Andrea, had kept on him until he agreed to give therapy a try. He was having problems he could no longer avoid. He needed to learn to face them and deal with them. She hoped the program would do him some good.

Andrea. He had known her since high school. The lock screen on his phone was her sky-blue eyes and blond hair, her perfect smile. He considered her his best friend. He didn't know where he would be without her. Divorces were common in the SEAL Teams, but they had held it together through multiple stints overseas. They were raising three kids. To anyone who asked, he said she was his rock, the one who held him steady. Sure, they'd had their scrapes. What SEAL couple hadn't? He was gone so often between training and deployments that maintaining a relationship took real work, especially since he couldn't talk about a lot of what he did. A lot of military couples who lived such separate lives eventually became strangers, even if they stayed together. Andrea had never given up on him. They had tried to learn to communicate better, even if their worlds had to be separate. He felt that they were as strong as ever. So when she pushed him to do this whole Intrepid Spirit thing, even though he doubted that listening to a bunch of hippie music would do any good, he agreed to go. Granola or not, he told himself, if he was going to do it, he would do it like a SEAL: all in, full speed ahead, with all his focus and effort. And actually, after he opened his mind to it, a lot of it was kind of cool. After years of jumping out of planes, fast-roping from helicopters to the decks of bucking ships, and kicking in doors in failed countries where even a lot of the friendlies probably wanted you dead, the granola stuff was a pretty nice change.

There also had been plenty of time to work out, which was Eddie's big thing. He was five-foot-eight and 165 pounds, all of it sculpted muscle. In twenty years he had barely missed a day of running and lifting weights.

Stopping to take a breath and reassess had new resonance for Eddie because he was planning to retire from the SEALs in a few months. That meant for the first time in years of constant training and deploying, he had a few moments to reflect. By nearly any measure he'd had a hell of a career. After spending a lot of his teenage years in trouble, he had decided to set himself straight. One morning in 1999, without telling his family, he had walked into a Navy recruiting station in a strip mall in Fort Wayne, Indiana, determined to enlist. On the wall there was a poster of a SEAL commando coming out of the water with night-vision goggles and a glistening assault rifle. Eddie told the recruiter that was what he wanted to do. The recruiter laughed and said the SEALs are not something you just sign up for. They had to pick you. First Eddie had to decide on a Navy career field, then he could apply and hope to get into the SEALs.

Right now the Navy needs corpsmen, the recruiter told him.

"Sweet, I'll do that," Eddie told him. He had no clue what a corpsman was.

He went to basic, then to the Navy's corpsman school, where sailors learn to be combat medics. He tried to get into the SEALs right away but a war was on and the Navy needed him as a medic. He deployed to Iraq right after the 2003 invasion. He came home and became the medic for a group of Marine snipers. He kept applying to the SEALs. He kept getting told no. But if Eddie had one trait he was known for—aside from aggression—it was that he never quit.

In 2004, after multiple rejections, he finally got the green light to try out for the SEALs. That in itself was another ordeal. The SEALs had a six-month course at their West Coast base in Coronado, California, called Basic Underwater Demolition/SEAL training, or simply, BUD/S. It was designed to attract tough guys who thought they were unbreakable—and then break them. For months the trainees had almost nonstop physical punishment, running on miles of soft sand, swimming in frigid water, carrying heavy logs, sleep deprivation and harassment devised to make students quit. No one got off easy.

The SEAL instructors that trained Eddie were pure muscle and menace. As the students ran through the surf each morning in twin lines, the instructors ran beside them, dealing out endless push-ups in the sand or freezing-cold sessions of sit-ups in the pounding Pacific surf, striking down hubris like ancient gods. If it looked like a guy wasn't suffering, the instructors would make sure to fix that. They wanted to strip students down to nothing to reveal if they had the will to keep going. When things were darkest, when the students' muscles felt like rags, when their feet were too swollen for their boots, when the rasp of the ocean cold rattled in their chests, the instructors encouraged the students to quit. Go ahead, get a hot meal, get some sleep, stop the pain. We understand. Go home. You don't belong. We don't want you here.

There was a brass ship's bell in the northeast corner of the BUD/S training compound. Any student who wanted to quit only had to ring the bell three times. By the time six months was up, seventy-five percent of the students had rung the bell. Eddie was not one of them. After five years of trying to get even a chance at tryouts, he was so energized that the beatdowns and sleep deprivation felt like a reward. They were recognition that he had made it. All he had to do was take the pain. He graduated in 2005 with Class 252. He later called it "the best time I never want to have again."

After becoming a SEAL, Eddie was stationed in Coronado and steadily climbed the ranks of the Teams. He was smaller than most SEALs but tried to make up for it with grit. There was no assignment he would not take. Already a solid combat medic, he focused on building out other skills. He became an expert marksman and sharpshooter with a pistol. He learned to work with explosives and also became a free-fall jumpmaster and an ace with a rocket launcher. He was determined to become the badass he had seen years before on the recruiting poster.

In the down times, Eddie was laid-back. He liked to laugh. He was easy to get along with and usually got the job done. Before long he had a reputation in Coronado as a good dude, a solid Team guy, a real frogman.

Eddie also showed he was a fearless fighter. Along with the seven medals he had for good conduct and achievement, he had two Bronze Stars for heroism with a "V" pinned to the ribbon of each that denoted valor under fire. He'd gotten the first as a journeyman shooter in Afghanistan in 2009, when his squad was searching stalls in a bazaar and came under fire. The write-up described how Eddie rushed through the kill zone, set up an assault on a rooftop, and launched two shoulder-fired rockets, obliterating the enemy position.

The music shifted again. The Tibetan bells faded and the notes of a Native American flute rose in the room like a summer grass. They drifted and bowed. Somewhere behind them the therapist urged the class to focus on their own emotional self, to be aware of the feelings rooted deep inside.

After two Afghanistan tours, Eddie came back, shaved off his big, bushy operator's beard, and in 2010 became an instructor at BUD/S. Now he was one of the bronzed, ripped gods running students through the freezing surf, punishing hubris, and telling men to quit. It wasn't a kind and supportive environment, but that was the idea. Neither was combat. If any shred of weakness made it into the Teams, it could cost lives. The instructors were quality control, the first line of defense.

After a stint as an instructor, Eddie tried to find a way overseas again. Being a Team guy in a platoon, operating in the field, kicking in doors—that was more his speed. He craved action. He wouldn't shy away from any mission. He liked to think of himself as one of those operators the nation could call in to take care of any situation, the shadowy group of pipe hitters who got the job done no matter what. He left BUD/S, transferred to SEAL Team 7, and did a stint in Iraq in 2013, then another in 2015 in an undisclosed country in the Middle East, where his squad was part of a quick reaction force—ready to be dropped anywhere in the region at the first sign of trouble. After a decade in the SEALs, he had built a reputation as a seasoned badass. In the SEAL Teams, where there's no shortage of overachievers revved up on testosterone, that was saying something.

Eddie was promoted to chief right as the SEALs were going from a somewhat obscure commando force to America's military crush. The nation was years into the wars sparked by 9/11 and the American public had stopped trusting leaders who said victory was near. Hope for spreading democracy in foreign lands was in a nosedive; even a grim status quo seemed unlikely, but people still wanted fighters who could take out the bad guys. Enter the SEALs. They were the men who in the absence of broad strategic victory could still deliver wins—the guys who shot terrorists in the face and dropped from helicopters onto cargo ships to free hostages, the guys who killed Osama bin Laden. They were evidence that in the face of repeated military failures, America was still great. And the nation loved them for it.

Men joined the SEALs for all kinds of reasons. Some saw it as a service to the nation or the world. Some were seeking the ultimate physical challenge. Some had something to prove to someone, often themselves. None of those fully described Eddie. Growing up, he loved combat movies, especially the ones that focused on small groups of fighters on the ground: Arnold Schwarzenegger spraying a machine gun one-handed in *Commando*, Charlie Sheen dealing out head shots to terrorists in *Navy SEALs*, and Tom Berenger, slaked in green face paint, stalking through the jungles of Vietnam in one of Eddie's favorite movies of all time, *Platoon*. From those screen-lit hours in movie theaters, he knew that was what he wanted to do. He wanted to be a fighter. When a doctor at the Intrepid Spirit Center later asked Eddie why he joined the military, he said simply, "To go to war."

His last deployment had checked all the boxes. Eddie had been put in charge of Alpha platoon, SEAL Team 7. As chief, he had whipped that group of eighteen men into an elite team of operators. Top marks in almost every measure. And because Alpha was far and away the best, they had been picked for the toughest assignment. In early 2017, they were sent on a classified mission to clear ISIS from the Iraqi city of Mosul. That was real war with a real enemy. The chance of a lifetime. Thousands of hardened jihadi ISIS fighters entrenched in an ancient warren of narrow streets with no choice but a fight to the death.

The mascot of Alpha platoon was a she-devil in thigh-high red stockings with a forked tail and one leg kicked high in the air. Platoon members had her patch Velcroed to their body armor and a mural of her on the wall in their headquarters. They called her the Bad Karma Chick. She got her name from the idea that every good or bad deed piles up on the scales of universal harmony and eventually tumbles down on the present. To most people karma is an invisible, nameless, uncontrollable force. The SEALs saw it differently. They believed that karma was not just visible, it was their job. They were the embodiment of bad karma coming down on bad people. An evildoer could only keep piling negative mojo on the universe for so long before a group of SEALs kicked down his door. The origins of the Bad Karma Chick's name were lost to the young SEALs Eddie led, but the concept had sunk deep into the culture: Alpha was there to make sure that bad things happened to bad people.

Mosul had been something to see—like the setting of the bleakest zombie movie, with a cinematic intensity that made it hard to look away. The coalition hit the city with thousands of air strikes, splintering bridges and smashing buildings to rubble. Iraqi ground forces clawed the city back, block by burned-out block. ISIS responded with truck bombs, booby traps, women in suicide vests, even poison gas. Eddie had been in the thick of it, fighting side by side on the ground with the Iraqi special forces. It was combat all day, every day, in an urban maze that seemed almost designed for killing.

In a few weeks at the height of the battle Eddie saw more action than he had in the first seventeen years of his career. The platoon launched scores of shoulder-fired rockets and missiles and called in more than a hundred air strikes. The chief fired his sniper rifle so much that it seized up and stopped working by the end of deployment. The official count of ISIS fighters killed by the platoon was somewhere around five hundred, but Eddie would often say the real number was probably higher.

It was exactly what Eddie had signed up for: Doing bad things to bad people. Karma. He loved it. When the fight was really revving up, Eddie refused to take a day off. He was either on the heavy machine gun or the sniper rifle day after day. He estimated his personal tally of kills just on the rifle was more than one hundred. He sometimes mentioned offhand that he might have the most kills in the history of the SEALs. Mosul was the type of fight SEALs would talk about for generations. It was Fallujah. It was the bin Laden raid. It was history. Eddie was proud to be a part of it.

After the fall of Mosul in the summer of 2017, the platoon returned to San Diego triumphant. The SEAL leadership gushed about how the guys from Alpha were rock stars. Eddie was rated the number one platoon chief in Team 7. The Navy was going to give him a Silver Star for heroism. His written evaluation from the brass was so polished it almost glowed. At the bottom of the write-up, the commander urged an immediate promotion, typing, "THIS IS A MAN I WANT LEADING SEALS IN COMBAT!"

But rather than pursue a promotion, Eddie decided to retire. When asked why, he said he had seen what happened when enlisted guys like him climbed the ranks. They planned operations instead of doing them. They ended up spending all their time filling out paperwork. They stopped being operators and became managers. Eddie was gifted at war, but he knew he was no ace behind a desk. That had been clear since at least eighth grade. So he figured he would get out of the Navy and get a job as an overseas security contractor—maybe do some of the same work he did in the Navy, but with better pay and less bureaucracy. He was proud of what he had accomplished. Even if the wars he had lived in were endless, he sure as hell had done his part.

So that summer, he and Andrea bought a house near the beach in the Florida panhandle where the water was turquoise and the home prices were half what they were in San Diego. It had a big front porch with a swing and a garage that Eddie could use for his workout cave. Just a few weeks before starting the program at the Intrepid Spirit Center, he had moved the whole family down and gotten them settled. Then he flew back to California. Now with the medical evaluations and meditation classes, he was starting to finally get settled in himself.

The Native American flute swirling in the room was joined by recordings of human voices chanting. Eddie drew in breaths and let them escape. The teacher told the class to sense each part of their bodies, find the tension and pain, recognize the feeling, and then let it drift away. Eddie floated on the lake.

Abruptly the still surface was broken. A voice was speaking to Eddie—not the instructor's voice. He opened his eyes and there was someone else from the Intrepid Spirit Center telling him he needed to come out into the hall for a moment. Eddie sat up and asked why. The man told him that some salty old master chief from the SEALs was out there asking for him—a guy named Brian Alazzawi.

Eddie pushed himself up to his feet. Good ol' Alazzawi. They had deployed together to Mosul. Eddie considered Alazzawi a good dude and the antithesis of the paper-pushing manager type. He was big and bald with a bristly mustache and lots of tattoos. Despite his rank he somehow managed to get out with the boys in the field regularly. They had spent days together in a sniper hide in Mosul, two old-school Team guys hunting terrorist dirtbags. But why was Alazzawi at the Intrepid Spirit Center? The center was at the Camp Pendleton Marine Corps base, an hour north of the SEAL headquarters at Naval Base Coronado.

Eddie grabbed his stuff and walked out of the room. He stopped when he saw Alazzawi. The master chief stood in the hall, flanked by two sailors in camouflage. Their uniforms showed that they were not SEALs but military police. The SEALs didn't often mix with the rest of the Navy and certainly were not in the habit of hanging around with cops. Not a good sign.

"Hey, I need to talk to you real quick," Alazzawi said. He ushered Eddie into a small office just off the hall. One of the police officers closed the door after Eddie stepped in. Small room, two cops: Whatever was going to happen, it wasn't good.

Eddie had other reasons he was trying to get out of the SEALs, things he didn't often mention. There were rumblings about things that had happened in Mosul. There was a formal investigation. It was all bullshit, Eddie assured his wife and friends, but that didn't mean it wasn't real trouble. Eddie had spent months watching the investigation smolder until it abruptly flared up. Naval Criminal Investigative Service agents had raided his house. They had seized his computers and phones and some of his equipment from Iraq. Then they had done nothing for months. Things quieted down, leaving Eddie wondering if the investigation had died or if, at some point, after he had spent the majority of his life doing Uncle Sam's dirty work, his own government was going to come after him.

Now here it was. He watched the master chief pull out a piece of paper.

"We're taking you to the brig," he told Eddie.

Eddie took the paper in his hands and read. It was a signed order calling for his immediate confinement. Eddie had been planning on a week filled with art therapy, meditation, yoga, and a few more sessions with doctors to scan for brain injuries. Instead he was going to jail.

"Can you explain this to me?" Eddie said, looking at his friend.

Alazzawi looked at Eddie, then looked down at the floor. He said he wasn't sure what was going on, he was just following orders, but both men knew what was happening. Eddie saw it as the ultimate betrayal. He had risked his life multiple times for his nation, executed its missions, killed its enemies, done the covert work politicians would probably deny even existed. And now he was going to take the rap.

The two military police officers took Eddie's phone and dropped it in a Ziploc bag. They handcuffed him and led him down the hallway past the meditation room and out into the sunny parking lot, where they put him into a van.

It was the start of a nearly two-year court-martial that hit the Navy SEALs like a missile. Within hours news rippled through the SEAL Teams of the arrest of the great Eddie Gallagher, the platoon chief who had just returned from kicking ISIS ass in Mosul. But as it did, a different story emerged from his platoon. In that story, told by a number of the men who served under Eddie, the enemy had not been ISIS but rather their chief. According to those men, the official accounts of triumph hid a darker reality: that Eddie Gallagher had come unglued, that he had lied to get medals, put men in danger to build up his own glory, shot at women and children and crowds of civilians, and murdered a prisoner in cold blood.

Eddie denied it. And there were few who had reason to doubt him. He was a true warrior and experienced fighter in an organization that prized both, a rising star in the SEALs destined for great things. Also, he was a good dude and friend to many. For them, it was easier to believe the explanation Eddie gave, that the whole thing was a lie. The accusations, he said, all came from misguided, inexperienced new guys in Alpha who in the face of combat had refused to go out on ops and instead had concocted stories to try to cover their own cowardice. Eddie had tried to set them straight in Mosul, and he hadn't done it nicely. He had called them out as the cowards they were. In the Teams, where courage and reputation are everything, the young SEALs knew that if they didn't take the chief down, word would get out and take them down. So they hatched a plan. It's fucked up, Eddie would tell people, I'm being framed.

The battle that emerged over what really happened in Mosul would play out both in public and in private over the next two years. And the collateral damage was so great that it swept through the SEAL Teams and the Pentagon to the White House and ultimately cost the secretary of the Navy his job. It also revealed a darker side of the SEALs, one that had been scuttling beneath the shining white image and heroic Kevlar exterior, down where many SEALs valued loyalty over truth and image over honor, and saw bloodshed as the true yardstick of worth. The battle over Eddie Gallagher became a battle over what the SEAL Teams stood for, and what they would become. The consequences would reverberate for years.

Eddie didn't realize any of what was coming as he was led out of the Intrepid Spirit Center in cuffs. He just knew he was in trouble. He wanted to call his wife. He wanted to call his lawyer. He wanted to call his buddies in the SEALs. He wanted to figure out what the fuck was going on. He kept asking, but Alazzawi and the two cops weren't giving him any answers.

A short van ride brought Eddie to Naval Consolidated Brig Miramar, the largest military prison on the West Coast. He was put in shackles and led through the bureaucratic prison in-processing: name, rank, address, emergency contact.

"Know why you're here?" one of the guards filling out paperwork asked.

"No idea," Eddie said.

"Well, you need to give us a reason," the guard said.

"I don't know," Eddie sighed. "Killing ISIS?"

ALPHA

CHAPTER 1

ALPHA PLATOON

CRAIG MILLER SCANNED the sweaty faces of the SEALs in Alpha platoon, crossed his arms, and allowed a rare, satisfied smile. It was a hot night in the California desert, and they were all pressed into a ramshackle barracks kitchen after a hard week of training—twenty big men yelling and laughing, circling like jackals, shirts off, spilling beer. As he watched the SEALs holler and strut around one of Alpha's newest members, he felt the pride of a job well done. He knew they were one of the best commando teams in the Navy. With Eddie Gallagher above him and a stable of solid guys below, things were finally coming together.

Miller was Eddie's second-in-charge, the lead petty officer of Alpha platoon. Everyone in Alpha called him "the Sheriff," not just because he was the best and fastest gun in all of SEAL Team 7 but because he was a tall Texan who liked to wear cowboy boots and didn't fuck around when it came to laying down the law. The Sheriff had a slim, powerful build, sharp features, and alert, searching eyes like an eagle. He was strict with everyone, including himself. He believed, at his core, in rules, discipline, and order. There was a right way to do things, and if anyone was going to screw around with regs, there better be a damn good reason.

Miller was twenty-eight years old but appeared to most of his men to have stepped through a wormhole from another era. He drove a sun-bleached Jeep CJ that was older than he was, and that he had repaired top to bottom. He wore a classic windup Rolex Submariner watch that was standard issue for frogmen in the 1960s. He loved old architecture and collected postcards of nineteenth-century courthouses. While many SEALs were focused on their next op, Miller studied SEALs lore and traditions.

Miller's father had been a SEAL before him, but his father had refused to steer his son toward the Teams. The crucible of SEAL life was so unimaginably intense that Miller's father believed a man had to reach for it on his own. Miller made up his mind early. He was a high school freshman in 2001 when the towers came down, and from then on was convinced that the nation needed good men to counteract all the bad in the world. Over the next several years he learned to swim and shoot and lug heavy packs while saving up more than $5,000 from summer jobs to buy his own Rolex Sub. The watch was his way of swearing his commitment to the SEALs long before he was old enough to sign papers. He had worn it nearly every day since.

Miller didn't talk a whole lot, but his taciturn bearing hid an iron will. Few in the platoon knew it, but Miller had barely made it through BUD/S. Halfway through training, he had broken his foot. He could have quit or gotten a do-over on medical grounds. Instead, he laced his boot tighter and pressed on. They can carry me out on a stretcher, he told himself, but I'm not ringing that bell. That determination and his skills with a gun had helped him climb fast in the ranks of the SEALs. His formal evaluations dripped with superlatives. Five years after joining, he was the youngest lead petty officer in Team 7.

Well after the sun went down it was still 100 degrees in the desert. Miller looked on as Eddie and the rest of Alpha's SEALs crowded around the kitchen table, their shirts off in the heat. They were all sculpted but lean, pro athletes whose chosen sport was combat. They bellowed like ancient warriors around a fire. At the center of the scrum, seated at the table, was Alpha platoon's newest member, Special Operator Second Class Josh Graffam. His muscles were as tense as a drawn bow. On the table in front of him, the platoon had spread four black pieces of steel. Assembled, they would make a Navy-issued Sig Sauer 9mm pistol.

Six feet away at the other end of the table, also stripped to the waist, sat the newest SEAL from one of Alpha's sister platoons, Bravo. The new SEAL was a mass of muscle, rising so big and broad above the table that he looked like a shaved grizzly bear. Graffam was five-foot-seven and wiry, a fraction of the size. But that didn't matter. This was a contest of skill and speed. Spread in front of the bear was the same array of pistol parts. In the middle of the table, a short lunge from both men, stood a magazine holding a single round of ammunition.

It was April 2016—almost a year before Alpha platoon deployed to Mosul. Eddie had become Alpha's new platoon chief just a few months earlier. The two platoons were at a remote Navy installation called La Posta in the dry, rocky Laguna Mountains fifty miles east of San Diego. They were there for close-quarters combat training: four grueling weeks of high-intensity shooting, room sweeps, and hostage scenarios that drilled into the men both the art and arithmetic of making quick life-and-death decisions at close range.

La Posta had a massive indoor training facility informally known as the Kill House. The building was nearly the size of a Walmart, its interior a warren of rooms and corridors. Each day the platoon ran shooting scenarios over and over in the Kill House while instructors watched with clipboards from catwalks above, like scientists studying rats in a maze. Each night the whole platoon slept in a spartan double-wide nearby—one long room with rows of bunk beds. At one end was a kitchen with an old fridge, a basic stove, and just enough room for two long tables. After a few long weeks of training, someone usually bought a keg.

That night, as the beer flowed, the platoon turned the kitchen into an arena for new-guy initiation games. The games had been going on in the SEAL Teams since the first groups of Navy frogmen generations before, and showed no signs of conforming to contemporary attitudes toward hazing. All freshly minted SEALs coming into a platoon were expected to go through them. There was no formal playbook, only ideas passed down from platoon to platoon with improvisations added by every generation. Games could take any form, but in an intense brotherhood of warriors like the SEALs, where unconventional thinking was prized and platoons had ready access to materials like flash grenades and tear gas, they were rarely dull.

Miller wouldn't have stood for anything truly abusive, but he loved a good new-guy game. The best games tested resolve and creativity under pressure, which in their line of work was critical. At the same time, of course, a good game had to have the promise of enough pain to make it entertaining.

The game devised by Alpha and Bravo contained all three. Graffam and the shaved grizzly had to assemble their pistols as fast as possible. The first to finish could grab the magazine holding the single round in the center of the table, slam it into his gun, and shoot the other new guy in the chest. It was a test of weapon knowledge and performance under pressure. The single round in the clip was a high-velocity paint round. It was nonlethal, but on bare skin from point-blank range, it was going to hurt like a bitch.

Standing near Miller was the boss of a troop of three platoons in Team 7, Senior Chief Brian Alazzawi. At forty-three, he had been on eight combat deployments, including six to Iraq. The Navy officially frowned on this type of stuff, but even though he was in charge, he was enjoying the game as much as anyone. He was an old-school guy and believed in old frogman traditions. There were limits, sure. Guys didn't need to get *too* hurt. Both men were wearing eye protection. But a little pain wasn't a problem—in fact, it was the point. He expected his SEALs to be hard. They had to be. The job was to kill, sometimes fast and up close. Their language was raw. Their lives were intense. They were the nation's door kickers and had to be ready to get medieval on whatever crazy mission they were given. They didn't do nice, or polite, or easy, and if you didn't like it, you could go back to the regular Navy.

Someone made a wager: Not only would the loser get shot, but his whole platoon would have to pick up all the spent shell casings after close-quarters combat training the next day. It was a chore nobody liked, made worse because every piece of brass they picked up would serve as a reminder that their platoon had gotten beat. And SEALs hated getting beat.

The men from Alpha and Bravo crowded around and howled for the competition to start. The new guys at either end of the table eyed each other, their hands hovering, trembling, ready to grab the pistol parts. Then someone shouted, "GO!"

Hands scrambled for steel. Assembling a gun was something both had done hundreds of times: Slip the black barrel into the hollow underside of the slide, then pull down and back into position. Grab the recoil spring and push forward until the steel pin clicks. Guide the slide onto the main frame that houses the grip. Hit the takedown lever just above the trigger, and *snap!* All the parts are in place. Then grab that magazine. Straightforward, but not with forty SEALs screaming at you. Both men started to fumble. Their hands shook. Simple movements became blurs.

"Come on, Graffam! Come on!" Miller yelled above the crowd. Eddie was just a few SEALs away, yelling even louder. They had trained the guys hard and suddenly felt like coaches on the sidelines. It was Eddie's first time being a platoon chief and Miller's first time as LPO. The win said as much about them as it did about the new guy.

Just past Eddie, Miller could see Alpha's senior snipers, Dylan Dille and Dalton Tolbert, laughing hysterically. Miller had served side by side with them for five years and they were practically family. Dille was lean and unimposing but deadly accurate in his craft. He had grown up hunting in the Rockies and was one of the top snipers in Team 7. Tolbert was his best friend, an expert shooter, dark hair, short and broad-shouldered. He was part Choctaw and, he liked to joke, all redneck, complete with a wife who was a stripper and a childhood in a trailer park hit by a tornado. Both snipers had joined Alpha with Miller in 2011. The three had come up together in the SEALs. They'd spent hundreds of days deployed together. They'd gone to one another's weddings. That night they were all clapping and laughing in part because they knew Alpha platoon was finally on track.

At the table, the grizzly had a slight lead, but he was so amped up that he struggled to fit the slide onto its rails. Graffam caught up. He clicked his recoil spring into place and raced to fit the slide onto the frame. Almost done. Was the grizzly catching up? There was no time to look. He hit the takedown lever and with a hard, metallic slap the parts fell into place. He swept his hand over the table and grabbed the mag. Roars shook the crowded kitchen. With a grin, Graffam pushed the magazine into the gun, then pointed the pistol at the massive target at the other end of the table, paused just enough to make the grizzly wince, and fired.

A YEAR OR TWO before that night, it might have made sense to bet against Alpha. Not anymore. Alpha had been known for a number of years as one of the worst platoons in SEAL Team 7. But it had quickly become the best. A big reason for that, they all knew, was Chief Eddie Gallagher.

The modern SEAL Teams operate on a two-year cycle of training and deploying designed to ensure that no matter what is going on in the world, there are always SEAL commandos ready to deploy to a hot zone. The cycle is known as workup. A new platoon forms at the start of the cycle, then during workup members spend six months training in individual specialty skills like sniper craft, underwater explosives, evasive driving, combat medicine, foreign languages, and surveillance. Then they spend six months on unit-level training, practicing how to navigate silently at night as a team, call in air strikes, raid ships, clear houses, rescue hostages, and do all the other things small teams of commandos might be called on to do. Then they spend six months on squadron-level training, where multiple platoons work together on complex battle scenarios with other Naval Special Warfare groups—fast boats and helicopter teams, intelligence and cryptography techs. The two-year workup ends with six months of deployment overseas. Then some new SEALs get mixed in and others leave, and workup starts over again.

During a workup, commanders watch for the best platoons and reward them with the live-or-die, must-succeed missions. Lackluster platoons are given less demanding work, much of it little more than foreign relations. A top platoon might get a covert insert to take out a terrorist cell in Yemen. A struggling platoon might spend six months training partners in Estonia or the Philippines. It says something about the SEALs that the deadliest missions in the most dangerous places are the most sought-after reward, and an assignment to a safe place with friendly people, good food, and gorgeous scenery is seen as punishment.

Alpha had not been awarded a dangerous deployment in years. On their first deployment together, as new guys in 2013, Miller, Dille, Tolbert, and their longtime medic Corey Scott had deployed to a somewhat hairy corner of Afghanistan where they saw regular, if not exactly heavy, combat. But on the next workup things fell apart when new leaders came in. The platoon chief and the officer in charge didn't get along. Bad blood complicated simple decisions. Without clear leadership the platoon couldn't find a rhythm. They struggled in training. Among the nine platoons of SEAL Team 7, Alpha consistently finished near the back. Their failures cost them a chance at the high-stakes deployments that all SEALs crave. Instead of Iraq or Afghanistan, they ended up in Guam.

It wasn't that Alpha was short on solid operators. Miller was the best close-quarters shooter in Team 7. Dille was a top sniper. Tolbert was being groomed for the Navy's classified antiterrorist unit, the unit once called SEAL Team 6 that now went by the benign-sounding name Development Group, or simply, DEVGRU. Even in an elite force like the SEALs, which only took the best, many of the guys in Alpha stood out. They were smart, motivated, and experienced. The senior guys had deployed twice together; they knew how to operate in near-perfect sync. Alpha was an all-star team. It just hadn't found the right coach. Eddie changed all that when he took over as their chief. He walked into Alpha's high bay in the fall of 2015, introduced himself, and announced he was going to make Alpha into the best platoon in Team 7. It was the beginning of a period some of the guys would later call "worst to first."

The high bay was home base for the platoon. Each platoon in Coronado had one. It was little more than an oversized garage that opened onto a narrow ribbon of asphalt, beyond which lay a creamy stretch of beach and the limitless Pacific. Inside, the high bay looked like Rambo's toolshed: stacked shelves overflowing with combat gear, including ropes for dropping out of helicopters, rigging for parachutes, scuba gear, and other equipment, all ready to go so that the platoon could get on a plane and drop into a hot zone at short notice. Each man had a closet-sized operator's cage packed with personal gear. At the back of the high bay the guys had built a man cave of mismatched, ratty, secondhand couches where Alpha gathered at the beginning and end of each day. A painting on the wall of the Bad Karma Chick in her red she-devil bustier looked down on it, her mischievous smirk offering a constant reminder to the platoon of their role in the universe.

When Eddie walked in that first morning, knowing grins ricocheted around the high bay. Eddie had a reputation around Coronado as a hard dude and a proud guardian of the roguish traditions of the SEALs. He liked to fight. He liked to drink. He never shied away from fire. Even at a base full of gunfighters, Eddie had a reputation as a badass. Some of the guys in the platoon had never spoken to him, but almost everyone knew who he was: aggressive, nononsense. He had an understated way of communicating, rarely using two words when none would do. He went by several nicknames. Some called him "Fast Eddie." Some called him "Blade." Whatever guys wanted to call him, they knew this time workup was going to be different. They had scored.

Many of the senior guys in Alpha knew Eddie personally. He had been their instructor at the BUD/S school just down the beach from the Alpha high bay. When they arrived as students, he was one of the first SEALs they met. It had been a harsh introduction. The SEALs had a word for men who were too weak in body, mind, or character to earn a place in their brotherhood. They called them "turds." SEALs tended to be terse and black-and-white in their judgments. In the SEALs you were either a good dude or a turd. Good dudes were not only strong and fast, but trustworthy and loyal toward their teammates. Turds were slovenly, lazy, weak, selfish. The only thing more despised than a turd was a coward.

As an instructor, part of Eddie's job was to make sure no turds got through training and earned the SEAL Trident. To the SEALs the Trident symbolized everything. It was a golden pin featuring an eagle, its talons gripping a pistol and Neptune's trident, but unlike all other eagle insignias in the United States military, which had their wings spread wide, this one was crouched defensively, wings down, ready to fight. When a new SEAL earned his Trident, the other SEALs bringing him into the fold pounded the metal barbs of the insignia into his chest, signifying a blood brotherhood. The Trident was more important than rank; it literally left a mark that would be there forever, even after SEALs took off the uniform. The SEALs had to make sure no one earned it who could not live up to their standards.

Eddie performed his job as a guardian of that brotherhood with biting intensity. Many of the men still had painful memories of being a student running up the beach as Eddie ran alongside. Eddie loved to run students up the beach. He got the nickname "Fast Eddie" because he could run six-minute miles in soft sand with students trying to keep up. Those who fell behind ended up in the goon squad—the back third of the group. At intervals, the class would stop, and Eddie would punish the goon squad with push-ups, sit-ups, bear crawls, and flutter kicks until they could barely move. Then, because their push-up form was poor, he punished them with more push-ups. He sent them to lie in the bone-chilling surf, their arms locked together as the waves crashed over their heads. Then he would make them run again. If you turds don't like it, Eddie would shout at them, all you have to do is quit. And you should quit now, because tomorrow is going to be worse. "The only easy day," he would tell them, "was yesterday."

Eddie never talked about how he got his other nickname, "Blade," but he didn't try to sugarcoat what the SEAL Teams were all about. It wasn't an exercise club. It wasn't a way to impress women. It was an elite group of warriors, and the students would be expected to perfect its lethal craft. They had to be killers; they couldn't ever shy away. They had to be ready to kill with their bare hands.

Eddie liked to tell war stories while he was punishing the students so they understood what they'd be up against. One time in a house raid in Afghanistan, he told students, an enemy came at him and he had to smash the guy's head in with a toaster. On another day, when he was a sniper, he told students, he had his scope on a high-value Taliban fighter in a village. His team had been watching the guy for days, but the fighter must have known the Americans were tracking him because each time he left his house, he would carry a little girl in his arms as a human shield. The team was growing frustrated. The man was a danger and had to be taken out, but he was taking advantage of the Americans' rules of engagement, using their own sense of decency against them. One day, Eddie told them, the fighter appeared carrying the little girl as usual and Eddie put him in his crosshairs. If he took the shot, he risked killing the girl. If he didn't, Americans might die at the fighter's hands. There was no easy choice.

He looked at his BUD/S students with no hint of feeling or hesitation. I pulled the trigger, he told them. The bullet went right through the girl and hit the target, killing them both. Remember, he told students: It's war you're preparing for, and you'll be forced to make these kinds of decisions.

Day after day Eddie gave the students little rest. The crux of BUD/S was something called Hell Week: five days with almost no sleep, wet, cold, and miserable the whole time, crawling through the sand, paddling rubber rafts out through the surf in the dark, running in wet boots, stumbling under the weight of heavy logs, crawling under barbed wire while instructors fired off automatic weapons and threw flash grenades. Eddie was one of the instructors who made sure that getting through Hell Week would be the hardest thing students ever experienced. He was one of the toughest instructors, and proud of it. "When some of the instructors were hard on students, it seemed like an act," one of Alpha platoon's older members, David Shaw, wrote in an evaluation after BUD/S. "With Eddie, it wasn't an act."

It wasn't that Eddie was a mean guy. In fact, a lot of students looked up to him. He was just demanding to a level that was scary. But when it was all over, he was also one of the first to shake the hands of the men who survived and welcome them to the brother-hood.

For students molded in that crucible, Eddie was their first close-up look at a real SEAL and shaped the idea of what a SEAL should be. He became their mentor, their model, their aspiration. Many of the guys in Alpha still felt that way when Eddie walked into the high bay and announced he was their new chief.

Eddie brought the same hard-charging discipline to Alpha that he used in BUD/S. Since he was a platoon chief now and not a BUD/S instructor, his job wasn't to run guys into the ground until they washed out, but his expectations were still high. Alpha was a group of warriors, he said, and they would focus entirely on preparing for war. He would do what he could to ensure they got the best training and the best opportunities. If they worked hard, he said, they would become the best. And if they were lucky, there would be no more deployments like Guam. They'd be sent right into the middle of whatever shitstorm was kicking up, which is exactly where all the guys in Alpha wanted to be.

A lot of platoons at Coronado took Fridays off during training. Eddie shut that down. Instead Alpha set up an extra day of close-quarters combat practice, kicking in doors and clearing rooms again and again until every step through the threshold and sweep of the rifle was reflex. Eddie described his leadership style as "no bullshit." He asked a lot and expected it to be done. He didn't care as much about rules and regulations as he did about being ready for combat. It was something he honed on repeated deployments during the hectic combat surges in Iraq and Afghanistan. He was immediately impressed with Alpha. When he told them about the extra training, there were no complaints. Everyone was down to be the best. He had some of the most accomplished SEALs in Team 7 at his disposal, and after years of being misfits, they were eager to make things happen.

The one criticism Eddie had of the platoon during workup was that they were . . . nerds. First with the Marines and then in the SEALs, Eddie had come up surrounded by guys who liked to fight hard and party hard. Group drinking binges were a rite of passage.

Drunken brawls and late nights at strip clubs became legend. But with Alpha it was different. All of the senior guys were married and tended to go home after work. His lead petty officer, Craig Miller, was so straitlaced he seemed like something out of a *Leave It to Beaver* time warp. When Eddie said they should go out for beers, Miller often said he had plans with his wife. He would talk about how he was planting fruit trees in the backyard or building a chicken coop. The snipers were just as domestic. They liked to go for trail runs. One of the medics was volunteering at a hospital on the weekends. The man in the platoon who specialized in calling in air strikes was always out rock climbing or mountain biking. Some of the guys seemed to prefer playing videogames to going to the bar. They talked about how drinking during the week hurt their performance. They did yoga. There hadn't been a single bar fight or drunk driving arrest. The platoon was a bunch of boy scouts. It was a big change from the lifestyle Eddie's generation grew up in. Sometimes he missed the antics and the camaraderie. But at least, he joked to other chiefs, he wouldn't have to worry about bailing anyone out of jail.

WHEN ALPHA GOT a new platoon chief, it also got a new commanding officer, Lieutenant Jake Portier, who had been handpicked by Eddie. Eddie was a master of deals. He had a reputation as a good dude and had friends and connections all over the Teams, and it allowed him to get what he wanted. He knew a good lieutenant was critical to a good deployment, so he had looked around until he found Portier, then worked it so he ended up with Alpha.

SEAL platoons, like almost every military platoon everywhere, relied on dual leadership: one officer and one senior enlisted man. The officer gave the commands, but because that officer was almost always a young, inexperienced lieutenant, he relied on an enlisted chief with years of experience who had the know-how and credibility with the troops to make it actually happen. The lieutenant relayed orders, the chief deployed the platoon with a strategy that got it done. It was a time-tested but delicate arrangement because while the lieutenant was technically in command, the chief almost always had more experience and street cred with enlisted SEALs, so he effectively had all the power.

Eddie and Portier had deployed together to the Middle East right before joining Alpha. It was a quiet tour. They were staged as a crisis reaction force in case something bad happened in the region. Nothing bad had happened, so they spent the whole time training and lifting weights. But during that time, Eddie had gotten to know Portier, and he liked what he saw.

Like many SEALs in Alpha, Portier had been one of Eddie's students in BUD/S. Others in Alpha still remembered what a stud Portier had been in the course. In a timed relay of running, pull-ups, and sit-ups after Hell Week, he had finished first, even beating some of the instructors. He had graduated from Ohio State with an engineering degree and never talked about trying to make a career as a Navy officer. He wanted to do a couple platoons, then get out as soon as the Navy tried to put him behind a desk. Just like Eddie. He seemed to have a proper frogman perspective on Navy regulations, focused more on getting the mission done than making sure every rule was followed.

Jake is like an enlisted guy, Eddie told the rest of Alpha. With him as officer in charge and Eddie as chief, he said, Alpha is going to be a dream team.

Portier was twenty-nine years old, a full decade younger than Eddie. He had next to no experience leading troops in combat. As Mosul neared, Eddie took him under his wing and assured him he would show him the ropes and make him a great officer. In many ways, it was a continuation of the teacher/student relationship they'd had in BUD/S. The Navy, like the rest of the military, has strict rules forbidding fraternization between officers and enlisted troops, created to keep the command structure from being undercut by personal relationships. But the regulation, like so many others, was often ignored in the SEAL Teams. Eddie and Portier would go out for beers together or hang out and barbecue. Eddie never called his commander "sir," or even "lieutenant." He called him "Jake." Senior

Chief Alazzawi later said the two were as close as any command team he had ever seen, so close that Portier told Eddie he was going to pop the question to his fiancée before she even knew.

That wasn't a bad thing, in the eyes of Alpha. Eddie and Portier appeared to click: Eddie was the kind of door-smashing tactician who could make things happen. Portier was a detail-oriented engineer who could manage the bureaucratic red tape to clear a path for Eddie. After years of dysfunctional leadership teams, everything was finally coming together.

The platoon's mojo showed when Alpha and Bravo arrived at close-quarters combat training in La Posta in the spring of 2016. During the four-week course, instructors ramped up training steadily, starting on the first day with solo shooters clearing one room, then two, then three. They started with no ammunition, then paint rounds, then live ammo. As soon as the platoon was getting confident, instructors blacked out the lights and made them operate with night vision. Eventually training got to the point where the whole platoon would sweep in a coordinated wave through a house filled with a complex and unpredictable mix of armed enemies and civilians, no lights, live rounds.

The instructors' job was to sweat every detail and mistake. Step through a door with the wrong foot, they would make a note of it. Have your trigger finger in the wrong place, you would hear about it afterward. They marked down every screwup on a whiteboard. Even if things ran smoothly, they'd find something. Bravo platoon often had so many mistakes that they had to stay late to run drills over again. Not Alpha. The extra practice and demand for perfection from Eddie and Miller showed. Often the instructors had little to offer but praise for Eddie and his guys. Once, after a particularly complicated run where the Sheriff and a few guys had cleared several rooms at lightning speed even though half of the platoon was pinned down, the instructors at the debrief had written just three letters on the giant whiteboard: "SAF," Sexy as Fuck.

THE SWEATY PACK of jackals in the kitchen were still howling as Bravo's shaved grizzly rubbed a neon-pink spatter of paint on his chest where a welt was rising. The Sheriff laughed. He was proud that his new guy had won. He expected nothing less. The platoons refilled their beer cups as the din of good-natured shit-talking filled the room. Miller could hear his men reminding Bravo that there was going to be plenty of shooting the next day. Be sure to pick up every round, they said.

Bravo wanted a rematch. Two out of three, they shouted. Eddie and Senior Chief Alazzawi stood by as the cries of the pack grew louder. Miller smiled as the snipers in the platoon pushed Alpha's new guy to do it again. One of the most aggressive SEALs in Alpha, a big, fast, young sniper named Josh Vriens, started shouting, "You got this! You got this!"

The SEALs took apart the pistols and laid them out on the table. The new guys sat down at either end. The platoons crowded in, powered by beer and testosterone.

On the word *go* the new guys jumped to life. They grabbed the barrels, jammed them into the slides, flung in the recoil springs. But when the takedown lever signaled the final piece in place with a loud snap, it was again Graffam who was holding the magazine. He stood up and smiled. The pack circled. They screamed for their new guy to take the shot. But Graffam lingered. With ceremony, melodrama, and a broad smile he racked back the pistol and slowly lowered it at his target, savoring the victory. The room quieted as the men waited for the shot. Graffam lingered. He was one of the platoon clowns, always joking around. Several of the guys in Alpha snickered.

"Just do it!" Bravo's grizzly growled, wincing. "Fucking do it!"

Graffam continued to wave the pistol and tease. Suddenly, the grizzly bellowed, hurled the table to one side, and dove at Graffam, fists swinging.

The pack erupted, then collapsed into a melee. Some SEALs tried to pry the belligerents apart; others tried to get a few hits in. At one point, Bravo's chief, a big brawler with a shaved head, punched

Alpha's assistant officer square in the mouth. The volume soared. Then the chief stepped in and pushed toward Bravo.

"Fuck this!" Eddie roared. "You want to go platoon-on-platoon? I'm not fighting with fucking fists! I'm going to stab motherfuckers!"

Everyone froze. SEALs instinctively trained to search for weapons noticed one of Eddie's hands was in his pocket. The smile drained from Miller's face and he looked over at Dille and Tolbert, who looked as stunned as he was.

No one had a problem with brawling. They were a rough crowd in a rough business, and not averse to pain, but suddenly a guy had taken it too far. And it was one of the oldest, most experienced, and most trusted guys there, the guy who was supposed to be the mature one, the chief. An awkward silence spread over both platoons. Was Eddie making a threat or a joke?

A sniper from Bravo whispered to Josh Vriens, "Dude, what the fuck's up with your chief?" The big sniper shrugged. He viewed Eddie as a badass and a mentor. He wanted to someday be just like him. "No idea," he whispered back.

Senior Chief Alazzawi stepped between Eddie and the Bravo guys. "Whoa, whoa," he said. He put his hands up. His thick forearms were covered in dark sailor tattoos that had grown blurry with age. "No one needs to be talking about stabbing anyone."

A few SEALs stepped back. The Sheriff looked at the young faces ranged around the room and almost felt embarrassed for Eddie. The sudden, aggressive threat had, for the first time, showed Miller a flaw in his chief. Lethal force was the core of their profession, but to flash it outside of combat was bush league—the move of a gangbanger or a street punk, not a trained fighter. It showed lack of control. Maybe it was just bravado, Miller thought. Maybe Eddie was making the threat so that he could claim the title as the biggest badass in the group—the most alpha in Alpha. But over the years Miller had learned that the guys in the SEALs who focused most on being the most badass often were the *least*. Despite his reservations, Miller said nothing. As lead petty officer his job wasn't to find flaws in his chief, it was to back him.

Alazzawi pushed the two factions apart. No one was going to

stab anyone. Alazzawi was going to make sure of that. But no one was going to report a fight or a threat to use a knife either. Over the generations as a tiny land force in a big Navy full of ship drivers, the SEALs had learned to solve their own problems. The small tribe of frogmen was suspicious of the larger Navy and its antiquated bread-and-water discipline system. They had come to believe little good could come of it. SEALs dealt with things in-house, as SEALs.

Alazzawi ordered the new guys separated. He sent Bravo's grizzly bear outside the barracks, telling him he needed to cool off and learn to control himself. He told the Bravo chief who threw a punch to apologize. Then he looked at the Alpha junior officer who'd been hit and was bleeding from a split lip. Alazzawi said he needed to accept the apology. The junior lieutenant nodded sheepishly.

"Okay, good," the senior chief said. He looked around at all the other guys. His eyes connected with Eddie and his officer, Jake Portier, and then with the command team from Bravo platoon. "This never happened."

THE BRAWL IN the kitchen confused a lot of the guys in Alpha, like children noticing for the first time a parent who made a mistake. But that was the most confusing part. *Was* it a mistake? When Eddie said he'd knife someone, was it an honest threat or a calculated bluff meant to defuse the situation? Was he going to recklessly escalate the fight with lethal violence or was he actually de-escalating it with a little street-gang psychological warfare? Did the threat mean that Eddie was not quite the leader Alpha had hoped for, or just the opposite?

It took Miller a while to realize that the brawl in the kitchen was an omen for the next six months of workup to deployment. Alpha would continue to excel. Eddie would continue to push them, just like he did in BUD/S. But wrinkles started to appear in Eddie's godlike persona. He would do and say things that no typical frogman would do. . . . But it was hard to know if he was *screwing up* or just *screwing with* his less-experienced SEALs. Maybe he was such a badass that he didn't have to do things like everyone else.

Whatever the explanation, Eddie never appeared to suffer consequences from above. No one ever yelled at him. No one punished him. Eddie always seemed to find his way out of every fuckup. The SEALs above him seemed bent on smoothing problems over quietly so the platoons could stay focused on the larger mission. The SEALs below him didn't complain because he was their ticket to a real deployment. It all just faded away. Like Alazzawi said, "This never happened."

A few days after the brawl in the kitchen, Alpha was back in close-quarters combat drills doing live ammo runs. It was one SEAL at a time clearing rooms. The scenarios were getting progressively gnarlier. What had started as clearing empty rooms with no ammo now included furniture and barriers, live ammo, and life-size cardboard cutouts—some armed enemies, some friendlies. Often the instructors tried to trick the SEALs. A figure with a gun one run might hold a cellphone the next. Accidentally drilling the wrong target was a safety violation—one of the biggest mistakes a SEAL could make. One safety violation, you got written up. Too many, you'd be kicked out of the platoon. Everyone understood the seriousness of what they were doing. They were using real bullets in complex situations. No one wanted to come around a corner into a hallway and accidentally get smoked.

Eddie did not do well. One morning the instructors added a cutout of an unarmed American soldier in a camo uniform. One by one the platoon went through the scenario, sweeping the corners of the room at warp speed, spotting the soldier and scanning his hands for weapons, then moving on. No one shot him. But when it was Eddie's turn, he shot the soldier right in the chest.

Instructors noted the violation and talked to Eddie about his mistake. But when the platoon ran through another scenario that day, Eddie drilled the same cutout. And when they ran a third scenario, he drilled it again. The senior guys in Alpha watched from the catwalk above. Miller was worried. Either Eddie couldn't do the drill right or didn't care. Both were a problem. Miller respected Eddie. He loved what he was doing for the platoon. But he was starting to realize that maybe tactics weren't Eddie's strong point. He made a note in his mind that he would have to do more to help his chief.

In the end, Eddie didn't get in trouble for the bad shots. The instructor in charge of the close-quarters combat had served with Eddie for years. The two were tight. Eddie told the platoon later in the bunkhouse that the instructor had tried to scold him, but Eddie just smiled at the instructor as if to say, *Are you really giving Eddie Gallagher pointers on how to shoot?* From now on, he told the instructor, I'm going to shoot that cutout every fucking time. The instructor, Eddie said, just shook his head and laughed.

A few days later, Alpha was going through an exercise that tested quick reaction to an unexpected scenario: One by one SEALs had to come through the door ready for anything to happen on the other side. No one knew how many rooms or how many people were waiting. It could be an ISIS bomb factory, or it could be a ladies' tea party. Each SEAL in Alpha had only seconds to decide how to move and shoot.

That day each SEAL through the door immediately faced three armed enemies at close range. The targets were played by real people. All guns were loaded with paint rounds. Each platoon member had to drop all three combatants in a few seconds, then press forward, rifle raised, through a doorway leading to a second room. There they encountered a SEAL in uniform with no gun who rushed out with his hands up, yelling, "Don't shoot!" Platoon members were expected to rush past the friendly into the second room, which held three more men: one armed enemy and two unarmed SEALs. The goal was to shoot the enemies and secure the rooms but not harm the SEALs. The whole run was expected to take only seconds.

It was a vital skill. In a real combat scenario, squad members raiding a terrorist cell or rescuing a hostage could easily run into one another, guns drawn. They had to train their reflexes. Mistakes were deadly. The whole platoon went through one by one with few problems. As they finished, they went up to the catwalk to watch their buddies. When it was Eddie's turn, he shot all the enemy fighters. Then he shot all the SEALs.

The Alpha guys on the catwalk looked down in disbelief. Three safeties in one run. If that had happened to anyone else in the platoon, they'd be toast. When Dylan Dille saw his chief shoot a SEAL with his hands up, the sniper thought to himself, *What if the same thing happens in combat?* Miller had a sinking feeling as he watched. The first safety violation could have been a fluke. But Miller was starting to wonder if Eddie just couldn't differentiate. Maybe his default was kill. That could get ugly in a war zone. Afterward, Eddie just laughed about it. *Maybe he's just joking around,* Miller thought, *but if he is, it's going to make it a lot harder to get the guys to take this seriously.*

Nothing happened to Eddie after the safety violations. Just like nothing had happened the time before. Eddie had been in the military for nearly twenty years. Guys he'd come up with were now the top enlisted senior and master chiefs running the show. Loyalty ran deep, especially with SEALs who had deployed together. If you were seen as a good dude, other dudes would look out for you. No one was going to report a guy like Eddie for showing up late and screwing up in training. And if anyone did report it, chances were that the leaders who would look into it were Eddie's buddies.

The leadership's willingness to look the other way seemed to increase as the workup went on. Eddie skipped training and slept through classes. He didn't show up for drug screenings. He missed a mandatory muster of the whole team because he had flown out to Cabo San Lucas without clearance. It was stuff that would have gotten a normal SEAL flattened. With Eddie nothing happened. The snipers started to joke that the chief was the SEAL equivalent of a made man in the Mafia. Eddie was untouchable. By September 2016 he was openly complaining about the workup to his boss, Alazzawi. "I'm over this training. It's fucking gay," he texted. And the instructors, he added, "are a bunch of morons."

Alazzawi saw it as healthy discontent. Eddie was a natural fighter. He wasn't the type of guy who wanted to train; he wanted to be in combat.

Miller didn't mention his concerns about the chief to the platoon. No need to cause drama. If the Sheriff showed confidence in the chief, the other SEALs would have no reason to raise doubts. After all, they weren't looking for problems. They liked Eddie. He hooked up guys with the best training schools and wrote them glowing recs that would help with their next assignments. As a chief he pushed them to focus on the stuff they'd need in combat but didn't sweat needless stuff like uniform standards and haircuts. He was their leader, their mentor, and their friend. He would have them over to grill up tri-tip and drink Sculpin IPA. A couple of the guys even went to Bible study at Eddie's house. He might have his flaws, but he was a good dude. And if the higher-ups were willing to overlook his screwups, it benefited Alpha as much as Eddie. His status as a made man was lifting them all. The Team leadership saw Alpha as hands down the best platoon. With any luck, they would get the pick of assignments. And that was good, because the SEALs were facing a dangerous and virulent new enemy.

In December 2016, with only a few months before deployment, Alpha still didn't know where they would be going, but at the top of their wish list was the largest concentration of terrorists in the world, the ISIS-held city of Mosul. During workup, the specter of ISIS had grown darker and more real with every passing week. In 2014 militants had taken over a swath of Syria and Iraq the size of Indiana. Since then they had started to expand their reach and influence until they seemed to be everywhere. In November 2015, coordinated ISIS attacks on cafés and a concert hall in Paris killed 130 people. Three weeks later, a married suburban couple inspired by ISIS gunned down fourteen government workers in San Bernardino, California. The grim headlines never seemed to end: ISIS was enslaving women, crucifying Christians, beheading journalists. ISIS was taunting America on Twitter, saying that one day the black ISIS flag would fly over the White House. Alpha was hoping for a chance to take the fight to ISIS territory. After all, they figured, if anyone needed bad karma, it was these assholes.

Eddie sent a text to Senior Chief Alazzawi, pressing him on where the Navy planned to send Alpha.

"Wherever there is trouble," Alazzawi responded. "Bottom line up front, need smart dudes in the worst place to do great things without people worrying. Where that is is still up in the air. Just know we need to send our best."

"Cool," Eddie wrote. "Jake and I are def down to go to the shittiest place if there is for sure action and work to be done. I just don't want to try and chase it and end up getting a raw deal. We don't care about living conditions or per diem, we just want to kill as many people as possible."

That's what Alazzawi liked about Eddie. He was a hard dude and he loved what he did.

"We trust u guys to be in a fucked up place doing great things," Alazzawi wrote.

"Fuck yeah, I appreciate you looking out for us," Eddie replied.

At the very end of December, deployments were announced and Alpha learned that their hard work had paid off. At the beginning of February, they were getting dropped in Iraq. The Iraqi Army was putting together a massive assault force, bigger than anything seen since the U.S. invasion in 2003. The force would roll straight into the city of Mosul. And Alpha would be right there with them.

CHAPTER 2

MOSUL

A TEXT FROM THE SHERIFF popped up on the phone of Alpha's senior sniper, Dylan Dille: "Hey, call me on the red phone now."

It was dawn on the day in early February 2017 when Alpha was taking off for Iraq. Most of the combat gear was already packed in pallets and waiting on the runway. Dille had come to the high bay before dawn to pack the last of it.

He watched the last pallet bound for Iraq as it was loaded onto a truck in the dawn light. Behind it, he could just make out the twin lines of exhausted students running through the surf on the beach—the latest class of potential SEALs struggling through BUD/S. He was almost ready to go to the airport. And here was a text from Miller, telling him to call. And to use the red phone.

The platoon had a green phone in the high bay for run-of-the-mill communications. The red phone was a secure line for classified communications only. To get to it, SEALs had to leave the high bay and go up to the third floor, where the Team 7 brass worked. It required putting on a uniform and scanning a badge to get into a secure area. Generally, the enlisted SEALs tried to avoid the third floor at all costs.

Dille walked back into the high bay looking for Dalton Tolbert.

Tolbert was one of the wildest men in Alpha platoon. Craig Miller had been raised in a law-and-order household by a father who was a cop. Tolbert most definitely had not. His father drank and wasn't in the picture. He grew up running free in the Ozarks, wearing black death-metal shirts and hanging with a rebellious crowd. He regularly grumbled that the Sheriff was wound way too tight. He was not the typical military man. Before joining the SEALs, he had won his rural Missouri high school talent show by performing a song-and-dance routine in a fuchsia chiffon dress. Years of SEAL training had not worn down a vicious sense of humor. In the platoon, he could be counted on to deliver a one-liner that summed up what everyone was thinking.

"I just got a text from Craig telling me to call him on the red phone," Dille said when he found Tolbert.

Tolbert walked out of the depths of the high bay with his phone in his hand. "Yeah, me too. Weird," Tolbert said, furrowing his brow. "But then again, it's Craig."

As lead petty officer, Miller was the boss. Dille and Tolbert both respected him. He was a standup guy, a good dude, and a phenomenal operator. But to Tolbert, what made him so good also sometimes made him a pain in the ass. If Eddie let things slide, Miller was the opposite. Guys in Alpha would roll their eyes when the Sheriff demanded that every detail be followed to the letter of regulations. No detail escaped him. Even camouflage face paint had to be applied a certain way.

Miller and Eddie had flown to Iraq early to spend a week scouting with the Iraqi partner force and getting briefed on the combat plan so that the platoon could hit the ground running. "You know Craig, he probably just wants to check again that everything's been checked," Tolbert said.

"Why talk about it on the red phone, though?" Dille asked.

Tolbert's wife was waiting in the parking lot to take him home. They had just a few hours before he had to get on a plane for six months in Iraq. "Who the fuck knows? I'll tell him we'll talk to him later," Tolbert said as he tapped out a text.

Almost immediately a reply came back. "Just make sure when you get here you get in my truck. We need to talk. Something's up with Eddie."

Dille's and Tolbert's eyes met. Miller could be a stress case, but he was also smart. Whatever was up, it was serious. And he didn't want anyone else to hear.

A few hours later, Alpha platoon's sixteen SEALs and a handful of explosives ordnance disposal specialists, or EODs—bomb gurus attached to the platoon—loaded onto an enormous gray C-5 cargo jet and lifted off over the Pacific for the flight to a military airstrip in the Kurdish-controlled region of northern Iraq. It was a long, dull flight, but the platoon buzzed with excitement. They expected a historic battle in Mosul against a foe of an almost comic-book level of evil. There was no question in their minds that ISIS deserved a lethal dose of karma. And not only did they manage to get selected for the mission, but they had the good fortune to be flying to Iraq just a few weeks after Donald J. Trump had become the forty-fifth president of the United States. In the SEAL Teams, Trump was a hero. The Teams were overwhelmingly white and entirely male, and were predisposed to Republicans. Fox News was their default news source. But Trump had a special appeal. For years Barack Obama had been pulling troops back and limiting combat operations. Trump, on the other hand, talked tough, vowing to "knock the hell" out of ISIS and "bomb the shit out of 'em." Trump had promised to take the gloves off, and he had. He picked retired general James Mattis as secretary of defense, and Mattis was vowing to use "annihilation tactics" to destroy ISIS completely. After years of the Obama administration winding down military operations, the SEALs were going to get a chance to really fight, and they were pumped.

Almost twenty-four hours later, when the snipers filed off the jet into the bright Iraqi sun, a convoy of tan cargo trucks rolled onto the tarmac and parked. At one end the snipers saw the six-foot-two frame of the Sheriff get out of a white Ford F-150 pickup and fix them in his eagle's gaze. Dille and Tolbert maneuvered to make sure they ended up in the pickup once everything was loaded. There was a ninety-minute drive east from the air base in the city of Erbil to the platoon's new safe house on the outskirts of Mosul in Kurdistan. It might be one of the only chances to have a real conversation away from the rest of the platoon for a very long time.

"I'm worried about Eddie," Miller said immediately as the convoy steered out of the city and headed out onto a highway. "He's acting like he's lost his mind."

In the week Miller and Eddie had spent scouting for the deployment, Miller said, Eddie had changed dramatically. The chief, who had generally been an easygoing, if tough, leader, was brooding like a character in *Heart of Darkness*. He seemed lost in his inner thoughts much of the time. His tone had turned grim. He seemed consumed by the idea of death. Miller knew something was off but couldn't figure out what. "You feeling okay, Eddie?" he had asked repeatedly. "Everything good with your family?" Miller knew sometimes home could weigh heavily on a SEAL. Miller's wife was six months pregnant with their first child, and it had not been easy to leave. Maybe something was going on with Andrea or the kids. The lead petty officer was supposed to support his chief. He told Eddie if he could help in any way, to let him know.

Miller told the story as he drove. His Rolex Sub hugged his wrist. He had purposefully brought it on the deployment because he planned someday to give it to his son and, when he did, tell him the story of the epic battle of Mosul. The snipers listened, watching the squat houses and dusty winter fields of the Iraqi countryside fly by.

The weird behavior started around the time Eddie met with Chief Stephen Snead, Miller told them. Alpha platoon SEAL Team 7 was taking over a sector of Iraq from Charlie platoon in SEAL Team 5. Snead was chief of Charlie and an old buddy of Eddie's. They had deployed together to Afghanistan in 2010, during the tour where Eddie said he shot through the little girl. When Eddie had been caught during workup sneaking off to Cabo San Lucas, it was to go to Snead's wedding. Both had patches from that platoon that declared them "The Good Old Boys."

In addition to being a buddy, Snead was a mentor. Both men came from the same town in Indiana. Snead was a few years younger, but he had advanced ahead of Eddie in his career. Since he was always a step or two in front, he was there to pass Eddie advice when he arrived at the same point. During Alpha's workup, Snead fed Eddie tips on what tactics to study and how to make it through training as a new platoon chief. He had been on the ground in Iraq for six months and was now, once again, there to hand the baton to Eddie.

Snead met Eddie and Miller at the airport and took them to a spacious mansion in Kurdistan that the SEALs called the Sheikan House. It was their safe house far from the front lines, a place where they could rest and refit. It had running water and a working kitchen, a ping-pong table and a crude rooftop bar. Once Eddie was around Snead, Miller told the snipers, he turned suddenly morbid. It was as if a switch had flipped. Suddenly Eddie seemed to be consumed by the dark possibilities of the next six months in combat, as if the prospect of mayhem, killing, and death were some ghoulish type of opportunity.

The first afternoon at the house, Eddie, Snead, and Miller were sitting at the kitchen table, and Snead was talking about all the shit that had happened on his deployment. He brought up the day one of the EODs attached to his platoon had been killed. The bomb specialists were trained in many arts, but one of the most critical was spotting and diffusing improvised explosive devices. Snead said he was driving with three of his guys in an armored truck through a village they had just taken from ISIS. The EOD was in the back seat next to Snead. Someone in the truck spotted what looked like an IED ahead of them. The truck stopped. Snead told them to reverse. The EOD opened his door so he could watch the path of the rear tire for other possible IEDs. He had his head cocked out, scanning, when the truck triggered an unseen explosive. The force of the blast slammed the heavy armored door closed and crushed the EOD's head. Eddie seemed fascinated, and probed with questions, asking for every visceral detail.

Miller sat at the table listening and was struck not so much by the details of Snead's story but by the tone. There was no sorrow or remorse. It wasn't that he was laughing about it, more that he seemed locked on it with the primordial focus of a coyote tracking a rabbit. To Miller, it sounded like Eddie and Snead were describing some elusive mystical beast that was their quarry—the raw presence of combat, the one real thing that forged true SEALs.

As Miller listened, a chill went over him. When the EOD sailor died, scores of SEALs showed up to the funeral in San Diego. Miller had been there. He had watched the parents weep by the coffin, holding a little boy still too young to fully grasp what had happened. All that seemed lost on the chiefs. Miller only knew Snead in passing, and he didn't know if he had grown callous after years of deployment, but what Miller heard was two guys whose profession was war talking shop, fascinated with possibilities of chaos, hardened to loss and sorrow, as if death was nothing but a résumé-builder.

Snead went on with the story. He said when the blast hit, he caught a few blast fragments in the leg and he was being awarded a Purple Heart for being wounded. He said he was also put in for the Silver Star, the nation's third-highest battlefield decoration for heroism. Miller noticed Eddie immediately perk up.

"It felt like all he heard was that Snead was getting a Purple Heart and a Silver Star, and those were two things Eddie didn't have," Miller told the guys in the truck. "I don't know if he's jealous or insecure, but you could just tell that it got to him."

After that, Eddie was different. For the rest of the handover, Miller said, the chief kept talking about how SEALs were going to get shot on the deployment and that it wouldn't be a real deployment unless someone got killed. He seemed resigned to it, but also energized. Eddie would be touring the region with Snead, looking at a bombed-out village, and turn to Miller and smile and nod and say things like, "There's going to be a lot of Purple Hearts this go."

Long before arriving in Iraq, Miller had accepted that the fight to clear Mosul was going to be big and ugly and dangerous and that some SEALs might not come home. It was a reality all SEALs accepted when they signed up. Miller had been shot at in Afghanistan. It didn't worry him too much. Actually, he kind of enjoyed it. He was looking forward to the fight. What worried him was that his chief seemed not just resigned to losing dudes but almost eager.

As the pickup sped across the Iraqi desert, Dille didn't immediately react. Of all the men in the platoon, he had a reputation as a reader and a thinker. Right before the SEALs he had been accepted to the Coast Guard Academy but pulled out at the last minute because he wasn't sure it would be challenging enough. He wanted to do something real, to make a real difference. Growing up hunting, he learned that the most important tool a hunter can have was not a rifle, but patience. Being a good sniper was about more than just hitting targets. It was about watching until patterns emerged and not pulling the trigger until you were dead sure, because there wouldn't be another chance. He used the same instinct when judging others.

"Maybe this is just talk," Dille suggested after a few moments. "Maybe it's just Eddie being Eddie."

In two years of observing Eddie during workup, Dille had come to the conclusion that the chief was mostly show. He wasn't that good a shooter. He wasn't that good a strategist. He wasn't even that good a brawler. A few SEALs from Alpha had sparred with Eddie and had beaten him pretty badly. Dille wasn't even sure the chief was a good person. He had seen the chief make mistakes, then blame other SEALs. He'd heard him lie and make racist jokes.

Dille had decided Eddie was all talk. He was one of the few who didn't believe any of Eddie's war stories. Many of the guys in the platoon had heard Eddie tell the story in BUD/S about shooting through the little girl in Afghanistan to kill the Taliban target. When Eddie took over as chief, he told the story again in the high bay. The high bay version was less like a parable and more like a joke. Eddie said he had been with a group of Army Special Forces in Afghanistan in 2010, trying to hit a high-value target who was carrying a child. The Green Berets didn't know what to do, so Eddie just fired straight through the girl. The Green Berets' jaws dropped. They looked at him like, *What the fuck did you just do?* Eddie told the SEALs. Then came the punch line. Eddie grinned as he looked at the guys. "Hey," he said he told the Green Berets, "you gotta break a couple eggs to make an omelet." Guys chuckled. Dille didn't think it was funny. Dille remembered hearing Eddie tell a third version of the story years before to his BUD/S class about making tough moral decisions. In that one, Eddie got the girl in his sights and decided *not* to pull the trigger. Maybe one version of that story actually happened. Maybe none did. Dille increasingly believed his chief would say just about anything to make himself look good. And his idea of what looked good was pretty warped.

"It's just Eddie talking," Dille told Miller. "He always has to be the biggest badass in the room, and half of his stories aren't even true."

Yeah, but there's more, Miller said. In Mosul, U.S. military leaders had created rules of engagement that required the SEALs to stay 1,000 meters behind the Forward Line of Own Troops, or FLOT, and let the Iraqi soldiers do the door-to-door fighting. The SEALs were there to be advisors, not door kickers. Miller had tried to talk to Eddie about the strategies the platoon could use to get in the fight anyway. Being that far back, maybe they'd still be able to use mortars and hand-launched drones to hit the enemy, he said. Eddie shook his head. Fuck that, Miller said the chief told him. Alpha wasn't going to stay 1,000 meters back. They were just going to get right up in it, kick in doors, clear houses, and get close enough to shoot ISIS in the face.

Dille shrugged. "That's what we want though, right?" The brass always had too many rules, and one of the skills of a frogman was figuring out how to get around them.

Yeah, but maybe not, Miller said. The Sheriff was okay with sidestepping some regs as long as the platoon had a purpose and a plan, but he told the snipers he had tried to ask Eddie about their strategy and got no answers. They'd be driving through recently cleared villages on the outskirts of Mosul, looking at the pulverized buildings left from coalition air strikes and artillery. How were we going to move up while all this was going on? Eddie would just tell Miller to quit worrying.

"Zero interest in how he was going to make his plan work," Miller said. "Just 'let's go in and get 'em.'"

In the Teams, guys valued hard-charging gunfighters. But that aggression had to be combined with a foxlike cleverness that stayed a step ahead of the bad guys. Eddie didn't seem to want to figure that part out. During the turnover, Miller never saw his chief talk to Snead about how things worked on the battlefield. The day before Snead left, Miller suggested to Eddie that they sit down and pick Snead's brain about the previous six months. "Nah, we're good," Miller said Eddie had told him.

There was silence in the truck as Miller's words sank in.

"Great," Tolbert said. "We finally get a good chief and he turns out to be a psycho."

The rest of the drive was devoted to how to manage this new intel. No one was going to whine about getting in an up-close fight with ISIS. Hell, most of the guys would be thrilled. And no one was going to tell a chief no. That would be seen as insubordination or, worse, cowardice. Miller liked what Eddie had done for the platoon and was determined to make things work. Best thing to do, he decided, was support the chief with whatever he was going through. If Eddie wasn't going to sweat the tactical details of operating on the front line, then Miller would take on that part of the job. After all, if Eddie didn't succeed, none of them would.

"Okay, if we're doing this, which it looks like we are, we need to be on our A game," Miller told the snipers. "We need to focus on medevac, maybe take blood out with us and have it in every vehicle." They'd have to make sure all their procedures were checked and double-checked. Guys couldn't get lazy, and no cowboy shit. They would need to stay in the armored trucks whenever possible, stay away from windows, always wear helmets. Miller wasn't going to shy away from a fight, but he also didn't want to get careless and end up bringing someone home in a bag.

"Welp, if Eddie's going Rambo we should probably let medics know," Tolbert said.

Dille nodded. He was still in observation mode, waiting to pull the trigger. Eddie was Eddie, but maybe this whole conversation in the truck was just Miller being Miller. He didn't want to say anything that might needlessly freak anyone out.

"We can handle this," Dille assured the others as they neared the safe house. "Maybe it won't be that bad."

ALPHA GOT ITS first view of Mosul through the bulletproof glass of its armored trucks a few days later. The platoon had four M-ATVs—

blast-proof five-seat trucks that looked like oversized Jeeps, each topped with a remote-controlled .50-caliber heavy machine gun. The platoon pulled up onto a hill on a hazy afternoon in late February 2017 and saw the city spread out in a lattice of dust-colored urban blocks on a table-flat plain. The beige expanse was punctuated by eruptions of black smoke, as if dozens of urban volcanoes had pushed through the cracks in the city streets and were venting from hell below. ISIS was lighting mounds of car tires to form an inky smoke-screen in an attempt to hide their movements on the street from the coalition drones, fighter jets, and attack helicopters that churned above the city at all hours. In the checkerboard of haze and tire fires swirled larger columns of smoke—the gray plumes from coalition missile strikes.

The only clear landmark was the dark thread of the Tigris River weaving south toward the sea. The river was the reason for the city of Mosul. On the ancient Silk Road between East and West, it was one of the easiest places to cross the Tigris, and a settlement took root on the bank. The natural crossing had traded hands many times over the millennia, and each wave of traders and invaders had left its mark on the city. Its ancient, meandering streets hosted markets that dated back to the Babylonians, stately Ottoman houses, and ancient stone mosques standing near Assyrian churches that in some cases had been holding daily worship for more than a thousand years.

The latest invader was the Islamic State—a hardcore group of militant Sunni Muslims in Iraq and Syria, long kept in check by sectarian governments in both countries and suddenly freed as both governments crumbled. Now they were determined to create a fun-damentalist Sunni caliphate of their own. Sunni fanatics from all over the globe had gathered to form a state based on a strict interpre-tation of Islamic law. ISIS arrived at Mosul from the west in hun-dreds of stolen Humvees and pickups in the first half of June 2014 to sack the city just as the Mongols had centuries before. They shot their way through checkpoints, stringing up Iraqi police and setting government buildings on fire. Tens of thousands of residents fled. So did nearly all of the Iraqi soldiers in Mosul.

Over the course of four days, a ragtag force of about two thousand ISIS fighters took control of Iraq's second-largest city, home to more than two million people. ISIS crushed anyone who didn't follow its interpretation of Sunni Islam. Young men were pressed into the ranks; women were forced to marry ISIS fighters. Assyrian Christians who had lived in the city for centuries were executed. Students and intellectuals were killed. Though hundreds of thousands of Mosul residents fled at the coming of ISIS, two and a half years later hundreds of thousands still remained captive in the city. Anyone who tried to flee was shot.

The offensive to free Mosul had started in October 2016 on the rural outskirts to the east of the city. A vast force of Iraqi Army troops backed by American and European forces moved in. Heavy artillery pounded enemy strongpoints. Circling drones vaporized ISIS vehicles and heavy weapons. Iraqi tanks swept across the scatterings of villages, moving fast on open ground. ISIS fell back into the urban heart of Mosul, where the dense population and warren of narrow streets erased the Iraqi Army advantage. The army stopped on the perimeter of the city to prepare for the final battle. That was when Alpha arrived.

Somewhere between two thousand and eight thousand ISIS fighters were barricaded in the city. There was no escape. Iraqi tanks and army battalions outnumbered the ISIS force by at least ten to one. They were better equipped and better trained. Coalition jets owned the skies and could hunt over the city day and night. But the fight was not going to be fast or easy. ISIS had spent years preparing for the assault. Mosul was infested with trenches, tunnels, and hidden bombs. ISIS had makeshift factories to churn out suicide car bombs and chemical weapons. And because they had no retreat, it would be a fight to the death.

The coalition had enough air-to-surface firepower to flatten Mosul in an afternoon, but couldn't use it. Mosul was a jigsaw puzzle of urban blocks that held the largest concentration of terrorists on the planet, but also had about a half million civilians. An all-out assault would leave tens of thousands of innocents dead. The only option was to clear Mosul on foot, house by house. That's where the SEALs came in.

The idea was to put a noose around the city with conventional Iraqi forces and slowly tighten from all sides. Teams of Iraqi commandos would be at the front, taking the city back block by block. The SEALs would be right there with them. As they won ground, conventional army forces would follow, tightening the noose until ISIS was strangled. It would be bloody urban combat. Every block was a stronghold where ISIS had pecked sniper loopholes and rigged doors and hallways to blow if someone made the wrong step, but the coalition had the advantage of the skies. Drones and gunships hovered over the city waiting to send precision air strikes in on ISIS positions. One of the main jobs of the SEALs was to call in those strikes. Chiefs on the ground would coordinate with their Iraqi counterparts, pinpoint enemy positions, and target precision American firepower.

Alpha teamed up with the Iraqi Ministry of Interior's elite Emergency Response Division, or ERD, which was the Iraqi version of the SEALs. ERD had a grueling selection course modeled on BUD/S, complete with the SEALs' signature brass bell students could ring if they wanted to quit. The force also had plenty of experience. By the start of the offensive against Mosul, it had already led a bloody street fight to take back the city of Fallujah. The soldiers were battle-hardened and well armed. And because they were mostly Shia, they instinctively hated the Sunni-dominated ISIS. ERD's mission was to find and kill ISIS fighters as it took back the city street by street. Alpha was supposed to hang one kilometer back and help by calling in air strikes from the rear. It was not a direct combat mission. It was what's known as Triple A: Accompany, Advise, and Assist.

Even though Alpha had to hang back, it still had an arsenal of ways to rain fury down on ISIS. It had mortars and truck-mounted heavy machine guns that could easily kill at a kilometer. It had MK-13 sniper rifles and MK-47 automatic grenade launchers, both lethally accurate up to 1,500 meters. It had Carl Gustaf recoilless rifles—shoulder-fired rocket launchers that could shoot both armor-piercing anti-tank rounds or anti-personnel rounds designed to shred an area with deadly shrapnel. The platoon had hand-launched drones that could hunt the city for targets and shoulder-fired Javelin missiles that could lock on a target from miles away. Perhaps most important to the Iraqis, the platoon had Joint Terminal Attack Controllers, or JTACs—SEALs trained to call in strikes from the gyre of bombers and attack helicopters circling Mosul at all times.

In such a massive operation, guys on the ground had to worry about their own allies as much as ISIS. Several different kinds of Iraqi ground troops were converging on the same city from different directions. So were European commando teams, U.S. Marines, U.S. Army Special Forces, and SEALs, all with different commands, often speaking different languages, all completely capable of accidentally mistaking a friend for an enemy and cutting them down with a .50-cal or vaporizing them with a missile. To cut the risk, every coalition troop and every SEAL in Alpha platoon carried an electronic tracker called an Android Team Awareness Kit, or ATAK. Each SEAL with an ATAK showed up as a blue dot on all coalition maps, letting commanders in headquarters, pilots overhead, and Iraqis battling in the rubbled blocks know exactly who was where. The trackers would let the SEALs get close without getting killed.

Alpha's armored trucks idled on the hilltop, watching the city below. ERD troops were blasting away at the airport. The SEALs could hear the spray of machine gun fire and see people running. American helicopters circled overhead, sending in Hellfire missiles. The black tire smoke grew thick as ISIS lit its defensives. The SEALs could see Iraqi soldiers on foot moving in squads through a collection of industrial buildings north of the runway.

How can we help those guys from all the way up here? Miller asked himself. He wondered if Eddie was right. Maybe it was pointless to follow regulations and stay so far behind the FLOT.

Before he could discuss it with Eddie, a mortar exploded at the base of the hill, sending up a column of dust and a deafening *crump!* that Miller could feel even through the thick armor of the M-ATV. Then a second mortar hit higher on the hill. Then a third. ISIS had spotted the trucks and was steadily walking in rounds, adjusting after each hit until they were on target. Eddie radioed the other trucks:

Time to get the fuck out. It was a fitting introduction to Mosul. If Alpha was capable of hitting from behind the front lines, so was the enemy.

DYLAN DILLE WALKED into a squat, dirty abandoned house that Alpha had commandeered as its operating base and stopped cold. The family that had once lived there had fled in such a hurry when ISIS first arrived that a little girl's drawings were still taped to the wall of the room he planned to use as a bedroom. Schoolwork and clothes were scattered in a closet with a pink door. The furniture was still somewhat arranged in the family room; photos of parents and grandparents, birthdays and weddings, were scattered here and there. For Dille, walking through the rooms made the war more real than the mortar strikes on the hill. For the first time the sniper could see the human toll. During workup he'd always pictured the fight against ISIS as a gunfight against a bunch of armed fanatics in beards. He realized that mixed into the fighting were thousands and thousands of lives torn apart, little girls who couldn't go to school, old women forced to flee when they could barely walk. The fighting was much more complex and the cost more real. He could feel his anger at ISIS sharpen. As he set up his cot in a corner of the room, the drawings on the wall made him more eager than ever to lay down fire.

Alpha's combat house was in a smashed-out village called Hammam al-Alil a dozen miles downriver from Mosul that had recently been retaken from ISIS. The platoon walked in loaded down with combat gear and divided up rooms. Eddie, Jake Portier, and Portier's assistant officer in charge, Tom MacNeil, took one room. Miller, Tolbert, and the other senior enlisted guys moved into the room Dille had picked. The rest of the platoon crammed their cots into a separate one-room building that had been a family prayer room. There were no showers, no running water, very little electricity. Because of the prayer room's tight quarters and the smell it took on after nearly a dozen unwashed men started sleeping there, it became known as the Sardine Can.

The house right next to Alpha was used by Iraqi ERD. The house on the other side held another SEAL Team 7 platoon, Golf. In a house just behind Golf was a platoon of Marine Raiders—the Marine Corps' version of the SEALs. British special forces were also a few houses away. Each commando platoon was paired up with a different Iraqi force. All of them fell under the command of one United States Marine Corps colonel known as the Special Operations Task Force commander, or SOTF. The colonel directed the missions and set the rules. From a small command center across from the SEALs' house, the SOTF team could see the feeds from drones, track the location of aircraft, chart the slow tightening of the noose, and see the hundreds of dots of different platoons moving through the battlespace as their ATAK trackers pinged on the map. Like a conductor, the SOTF made sure all the players performed their parts and no one got fried by an air strike.

Every day, Eddie and Portier had to debrief the SOTF on their missions and coordinate plans for the next day. The Marine colonel had to give the green light for all missions. He set the guidelines, he enforced the rules of engagement, he approved the air strikes, and he made sure no one in the commando teams was going rogue in a way that was going to blow up in Uncle Sam's face. The platoon knew they had to keep the SOTF happy. Step out of line and Alpha could be put on time-out at the safe house in Kurdistan. Get too wild and the Marine colonel could easily send the whole platoon back to California.

Eddie's voice came over the radio: "Turn off your ATAKs."

Alpha's big armored trucks were rolling toward Mosul in a dusty line behind a convoy of ERD Humvees when the order crackled over comms. Dille looked at Tolbert and wondered if he had heard the chief right. In the truck behind them, Miller looked at Tom MacNeil, Alpha's junior officer, a Naval Academy grad. Amid the roar of the big diesel engines they said nothing. The men knew it was crazy to turn off their trackers, because it would drastically increase the risk of getting vaporized by friendly fire. But they trusted Eddie. He had been in way more combat. If the leader wanted to do something covert, he probably had a good reason. And maybe it would mean they would finally get into the fight.

Eddie had only half of the platoon with him that day. He'd divided the platoon into two squads so they could rotate on missions. Splitting the platoon made it more nimble and would give each squad a chance to rest, he told them. That day Squad 1 was with him. It included Miller, Dille, and Tolbert, and it was by far the more experienced of the two squads. They were driving north along the Tigris through a green patchwork of farm fields that ran up to Mosul. That morning ERD had taken over a house at the southern edge of the city, at most 200 meters from the FLOT. Eddie told the others over the radio that ERD needed sniper support. Even if they had to bend the rules, they were going to help.

They were about a week into a six-month deployment, and Eddie had been bitching constantly about staying a kilometer behind the fighting. The biggest battle of his career was kicking off, and SOTF's rules threatened to reduce Alpha to little more than a bunch of well-armed tourists on combat safari. Frustration was growing in the platoon, too. All the guys in Alpha had chosen combat as a profession. They had studied and practiced the art of lethal force to near perfection. They wanted action. It didn't sit well that they might watch tire fires and air strikes from a distance for six months, then go back to a lifetime of doughy civilians saying, "Thank you for your service."

The SEALs were unconventional forces, and they did things unconventionally. If a platoon could get a mission done by getting a little creative, that wasn't just accepted, it was encouraged. It had been drilled into them again and again. But even to guys who had misgivings, expressing them wasn't how a SEAL platoon worked. It was a strict military hierarchy. The chief told you what to do, and you did it. Working around the rules was expected, but second-guessing the boss was not.

So when Eddie gave the order, they all pulled out the smartphones that ran their ATAK trackers and switched them off. Their little blue dots disappeared from the screen in the SOTF command center, where there were so many other blue dots churning around Mosul that it was unlikely anyone noticed.

The trucks rolled north. On the left was the Mosul International Airport, still smoldering from the fighting a few days before. Ahead was Mosul itself.

Dylan Dille was driving. He pulled his armored gun truck up at an abandoned farm compound on the bank of the Tigris. A high wall surrounded a few buildings, providing cover. As soon as they arrived they could feel how close they were to the fighting. The FLOT was just ahead. The rattle of machine gun fire and the zip of stray bullets from ISIS filled the air overhead like summer insects.

ERD soldiers were pushing up through an industrial neighborhood a few blocks away. ISIS was springing its defenses. They had built hundreds of armored suicide vehicles, welding *Mad Max* plates of iron onto civilian cars, trucks, and even bulldozers, leaving only small slits for windshields, then packing them with explosives made from fertilizer and other looted chemical stockpiles. They were crude but powerful enough to take out an M-ATV and were one of the few heavy weapons ISIS still had in good supply.

As Dille parked his truck, the whole street shook as a fiery mushroom cloud rose above the FLOT. A car bomb had just blown. The boom felt powerful enough to bend the thick blast glass of his windshield.

Miller felt the blast and instinctively glanced back at the other trucks to make sure everyone was okay. He remembered his conversation with Dille and Tolbert in the pickup a few days before about taking every precaution. He remembered the story of the EOD technician who had his head smashed in by an open door. He got on the radio. Everyone stay in the trucks unless you have a reason to be out, he said. The area hasn't been swept for IEDs yet, so there's no reason for anyone to be walking around, even behind cover. Before Miller could fully take in what was going on, Eddie was out of his truck, walking past Miller's window wearing just a ball cap.

ERD had set up a hasty command post in the farmhouse. The Iraqi general in charge was poring over the maps and directing squads over the radio. Eddie had a brief conversation with the ERD officer, then came back to one of the trucks and announced over comms that ERD needed a sniper, so Eddie was going to the roof.

Dille wasn't sure he had heard right. Eddie had been a sniper years before but was not one anymore. He hadn't trained on the rifle in workup. He didn't even have his own sniper gear. Why was he going to the roof? Dille watched through the thick glass as Eddie grabbed another SEAL named Joe Arrington—who actually was a sniper—took his gear, and told him to come help as his assistant and spotter. Eddie had Arrington's rifle in his hand. The two climbed to the roof of the farmhouse.

Dille waited for Eddie to give the signal to the other snipers to get in the action. It never came. Dille and Tolbert were left sitting in the trucks, wondering what was going on. Something was off. Why had the chief gone to the roof without them? Eddie was supposed to be the tactical lead—the coach of the team. He should have been down at the trucks directing strategy. If he wanted a sniper rifle on the roof, he could send one. The chief getting behind the narrow scope of a rifle alone on a rooftop during their first real combat operation was a bit like a basketball coach tossing aside his playbook at the first whistle of the game and going in for a dunk.

Miller was in his own truck thinking the same thing. Eddie had walked off without making a tactical plan for defense or even telling Miller where he was going. The Sheriff sighed, *Not good.* He was annoyed that the chief had left without first doing his job. Then Miller stopped himself and remembered that part of SEAL training is learning how to react when things don't go according to plan. You had to deal with it. If Eddie wasn't going to do his job that day, fine. Miller knew he could do the job just as well, maybe better.

A road ran straight down to the farmhouse compound from the FLOT, where a row of abandoned houses was getting rocked by the staccato of machine guns and the boom of mortars. It was a straight shot for another *Mad Max* suicide car. Miller ordered one of the gun trucks to park at a corner looking down the road toward the front lines. Any car bombs speeding toward them would be stopped by the armor-piercing rounds of the heavy machine gun on the truck's roof. He parked another truck at the rear to guard their flank and told a third truck to back into an area where the gunner had a view of the fighting and could watch for ISIS fighters on rooftops. Now if something went wrong, at least they'd be ready.

Miller told medic T. C. Byrne, who was also the platoon's drone pilot, to launch the Puma. The Puma looked like an overgrown child's toy, a garage-built radio-controlled plane. It had big white wings and a simple propeller, but it also had cameras and targeting software that could circle over Mosul to pinpoint enemy positions.

As the drone circled, Eddie lay on the roof scanning for targets. He was up there for a long time, but he didn't take any shots. By that spring, many of the ISIS fighters had been battling the Iraqis for months and knew better than to stick their heads up. Instead they shot through small "murder holes" pecked in the walls. Eddie had also set up in a bad place, the snipers knew. The farmhouse was right next to the river on ground too low to look down on the city. There were simply no targets. As they waited, a few SEALs got out of the trucks to help ERD. Late in the afternoon Eddie climbed down and told the platoon to break down their gear. He passed by Byrne, who was still flying the Puma. Pack it up, Eddie said with what sounded like frustration, we're going home.

Byrne brought the drone around in a wide swing over the Tigris and angled toward the small courtyard where the trucks were parked to bring it in for a landing. He was aiming to glide just over the courtyard wall and skid the drone to a stop in the gravel lot. But landing the Puma wasn't easy. The Puma came in too low and crashed into the wall outside the compound, bounced back like a dodgeball, and tumbled down onto the riverbank.

The impact didn't damage the drone, but it presented the SEALs with a serious problem. They needed to get the Puma back so they could use it on the next day's operations. But when the Puma landed on the riverbank it became in effect a big white X that could be easily spotted from thousands of windows and murder holes in Mosul. Any enemy sniper just had to dial in the wings and wait for someone to come grab it.

Nearly all of the SEALs were still in the trucks, oblivious to the situation. Eddie and Arrington were crouched behind some rubble closest to the downed drone, but neither wanted to risk running out to the white X. Eddie said he had an idea—they would send an Iraqi soldier instead. The chief relayed a message to the Iraqi officer in charge and a minute later an Iraqi in camouflage sprinted out to grab the plane. As soon as he reached it, he suddenly jerked and fell to the ground. A sniper had shot him right through one of his butt cheeks. The soldier writhed on the ground and called for help. Eddie and Arrington ducked out from behind the rubble where they were hiding and sprayed a quick burst of cover fire as the Iraqi stumbled to his feet and lurched back to safety. Eventually, the Iraqis drove a battered armored Humvee down to the riverbank to block fire while a soldier opened the door and grabbed the drone.

Eddie came back to the trucks clearly pumped. It was the platoon's first taste of combat in Mosul, and he wanted to tell the guys about it.

I actually saw the sniper who shot the Iraqi, Eddie told Dille.

"No shit?" Dille said.

Yeah, he was running up a hill across the river, Eddie said. He told Dille he took a few shots, but the sniper got away.

Eddie left to go to his truck, and Dille went to find out more about the firefight from Joe Arrington, the SEAL who had spotted for Eddie. The two had known each other for years. Dille asked about the sniper Eddie had fired at. Arrington just shook his head and smiled. Eddie may have shot his rifle, he said, but he was just spraying at nothing—we didn't see anyone.

Dille nodded. Part of him had hoped the story was true. But given what he knew of Eddie, finding out it was bullshit didn't surprise him.

That was it: the first day in combat. All in all, the guys saw it as pretty stupid. A squad of elite commandos had snuck into the biggest firefight on the planet. Then most of them sat in their trucks all day while the chief played American Sniper on a roof and an Iraqi got shot in the ass. Not the type of stuff that would ever make it into a Hollywood screenplay about SEALs. But if nothing else, it suggested to the snipers that Miller was right. Eddie really did intend to get right up on the FLOT, and when he got there, he might be more concerned with getting some action than he would be about devising tactics. In fact, he might not even do his job as chief at all.

As ALPHA's M-ATVs bumped down the dusty road back to their house in Hammam al-Alil, Eddie came over the radio to speak to all four trucks. "Hey, no one says anything about this," he announced. One of the other trucks radioed back. They didn't understand what he meant. "Don't fucking talk about it to the other guys," Eddie clarified. The radio clicked off with no further explanation.

The "other guys" were Alpha's Squad 2. When Eddie had divided Alpha in half at the start of deployment, he had presented the idea as a way to alternate combat missions to give everyone a rest. But soon it became clear that for Eddie, the squads were not equal. Eddie was building a varsity and a JV. Squad 1 was packed with guys Eddie considered the hardest and most experienced: Craig Miller; the senior snipers Dylan Dille and Dalton Tolbert; Joe Arrington, a strong sniper who was also the platoon's most experienced JTAC; and the best medic, T. C. Byrne, whom Eddie had handpicked from another platoon because of his skill. Eddie filled out the crew with Alpha's newest new guy, Ivan Villanueva, whom the chief saw as a reliable gopher.

Squad 2 was stocked with SEALs with less experience and fewer accolades, guys Eddie often badmouthed in front of Squad 1. There was Josh Graffam, the new guy who had won the pistol contest back in training. Eddie never particularly liked him. There was David Shaw, a JTAC who was an outlier because he had become a SEAL after spending years as a Navy diver and getting a master's degree at George Washington University. He was so much older than the others that the platoon called him Shaw-daddy. Eddie seemed wary of Shaw, and talked openly about how he thought Shaw was bad at his job, though no one else seemed to agree. There was Corey Scott, the other medic, who was senior to Byrne, but not quite the go-getter, and there was Josh Vriens, the most junior sniper.

Vriens was a tall, powerfully built sniper from Southern California whose resting expression was a bemused smile. He had been a water polo coach before joining the SEALs and had the loud, friendly confidence of a jock who liked to win. He prided himself on being the most aggressive SEAL in Alpha and all through training yelled at everyone to be faster, harder, meaner. He believed SEALs should always be like pit bulls straining at their leashes and should let the chief worry about when to set them loose. Vriens was also a devout Christian. He saw no contradiction between the two, so long as the fight was righteous. And he saw Mosul as a very righteous fight.

Bullies had always infuriated Vriens, especially men who victimized women. The SEAL ethos that all new SEALs were required to memorize read in part, "I humbly serve as a guardian to my fellow Americans, always ready to defend those who are unable to defend themselves." That was right up his alley. After college he had wanted to become a cop, then a detective, then eventually an FBI agent specializing in sex traffickers. What better way to express his faith than through good works? But before he could apply to any local police forces, a Navy veteran who had gotten to know him as a mentor pulled him aside. Since Vriens had grown up playing water polo, he was a powerful swimmer. With your skills and motivation, the mentor said, you'd make a great SEAL. Vriens never looked back. He breezed through BUD/S and excelled at everything he did. He planned to stay in the military until he retired and hoped he could find a way to do the whole twenty years behind a gun.

Vriens loved Eddie. He admired that the chief went to church regularly yet was a savage badass. He was pumped to be serving with such an aggressive frogman who didn't keep the leash too tight. But when Alpha got to Iraq and Eddie put Vriens in Squad 2, away from the best SEALs in the platoon, the sniper began to worry. He started seeing signs that Eddie was planning to push his squad aside. Eddie told Vriens to give Squad 1 his best weapons—the rocket launchers, the grenade launchers, the Puma, the Javelins. There was little left for Vriens to work with. Vriens started getting a sinking feeling that Eddie planned to do all the real fighting with Squad 1 and leave him on the bench.

That same creeping feeling spread through Squad 1 when Eddie gave the order over the radio not to tell Squad 2 anything. No one radioed back to ask why the chief didn't want to talk about their first enemy contact. He was the chief. But the order caused them to glance around at one another. Debriefing was a daily part of life on deployment. What one squad saw on one day could provide life-saving intel for the squad going out the next. Guys understood the logic behind turning off trackers to get in the fight. But why hide details of the first contact from the other squad? That wasn't just weird, it was dangerous.

Everyone in Alpha wore a platoon patch bearing the Bad Karma Chick. Everyone except Eddie. He wore a black-and-red "Good Old Boys" patch from his crew that deployed to Afghanistan years before. It was a small detail that at first just struck guys in the platoon as a little odd. Why wouldn't the platoon leader wear the platoon patch? But after that day, the guys couldn't put it out of their minds. Some began to wonder if Eddie's loyalty was really with Alpha.

Vriens was waiting in the doorway of the Sardine Can when Squad 1 came home. "Yo, how'd it go today?" he said, smiling as he walked up and met the trucks. He'd spent all day wishing he was up at the FLOT killing ISIS and now wanted to hear about the action. It was getting dark, but even in the low light the eagerness showed on his face. Dylan Dille looked up at him as he shouldered his sniper bag and shook his head, then looked down. "It was . . . kind of slow," he said.

"What do you mean, 'kind of slow'? Like what happened?" Vriens pressed.

Dille kept walking to the house, weighed down by gear. "I'll tell you later."

Vriens and Dille had been friends for years, and Dille was dying to tell him all about the bullshit Eddie had pulled. But he wanted to do it quietly, covertly. Not while the chief was right there.

Vriens turned to Craig Miller, who had just stepped down from his truck, and asked where the squad had gone. Eddie stood near the door to the house, just a few steps away.

"Can't talk about it right now," Miller said. He pushed past, fol-lowed by the rest of Squad 1. Maybe Eddie had reasons for keeping things quiet, Miller kept thinking. As LPO, Miller had to make sure the guys respected the chief's orders.

"Are you fucking kidding me? What, are you, like, *too* busy?" Vriens said sarcastically. He looked around as if to see if anyone else had noticed what was going on.

Then one of the interpreters, whom the SEALs referred to as "terps," spotted Vriens. He was a rotund, jovial Kurdish man the platoon called Phil. "Oh, Josh, it was crazy," he said with a grin. "The Puma crashed, and when they went to get it, bullets were flying. This one Iraqi got shot."

Bullets flying? A guy got shot? Vriens looked around. The cold shoulder he was getting from the squad confirmed his worries about the future of Squad 2. The chief would probably have Vriens doing laundry at the safe house before long.

"Fuck this!" he said. He marched back to the Sardine Can with a clenched jaw, pushed open the door, and started swearing. ISIS had shot a guy, and Dille and Miller were trying to say that nothing had happened? It wasn't just the silent treatment that pissed him off. It was the implication. Vriens was probably going to miss the most epic battle that his generation of SEALs would experience. And friends like Miller, Tolbert, and Dille, the men he had eaten with, slept with, and jumped out of planes with for years, the guys he was ready to die with, were cutting him out of it. It was the betrayal of everything he believed about the brotherhood of the SEALs.

Vriens began to boil with rage. He pushed open the door and went out into the yard to confront his friends. He found Miller and Tolbert still pulling gear out of the truck. "What the fuck!" Vriens said. He had his arms cocked open and his chest out so that his whole body demanded an answer. "Why aren't you telling us anything?"

Miller glanced across the yard. Eddie was still on the steps, talking to the lieutenant. "You need to calm down," Miller said.

"What do you mean, *calm down*?" Vriens shouted. "You're not even going to give your boys a debrief?"

Then Tolbert, several inches shorter than Vriens, got right up in his face and pushed him back. "Calm the *fuck* down!" he hissed.

Tolbert was as pissed about Eddie's bullshit as anyone. Ever since the ride from the airport, he had been angry that he was going to have to figure out how to deal with stupidity rather than focus on fighting ISIS. He had worked hard to get to the SEALs and even harder to get to Mosul, only to be confronted with the same backwoods bullcrap he'd left behind when he joined the Navy. He was one of the best snipers in the platoon, but he had spent all day stuck in a truck like a dog at a Walmart parking lot. And this shit about one squad not talking to another made no sense. It confirmed to him, just like Miller said, that Eddie had gone way upriver.

"This is not your fucking problem right now," Tolbert hissed at Vriens, trying to lower his voice, but still speaking through gritted teeth. "You'll find out when you need to know."

Vriens pushed back. His eyes were wide open; he was clearly ready to fight. "Oh, it's like that? When I *need* to know?" he said.

The Sheriff stepped in the middle. Just chill out, both of you, Miller said. He looked over and saw that Eddie had gone inside the main house. Other SEALs from Alpha, drawn in by the standoff, had gathered around. Miller realized that Eddie had pushed him into a corner. He now needed either to support his chief or to support his men. He couldn't do both. Eddie's order was about to spark a brawl and quite possibly cause a split in the platoon for the rest of the deployment.

"All right, everyone," he said in his most authoritative voice. "Meeting in the Sardine Can."

The platoon piled into the prayer room and crowded onto the scattering of cots. A lot of them still had their sweaty body armor and helmets on. Miller made his way to the front and explained everything that had happened that day: the trackers, sneaking to the FLOT, Eddie's one-man sniper mission, the crashed Puma, Eddie spraying bullets, and the Iraqi who got shot in the ass. Miller ended by describing how Eddie had told everyone on the way home not to talk about it to anybody.

There was silence as Alpha took it all in.

"Well, that's . . . stupid," volunteered one of the EOD technicians.

"None of this makes any sense," Vriens said. His anger had dissolved into bewilderment. "Why wouldn't you want to share that stuff? Like, what's the point?"

Miller shook his head. "I don't know, I really don't," he said.

There were other questions. Guys wanted to know tactical details about the gunfire and the suicide cars. But most of the questions focused on Eddie. What was his reason for hiding things? What was he trying to do? Was he trying to divide Alpha in two?

Miller crossed his arms. He kept shaking his head.

"Look, this is coming from Eddie, not me," he finally said. "But we're not going to let it happen, okay? I promise I will never keep anything from you. Never. No one is ever, ever going to divide Alpha."

CHAPTER 3

AMERICAN SNIPER

EDDIE WOVE HIS way through a blown-up, burned-out elementary school, past tangles of broken desks covered by the dust of explosions. A heavy pack of sniper gear hung from his shoulders. In the dark hall, he stepped past an IED set to blow if anyone opened one of the classroom doors and moved toward a stairway to the roof. Right behind Eddie was Dalton Tolbert, lugging his own sniper pack, an assault rifle in his hands, silently sweeping his eyes over every desk and corner, looking for stay-behind ISIS fighters.

It was a few weeks after Alpha's first combat mission, and the platoon had pushed deeper into Mosul than ever before. The noose around Mosul was tightening, and as it did, Eddie was establishing a pattern. Most mornings Eddie would have the platoon give false locations in official radio transmissions to the SOTF, then turn off their trackers and move up to the FLOT. Once they were close to the action, the chief would grab a few SEALs for security and walk off to find a rooftop or window with a view of the city that would be his sniper hide. There he would spend the day behind the scope of a high-powered rifle, cracking off shots.

That morning, Eddie walked up the school's abandoned stairway and stepped out into the sunlight of the roof with Tolbert. As their eyes adjusted they saw the bright sprawl of Mosul stretching out in front of them.

Craig Miller was a few blocks away running the platoon's main operations with ERD while Eddie was on the rifle. It was becoming clear to the Sheriff that his boss wasn't the least bit concerned with the basic requirements of being a platoon leader. He rarely told the men the plan for the day, and he didn't do much of a debrief when the day was done. Miller noticed that Eddie even neglected basic safety steps like memorizing the head count before going out on missions so he wouldn't leave anyone behind.

Was someone in the leadership to smack Eddie and tell him to do his job? Miller thought maybe the young lieutenant in charge, Jake Portier, would eventually be forced to say something. But so far, no luck. Portier was a big, confident man with authority in his voice. The guys liked him. He was smart and funny and strong. He liked to blast music in the trucks on the drive to Mosul. But as the weeks went on, it became clear that while he was their commanding officer, he wasn't much of a leader, and he definitely wasn't in command. During missions Portier spent much of his time on the radio in a truck coordinating between the Iraqis and the SOTF, acting more like a dispatcher. Officially, his job was to make the orders that Eddie would carry out, but guys regularly heard Portier try to give commands over the platoon radio, only to have Eddie's voice crackle back with something like "No, Jake, we're not fucking doing that." Eventually they noticed that Portier just started asking Eddie to tell him the plan. And Portier didn't seem to mind. He was one of Eddie's biggest cheerleaders. He appeared enamored of Eddie's experience and swagger. It was as if the BUD/S instructor relationship from years before had never gone away.

Eddie was choosy about which team members he took to the sniper hides. He picked favorites, and Dalton Tolbert was one of them. Eddie saw potential in him. Tolbert had a hunch it was because he had a wild streak and the chief saw him as a fellow rebel who didn't seem too caught up in rules and regulations. Eddie would tell him he had the makings of a real frogman. Dylan Dille, on the other hand, was more serious, almost too cerebral; he seemed to think about war too much to really enjoy it. Joe Arrington was the other choice, and he didn't click with Eddie. Arrington had deployed as a new guy with Eddie in a different platoon years before, and it hadn't gone well. Eddie had hazed him relentlessly. Arrington had appeared in a platoon skit in a dress as a character named Bubbles, and Eddie had never let him forget it. He considered Arrington a hippie and a goof. He was still calling him Bubbles years later. Of the snipers in Squad 1, that left Tolbert.

On the roof they set up their rifles and dialed in the range. A platoon of ERD had pushed ahead and a firefight was blowing up about 1,000 meters north into the city. Through their scopes, Eddie and Tolbert could see Iraqi Army trucks moving into position and squads of soldiers maneuvering around corners. Puffs of smoke rose over the neighborhood as grenades and mortars fired off. The two snipers hunted the rooftops, ready to pick off ISIS fighters, but buildings were blocking their view of the main fighting. They scanned for nearly an hour but took no shots.

Then Eddie hissed, "I got something."

Tolbert lifted his eye from his scope and tried to line up with Eddie, then peered back through the glass as Eddie talked him onto a courtyard in the middle distance. It took a moment for Tolbert to take in what was happening. The fighting was only a few blocks away, but there was no hint of it in the courtyard. In the morning light, a middle-aged man leaned one shoulder against a broad doorway and cocked his head to one side, watching a young boy chase after a soccer ball as it bumped across the dirt.

"What, the kid?" Tolbert said.

No, Eddie said, the man. Go ahead, Eddie said, shoot him. It was as if Eddie was doing Tolbert a favor by offering him the first shot.

Tolbert scanned for a gun or some military gear, a radio—anything that might make the man a target. There was nothing.

Come on, shoot him, Eddie said. The chief was looking down his own rifle, finger on the trigger, but he wanted Tolbert to make the kill, like it was some sort of an initiation and he was daring the young sniper to do it, maybe even grooming him. Tolbert centered his scope on the man. But if Eddie thought Tolbert's trailer-park roots made him an outlaw, it was just the opposite.

It was true that Tolbert had grown up with nothing and clawed his way up like a character from a Victorian novel. His mother had multiple sclerosis and couldn't work. His father was almost never around, and when he was, it was usually trouble. He spent much of his boyhood in the Ozarks in a single-wide so decrepit that when the family finally moved out, the local authorities had it condemned. They were poor enough that at times Tolbert shot squirrels and speared frogs to put meat on the table. "This is where you don't want to be," his mother once told him, gesturing around the trailer. "So go out there and find something better."

Tolbert had every excuse to amount to nothing, but he just didn't have it in him. He wanted to be the best at something. There was no money for college, and his tiny rural high school was too small to have sports teams that might get him noticed, so the military seemed like the best way out. Both his parents had been in the Navy. He decided to go the same route. And when he heard in middle school that the elite of the elite in the Navy was the SEALs, that's what he announced he planned to do. His own mother just laughed at his announcement and told him he couldn't even pick up his own socks, so she didn't see how he was going to be a SEAL. That made him want it more. During high school, he trained relentlessly. He would pack the heaviest pots and pans in a backpack and go rucking through the woods or sit in a bathtub of icy water for as long as he could to try to toughen up for BUD/S.

Because Tolbert grew up with nothing, the SEALs to him meant everything. He pushed hard and refused to quit. Early in training he fell off the back of a moving cargo truck and ended up in a medically induced coma for several days with serious internal bleeding. The Navy offered him an early medical discharge, but he wouldn't take it. He wanted to be someone that mattered. He wasn't going to let a near-death experience get in the way.

Growing up, Tolbert had gotten a close-up view of every dead-beat vice and destructive lifestyle imaginable. He met scammers and liars, many of them supposed authority figures. He didn't consider it a bad upbringing because it forced him to decide early who he was and what he wanted. It made him disciplined and hardened to outside influence. He didn't have to worry about fitting in, because he never had. And so even if the chief he had admired was saying to do it, there was no fucking way Tolbert was going to shoot a guy who was just watching a kid play.

At the same time, Tolbert also wasn't ready to tell his chief and former BUD/S instructor to fuck off. Eddie had given him an order. Defying it would have consequences. He had to make it look like he was obeying. If he did it just right, he could scare the man and the boy inside, away from the gunfire. He shifted his crosshairs off the man's torso, put them on a wall just over his head. He pulled the trigger. The high-velocity bullet smacked against the building, spraying concrete. Through his scope Tolbert saw the man wince. Eddie, seeing that Tolbert had missed, immediately fired. His shot went wide. The man waved frantically to the boy and they scrambled inside. Tolbert breathed a sigh of relief. He had just seen Eddie try to shoot a civilian for no reason. But at least the chief wasn't a very good shot.

Over the next weeks Tolbert was one of the few SEALs consistently given a front-row view to Eddie in action. He quickly realized that Miller had been wrong about Eddie. Things weren't just bad. They were, in fact, much worse. The after-action reports Tolbert quietly passed to the other snipers at the end of the day recounted a mix of sloppy practices, screwups, and bizarre behavior he could only call madness. At times, Eddie would say he saw a target and fire, but Tolbert would swing his scope to see it and find nothing. Other times, he saw Eddie shoot at targets and miss, but still claim a kill.

Eddie liked to regale the platoon with stories about kills at the end of each day. A few days after Eddie tried to shoot the man from the schoolhouse, he and Tolbert set up on a nearby rooftop, once again leaving the rest of the squad waiting down below in the trucks. The guys below heard the chief's sniper rifle echoing repeatedly over Mosul. *Must be a lot of action*, Dille thought. Eddie came down at the end of the day, pulled off his sweaty body armor back at their house, and announced he had shot fourteen that day. The snipers gathered around to hear more. Eddie said he had seen squads of ISIS fighters in camo moving tactically to the northeast, block to block. He dialed in and picked them off one by one.

Shit, fourteen, thought Dylan Dille. No one else had even seen ISIS yet. One kill would be headline news. Fourteen was epic.

Eddie left to go change out of his gear. Tolbert remained behind, shaking his head and smiling. "Total bullshit," he said. Eddie had fired a ton of shots, but he'd been firing almost directly to the east. The front line was several blocks north. "He might have shot *at* fourteen guys, but if he did, I'm pretty sure they were all ERD," Tolbert said. "And he didn't hit any of them."

Every day Eddie kept shooting and boasting about more kills. Two here, five there. He sounded like a fisherman whose catches got bigger with every telling. Tolbert and Dille were quickly starting to wonder if part of the reason Eddie had such a reputation as a badass when he joined Alpha was that he relentlessly built up his own lore. After a month in Mosul, almost everyone who had spent any time in a sniper hide with Eddie had a story. Eddie would fire like he was in the Alamo. He shot ten or sometimes twenty times as much as other snipers. The crack of his rifle was almost always followed by him announcing, "Got 'em!" But when other snipers swung their scopes to check out the hit, they almost never saw anyone. Even so, Eddie kept casually mentioning a mounting tally back at the house.

I shot a guy today, he told Dille. *The guy slumped against a wall but didn't fall down, so I kept shooting and watched the body dance as each bullet hit.* Joe Arrington overheard the story. After Eddie left the room, Arrington told Dille that Eddie had told him the same story years ago about another deployment in Afghanistan.

Eddie also appeared to be making up stories about close calls that never happened. He would tell the platoon a mortar landed ten meters from him. Guys who had witnessed it would quietly correct the story once he was gone—it was more like a hundred meters. One afternoon Eddie rushed in from a rooftop sniper position, breathlessly claiming that he had been shot in the helmet. He texted his buddy Snead to make sure he knew, adding, "They flanked us pretty good. Shit is crazy." That night, while Eddie was meeting with the colonel at the SOTF, Tolbert, Dille, and a few others quietly inspected Eddie's helmet. There were no bullet holes. No marks at all.

The real firepower in Mosul was in the hands of the JTACs, who could call in air strikes and obliterate a whole building of ISIS fighters, but Eddie argued he probably had more kills than any of the JTACs. He told the platoon he averaged at least three kills a day, then told them, "Do the math." He suggested he probably had more kills than any sniper ever in the SEALs, even more than Chris Kyle, "the American Sniper." He appeared to be trying to build the mystique that would make him a legend when he returned home. It became so ridiculous that Tolbert started to respond with mock excitement at each shot the chief took. "What you got, Eddie, what you got?! Talk me onto the target!" he'd yell, adding just enough melodrama to his voice to go undetected by the boss but still make Dille giggle under his breath.

Guys in both Alpha and Golf platoons started making fun of Eddie's bravado and suspicious body counts behind his back. On the walls of some of his regular sniper hides they started writing one-liners about what a badass he was. One read, "Eddie G puts the laughter in manslaughter."

THE SENIOR CHIEF in charge of the troop, Brian Alazzawi, came for an inspection halfway through the deployment. Eddie respected Alazzawi because he was an old-school, door-kicking dude who still took every chance to get out in the field with the boys. Alazzawi respected Eddie because he carried himself like he was the toughest guy ever to wear a SEAL Trident. "Everyone's a pussy to Eddie. Everyone. If you're not Eddie Gallagher, you're a pussy. That's one of the things I love about him," Alazzawi later said.

Eddie took Alazzawi up in a sniper hide to give him a taste of what Alpha was doing in Mosul. The senior chief noticed something was screwy with Eddie, too. They were in an abandoned concrete room, three stories up. Eddie was on the rifle, shooting through a narrow window. The senior chief stood directly behind Eddie, spotting with binoculars. After scanning over the dense urban blocks for a few minutes, Eddie said he spied a group of dudes in ski masks carrying AK-47s. *Boom.* The bang of his high-powered rifle echoed through the concrete room.

"Got 'em!" Eddie said.

He fired again. *Boom!*

"Got 'em!"

He fired again. *Boom!*

"Got 'em!"

Alazzawi scanned with the binoculars, eager to see ISIS dirtbags getting smoked. After a moment he lifted his eyes to make sure he was lined up with Eddie, then scanned again. There was nothing there. *Either I'm going crazy,* he thought to himself, *or Eddie is.*

Eddie shot again. A deafening crack echoed through the room, sharper and louder than the others, followed by a shower of concrete shards and dust.

"What the fuck?" Alazzawi shouted as he ducked. He looked around and realized Eddie had panned too far to one side, missed the window entirely, and shot the wall of his own sniper hide.

Eddie didn't seem to notice. Or at least he didn't react. He just kept shooting.

It should have been a red flag, but Alazzawi had bigger things to worry about. He was overseeing three platoons in Iraq, and the other two teams of so-called elite commandos were barely functioning. One had a fresh, inexperienced chief because the original chief had been shot. Another had a command team so dysfunctional that he had to fire them halfway through deployment, and he now had to babysit the new team. At least Alpha's chief was competent enough to be left on his own.

The platoon wasn't so sure. The actual mechanics of clearing the city seemed far less important to the chief than the appearance of being a warrior in an epic battle. Guys in Alpha noticed Eddie seemed determined to use as many rockets and shoulder-fired missiles as he could, even when the SEALs saw no apparent targets. He was firing on the dense neighborhoods like they were a training range. He had guys launch toward random buildings in the city, arguing that he was doing recon by fire—stirring up the hornet's nest to see what came out. Sometimes he would gather the guys together and shoot a video posing with an American flag while a SEAL in the background shot a rocket into the city. He texted one of those videos to his buddy Snead. It was almost as if he was shooting rockets just to get his stats up so he could gloat back in Coronado that he was getting more combat than his friends.

Golf platoon, the other SEAL outfit trying to operate in Mosul, was not happy. They often went to the same sniper hides as Alpha on different days, and the way Eddie operated was pissing them off. Every time a sniper took a shot from a hidden nest for no reason it let ISIS know where they were. When Eddie took ten, twenty, or thirty shots a day, that meant enemy fighters would stay hidden and snipers couldn't work. Or worse, it meant ISIS would zero in on the spot and send mortars raining down. There was a very real possibility Eddie's shooting at nothing was going to get guys killed.

Golf's chief would get into shouting matches with Eddie, accusing Eddie of sneaking up to the FLOT or burning sniper positions. Eddie would say he was just jealous because Eddie was getting more action. Then Eddie would bash the chief behind his back with Alazzawi. "Bro he is the dumbest motherfucker I have met," he wrote in one text. "I don't know how this guy fakes that he was any good at his job."

Every day, Portier went to briefings with Eddie and the SOTF. Miller and the snipers knew the lieutenant had witnessed the infighting, the lying, and the weird behavior of the chief, but day after day, he did nothing. The officer was closer with Eddie than with anyone else in the platoon. They slept in the same room. Often the snipers next door could hear them yelling at each other through the walls. Eddie insulted and browbeat the officer so often that the platoon started joking darkly that Portier had some kind of codependent abusive relationship with Eddie and could never leave him. The chief's constant disapproval only made the officer try to please him more.

Many of the guys tried to put Eddie's antics out of their minds. After all, they had a job to do. Their platoon drama was just a play within a play—a petty nothing in the epic saga of Mosul. Block by block they were helping ERD, pinpointing ISIS with drones, hitting them with mortars, and calling in air strikes. They could focus on how their boss sucked, or they could focus on destroying a brutal criminal theocracy that had vowed to spread violence all over the globe. Every day they had a chance to be the bad karma that ISIS had coming. The stuff with Eddie? They might grumble about it, but most of them figured they'd probably laugh about it eventually.

In the worst moments, though, it didn't seem funny at all. There was a war going on—the biggest armed conflict on the planet. Thousands of Iraqi troops were slowly tightening the noose on an increasingly desperate and mean group of ISIS fighters. Almost every day Alpha took fire, often from heavy machine guns, sometimes from rockets. Two SEALs had close calls from rocket-propelled grenades. An interpreter was nearly cut in half by one of the explosions. ISIS dropped a grenade from a drone and nearly killed Craig Miller, knocking him backward and sending a hot shard of shrapnel into the body armor on his chest.

One afternoon Dylan Dille was walking from his truck to a sniper hide when a mortar hit just a few meters away, showering the street with stone blocks. It was the closest he had ever come to death, and he was surprised and a little pleased to find he felt almost no fear. His instinct was not to panic but to focus. ISIS had spotted the squad. He needed to warn the others that it was time to bail. He ducked into a house being used by Portier as a command center and told him, then hurried back past where the mortar had hit to a building where Eddie and the snipers were set up on the roof. As he passed the crater he smelled the unmistakable scent of garlic. It was strong, so strong it burned. He began to cough. He realized ISIS had hit the platoon with homemade mustard gas. The word passed fast and guys took cover in their trucks, wiped down with decontamination sponges, and got out of the area as fast as possible. The mustard was poorly made and didn't cause anyone serious harm. But it showed how vicious the fighting was getting.

———

JOSH VRIENS WATCHED the sun rise from behind the barrel of a .50-caliber sniper rifle on the top floor of an abandoned police station above the Tigris River. The growing light slowly stitched detail into the silhouettes of the ancient city's domes and minarets as he scanned the rooftops. The city was quiet. A half dozen other SEALs from Alpha were set up with him in the police station. Eddie had set up with other SEALs a block south in an abandoned university building. All of them had their rifles fixed on the old city, but there was no action. It was too early. No one was out on the street.

Suddenly a high-pitched *whoosh* cut the air—the telltale scream of a Javelin. Vriens caught the flash of the $100,000 missile streaking across the river. It arced up, then slammed down into the ancient, hand-built stone dome of a four-hundred-year-old mosque on the other side of the water. The boom echoed through the silence as showers of stone plinked onto the street and smoke rose above the city.

The missile had come from Eddie's position at the university. Vriens knew Eddie loved firing Javs and often shot missiles and rockets to try to stir things up. Eddie explained it like it was an established tactic, but in a crowded city, it struck Vriens as a pretty bad idea. In workup SEALs practiced over and over to make sure they didn't endanger civilians. It was a point of professional pride. Vriens started to worry that it seemed to matter little to Eddie.

It was March 22, 2017. Alpha had been in Mosul for a month, and both squads were out together. For their first big operation with the entire platoon, they were trying something different. The Tigris cut the city into two halves. ISIS was holed up in the west. On all their previous missions the SEALs had attacked western Mosul from the desert edges, pushing the enemy back toward the river. The eastern half was an abandoned expanse of rubble and skeletal buildings. The plan was to sneak into those buildings, surprise the enemy pushed up against the river, and shoot them in the back. It was a classic stealth SEAL mission.

Vriens and his squad inserted well before dawn, climbing the dark, abandoned stairwells of the police station using night vision while Eddie and his crew went up into the university. The police station looked like someone had kicked in its teeth. All the glass was smashed out of the windows. The concrete and stucco walls were a plague of dull gray pocks caused by showers of machine gun fire and exploding shells. Inside, the walls were spray-painted with ISIS flags and propaganda. ISIS had lugged barrels of oil to the top floor and dumped them down the stairwell, perhaps planning to set the place on fire as they retreated, but the oil was still there, dark and slick as the SEALs crept up the stairs.

Miller and Dille set up a mortar pit in a courtyard between the two buildings. The armored trucks with their heavy machine guns were positioned to the north to provide flanking cover fire. Just across the water stood Mosul's old city, where for centuries merchants and traders had built up a warren of stone houses. Many of the streets were no wider than a man's reach. They branched into dead ends and hidden courtyards. Jumbles of flat roofs provided hiding spots at every level. It was the perfect place for ISIS to make a last stand.

As the rumble of the Javelin explosion ripped up the river, Vriens scanned the streets for fighters who had been flushed out. He wasn't exactly cool with firing missiles randomly, but if it actually worked, he didn't want to miss the chance to smoke an ISIS fighter with a .50-caliber rifle. No luck. ISIS had bashed networks of rat holes through the shared walls in the houses of Mosul's old city. They could go for blocks without venturing out. Vriens scanned the open streets where he thought fighters might be forced to expose themselves, but all was quiet. The Javelin had blown a hole in the side of the mosque, but it hadn't stirred up anything. All it had done was announce to all of old Mosul the location of the SEALs.

Vriens shook his head in frustration but stayed in position. If he bailed on every mission where Eddie did something stupid, he'd never leave the Sardine Can. He sat patiently for hours, listening to the echo of gunfire from a battle several blocks south where the Iraqis were pushing toward the old city. Then finally, he spotted a man stepping out onto a top-floor balcony across the river. Vriens had taken a break from the sniper rifle, and he studied the man with his binoculars. The man was of military age, looking south toward the front line of fighting, talking into a boxy handheld radio.

"Whoa, whoa, I got something," Vriens said to the other SEALs in the room. But he wasn't sure the man was a legit target. The man didn't have a gun. If he was just a civilian ham radio enthusiast, he was off-limits, but if he was coordinating fighting positions for ISIS, he was cleared hot. Vriens turned to one of the platoon's Iraqi interpreters, "Hey, do people in Mosul usually talk on walkie-talkies?"

"What? No, man, this is Mosul," the terp said. "They talk on cellphones like everyone else."

Vriens studied the man. He was looking toward the front lines. He appeared to be relaying information on the battle. Vriens could make out five or six other men in the room off the balcony. No women. No children. It was the first real target of the day. Two other SEALs had their crosshairs on him.

"Okay," Vriens said. "When you're ready, take the shot."

One of the snipers squeezed off a shot but missed. The bullet exploded against a wall and the man flung himself down and crawled inside.

The team decided to try a Javelin missile that could take out the whole room, but they needed clearance to fire. Vriens had another SEAL radio Portier and relay what he was seeing. Portier then radioed the SOTF. While Vriens was waiting, he told Corey Scott to get the missile ready.

Scott was a platoon medic but also one of the more experienced fighters in the platoon. He had been with Alpha as long as Miller, Dille, and Tolbert and had deployed with them to Afghanistan. Nothing in his demeanor immediately screamed that he was trained as a saver of lives. He had a low, prominent brow, a shaved head, and the broad, powerful shoulders of a brawler. He looked more like a longshoreman from an old movie. The team's other medic, T. C. Byrne, was always geeking out about medical procedures and anatomy. After missions he volunteered to help the surgeons working on Iraqi soldiers in order to build his skills. Not Scott. He was there to do a job, but first aid did not seem like his passion. In Coronado he had a reputation for arriving at the Alpha high bay a bit late and leaving a bit early. Because he was rarely around, the guys called him "the Ghost." If he had a reputation for anything else, it was for being a serial entrepreneur with a shaky record. Scott seemed to always be looking for an easy way to get ahead and he was vulnerable to get-rich-quick schemes. He once bought a small avocado farm in the hills above San Diego, sure that he would soon be rolling in dough and guacamole. It didn't pan out. He tried to start a moving company and got a few other guys in the platoon to invest. They lost money. None of that, though, meant he wasn't a solid SEAL. He was even-keeled, fearless, and loyal. And like everyone in the platoon, he wore many hats. He could shoot a rifle, launch a missile, and then stop a bleed.

Scott pulled out the Javelin and balanced the launch tube on his shoulder. Attached to the tube was a laptop-sized computer with a small screen used to lock in on the target. Scott used his thumbs to zoom in on the door of the balcony. Portier gave the green light to fire. Scott positioned himself in a window, got a lock on the door, and launched. There was a modest click, a second of silence, then a fierce hiss as the missile popped out of the tube. It floated for a fraction of a second as ten steering fins popped out like a chandelier of switch-blades. Then the main thrusters kicked in and it roared away.

The missile went right through the door. Smoke and debris punched out of every window. As the dust cleared, the team could see a survivor dragging out the wounded. The snipers started firing on anyone still moving. Then the battle started heating up. The SEALs could hear the shooting to the south, where Iraqi soldiers were pushing north along the river. The fighting was growing more intense. Vriens spotted files of ISIS fighters in combat gear darting between buildings and moving toward the front line. The SEALs began firing. Soon everyone was shooting almost as much as Eddie usually did. The ISIS forces battling the Iraqis to the south realized that they were being hit from the east, and turned their guns across the river.

Rocket-propelled grenades shot toward the SEALs, leaving

white smoke trails across the green water. Tracer fire from an ISIS heavy machine gun streaked over the police station. The Puma drone was up, circling above the neighborhood. With its black-and-white camera, it zeroed in on enemy rocket teams and relayed the locations to the mortar team. Miller and Dille dropped mortars as fast as they could. ISIS responded with its own mortars. The SEAL gun trucks dumped rounds back, using a mix of armor-piercing rounds and exploding anti-personnel rounds that the SEALs called "party mix." Soon the SEALs were throwing everything they had across the river: mortars, snipers, machine guns, and shoulder-launched rockets from the Carl Gustafs.

For maybe the first time since landing in Iraq, Alpha was working as it was supposed to, a whole platoon focused on a surprise mission, sucker-punching ISIS in the gut to take pressure off the Iraqis taking back the city. That Eddie was acting more like a shooter than a chief didn't seem to matter. The guys all knew their roles; no one needed direction. Snipers spotted for gun trucks. Gun trucks provided suppressive fire for snipers. The camera in the sky relayed enemy positions, and the mortar team pounded them. Carl Gs flew into buildings where ISIS scurried for cover. It was, as noted in a write-up for a Bronze Star awarded months later to Jake Portier, a "lethal symphony of focused combat power." The crescendo was a five-hundred-pound bomb called in by one of the JTACs that screamed in on an ISIS command post and swallowed the entire building in a whip of smoke and dust caused by its own ruin. Vriens watched it all from a blown-out window. Karma was raining down. All the mayhem was . . . beautiful.

By the time it was all over, darkness was falling. Eddie sent the call over the radio to break down the operation and regroup at the university. They were headed home. The mission had been going on for twenty-four hours and they were wiped. Vriens lugged his gear down to the gun trucks, exhausted. The adrenaline was wearing off, and the cold of the spring evening made him shiver in his sweat-soaked uniform. But he was also pumped. Alpha had pulled off a coordinated, complex attack with nearly every weapon at their disposal and sent ISIS fighters cartwheeling through the air. It was what he had joined the Navy to do. Even with the Eddie situation, Vriens saw that Alpha was going to work. It felt fantastic.

Everyone piled into the idling trucks, ready to go. But orders came down from the SOTF to wait. The colonel in charge was sending Golf platoon to replace them. Alpha had to hold until the other SEALs arrived. A few minutes went by, then a few more. Everyone wanted to go home and get some rest. As they waited, Eddie came over the radio. He wanted to know if anyone had any ammo left.

"Not really," Vriens replied. "Just a couple cans of forty mike-mike."

Sweet, Eddie replied. He told Vriens to grab the cans and meet him on the roof. Also, he added, bring the new guys, Graffam and Villanueva. He wanted to get them some experience.

"Forty mike-mike" was the nickname for the MK-47—a squat, laser-guided grenade launcher that spat out forty-millimeter grenades at a rate of 250 rounds per minute. It was impressively lethal, but in the dense urban landscape the SEALs hadn't had much chance to use it. Vriens lugged the MK-47 up the stairs with more than a little excitement. It was a badass gun, why waste the opportunity? He and the new guys set up the launcher on the roof facing the city. By that time the sun had set. All power to occupied Mosul had been cut, so the city looked darker than it probably had for a thousand years. The new guys needed to learn the gun, Eddie said. Some practice would be good for them. Fire into the neighborhood across the river, Eddie told the new guys. There wasn't much more instruction than that.

Why do it? Eddie didn't say. Vriens didn't ask, and neither did the new guys. To question an order was to create a problem. When guys were a problem, Eddie sent them back to sit at the safe house. Graffam and a few other guys had already been benched for a few weeks for hesitating at some of Eddie's tactics. Whatever guys thought of the chief, they knew they had to be very careful not to piss him off.

The guys took turns spraying the city with grenades. In the dark the burst of hundreds of bomblets put on an impressive fireworks show. They drained one ammo can, then another. It looked cool,

Vriens thought as he watched. But as they continued to launch grenades over the river it dawned on him that it was also incredibly stupid. They were exposed on a rooftop. At any moment an ISIS sniper could tag one of them in the head. It was dark, but the enemy had a few night-vision scopes. Vriens was the last person to shy away from risk, but what was the reward? Eddie was putting his own guys out there for no reason.

Vriens was hunched over in front of the gun, holding down the tripod as the new guys shot. He started to think more and more about who might be hiding in the ghostly, blacked-out buildings on the receiving end of the fireworks show. It occurred to him that some of them might hold ISIS fighters who had been shooting at them all day, but others might hold families trapped in the crossfire, cowering as grenades smashed into their rooftops. In the dark there was no way to know.

Vriens had joined the Navy to help the helpless. He was convinced Mosul was a righteous fight. For years he had craved unfettered combat and now here he was, in the thick of it, launching hundreds of grenades blindly into a city. He wondered how it had gotten to that point and felt himself recoil. He looked over at Eddie. In the flashes from the grenades he could see the chief's face. His eyes were locked on old Mosul. His mouth wore a broad grin. He seemed to be enjoying himself.

CHAPTER 4

PIRATES

NO ONE COULD make sense of Eddie. Two years of intense training in which every step and sweep of a rifle was graded seemed to evaporate once he hit Mosul. The bold leader who had pushed Alpha to the top spot in Team 7 seemed to abandon the platoon as soon as he stepped into combat. To the men, he appeared to lose sight of any larger purpose of the targeted lethality that the platoon could unleash, and instead became fixated on the lethality itself.

In the context of Alpha's short time in Mosul, Eddie's actions made little sense, but in the longer memories of the SEAL Teams he was no anomaly. He was a SEAL raised by other SEALs. His actions reflected a learned behavior passed down from the men who had come before him. He was part of an unsanctioned subculture in the SEALs that prized killing above nearly everything else, including, in some cases, the rule of law. And in his own way, he may just have been trying to fit in.

The SEALs had a reputation as heroes, but also a troubled past the organization had done its best to hide, even from itself. For generations the SEALs had secretly clashed with a dark subgroup in their own ranks—parasites who fed on the same core values and lore that the SEALs held most dear and used them for their own ends. It was a loose, informal, and secretive group—not a club but a culture.

They considered themselves the real SEALs, the best of the best, artisan killers—the true warriors unafraid to perform the grisly acts of war that politicians and admirals too often pretended didn't exist. Because war was dirty and lawless, they saw no point in trying to be any different. There was no membership in the group, though its influence could be seen everywhere. It went by many names and as often by no name at all. The followers were at different times called "hunters" or "pipe hitters." Since they were sailors, but also the bane of the Navy, they often just called themselves "pirates."

THE NAVY SEAL Teams were created in 1962 by President John F. Kennedy, who as a commander of a small patrol torpedo boat in World War II had seen the outsized value of small units in big fights and understood, as one early SEAL put it, "that a well-trained David can kick Goliath in the balls." *SEAL* stood for "Sea, Air, and Land" and represented all the capabilities of the new force. The Navy wanted commando troops able to strike underwater, on the beaches, or from the air. They wanted small, independent teams smart and flexible enough to blow up bridges, cut communication lines, train resistance fighters, and assassinate foreign targets, then slip away unnoticed. They needed to be able to adapt and react with almost no oversight as conditions changed, so the Navy gave them a level of independence unheard of in the rest of the force. In the Navy's fleet of ship drivers and jet pilots, there was only one group that seemed suited for such a dangerous and physically demanding mission: the UDTs, or Underwater Demolition Teams—the original Navy frogmen.

Twenty years earlier, at the onset of World War II, the American military realized that defeating the Nazis and the Japanese would depend on making a series of successful amphibious invasions, but many of the critical landing beaches bristled with mines and massive iron obstacles scattered on the sand like jacks to keep Allied ships from hitting shore. Other beaches, especially in the Pacific, were guarded by coral reefs.

The Allies learned early that they could have the best ships and the best troops, but if they couldn't land and seize critical ground, they had nothing. In one early battle in the Pacific, on the island of Tarawa, Marines trying to land hit an unseen reef hundreds of yards from shore. Under withering fire, men laden with heavy equipment jumped into the water. Some immediately sank and drowned, others were mowed down by Japanese machine guns as they tried to wade in. More than a thousand Marines were killed trying to take the tiny island, another two thousand were wounded.

In desperation, the Navy created the Underwater Demolition Teams. The UDTs' mission was to swim silently to beaches before amphibious landings, chart the depths, defuse mines, and blow up obstacles by hand to clear the way. The work was basic but harrowing. Sailors had to swim hundreds of yards to shore, often under fire, using only primitive swim fins and masks. They worked with simple plumb lines and slates for recording depths and satchels full of explosives for destroying obstacles. The frogman's weapon of choice—his only weapon—was a fixed-blade knife. It was the only thing a diver could carry, and it was guaranteed never to jam or misfire. It became a symbol of the Teams. To this day, as a reminder of the frogman heritage, every new SEAL is given a ceremonial version of the same fixed-blade Navy knife that the frogmen carried.

With World War II going full steam, the Navy didn't have time to train explosives experts, so it rounded up anyone with workable civilian experience: hard rock miners, roughnecks, and demolition crews. Then UDT leaders put them through a punishing physical gauntlet of running and swimming. The idea wasn't so much to train men to do a job but to strip away those who didn't have the right stuff. If the Navy could find the men who wouldn't quit despite cold, exhaustion, pain, and psychological punishment, then it had found men who would not question an order to leave the safe, armored hull of a destroyer and slip alone, nearly naked, into the dark sea to swim toward an enemy island armed only with a knife.

Often the frogmen had to swim to the beaches while the Navy was bombarding the shore and the enemy was firing back. Casualties could be high. During the D-Day invasion of France, UDT swimmers were the first ashore on Omaha Beach. Swimming through waters choppy with machine gun fire, they dashed onto the sand to clear the way for the first landing craft. With no cover, they were shot to pieces. The casualty rate for the frogmen that day was fifty-two percent.

The men who volunteered for that kind of work were like nothing the Navy had ever seen. Over centuries the Navy had developed a culture of white-tablecloth order and discipline that had changed little since the time of British frigates. A ship captain acted as lord and commander. A strict hierarchy of officers and sailors ensured that the many specialized operations of a ship ran smoothly. The frogmen were a different breed. They had been formed from civilian workmen in New Deal 1940s America, and they embraced the era's informal attitudes of blue-collar solidarity and equality.

They operated in small teams—usually just a half dozen men in a rubber boat. There was little distinction made between officers and enlisted sailors. They all endured the same training, ate the same chow, slept in the same bunks. During missions, they all jumped into the same dark water where, as the early frogmen noted, there was no place on their bare shoulders for rank or epaulets. Low-level enlisted men and officers all routinely used only first names.

For generations the military ground forces have insisted on discipline and attention to detail. Haircuts, uniform standards, exact marching, and crisp salutes were all part of a tradition of obedience hammered into every activity to keep troops in line when the shooting started. The frogmen, with their New Deal culture, had little use for any of it. After all, they were not an attack force, they were a crew of workmen out to do an insane job. They could be as crazy as they wanted.

On ships the Navy and frogman cultures clashed immediately. Sailors were forced to wear uniforms and keep busy in the sticky South Pacific while frogmen lazed about the decks in shorts, smoking and playing cards. One admiral complained in frustration to the officer in charge of the UDTs that he considered the frogmen "the most unruly bunch of Navy men" he had ever seen. The officer reportedly replied, "Yes, sir, but they got the job done."

The UDT swimmer's dangerous work gave the low-ranking frogmen a special status in the Navy. They had a swagger that transcended rank because no one in the Navy could succeed without them, and no one in the Navy wanted to trade places. "They considered all of us as crazy as they had ever seen," said a frogman who had helped clear the beaches on Okinawa in 1945. "They thought the idea of swimming into the beaches almost naked was insane, and they wouldn't have our jobs for anything."

That World War II experience created the mold for the frogmen for generations. They were part of the Navy, but not really sailors. The Navy needed them but didn't necessarily want them. And the frogmen didn't just accept that rogue outsider status; they wore it like a badge of honor.

When Kennedy ordered the Navy to create the SEALs, the Pentagon naturally looked to the UDTs. Though the SEAL mission was far outside the scope of the Teams' beach-clearing missions, the frogmen were better suited for the job than anyone else in the Navy. They were tough, fearless, and in great shape. Nearly all of the first SEALs came from the UDTs. And they brought the frogman culture with them. They had the same egalitarian brotherhood of shared burdens and first names. They had the same rough edges and disdain for Navy hierarchy. And they had the same attitude toward military rules and regulations: What may be necessary on a battleship or submarine or even in a traditional infantry battalion wasn't just a burden for a small squad of crack commandos inventing a whole new type of modern warfare, it was a joke.

The SEALs stressed independence and unconventional thinking, and they had a certain admiration for outsmarting the military bureaucracy. It all fell under a guiding principle they called "being creative." That principle became institutionalized as old frogmen rose in rank and trained new generations. The philosophy survived Vietnam and the Cold War and was passed down to the modern SEALs fighting in Iraq and Afghanistan. It was embraced at nearly every rank. "In a wartime environment, it is about being creative, and you can be very creative within the rules," Admiral William McRaven, who led the SEALs during the raid on Osama bin Laden's compound, said in an interview after he was named one of the four runners-up for *Time*'s Person of the Year in 2011. "The leadership gives them the opportunity to be creative because they're specially selected, they're specially trained, they're specially equipped."

THE SEALS SAW the freedom to be creative as their greatest tactical asset. That they weren't too rigid about old ideas of saluting or haircuts, that they gave relatively low-ranking enlisted men the freedom to make big decisions, and that they were not locked into dogmas about the right way to fight—these were what gave them the edge over enemies. But that freedom also gave SEALs enough slack to drift into dark waters.

If the original frogmen of World War II had the crucible of the South Pacific to mold their culture and identity, the SEALs created by Kennedy had Vietnam. It was a vastly different experience. The SEALs stopped being combat swimmers and became jungle fighters. The missions were different, and so were the potential dangers. Perhaps the biggest danger was one that has always stalked elite warriors: the danger of becoming so focused on the craft of killing that you forget why you are killing in the first place.

The frogmen of World War II had to be physically strong and almost recklessly brave, but they didn't have to know much about killing, nor how to create a culture that could protect against killing's corrosive effects. They had long been courageous and irreverent misfits, not proper warriors. But in Vietnam, the SEALs got dropped into a guerrilla war against a shadowy enemy force often disguised in civilian clothing. Their enemy fought dirty, with no respect for laws. And with the creativity and latitude to make their own tactics, some SEALs decided to fight even dirtier.

In 1962, just after the SEAL Teams were formed, small groups of SEALs started inserting covertly into South Vietnam. At first they worked only as advisors, helping to train South Vietnamese troops to counter Viet Cong guerrillas, but as the United States got drawn deeper into Vietnam, so did the frogmen. Teams started working with the CIA on a classified operation called the Phoenix Program, designed to destroy the political infrastructure of the Viet Cong. The CIA believed that the Viet Cong had a secret network of village leaders, tax collectors, and messengers spread throughout the country that allowed the insurgency to thrive while hiding in broad daylight. Taking out those civilians would strangle the enemy. By 1967, squads of SEALs were running Phoenix missions all over the country. The CIA had a web of informants gathering intelligence. That intelligence was passed to the SEALs, who ran ambushes, kidnappings, and assassinations.

Those groups of SEALs, often numbering fewer than two dozen, had almost no oversight. They were technically sailors under the command of the Navy, but the small groups of machine gun–carrying ground-pounders usually operated far inland from any Navy command. Sometimes their closest overseers were on the other side of the ocean. Army and Marine units overlapped in some of their terrain but had little say over the SEALs. "They essentially reported to themselves," former SEAL commander Tom Hawkins, who commanded a platoon in Vietnam, wrote in his book *The History and Heritage of U.S. Navy SEALs*. In ideal circumstances, that freedom to be creative cut through layer after layer of military bureaucracy. But it also meant SEALs could raid and kill with next to no accountability.

The SEALs started looking and acting less and less like professional American military troops and more like the guerrillas they fought. They pulled off identifying patches, dog tags, and any other insignia that could mark them as American. They often carried foreign-made weapons to look more like the Viet Cong. Their missions were classified, so other American troops often had no idea what to make of these small groups of men with long hair, strange weapons, and no identifying insignia. They moved almost exclusively at night, often wired on Dexedrine or other kinds of speed. When the mission was to slip in to snatch or kill the enemy, stealth and camouflage became critical. Many started wearing black pajama shirts and going barefoot so they wouldn't leave American boot prints.

On missions SEALs smeared themselves with camouflage paint, giving rise to their nickname during the war: the men with green faces. They carried pistols with silencers, called "hush puppies," that could kill without waking up a village. When silencers proved hard to come by, some settled for crossbows. "I wanted to be as sneaky as I could be and I didn't bother trying to follow Hoyle's rules," Lieutenant Commander Roy Boehm, who was one of the first SEALs in Vietnam, recalled in an oral history. "You can't play by the rules when you're the only person reading the book. The kind of enemy we would be fighting would be sneaky, underhanded, and fight as dirty as he could. So we had to be better at that than he was."

With the Phoenix Program churning out a steady number of targets for the SEALs, squads would sneak in silently at night, grab villagers, and bring them back for interrogation. Those straightforward night missions gradually branched off on darker avenues until it was hard to find the light again. The intel SEALs received was often suspect. A farmer might finger his neighbor over an old grudge. A corrupt official might turn in someone to whom he owed money. Fishing boats the SEALs ambushed because someone said they were used by Viet Cong couriers often turned out to be nothing but fishing boats. Purported Viet Cong bases burned to the ground were sometimes just poor collections of huts inhabited by simple peasants.

Not all SEALs crossed into such dark territory. Likely not even most. But in Vietnam the freedom SEALs had to be creative enabled pirates fixated on killing. Mike Beanan, a twenty-year-old new guy in the Mekong Delta during the height of the fighting, found himself assigned to a platoon full of pirates. In an account he published under an assumed name after he came home, he described how the whole squad descended into savagery. The job mutated from identifying and killing Viet Cong operatives to tasks like sneaking into a village at night to assassinate a village chief and making it look like the Viet Cong had done it. When intel told them to hit Viet Cong tax collectors, they would, according to Beanan, "rob them of all the money and, of course, kill them. And then report that all the money was destroyed in the fire fight." Then they'd use the money to party.

The SEALs carried machine guns and assault rifles, but the baddest, meanest, truest way to kill people was still the original frogman's weapon, the knife. It was silent; it was pure. It put minimal distance between the hunter and the act of killing, and for some pirates in the Mekong it became an almost ceremonial execution tool. "It's called 'getting wet,' cutting somebody's throat with your knife so the blood would go all over you so you . . . It was a ritual," Beanan recalled. He said his platoon leaders told him to do it to some villagers. He refused but said many others did not.

Often pirates would cut off an ear or other part of the body as a trophy. They would then smear their signature green face paint on the body and leave it as a calling card. "It was a business, and the business was terrorism," Beanan said. The techniques were designed to have the maximum impact on the villagers, he said. "Finding a loved one with a green face and stabbed—in the middle of the road—was incredible terror."

When SEALs snatched a sleeping target from a village, they would sometimes booby-trap the door of a hut with a grenade set to go off on the next person who came out. "And these are like families, little kids and stuff," Beanan recalled. "It was something you just didn't think about. You just did it."

The SEALs soon earned a reputation among conventional troops as savages. An Army general in Vietnam told Hawkins to clear his SEALs out of his area of operations, adding, "You SEALs are assassins. I don't want you here."

Often the shift toward terror tactics was done with the knowledge and sometimes at the direction of the officers in charge. Richard Marcinko, a young lieutenant who commanded a SEAL platoon in the Delta, went by the name "Demo Dick" and called his men "Marcinko's Merry Band of Murdering Marauders." Village by village, his team destroyed rice supplies, blew up fishing boats, and burned houses. Demo Dick liked to booby-trap the bodies of those his men had killed before they moved on from a village. "It made me feel good to hear an explosion after we'd left the area," he later wrote in his memoir, *Rogue Warrior*. As time went on, Demo Dick and his men began to not just dress like the guerrillas that they were fighting, "we began to think like guerrillas, getting spookier and spookier and dirtier and dirtier." Demo Dick's superior officers were largely on the other side of the Pacific, and he reveled in the freedom to be creative.

"There's something to be said about the purity of a small war," he said. "For the SEALs it was instant gratification. You would write up a patrol order, go out there, and shoot the bastard. Either you'd win, or you'd lose. It was black and white, no gray. And that's music, that's the epitome of life for a warrior."

Except it wasn't black and white. There was gray. Lots and lots of it. Small groups of heavily armed Americans who didn't speak the language and didn't understand the culture suddenly had to decide who in Vietnam was a friend and who was an enemy. Enemy often became the default. Civilian casualties were considered part of the equation.

Unsuspecting villagers could be silenced with a knife or hush puppy so a mission could go forward. In 1969 Bob Kerrey was a twenty-five-year-old lieutenant leading a squad of SEALs in Vietnam. One night they crept into a remote delta village to do a "take out" on a Viet Cong target. On the edge of a village they encountered an old man and woman sleeping in a hut with three children. Afraid that they might sound the alarm, the SEALs dispatched all five with their frogman knives. Down the path, the SEALs encountered another group of about a dozen women and children. The element of surprise now lost, they killed the villagers with machine guns.

Then, with the lieutenant watching, the unit covered up what they had done, reporting to commanders back at their base that twenty-one Viet Cong had been killed in action. Kerrey later became a United States senator.

Captives the SEALs brought in were routinely tortured by CIA and South Vietnamese authorities with electric shocks or beatings and often summarily executed. Some were interrogated aboard helicopters, then thrown overboard. During a 1971 congressional hearing after the Phoenix Program was shut down, the director of the CIA admitted that the program had killed 20,587 suspects. At the same hearing, an Army intelligence analyst who had witnessed torture and executions called Phoenix Program an "indiscriminate murder program."

With the hearings creating bad press at home, the Navy put all

SEALs in Vietnam in time-out in 1971 and forced them to take a written test on the rules of engagement. Most of the SEALs soon left the country. "Some members of the commando teams in the field have become afraid that their activities might bring down on them the kind of prosecution that convicted First Lieutenant William L. Calley Jr. in the massacre of civilians in My Lai," a *New York Times* reporter who visited the region that year reported, referring to Army soldiers' infamous slaughter of hundreds of unarmed villagers. On the wall in the Mekong bar the commandos frequented, the reporter noted, was a sign that read, "People who kill for money are professionals. People who kill for fun are sadists. People who kill for money and fun are SEALs."

The guys who didn't have a taste for blood tended to get out after one enlistment. The guys who did not only stayed, they got promoted. Soon many of the pirates were the men in charge, training the next generation. The Mekong jungle practice of silently killing unsuspecting targets became rooted in training, where one student going through in the 1980s noted that "the use of a knife, garrote, and sentry stalking are taught by men who have done it for real."

Many pirates who came home from Vietnam had even less use for Navy discipline and formality than the frogmen they had evolved from. One of them was Demo Dick. The world of the SEALs, he said, "was rough-and-tumble macho, full of fuck-you-very-much tough talk and I Am the Baddest Motherfucker on the Block attitude . . . T-shirts and shorts were the uniform of the day, and if your hair wasn't quite perfectly combed, well, tough titty, dickhead."

Vietnam created a divide in the SEALs. There were men, sometimes derisively called "boy scouts," who saw law and order as vital both to the mission and to the brotherhood's soul. And there were pirates who saw that stance as hopelessly naïve and against the very reason the SEALs were created. To them that law-and-order stuff was a useful beard for visiting dignitaries but not how things really worked. The purpose of the SEALs was to do the nation's covert dirty work. Commando groups like theirs were created specifically to go beyond what was officially sanctioned—and do it quietly and deniably. The Teams weren't there to look good, they were there to hit hard. And they had to be packed with pipe-hitting pirates willing to do the work. The pirates didn't see themselves as parasites in the SEAL Teams, they saw themselves as the true SEAL Teams, the real brotherhood. Everything else was just window dressing.

The two views of the brotherhood clashed repeatedly. Early in his career, William McRaven, who eventually rose to the rank of admiral in command of all SEALs, was fired from a platoon commander job by Demo Dick for being too much of a rule follower. "He was a bright guy, but he didn't like my rude and crude way," Marcinko later said. "If I was a loose cannon, he was too rigid. He took the *special* out of *special warfare*." Pirates and boy scouts never agreed to coexist, but neither side ever managed to get full control of the Teams either. The Navy repeatedly tried to put the boy scouts back in control, but the autonomy and freedom built into the foundation of the Teams always left enough crevices for pirates to survive and breed.

In pirate culture, killing was the purpose of the SEALs and its truest expression. That culture gradually influenced the entire Teams. The SEALs were a brotherhood of elite warriors, and lethal force was their craft. They took a certain pride in the art of doing it up close. In the hypercompetitive SEAL hierarchy, experience was everything. A guy who had been to combat had more cred than a guy who had not. A guy who had killed in combat ranked even higher. And the method mattered. Getting a kill from a distance with a rifle was one thing. Shooting a man point-blank after kicking in a door was another. And killing someone with the frogman's original tool, the knife—having the skill and the guts to stab a guy at arm's length, close enough to hear his breath and watch the life drain from his eyes—in some circles that was seen as the ultimate. The SEALs' arsenal evolved to include killer drones and Javelin missiles, but the reverence for the knife never went away.

IN 1986 A TEAM OF Navy SEALs emerged silently out of the dark Mediterranean Sea and crept onto a beach in Libya. They wore no patches and carried Soviet bloc weapons to hide their identity. Once on the beach they mapped out the Libyan defenses in case the United

States needed to invade, then blew up communications lines and other targets to cause calculated chaos. On their way out, they strategically dropped a few butts from Israeli and Syrian cigarette brands before silently disappearing back into the blackness of the sea. It was a textbook clandestine SEAL mission, a stealth strike designed to confuse and destabilize the Libyan dictatorship. Details of the raid have never been publicly disclosed by the Navy. The operators who completed the mission are still unknown.

That is the identity that the SEALs have always wanted to project to the world: elite, nameless professionals, part James Bond, part Aquaman, able to strike with such stealth and precision that they are long gone before anyone knows they were there. In reality, though, the pirate culture, fueled by aggressive overconfidence, ego, and a thirst for destruction, repeatedly led to fiascoes.

After Vietnam, Demo Dick Marcinko was put in charge of all SEALs on the East Coast. Then he was given a new mission that would shape the SEAL culture for generations: create a super-secret counterterrorism squad that could hit anywhere in the world. At the time there were only two SEAL Teams, one on the East Coast and one on the West Coast. In a feint meant to confuse potential enemies, he called the new unit SEAL Team 6.

Demo Dick packed 6 with his friends from Vietnam. Two of his four squadrons created unit patches that looked a lot like a pirate flag. To fill out the ranks he took a creative approach, rejecting top candidates in favor of middle-of-the-pack "shitbirds" who he figured would work harder and have a knack for unconventional thinking. In his memoir, he said he wanted "dirtbags." "Dirtbags with union skills—truck drivers, crane operators, bricklayers, electricians, longshoremen. But I wasn't looking for just any dirtbags. I wanted motivated dirtbags." He let his men wear earrings and grow long hair and bushy beards. Many looked more like members of a biker gang than a crack military unit. In 1980 he gathered his new team at a base auditorium near Virginia Beach and got up on stage in front of a huge American flag to give the assembled band of pirates, marauders, and dirtbags a welcoming address. "You know what we are here to do—counterterrorism. And what does counterterrorism mean? It means that we will fucking do it to them before they fucking do it to us." The men roared in approval.

"It's about goddamn time, right?" Demo Dick said, pacing the floor. "For SEAL Team 6, I am fucking lifting the rules."

The only rule he insisted on was loyalty, and not to the Navy or the nation or the Constitution. "Your loyalty must be first and foremost to your partner, your squad, your platoon, and the Team," he told them. "I am the law, gentlemen—and my law is simple. There will be unit fucking integrity." He paused and took on the accent of a mobster. "This command . . . will be like a friggin' Mafia," he said. "I . . . am the *Capo di tutti capi,* the *Padrone.* I make the offers nobody refuses. And I . . . I take care of everybody. What's more, we're a family. And you never talk family business outside the family." It didn't take long for the ideas of loyalty in Team 6 to spread through the SEALs.

The SEALs emerged from Vietnam as good guys. They were almost unknown to the public, so they carried none of the culture baggage of a despised war. In post-Vietnam pop culture of the 1980s, soldiers were often portrayed as damaged or even criminal: village burners and baby killers. Not the SEALs. The only pop culture SEAL to emerge after the war was Thomas Magnum from *Magnum, P.I.*—a cool private investigator who wore aloha shirts and drove a Ferrari. The darker internal struggle was effectively kept hidden.

Throughout the 1980s many in the SEALs quietly embraced Demo Dick's pirate philosophy, often believing so much in their own badass swagger that they spent little time on designing strategy, instead relying on needlessly complex frontal assaults. The product was one failed mission after another and a steady stream of body bags.

The first big test for the SEALs after Vietnam was the U.S. invasion of Grenada in October 1983. The tiny Caribbean nation had only a small army and almost no heavy weapons, but the Reagan administration feared it could become a springboard to spread communism throughout Latin America, so the United States invaded with nearly eight thousand troops. The SEALs were supposed to lead the charge by seizing the airport. Instead of just landing in helicopters on the runway, eight Team 6 commandos would parachute into the ocean with two speedboats, then make an amphibious land-ing. But delays caused the daytime jump to instead happen at night—and in a storm. The SEALs splashed down in seven-foot waves far from their boats. Four of them drowned and were never seen again. The mission was aborted.

It was the first of several tasks given to the SEALs in Grenada. All of them went hopelessly wrong. A stealth plan to rescue Grena-da's British-appointed governor-general, who was under house ar-rest, was undone by a botched helicopter rappel that came under fire from Grenadian troops. The helicopters pulled out after inserting only half the team, taking heavy weapons and radios with them. Sur-rounded, nearly all of the SEALs were soon wounded. With no ra-dios, they were reduced to using a calling card to phone the United States and relay instructions for air strikes from gunships circling above. Eventually a company of U.S. Marines arrived to rescue them. The whole mission was supposed to take forty-five minutes. Instead it lasted twenty-seven hours.

Nineteen Americans were killed in action during the weeklong invasion. Though SEALs made up far less than one percent of the forces involved, they were twenty percent of the casualties. In the aftermath the SEALs admitted they had been underprepared and had taken needlessly complicated approaches to missions better suited for conventional troops. It was an embarrassment and a trag-edy for the men who were lost. But in a culture that prized loyalty and aggression over transparency and caution, any lessons learned were quickly shelved.

During the 1989 invasion of Panama, the SEALs once again went after a series of high-value targets and once again charged into disasters. One mission was to cut off the escape of Panamanian dic-tator General Manuel Noriega by blowing up his Learjet. Forty-eight SEALs paddled silently up to an airport on the coast of Panama City and approached the general's hangar across an open runway with no cover. Guarding the hangar were more than a hundred Pan-amanian soldiers with machine guns who easily spotted the SEALs and started mowing them down. Within minutes seven SEALs were wounded and four were dead. The SEALs eventually drove the Panamanians back, captured the hangar, and destroyed the jet, but not before they had once again accounted for nearly twenty percent of the total casualties of the entire invasion.

Part of the problem was the frogman culture itself. The UDT men of World War II were picked in part because they had the courage to do something so insanely dangerous and difficult that no one else wanted to do it. They had the freedom in the Navy to create their own rules and culture, including a culture of working around the rules. It gave them the room to do great things, but it also gave them leeway, if they wanted, to be thoroughly mediocre. The belief that loyalty trumped all else built a hierarchy based on nepotism rather than merit. Demo Dick built what one SEAL later called a "cult of personality" around himself, drove a Mercedes bought with government money, and often held planning meetings in the back booth of a local bar. The belief that rules and regulations were an obstacle led to a lack of discipline and, in some cases, a poorly trained force.

The frogmen at their foundation also had a culture of daring. They had long been the ones who did jobs no one else was willing to do. Fear was one of the few things they had no tolerance for. That foundation resulted in groups of SEALs repeatedly concocting missions with pointless levels of risk because no one wanted to speak up and be labeled a coward.

DEMO DICK MARCINKO ended up getting convicted of a kickback scheme to help a buddy sell grenades to the Navy and was sent to prison in 1990, a short time after he retired. Men like Bill McRaven, whom Demo Dick had fired, moved up in the command structure and made strides to professionalize the force. Demo Dick's name was mentioned less and less. The SEALs became more formal and more disciplined, and in the years since have been responsible for countless military successes, many of which are still classified. The pirate culture ebbed, but its disdain for rules, its Mafia-like focus on loyalty, and its fascination with killing up close proved hard to eradicate, especially after 2001, when platoons of SEALs were sent to Iraq and Afghanistan to hunt terrorists.

In many ways, the war on terror was Vietnam all over again. SEALs were dropped into foreign countries with unfamiliar cultures where they didn't speak the language. They had to tell enemies from allies in a fight with no uniforms. Their commanding officers were often far away. They grew bushy beards and went around in civilian ball caps, advertising to other troops that they were too elite for regular military standards.

Just like in Vietnam, a force with a poor understanding of language or culture too often measured success in terms of kill counts. And just like in Vietnam, the SEALs got mixed up with CIA agents who didn't mind torture. A few months into the Iraq war, SEALs from Team 7 were working with CIA agents at the notorious Abu Ghraib prison, where, according to later court filings, they punched and kicked detainees, broke fingers, twisted testicles, and gouged eyes. One detainee was found dead in a prison shower. Photos emerged of his body packed in ice.

Faced with a vicious insurgency, just as in Vietnam, some SEALs decided the way to win was to fight even dirtier than the enemy. If the game was terror, they were determined to play to win. In 2006, a new commander took over one of SEAL Team 6's squadrons. In an homage to the Native American warrior on their unit patch, he presented each SEAL with a custom-made ceremonial combat tomahawk and urged them all while they were in Iraq to "bloody the hatchet." Several men started carrying their hatchets on operations and before long some guys were using them to kill enemies or hack their dead bodies.

As the wars in Iraq and Afghanistan got dirtier, SEALs got pulled into the muck. Operators began shooting enemy fighters through the top of the head in a way that split the skull open. They called it "canoeing" because the shot split the head wide open like a canoe. They left the bodies behind like a calling card, a way to telegraph terror to the enemy and the local population, just like the frogmen in Vietnam who had painted their victims' faces green.

Demo Dick was gone, but the idea of fierce loyalty to teammates remained. SEALs covered up for one another or stayed silent. In a decade of high-tempo operating, the SEALs were faced with uncounted investigations for misconduct, but less than a half dozen ended in criminal charges. At those trials, SEAL witnesses either refused to testify or testified that nothing had happened. In the longest period of war in the nation's history, when SEALs played an outsized role in combat missions, none were convicted of beatings or killings in war zones.

A new version of the pirate culture seemed to spring up organically in platoons all over the Teams. In Ramadi in 2006, American Sniper Chris Kyle and his platoon in SEAL Team 3 started spray-painting their trucks, body armor, and helmets with the scowling black skull emblem of a heavily armed comic-book antihero called the Punisher. The Punisher was a gun-toting vigilante who made his debut in 1974 and soon became a kind of Dirty Harry embodiment of white suburban outrage, fighting crime with massive handguns and none of the hindrances of the rule of law. Early promotional posters read, "If you're guilty, you're dead." He was the perfect symbol for a nation hungry for payback after September 11.

The Punisher emblem embodied the belief that rule of law was a hindrance to the true pursuit of justice and that guys with guns on the ground were far better equipped to decide who was guilty than officers in the rear. "We wanted people to know, *We're here and we want to fuck with you*," Kyle wrote in his memoir. Spray-painting Punisher skulls on all of the equipment was his platoon's version of psyops, he wrote. "*You see us? We're the people kicking your ass. Fear us. Because we will kill you, motherfucker.*"

Like Eddie, Kyle claimed to have more sniper kills than any SEAL in history. But by his own telling, he was repeatedly investigated for needless deaths of civilians, and members of his own platoon started to openly question his shots. In his memoir he described killing two insurgents riding on a scooter together in Ramadi with a single bullet. Kyle said he saw the pair plant an IED before he pulled the trigger. But the Army investigated and found no IED. A short time later, Kyle shot a man walking on a busy street in broad daylight, claiming he had a gun. The man's wife complained to authorities that he had been walking unarmed to a mosque. The Army again investigated and had enough doubts that it shut Kyle's whole platoon down for the rest of the deployment. SEALs in Kyle's platoon grew so suspicious of his shots, that while some SEALs called him "the Legend," others in his platoon called him "the Myth."

At the height of the wars in Iraq and Afghanistan, while platoons were quietly sharing photos of the enemies they'd "canoed" and Kyle was selling books celebrating all his kills, Eddie was coming up through the Teams, learning the ropes from older frogmen who carried knives and wore pirate patches on their uniforms. Pieces of the pirate worldview forged in Vietnam and Afghanistan lay scattered all over the Teams by the time Eddie arrived at BUD/S. An operator who wanted to embrace the pirate ethos had only to pick the pieces up.

CHAPTER 5

THE CAPTIVE

EDDIE DROVE ONE of Alpha's big, armored M-ATVs through a dusty farm field toward the FLOT, trying to get as close to the fighting as possible. The field ran up a gentle rise to a village of a few dozen flat-roofed houses. A vast cemetery stretched beyond the village, its centuries of headstones the only things sprouting out of the bare ground. Beyond the cemetery lay the edge of Mosul. Eddie parked the truck so that the .50-cal machine gun on the roof had a good sweep of the village. His ice-blue eyes scanned for targets.

It was dawn. In the distance the scratchy street-corner loudspeakers of Mosul sounded the morning call to prayer. Tire fires were already burning. The silhouettes of minarets rose up beyond the black smoke. In the growing light an American Apache helicopter gunship cut fast over the flat rooftops. It passed over the village and then over farm fields left unplanted for seasons because of the fighting. There, in the dirt, a line of Iraqi Humvees and six-wheeled armored troop carriers was kicking up a plume of dust as it lurched toward the village. The pop of gunfire echoed over the field, followed by a reply from the village. Then more gunfire, until soon the air was rattling with automatic weapons. Iraqi soldiers scurried forward on foot, using the steel hides of the trucks as cover. A massive Abrams tank clattered alongside, ready to smash through courtyard walls or entire houses to destroy any refuge for ISIS. Eddie's truck began pounding the village. All around was war. And if there was any other place Eddie Gallagher would have rather been at that moment, it was likely even closer to the action.

Of all of his combat deployments, Mosul was the most intense yet. And to anyone who asked, Eddie said it was the most badass. Laying siege to a city against a savage enemy was a chance he knew he likely would not see again. This was not some Podunk insurgency like so many platoons had experienced in Afghanistan, where the enemy fighters spent most of their time trying to pretend they were civilians. This was all-out war. ISIS was more vicious than anything Eddie had ever encountered. It was clear they were willing to fight to the death. Eddie finally had a chance to experience war like he'd envisioned it watching *Platoon* as a kid.

If ISIS was completely savage, the other side was almost as barbaric. The Americans might tiptoe around civilian casualties. Not the Iraqi Army. They were hunters. Many had adopted the Punisher logo and put it all over their uniforms. They were going to take back the city no matter what. Many of the Shias in ERD believed that the Sunni residents of Mosul were all ISIS sympathizers. If civilians were killed in the process, that was war.

It was May 3, 2017, the first day of a new offensive. For two months Alpha platoon and its Iraqi allies had slowly punched into Mosul from the south, grinding small bits of the city off block by block. But the fight had bogged down as they closed in on the honeycomb of the ancient city center, which had literally been built to withstand a siege. ISIS was dug in deep.

Full frontal assaults were a tactic for standard infantry. The SEALs always tried to strike where they were least expected. So the coalition was making a surprise run to hit from the west, away from the river, in the desert on the far western side of the city.

The village that was Eddie's target sat on a patch of high ground with a sweeping view of the western approach to Mosul. The farmhouses offered a clear field of fire across the fallow fields and ancient cemetery. No one trying to go in or out of Mosul could get past. Dozens of ISIS fighters held the strategic outpost and were firing on anyone who used the main road. But days before, Iraqi troops had circled the village, cutting off all escape. They waited as the fighters inside ran low on food, water, and ammunition. On May 3, ERD forces moved in to clear the village. The SEALs were there, as usual, to advise and assist. The Iraqi officer in charge estimated the village would be destroyed by lunchtime.

Eddie scanned with the .50-cal, looking for enemy fighters. The Iraqis' armored vehicles pressed into the village. He could hear the firing and the occasional punch of a grenade. He saw the smoke rising over the village. But he wasn't allowed to join the fight directly under the rules of engagement. The best he could do was fire from the flank.

Eddie was about 300 meters away and it likely tore him up to not be closer. Two months into what was probably the most epic urban battle of his generation, he had yet to get in an up-close gunfight. He had not even been within blocks of the enemy, and had never looked an ISIS fighter in the eye. The Marine commanders at the Special Operations Task Force were too hesitant. Too many lawyers and wannabe politicians were still holding the leash. The way to glory and status for the SEALs was by charging aggressively to the front. You didn't get medals sitting in a truck. There had to be danger and blood. But the brass in charge didn't see it that way. The American people by 2017 were tired of war; the United States involvement on the ground had to remain limited, quiet, deniable. No one wanted flag-draped caskets. So pipe hitters like Eddie were repeatedly told to stand back and stand by. He was somehow supposed to fight a war from the rear. It was increasingly clear the Pentagon wanted him to remain a spectator in the climax of the war he'd been fighting his whole life. "Dealing with this SOTF sucks," Eddie texted his boss, Senior Chief Alazzawi, during the deployment. "These guys are a bunch of vaginas and constantly tell us to stop being aggressive."

There was a saying Eddie sometimes repeated to young SEALs as they made their way through the Teams. "Special operations is a mistress," it began. "The mistress will show you things never before seen and let you experience things never before felt. She will love you, but only a little, seducing you to want more, give more, die for her. She will take you away from the ones you love, and you will hate her for it, but leave her you never will. If you do, you will miss her, for she has a part of you that will never be returned intact. And in the end, she will leave you for a younger man."

Eddie had known the mistress for much of his adult life, and he could sense that she was already moving on to the younger men. Chief was the last rank where a SEAL could count on seeing any action. If he stayed in the SEALs he'd almost certainly end up behind a desk. He was nearly eligible for retirement. At the end of it all there would be no victory, no peace accord, no ticker-tape parade. War would go on. Combat wasn't so much a question of peace but of score. How many bad dudes could a SEAL take out? And here, at the end of Eddie's career, was Mosul. One last big fight, if he could only figure out a way to get into it.

CRAIG MILLER DROVE up to a bombed-out building about 500 meters back from Eddie's position. He pulled into a walled equipment yard and the other trucks from Squad 1 followed. In growing light, the thick steel doors of the M-ATVs creaked open and boots crunched over the gravel. The platoon fanned out and began setting up the lethal symphony they had rehearsed so many times in the past few months: the Puma to scout for targets, mortars to pound them, snipers to pick off fighters, the kamikaze Switchblade drone for surprise strikes, shoulder-launched rockets, and Javelin missiles. If there was a normal rhythm to a massive urban assault against a self-proclaimed terrorist caliphate, then the day started out normally enough. It was how it ended that changed everything.

The platoon would later be asked to detail May 3, 2017, again and again, sometimes under oath. Where had they been? What were they doing? What had they seen? How had it happened? And why? Most of the answers came easy. The memory was often etched in high definition, not just clear but inescapable. But for the bigger question—why?—no one ever offered much of an answer, other than that Eddie was just Eddie.

Miller walked a few steps across the gravel yard and entered the building where the squad had parked. It was bigger than the low farmhouses sprinkled on the outskirts of the city, four stories high with a ten-foot wall surrounding it. Once it had been an office building or some kind of government bureau. But like every inch of the region, it had been conquered and reconquered and was now just a bullet-riddled shell. Everything of value had been stripped. Broken desks and filing cabinets lay in heaps. The windows were smashed. The perimeter wall had holes big enough to drive a tank through. A giant red-and-white steel radio tower that had once stood hundreds of feet above the building lay tangled on the ground. But the building's high, flat roof still offered a strategic view of the target village, and the perimeter wall provided cover from enemy fire. For a temporary command post, it was perfect.

As Miller walked into the command post, Dylan Dille pulled a mortar tube from the back of his truck and hefted it onto his shoulder. He looked for a spot with some cover and soft ground where he could set up. He crossed an open section of the yard where a massive hole in the perimeter wall opened the courtyard to enemy territory. Without warning the zing of bullets zipped past and slapped a nearby wall. He dashed across the gap.

"Careful, man. I almost got shot," he yelled back.

Dalton Tolbert was right behind him carrying the heavy baseplate for the mortar. Without hesitating he crossed the same alley, but at a sprint. Both SEALs stepped through a hole smashed in a wall during an earlier battle and found a sheltered spot in a vacant lot for a mortar pit.

Miller walked back out of the building, hooked his thumbs in the chest rig on his body armor, and surveyed the yard. Since Eddie was out in a gun truck doing his Eddie thing, the Sheriff was assuming the duties of chief, as usual. Miller was also increasingly on the lookout for threats. A few days before, he had almost been killed by a grenade dropped from a small, off-the-shelf drone that ISIS had rigged to kill. Miller stood up after the blast unhurt, but it had been a good reminder: ISIS could strike anytime from any direction. He ran through the different threat scenarios. Frontal attack, rear attack, mortar attack, and attack from within the walls by ISIS posing as

ERD or a stay-behind fighter hidden in the rubble. He directed two of the four gun trucks to move to strategic corners of the walled yard to protect the approach. He relayed to his ERD partners not to let any unknown Iraqi forces into the compound. Once everything seemed to be in position, he pulled out a sledgehammer and started knocking a new hole in the outer wall so he could pass mortars to Dille and Tolbert without exposing anyone to enemy fire.

As Miller ferried mortars across the yard, he passed by an armored truck where a Marine named Giorgio Kirylo sat studying the screen on a piece of electronic equipment the guys in Alpha universally referred to as "Gio's nerd box." Kirylo was a signals intelligence specialist that the SOTF had attached to the platoon because his classified equipment could intercept electronic communications and pinpoint ISIS locations for the platoon to destroy. As he sat in the truck, listening to chatter through oversized headphones, he wore a ball cap that read, "DEATH COMES KNOCKING."

Kirylo had joined the platoon a few weeks after they arrived in Iraq and had not made a great first impression. He criticized nearly everything the SEALs did, and constantly bragged about his combat experience, as if needing to prove he was more than just a computer geek. He was so loud and obnoxious that the Sheriff had pulled him aside and chewed him out. So had Eddie. Slowly, Kirylo had settled down and become more or less accepted.

One of the JTACs, Joe Arrington, passed Kirylo's truck and climbed the stairs to the compound roof. The bulky radios he used to call in air strikes jutted from the front of his chest, their stubby black antennas poking above his shoulders like wasp feelers. Right behind him was a second JTAC, Ryan Rynkowski. The SOTF expected the kickoff of the western offensive to get pretty hairy and assigned Rynkowski—who was an Air Force technical sergeant, not a SEAL—to help shoulder the air strike load for a few weeks. It was his first day working with Alpha.

At the top of the stairs both JTACs joined Alpha's lieutenant, Jake Portier, who was overseeing everything from the roof. Portier stood looking out at the battlefield with the commander of the ERD battalion, a gray-haired and slightly portly man with a mustache and green fatigues named Brigadier General Abbas al-Jubouri, who was directing the attack.

In the yard, T. C. Byrne, the lead medic and dedicated drone flyer, assembled the Puma's long white wings and launched it by hand like an oversized paper airplane. It skimmed the ground, then buzzed away and climbed slowly upward, circling to 1,000 feet. He set it on autopilot, circling above the city, and walked upstairs so he could relay what the Puma's camera was seeing to the command team.

Lying prone on the roof not far from the command team was the youngest SEAL in Alpha, Eddie's gopher, Ivan Villanueva, his finger on the trigger of a MK-48 lightweight machine gun, providing overwatch in case of attack. Beyond the outer wall that surrounded the compound, he could see the fallow fields stretching nearly a kilometer east to the Iraqi soldiers pushing in to clear the ISIS-held village. Near the village he watched Alpha's two dust-colored SEAL M-ATVs on the flank of the village, providing cover fire for the Iraqis. Eddie was in charge of one. The second was commanded by the squad's baby-faced assistant officer, Tom MacNeil.

Mosul was MacNeil's first time in combat. Like Portier, he had started out an admirer of Eddie, impressed by the chief's experience and resolve. He hoped to learn from him. And Eddie had enthusiastically taken MacNeil under his wing, vowing to raise him right. In combat MacNeil had proved organized and calm, even when things were exploding all around. He didn't squawk when Eddie turned off the ATAK trackers, and because of that Eddie had taken a shine to him. When one of Eddie's superiors asked how MacNeil was handling Mosul, Eddie replied he was "crushing it." But by that morning MacNeil was starting to grow wary of Eddie. What he'd once admired as aggression he was starting to see as recklessness. Eddie kept putting the platoon in pointlessly risky situations where they were either going to get shut down by the SOTF or killed. Just like Miller, MacNeil started quietly taking extra precautions. He practiced calling in medevacs at night before going to sleep. Every time they drove into Mosul, he memorized the locations of vacant lots where medevac helicopters could land.

Standard operating procedure required MacNeil's truck to stick with Eddie's for security, so when Eddie drove forward through the bare farm fields to fire on the village, MacNeil had to go with him. As usual, Eddie was going to try to push up as close as he could when the shooting started.

Back at the compound, the mortar pit was up and ready. Dille and Tolbert launched test rounds into an empty field. The Puma flying above spotted the rounds, and the medic piloting the drone relayed the hits to the mortar team so they could adjust.

Then Kirylo, the signals intelligence Marine, picked up some enemy chatter on the nerd box and triangulated the signal. He radioed the lieutenant and passed on the intel: It sounded like there was a group of ISIS fighters holed up in a small house at the northern edge of the village, including the local commander. Portier tried to radio Miller to hit the house with mortars, but Miller's radio seemed to be on the fritz. It kept cutting in and out, and he didn't get the message. The lieutenant turned to the JTACs. The skies above Mosul buzzed with aircraft day and night. That morning a pack of Apache helicopters circled just outside the city waiting for a call. Joe Arrington got on the encrypted radio and relayed the grid for the target. It was a one-story house with cinder block walls and only a few rooms. No friendlies nearby. No civilians. Arrington called for two laser-guided Hellfire missiles, both with 100-pound warheads set on a slight delay so that they wouldn't detonate until they punched through the roof and into the living room. The pilot radioed back confirmation. The package was out for delivery.

From the field where the trucks parked, Eddie and MacNeil watched an Apache sweep in and the missiles streak from its wing. Without a tail of white exhaust, they would have been too fast to see. The missiles crashed right through the roof and the whole place disappeared in a blast. There was no fireball, just a shuttering wave of pressure sending up a cloud that swallowed the house.

THE HELLFIRES WERE THE EXCLAMATION point of the assault. Dust and smoke drifted over the village and everything grew quiet. Within minutes ERD soldiers on the ground radioed back to General al-Jubouri that the village was clear. A few ISIS fighters had managed to escape, but most had been killed. ERD planned to sweep through the wreckage to make sure no one was missed, but barring any surprises, that was the end of operations for the day. It was about 10 A.M.

Dylan Dille headed in from the mortar pit to ask if he should pack the gear and get ready to head out. He scooted past the gap in the wall where bullets had nearly clipped him earlier and found his lieutenant in the courtyard conferring with General al-Jubouri. As Dille was about to ask what the plan was, he heard the general tell Portier his troops were bringing a wounded man back from the village. Portier got on the platoon radio and called for a medic. He wanted T. C. Byrne to stop flying the Puma and tend to the wounded Iraqi soldier.

Negative, Eddie cut in over the radio. He had overheard, and told Byrne to stay on the Puma. Even though the battle appeared to be over, Eddie wanted Byrne to look for targets so he could fire a Jav. Let the Iraqis take care of their own, he said.

General al-Jubouri shook his finger. No, he told Portier, his men weren't bringing in a wounded Iraqi soldier. They were bringing a wounded ISIS fighter. Portier keyed his mic and told the medic to stand down: *Never mind, T.C. It's not ERD. It's an ISIS guy.*

Dille suddenly perked up. In two months of combat and dozens of missions, the platoon had seen plenty of live ISIS fighters from a distance, and a fair number dead, but never a live one up close. This was going to be interesting. Eddie must have heard it, too, because Dille heard him immediately come back over the radio. "No one touch him," he said. "He's mine."

EDDIE'S TRUCK DID a U-turn in the field and headed back toward the compound, sending up a tail of dust. MacNeil, who had been worried about Eddie getting too close to the front line all morning, now watched mystified as the chief inexplicably drove away from the fight. He had no idea what was going on, or what Eddie meant by

"No one touch him, he's mine," but with Eddie's truck leaving, MacNeil's truck had to follow. Both left their position supporting the Iraqi troops and drove a kilometer back toward the compound.

Miller was walking to his truck to get something to eat when a battered green Humvee with a bullet hole in the windshield rolled into the compound. A gang of Iraqi soldiers hoisting assault rifles sat on the hood and hung off the sides, cheering and waving their guns in celebration. Draped across the hood was a wounded ISIS fighter. With his broken radio, Miller hadn't heard that the captive was coming, so this was a complete surprise. He strode across the yard to try to figure out what was going on. Like the rest of the guys, he had never seen a live ISIS fighter up close. He stared almost slack-jawed, forgetting what he had been on his way to do.

The Iraqi Humvee pulled in diagonally among the SEAL trucks and stopped. General al-Jubouri stood at the hood in his camouflage fatigues with his arms crossed, the captive spread out before him as if on a platter. The guy was conscious, but barely. He had shaggy, curly hair that was a few months past its last cut. He wore a dirty black tank top and baggy brown bottoms that one of the SEALs described later as "Aladdin pants." He was so skinny that his scrawny shoulders barely filled his tank top. He was covered head to toe with chalky dust, likely from the Hellfire strike, making him look a bit like a ghost or a statue. The only bright color on him was a fresh white bandage around his left calf with a small but vivid red blossom of blood on the gauze.

Iraqi soldiers pulled the fighter up by his arms and swung him down off the truck. The wound on his calf left a small smear of blood across the hood. As the soldiers lifted him down, he hung heavy and limp like a wet towel. He tried raising his head to see where he was, but he didn't have the strength. His head flopped forward, then slumped back as the soldiers laid him out in the gravel at the general's feet.

Word spread through the compound that the Iraqis had a live ISIS captive, and guys from Alpha flocked to see him. The idea of ISIS loomed large. The SEALs had heard so much about the wild-bearded, hardcore fundamentalists who tortured civilians, crucified priests, bombed Western cities, enslaved women, shot families, and were so fierce that they had chased the Iraqi Army out of half of their country. SEALs in full combat gear jostled for a view, eager to see their foe eye to eye.

The fighter in the gravel was not what any of them expected. He was young, tiny, pathetic. The first thing Joe Arrington noticed was that he had no shoes.

Dille pushed in, almost giddy, then stopped in his tracks. The guy was so skinny that when the Iraqi soldiers lifted him off the truck, his wristwatch slid all the way down over his biceps. He had smooth cheeks with no sign of stubble despite a siege that had lasted for days. *You gotta be kidding me,* Dille thought, *this isn't ISIS, it's a goddamned kid.* He turned to one of the platoon's interpreters and said, "Man, how old do you think that guy is?"

Iraqis crowded around with the SEALs, taking photos of the kid as he lay in the dirt. Dille felt a simmering disgust. He knew his Iraqi partners well enough that he was sure nothing good was going to happen to the captive. The house where the platoon slept in Hammam al-Alil shared a wall with a house ERD used to hold prisoners. At night the SEALs heard bloodcurdling screams. They could hear men being beaten and forced to bark like dogs, and the rhythmic jolted cries from what they guessed were electric shocks. The Iraqis would probably shoot the kid or, worse, take him back to that room.

Growing up in the Rockies, Dille had learned to hunt only in season, during daylight, and only if the tag matched the right age and sex. The rules were there for everyone's benefit. That's how he saw war, too. Lethal force was necessary, but so were rules of engagement. Trying to cut corners might seem like common sense but ultimately, over time, was self-defeating. No doubt this kid didn't give a shit about rules and would have shot anyone in the platoon that morning. Dille would have happily killed him or dropped a mortar on his house an hour before. But now he was out of season. To kill a captive was not just unprofessional and illegal but revolting, like shooting a bear cub in a zoo.

More Iraqis and SEALs showed up. They formed a wall of curiosity around the captive. Except for the gunshot on his calf, the captive had no other obvious wounds. Even so, he appeared to be in pretty bad shape. He lay limp on the ground, his eyelids drooped over pupils that barely bothered to scan the men crowded over him. His face was gaunt, his lips were going gray, his breathing was shallow.

General al-Jubouri knelt down and gently took the kid's hand. It was hot in the sun, well over 85 degrees. One of the aides splashed some water on the captive, and the general asked a few questions: Where are you from? How old are you? What ISIS unit are you with? How many fighters? The fighter could only mumble two or three words at a time. The general relayed the answers to an aide, who wrote them in a notebook. He was a local kid, from a neighborhood just a few miles away. He had joined ISIS only recently. There were twenty fighters with him. Five got away. The rest had been killed.

The general dropped the kid's hand and stood up, brushing off his palms. He turned to Miller, who was watching. "All right. We got fifteen of them," he said with a grin.

"What are you going to do with him?" Miller asked. Like Dille, he was feeling a twinge of pity for the enemy. It felt so incongruous that he tried to ignore it, but it wasn't going away.

"We'll take him back to Baghdad," the general said, then he winked at Miller.

Miller smiled and nodded like everything was fine, but the wink clearly meant something ominous.

What were the Iraqis really going to do with this kid? Miller tried not to think about it. That was Iraqi business he didn't want to get mixed up in. The SEALs weren't in Iraq to act as human rights observers. They couldn't fix all the country's problems. The United States had already tried that and failed. They were just there to help kill ISIS. Still, it didn't feel good to know a kid might suffer for no reason.

T. C. Byrne put the Puma on autopilot when the captive arrived and went down for a look. He wore a helmet camera that he switched on whenever something interesting happened. As he crossed the dusty yard toward the Humvee, he clicked Record. The cam captured the Iraqi soldiers beginning to lift up the captive to put him back on the hood of the Humvee. General al-Jubouri was done interrogating him. They were going to take him away and do whatever they planned to do. The general saw the men and put his finger up, scolding them in Arabic. "No, no, no, no . . . not in front of them," he said, referring to the SEALs. "Do not put him on the hood in front of them, not now." The general knew the Americans had strict rules about how they treated captives and seemed to want to avoid angering his partners.

Just then, the helmet cam captured a gloved hand slapping the general on the shoulder. Eddie had arrived.

General al-Jubouri turned and saw the chief. The two had worked together daily for two months; they had grown close. Eddie respected al-Jubouri because he was not afraid to get after it on the battlefield. Al-Jubouri liked Eddie because the chief was tough on his SEALs, just like al-Jubouri was tough on his soldiers. He called the leader of the SEALs "Chief Ed." He couldn't remember the lieutenant's name.

"Is he ISIS?" Eddie asked. Al-Jubouri said he was. Eddie nodded and said, "I got him, I got him."

Eddie had on a black ball cap instead of his helmet and a medical bag slung over his shoulder. All the other SEALs in the platoon wore an emergency first-aid pouch across the small of their backs. Not Eddie. He wore a small handmade hunting knife in a black leather sheath, horizontally woven into his belt loops. He pushed through the Iraqis around the captive, knelt down, unzipped the medical bag, and began cutting away the pant leg near the wound on the injured fighter.

Gio Kirylo, the Marine, came over excited. "Eddie's about to put him out, dude," Kirylo announced in a loud voice, as if he didn't want the others to miss out on the fun. "Hey, Eddie, this is from my sig-int strike!" Kirylo shouted, meaning the Hellfires that had been guided by his signals intel equipment. "Let me know if you need help!"

Eddie didn't respond. He reached down and checked the wounded leg. He pulled the kid onto his side to check the back of his legs for wounds. Byrne's helmet cam recorded as the kid winced in pain and tried to rise up. Eddie pushed him back down to the dirt. Then the camera clicked off.

Byrne stood above Eddie watching, trying to figure out what was going on. The more he watched, the more concerned he grew. Byrne's full name was Terence Charles Byrne III and he had one of the more unusual backgrounds in the SEALs. His stepfather was a banker who took the train into Manhattan from their leafy neighborhood in Connecticut. But his birth father was a black-market arms dealer who in the 1980s got mixed up with the CIA and its United Kingdom counterpart MI6 in a scheme to covertly sell high-tech artillery shells to both sides of the war between Iraq and Iran. After his cover was blown, he spent much of the rest of his life hiding out. Byrne had not only inherited his father's intensity and instinct for adventure, he had, decades later, inherited his war. In Alpha, Byrne was instantly attracted to Eddie's love for everything kinetic and became one of his biggest backers. He loved the chief's aggressiveness, his confidence. Byrne planned to go places in the SEALs. He wanted to try out for DEVGRU and thought Eddie's leadership and connections could help him get there. He was such a disciple of Eddie that in skits the platoon put on before deploying, Byrne appeared repeatedly as Eddie's boyfriend.

That started to change in Mosul after Eddie kept turning off the trackers and sneaking around. Those decisions fell most heavily on the medics. Byrne figured it would only be a matter of time before Eddie got someone hit by an air strike. It kept him up at night. He memorized everyone's blood type and ran through rescue procedures again and again, but never said anything to Eddie. He knew if he complained Eddie might just bench him at the safe house. And if he was benched, he wouldn't be there if anyone got hit. He had deployed to Iraq to work as a medic, so he shut up and did his job.

Now as he and half a dozen other SEALs watched Eddie work, an insistent barrage of questions hit his mind. The first was *What the hell is Eddie doing with a med bag in the first place?* Eddie had been a platoon medic years ago, but that wasn't his job with Alpha. No one in the squad had ever seen him even unzip a med bag. The platoon often encountered refugees straggling out of the city, some bleeding and broken from the fighting. Byrne treated them. So did the other medic, Corey Scott. Eddie never offered so much as a Band-Aid. The medics also treated wounded ERD soldiers. Not Eddie. Even with their own team, Eddie did little. Two weeks before, ISIS had fired a rocket-propelled grenade at one of the platoon's armored gun trucks and hit the open side door where Byrne and an interpreter were standing. The explosion showered the interpreter's legs with hot shrapnel and blasted Byrne into the back seat, knocking him unconscious. Byrne woke up in such a daze that he wandered out into the street oblivious to the enemy fire. Even in that state, it was Byrne who treated the interpreter's wounds, not Eddie. Now here was Eddie, working on an ISIS captive. Byrne couldn't make sense of it.

Byrne watched as Eddie cut away the pant leg. That raised a second question: *What the hell are we going to do with this patient?* By kneeling down and providing aid, Eddie had put the kid in the custody of the United States Navy. Would that mean after Eddie stabilized him they would have to evacuate him to a hospital? Would he end up in prison in the United States? Were they allowed to turn him back over to the Iraqis? In two years of training, the scenario had never come up.

Then a third question pushed to the fore: *Should I help?* The captive was struggling to breathe. Judging by the dust covering his body, the medic figured that the supersonic pressure wave from the Hellfire blast that blew out the windows and doors had also punched into the fighter's lungs, momentarily inflating millions of tiny air sacs to the point of popping, then letting them sag back, shriveled and injured. It was a condition called *blast lung*. If the kid had blast lung, he was going to need more than a bandage, and the medic wasn't sure Eddie was up to the task.

Byrne watched Eddie move from the captive's leg to his neck. The chief used a blade to make an incision for an emergency airway called a cricothyrotomy. It involved cutting a vertical slit down the center of the throat, then inserting a plastic breathing tube. It was the right move, Byrne thought. But Eddie fucked it up. Instead of inserting the tube through the trachea into the airway, Eddie had gotten it stuck between the skin and the cartilage. The kid was moaning in pain. Byrne instinctively knelt down to help. As he did, he clicked on his helmet cam. Now all the work on the captive was being recorded.

Dille was standing next to Byrne, growing increasingly uneasy. Eddie's declaration over the radio echoed through his head: "He's mine." Eddie had told Dille before deployment that if they encountered any wounded enemies, the medics could simply "nurse them to death." Now Dille wondered if that was what he was seeing. Was Eddie going to slowly kill this kid with medical procedures? He knew the SEAL Teams were full of pirates who cherished the idea of killing the enemy just for the sake of killing. And he knew Eddie liked to act like one. But would he really do it? Dille did not want to find out. He turned and walked away.

Miller stood watching, too mesmerized to look away. On missions Miller tried to be a step ahead of every scenario. He was constantly gaming out threats and devising responses. Now Eddie was providing first aid to a captive ISIS fighter. It was so outside any of the possibilities Miller envisioned that all he could do was stare. The only explanation Miller could come up with was that maybe the whole thing was a preplanned propaganda stunt: ERD would bring in a wounded captive, a SEAL chief would save a young ISIS fighter's life, then the Iraqi Army would put the kid on Iraqi TV to tell the story. It would give Eddie one more story to tell back in Coronado— the day he saved the ISIS fighter. It seemed laughable, but nothing else made sense.

As Eddie and Byrne worked on the fighter, guys in the platoon drifted away from the scene. The excitement of seeing the enemy was over. Some were turned off by the sight of a scrawny, shoeless kid; others had work to do. General al-Jubouri and Jake Portier walked upstairs into the building to keep an eye on the battlefield. Miller, unable to wrap his head around the general's wink and Eddie kneeling down to aid the prisoner, wandered away and tried to find something to keep himself busy. He remembered he had not eaten anything all day and went to his truck to find an MRE.

One of the few who stayed was Gio Kirylo, the signals intelligence Marine, who watched and listened as the pair worked.

Dille went back to the mortar pit. He had his rifle up and his hand on the grip. To anyone watching, he looked like he was standing security. In fact, he was lost in thought. What was about to happen? Was Eddie just going to rough up the kid or was he going to kill him? And if he did try to kill him, was anyone in the platoon going to stop it? Would the lieutenant? Would Miller? Dille wondered if he was the only one in Alpha who cared if an ISIS fighter died.

Combat had a lot of long, dull moments, even in a fight as vicious as Mosul. In those idle hours, Dille and Tolbert and a few other guys had often talked about what they would do if they actually got their hands on an ISIS fighter. It was an informal exercise of imagination—a combat version of truth or dare. They had tossed it around repeatedly. What would you really, no shit, do? Would you just shoot him, knowing the Iraqis surely would do worse if you didn't? Would you do it quickly or slowly? Would you canoe him? Would you use a knife? What if the fighter was a woman? What if the fighter was a kid? It was ghoulish but harmless talk with lots of posturing and gallows humor. Now it was no longer a game.

BYRNE LOADED A SYRINGE with ketamine and injected it into the captive's arm. Eddie had cut open the throat without any pain medication. The captive was weak, barely conscious, but clearly suffering. Byrne did not want to admit to the others that he was trying to ease the captive's pain, so he just told them that ketamine would immobilize the patient to make him easier to work on. Almost immediately, the kid went limp.

Byrne moved to address the breathing problems. If the kid's lungs had collapsed, Byrne needed to release air filling the spaces between the lungs and chest cavity. He inserted a wide-gauge decompression needle with a one-way valve through the ribs on the left side to let the trapped air out. He wanted a needle on the right side, too, but couldn't easily reach it. He looked up. The platoon's youngest SEAL, Ivan Villanueva, was standing just a few feet from the body, next to Kirylo.

It wasn't surprising to see Villanueva there. Right before deployment, he had gotten arrested for pulling a knife in a bar fight. Eddie had bailed him out and somehow smoothed it over with the command, then made Villanueva his assistant. In Mosul he was almost always right there to do what Eddie asked. Villanueva was like a sponge, eager to soak up as much experience as he could. He had assisted Byrne a half dozen times on other casualties.

"Get down here and help," Byrne told him. Villanueva knelt next to Eddie, and Byrne led him through how to insert another decompression needle in the right lung.

The platoon's other medic, Corey Scott, arrived. True to his reputation for not being around, the Ghost had been in a closed armored truck when the captive came in, and had missed the initial commotion. Then someone told him to grab his med bag and get over to the captive. With two medics and an assistant already working the patient, Scott knelt down at the head to monitor vitals. He noted the bandage on the kid's calf and the decompression needles sticking through his ribs. There were no wounds other than the gunshot on the leg. He felt the pulse on the neck. It was weak but even. He hovered his thumb over the breathing tube in the throat. He could feel steady breaths. The kid wasn't doing great, but he wasn't going to die.

Like everyone, Scott was confused about Eddie's plan. Once Eddie was done working on the kid, what were they going to do? No way they were going to medevac an ISIS fighter. The SEALs didn't even evacuate wounded ERD soldiers. And no way the Iraqis were going to take care of the kid. Scott had heard the ERD troops talk about murdering and sometimes raping captives. He had listened to the torture through the walls. If Alpha turned the kid over to them, best-case scenario, the Iraqis would just shoot him. Worst-case scenario would be, well, a lot worse.

Byrne tightened a band around the kid's arm and slapped the skin, searching for a vein to insert an IV. He couldn't find one. Eddie was kneeling next to Byrne. He was talking, but Byrne was too focused on his work to hear the words. He dug into the med kit for an alternative device called a Fast1—a multipronged, spring-loaded needle designed to punch down into the sternum and deliver fluids directly into the bone. He pushed it into the kid's chest and connected an IV bag, making sure the drip was barely on. Too much liquid could make the fluid leaking into the lungs even worse.

When the Fast1 was in place, Byrne sat back on his knees and took a breath. He had run through his checklist of care. The kid's airway was clear. Bleeding was controlled. Circulation was okay. IV was in place. The next step was transport to a hospital. Byrne had no idea if that was going to happen. Eddie or Portier would make that call. But if the kid was medevaced, Byrne would probably have to go with him. That made him remember something. The Puma was still circling on autopilot above the battlefield. The controller and the rest of the gear were still up on the roof. Byrne got up and told Eddie he'd be right back. He instinctively clicked his helmet cam off as he walked away.

Tom MacNeil left the truck where he was talking to the JTACs and went to update General al-Jubouri on the positions of enemy fighters. As he crossed the yard, the junior officer saw Eddie and Corey Scott kneeling by the prisoner. Then he saw Eddie draw out the knife he kept in a black leather sheath across his belt on his back. It was a stubby, handmade blade, only about three inches long. MacNeil recognized it immediately because he and Eddie were room-mates, and every night Eddie hung his pants on a nail by MacNeil's bed. The knife was one of the first things he saw when he woke up each morning. MacNeil walked by without pausing to think why Eddie had his knife out over the prisoner. He wasn't focused on Eddie; ISIS was still maneuvering on the edge of the city, and he had to relay information to the commander.

Miller found a pouch of combat rations in his truck, ripped it open, and had a few bites. Then he went back to making sure the platoon was ready for whatever happened next on the battlefield. The platoon might be moving farther forward. He was on his way from one truck to another, still chewing a mouthful of food, when he came around the corner of the bullet-riddled Iraqi Humvee. About ten feet away on the ground lay the sedated captive. Eddie was kneeling above the kid's right shoulder, facing away from Miller. In his hand he had the knife he always carried on his belt. Scott and Villanueva were kneeling across from him. Miller instinctively slowed his walk when he saw the knife. The kid was on ketamine and not moving. What was Eddie doing? Miller watched Eddie put the knife blade down at the base of the kid's neck, just above the right collarbone. Abruptly, without saying anything, Eddie shoved the blade all the way in.

Miller froze midstep.

He saw Eddie draw the knife out and hold it for a moment. There was almost no blood. Then Eddie pushed the knife in again. It wasn't a fast stab so much as an insertion: steady, even, intentional. This time blood flooded out—not a spray or a jet, but an eruption from a broad wound. The pump of bright red blood spilled across the kid's shoulder and onto the dirt. *Oh fuck,* Miller thought. All he could think to do was keep walking, as if nothing had happened. His face was calm as he passed the chief; his thoughts were on fire.

Scott saw the stabbing from just inches away. The medic was kneeling by the head, monitoring the kid's breathing. Eddie was next to him. There was no warning. Eddie didn't say a word. He pulled out the knife and stabbed the kid two or three times, right at the base of the neck. Scott was close enough to reach out and stop it, but he froze. He could have yelled out to Eddie, but he was too shocked to move. *Holy shit,* he thought. He looked around to see if anyone else was seeing what was happening. Everything became a blur. Eddie got up. He might have stabbed the fighter again in the side; Scott was too shocked to register what was happening. If Eddie said anything, it was lost in the panic.

Villanueva was kneeling just across the body. He was looking in a different direction when movement caused him to turn his head. He saw the chief with his hunting knife out. Without a word, Eddie stuck the knife in the kid's rib. Then Eddie walked away.

Scott lost it. He was too overwhelmed to think or act. His special operations medical training had readied him for scores of high-stress situations. The one where the platoon chief stabs a sedated POW was not one of them. Villanueva watched Eddie go. If the chief had said anything before or after the stabbing, he couldn't remember it later. He was as stunned as Scott. Villanueva didn't say anything or do anything. Blood pumped out of the captive's neck and saturated the dirt.

Miller saw Scott grab for a medical bag to try to save the kid. Someone put bandages on his neck and his side, though neither Scott nor Villanueva remembered trying to bandage the wound. Maybe, Scott said later, he had done it. He couldn't remember. But it didn't really matter, he said, it wasn't the type of wound you could put a bandage on. The next few minutes for him were a blank. Villanueva eventually stood up and walked away. "Once it's done it's done," he later said. "What do you do at that point?"

Scott was left alone. He'd seen the same issues with Eddie that everyone in the platoon had seen—the pointless gunfire and imaginary targets, the bullshit claims of body counts, the neglected duties. That was all manageable. Even funny. This was different. This was a crime. This was murder. Scott worried that he and everyone else could all go to prison for it. Eddie's stupidity was going to bring them all down.

Shit, he thought. *Now we have a problem.*

He knelt by the patient until he died.

BYRNE CAME DOWN from the roof with his Puma gear. He saw the kid lying alone on the sun-bleached gravel, pale and obviously dead. There was a big ball of gauze that someone had hastily stuck on the kid's neck and a big plastic sticker called a chest seal over the wound. There was another bandage on his ribs. Those bandages had not been there when Byrne left. A spurt of blood had splashed onto the kid's right shoulder and caked the dirt under his neck. That had not been there either. Something bad had happened.

Dylan Dille came around the wall from the mortar pit. Eddie passed him in the yard as he was walking away from the body. The chief looked strained but exultant, as if he had just beaten his record bench press. Dille saw the body lying abandoned in the yard with blue medical gloves and crinkled bandage wrappers wadded up all around it. *Eddie actually did it,* Dille thought. *This time he wasn't just talking. He actually somehow nursed that guy to death.*

A few steps away was one of the EOD techs, a guy named Josh

McCandless. He stood in the yard, staring silently at the body as he pulled nervously on a cigarette. He sensed Dille at his side. Without looking up he muttered, "Dude, that was just a brainwashed kid."

Dalton Tolbert came out from the mortar pit just behind Dille. He saw Iraqi soldiers coming up to Eddie laughing and smiling, congratulating him like he had done something incredible. Dille and Tolbert stood there, stunned.

Miller walked past at a fast clip, fury showing in his eyes. The Sheriff was trying to hold himself in check by focusing on his duties as a lead petty officer. If he could put them back in order it might help him get a handle on his reeling thoughts. *Control what you can control,* he thought. *Make sure the men are doing their jobs.* "Break it down, now!" he barked to the snipers. "We're getting out of here. This whole thing is fucked." Dille and Tolbert started packing up the mortar gear.

Miller stomped by the body. Iraqi soldiers he had never seen before were crowding around to take selfies. It was a dangerous situation. Any one of them could be an ISIS sleeper agent. SEALs milling around seemed unconcerned. Gio Kirylo, the Marine who had found the kid's hideout with his nerd box, dragged the body to a better location, and flashed a smile for a photo. So did the platoon's young dog handler. Miller saw Ivan Villanueva lifting up the kid's head by the hair for his own selfie. "Put that shit down!" Miller yelled. Villanueva dropped the head like a hot plate.

Miller was determined to get out of the area as soon as possible. Iraqis were walking around everywhere. One was holding a meat cleaver. Unable to wrap his head around the fact that he had just witnessed a murder, Miller instead latched on to the dangerously poor discipline it sparked. Half of the guys were ignoring their duties to gawk at the prisoner; dozens of unknown, armed Iraqis were in the secure area. They were taking photos of the body and of the SEALs. No one was watching the perimeter. They were vulnerable to attack. Elite Navy SEALs were acting like a bunch of idiots. The officer in charge was nowhere in sight.

The Sheriff stormed into the building and found Jake Portier on the roof. We've gotta get out of here, Miller told him. He was seeing red. He wanted to throttle Eddie, but he tried to stow his emotions and frame the whole debacle in terms of professional warfighting. The tactical situation was deteriorating, he said. Too many unknown Iraqis are in the compound. The guys have abandoned their positions and instead of doing his job, the chief is executing a prisoner. Portier nodded as he listened. At the mention of the prisoner he didn't respond with surprise or outrage. Instead he went down to get a look at the body.

EDDIE NEVER GAVE the platoon any real explanation for what he did. But many of the guys thought they understood the significance of the kill for a guy like Eddie. Eddie loved to tell war stories, even if many of them turned out to be exaggerated or flat-out invented. Eddie also prided himself on being an old-school frogman who knew more about fighting than the officers in the SOTF. For guys like him, the true measure of a SEAL was killing the enemy. And while the Navy over the generations had continually devised ways to add distance and safety to the violence—through artillery, missile cruisers, and unmanned drones—true frogmen still practiced the artisan craft of killing up close. There was nothing closer, more visceral, more badass, than the silent blade of the World War II frogmen and painted green frogmen of Vietnam. To a SEAL chief who liked telling war stories, being able to tell other guys that he had gotten a knife kill on ISIS was probably the ultimate. It would live on as lore at Coronado. It would forever cement his reputation. It was better than Snead's Silver Star.

That, at least, is how many guys later tried to make sense of it. And it still didn't make sense.

Even though the platoon knew the larger meaning of a knife kill, they had no idea how much Eddie wanted one. He appeared to have been hoping and planning to kill someone with a knife long before the captive arrived in the yard. In the months leading up to the deployment, Eddie texted an old SEAL friend named Andrew Arrabito. Eddie had served with Bito in Afghanistan when he was with the Good Old Boys. Bito was a crazy dude, Eddie told a few SEALs in Alpha. In Afghanistan, far from any of the Navy's watchful eyes, Eddie said, Bito had gone way off the reservation. He started wearing a ratty Mohawk and covering half his face in black war paint like a Native American warrior. He'd ride horses through villages wearing only a tribal loincloth. It was psychological warfare. The idea was to strike terror into the locals. Eddie would often tell the guys in Alpha that he and Bito had gone out and done some pretty crazy stuff in Afghanistan, but he wouldn't elaborate. Bito was one of the guys who called Eddie by the nickname "Blade." In Afghanistan he wore a big pirate flag patch on his body armor. In recent years Bito had started a boutique knife company called Half Face Blades. Bito's knives were all engraved with his company's logo: half of a scowling, Mohawked warrior's face that looked a lot like the way Bito had dressed in Afghanistan. Eddie wanted to make sure he had one of those special blades for Iraq. A few months before deploying he texted Bito to order one and asked him to put the Good Old Boys logo on it. He also wanted a custom hatchet, similar to the ones some Team 6 guys carried. The order wasn't done by the time Eddie shipped out, so he insisted that Bito ship the blades to Iraq. "I'll try and dig that knife or hatchet on someone's skull!" Eddie texted him.

Bito replied with one word: "Please."

Eddie waited weeks, but the package hadn't come. He followed up with Bito multiple times. Finally, just a few days before the prisoner came in, Bito said it was in the mail. Eddie texted, "Can't wait to get it. Def a good chance to use it here."

The knife hadn't arrived when Eddie came face-to-face with the enemy fighter. He only had the custom blade he'd been carrying on his belt for years.

MILLER WALKED OUT of the compound and into the sun of the yard. The mortar tubes were packed in the truck. The sniper rifles were broken down and put away. The midday heat rippled off the gravel yard. Across the bare farm fields the clutter of houses that had once been a village stronghold smoldered in silence. The Iraqi soldiers who had swarmed in when the captive arrived were almost all gone. The only thing still left from the morning was the dead kid himself, his thin body splayed out in the noon heat like a starfish on the beach. Someone had covered him with a scratchy green army blanket.

The platoon was quiet. They loitered around trying to pretend nothing had happened. Only a few guys had witnessed the stabbing, but the vibe quickly spread that something shady had gone down, and with a body lying in the middle of the yard, it wasn't hard to guess what.

The mission was over. Alpha just needed clearance from the SOTF to pull out and drive home. Miller paced around. He could not wait to get out of there. Then he saw Jake Portier step out of the building where he had set up the command post. The officer started gathering the guys together. Miller listened, hoping Portier was going to finally do something. For months the lieutenant had gone along with whatever Eddie wanted. Now that the shit had really hit the fan, it was the officer's job to show leadership. The death of the captive could not just be treated as nothing. Even if the guys were trying to skulk around and ignore it, the commander had to say something, Miller knew. It was too significant. He had to make some kind of statement.

Portier told the guys to gather around. Miller went over to listen. The lieutenant shared his plan of action. The dead enemy was the responsibility of many people. The sig-int Marine, the JTAC, the medics, and Eddie had all played a part. Given what had happened . . . they were going to take a group photo with the body.

"Come on guys, bring it in, bring it in," Miller heard the lieutenant tell the platoon. He turned away in disgust.

Dylan Dille was sitting in the front of his armored gun truck staring at nothing, feeling as though he was being sucked through a hole that stretched all the way back to when he first met Eddie. For a long time he had dismissed Eddie as all talk. Over and over again he had seen Eddie on the sniper rifle, plugging away at nothing, yelling out "Got 'em!" He and Tolbert had traded smiles as they listened to Eddie brag at the end of the day about how many bodies he'd dropped. Then there were all those stories from other deployments about killing a guy with a toaster and shooting a little girl that seemed obviously false. Once, while telling the story about how he got the nickname "Blade," Eddie told some of the guys he had stabbed some Marines in a bar fight and ditched the knife because he was sure he had killed one of them. Dille hadn't believed that one either. Now he was forced to consider that in every case Eddie might have been telling the truth.

Portier came around the open door of the truck and jolted him out of his thoughts.

"Come on, we're taking a picture," the lieutenant said. He was rounding up members and bringing them into the yard. Dille shook his head.

"*Come on,* get in the picture," Portier cajoled, as if trying to convince a shy co-worker to get in a picture at an office birthday party.

"I'm not getting in any fucking picture!" Dille shot back.

"Whoa, okay," Portier said, putting up his hands as if he didn't see what the big deal was.

Tolbert heard the lieutenant gathering people and quietly disappeared. He still wasn't sure what had happened, but knew he wanted no part in it. It was almost noon. Even if the kid had died on the battlefield and Eddie hadn't helped, there was no reason to take a picture with a corpse. They were SEALs, not trophy hunters.

Portier ushered other guys toward the body, saying, "Come on guys, bring it in, bring it in."

Eddie got down on one knee right behind the kid for a solo shot, threw off the blanket, and lifted the kid's head by the hair with his right hand, like he was holding the antlers of a prize buck. In his left hand he gripped his custom-made hunting knife. He looked straight into the camera, confident but not smiling, in a classic hunter's pose.

Then someone dragged the body a few feet to the south, perhaps to set up a better photo, away from all the medical trash and the pool of blood. Portier ushered the platoon in and arranged them in two rows, one standing, one kneeling, like a portrait of a high school soccer team, with Eddie as team captain at the center. In place of the ball was a teenage corpse. On either side of Eddie knelt two of the SEALs who also worked on the body, T. C. Byrne and Ivan Villanueva, each with an M-4 assault rifle resting on his knee. Byrne was ambivalent about the photo, but was determined not to piss off Eddie so that he could continue to go out on missions. Villanueva was compliant as usual. He was too junior to know what was normal and what wasn't.

Portier pulled in other guys to fill out the second row: the JTACs, Ryan Rynkowski and Joe Arrington, the junior officer Tom MacNeil, and Gio Kirylo.

Portier saw Miller off to the side with his arms folded and told him to get in the photo. Miller pressed his lips together in silent anger. He didn't want any part of Eddie's bullshit but didn't feel like he had a choice. At this point he had witnessed a murder and until he figured out what to do about it, he had to play it cool. He stepped in without a word and purposely moved to the back, next to one of the EOD techs, St. John Mondragon-Knapp. Portier noticed Corey Scott off by the corner of a truck and called the medic over. Scott was quiet as an undertaker. He had not told anyone yet that he had watched Eddie push his knife into the kid's neck or that he stayed with the kid until he died. He got in the photo but stood off to the side, almost out of the frame, hands in his pockets. When the lieutenant snapped the photo, Scott's face appeared to be shrouded in shame.

Portier wasn't done. He had mentioned several times in the previous weeks to guys in the platoon that Eddie was due to reenlist and wanted to make it special. This was the perfect opportunity. All enlisted troops in the military had to reenlist every few years to continue their career. It was a simple process of filling out some paperwork and swearing a quick oath. It could be done in five minutes in an office, and usually was. But the simple act of recommitting to defend and uphold the laws of the nation had increasingly taken on a ceremonial aura. And like other simple ceremonies, the advent of social media had turned it into a spectacle. Some sailors enlisted standing just above the water on the massive anchor of an aircraft carrier. Fighter pilots took the oath while in the cockpit. Divers did it underwater. It was like proposing to Uncle Sam. People wanted to show not only that they were committed but also that they loved what they did. Eddie had a tradition of reenlisting in combat to symbolize the essence of his profession. With the Good Old Boys he had enlisted right next to his sniper rifle in Afghanistan. This time he was taking the oath in front of the dead ISIS fighter.

Portier took out a small black pocket Bible and paper where he had scrawled the enlistment oath. A SEAL held up an American flag behind them. The body was at their feet. Eddie faced the lieutenant, raised his right hand, and began reciting the oath: "I, Edward Gallagher, do solemnly swear that I will support and defend the Constitution of the United States against all enemies, foreign and domestic; that I will bear true faith and allegiance to the same; and that I will obey the orders of the President of the United States and the orders of the officers appointed over me, according to regulations and the Uniform Code of Military Justice. So help me God."

The pool of blood spilled from the captive was drying in the hot sun in the yard. Flies buzzed around. Miller watched from the periphery, disgusted but unable to look away. The words of the oath hit him like a grenade. What had happened was not just bad tactics, or a crime, he realized, but an assault against everything he believed the SEALs stood for. How could Eddie swear to uphold the rule of law right after violating it in cold blood? He was not only taking a life, he was strangling the very values of the SEALs. It was an insult to the reason Miller had joined the Navy. The SEALs were supposed to be the good guys—karma in physical form working to wipe out the evil in the world, and here was Eddie, their pirate leader, acting as savage as any ISIS fighter. Miller thought to himself, *This is the most disgraceful thing I've ever heard in my life.*

He looked over and noticed the Air Force JTAC, Ryan Rynkowski, with a similar expression. "You okay with this?" Miller said. The JTAC shook his head. "This is fucking stupid," he replied.

The ceremony took only about a minute. Afterward, a few guys congratulated Eddie. Others just drifted away. For a long time after, it was quiet. The assault on ISIS had pushed east past the village and was now miles away. But the SOTF had ordered Alpha to stay in place until they were relieved by a Marine special operations platoon. So they sat there for hours. A thick, awkward silence settled in—the kind that saturates a dysfunctional household during the pauses in the yelling. Some guys avoided each other. Others pretended nothing was wrong. They organized gear. They waited in their trucks. They ate MREs out of brown foil pouches. They joked around. Dille flew a small quadcopter drone out over the village to assess the battle damage. Miller asked if Dille would teach him to fly, and for a while they practiced with the drone around the compound.

Then Eddie wanted a turn with the drone. He took over the controls. Byrne's helmet cam recorded as the chief circled the drone around the yard and zeroed in on the dead kid. He buzzed the corpse over and over again, zooming inches over the body. Gio Kirylo laughed and joked about the corpse as Eddie flew. Eddie said nothing. A lone Iraqi soldier stood in the yard, no more than ten feet from the body, with his hands on his hips. He looked at the drone, then looked back at Eddie in disgust. He picked up a dirty red quilt lying in the yard. As the drone buzzed around his head, he walked over and covered the body.

It was late afternoon when the platoon finally got back to their house. They parked the trucks and started restocking gear and ammunition as usual, but it was obvious something was wrong. One of the medics from Golf platoon came up to help T. C. Byrne unload the medical gear. The two had spent a lot of nights together in the aid station treating wounded Iraqi soldiers and had grown tight. The Golf medic immediately noticed that his friend looked like he'd eaten something bad and asked what was wrong.

"Eddie screwed us today, man," Byrne told him. "He screwed us big-time." Byrne looked down at the ground.

"What happened?" the medic asked.

"You promise you won't tell?" Byrne said. He led the medic to an out-of-the-way corner and laid out everything he knew. Eddie had done something to kill a prisoner. Byrne wasn't sure what. There might even be video of the murder, he said. Guys in the platoon took photos and videos with the body. The Iraqis had taken a bunch of photos and videos, too. It was only a matter of time before it all got out.

The Golf medic went white. The line between right and wrong could sometimes get fuzzy in Mosul, but killing a POW was way, way over it. And the photos were bound to find their way into the wrong hands. He was probably going to see it all on CNN. When the brass saw the footage, they'd go nuclear. Forget Alpha—*everyone* was toast. "Man, if people find out, you guys are done, we're all done," he said. "You just screwed the SEAL Teams."

Byrne nodded. "I know, man."

Josh Vriens noticed everyone was unusually quiet. The big sniper cornered Ivan Villanueva and made him tell him what was going on. Eddie's gopher told Vriens what he had seen: A teenage ISIS fighter came in as a captive, and Eddie had jacked him up with his knife.

Vriens liked Eddie, but it didn't temper his reaction.

"That's so fucking stupid," Vriens huffed. "If a guy is caught, he's caught. Go find another one on the battlefield and kill him." Vriens didn't always trust Villanueva, whom he saw as young and prone to storytelling. He went to find some of the senior SEALs.

Miller walked into the house where Alpha lived and went to the bedroom he shared with other senior members of his squad. He was still too overwhelmed to put words to how he felt personally, and anyway, it didn't matter. He knew he had to do something about the murder, but first he had to limit the damage by addressing the platoon. He had to put his foot down. He didn't want any guys thinking it was open season on war crimes. He was pulling off his body armor and wondering what to say when Dille and Tolbert came in. Their mood was dark.

"It actually happened, I can't believe it, the torture scenario actually happened," Tolbert said, as he pulled off his own kit and hung it on a nail.

"Yeah, except whenever we talked about it, no one actually said they'd do it," Dille said. He looked at Miller. "Any idea what Eddie actually did?"

Just then Corey Scott walked in. The medic looked tired and shaken. He told them he had watched Eddie stab the kid. He was right there. They were working on the guy. The chief didn't say anything. There was no heads-up, no explanation. Just fucking stabbed him. The kid had been too sedated to move. He wasn't a threat, Eddie just did it to get wet. Scott was clearly pissed. He had a young kid at home. He was worried he'd get tangled up in what Eddie had done. I don't want to go to jail for the rest of my life for that guy, he told the other guys.

The room was silent. No one knew how to respond.

It was only one murder in a city where murders were happening every hour of every day, in numbers and at levels of brutality that easily eclipsed the stabbing of a single sedated enemy prisoner. But for the platoon, the kid's death was an earthquake for two reasons. The first was obvious: It was a crime. SEALs vow to defend and protect the Constitution and uphold the rule of law, and under the rules of engagement set out by the United States military, killing an enemy on the battlefield was a service to the nation, but killing a captive was first-degree murder. The two sometimes might only be separated by minutes, but they were different. There is no eye-for-an-eye. Once a fighter became a captive, SEALs had to treat him with care and respect. Sure, ISIS didn't play by the same rules, but that was exactly the point. The SEALs and ISIS were different because one had laws and one didn't. Take away the laws and SEALs weren't much more than a better-armed version of ISIS.

The second reason that the kid's death shook the whole platoon was that everyone was now on the hook. As soon as Eddie killed that scrawny little dirtbag, he had forced a choice on all of them. Navy regulations required them to report him. Now they had to decide whether to obey the regulations or not. Would they be loyal to the platoon or to the rule of law? It was one or the other. And neither was a good option.

Doing something meant ratting on another SEAL. Not everyone in Alpha saw stabbing a wounded fighter who probably would have killed them and was going to die anyway as a huge moral outrage. In fact, on the list of tragedies they saw daily in Mosul, it ranked pretty low. But either way they were supposed to report it, which not only violated the frogman's unwritten code of loyalty but threatened to derail the entire deployment. If they reported Eddie, the whole platoon would likely get benched in Kurdistan while the authorities investigated. No one wanted that. The work was too important and a murder investigation would cloud the rest of their careers. There was a good chance it wouldn't just be Eddie who was fired. Portier would probably get fired. So might anyone who had been in the photos. Ruining SEAL careers for the sake of an ISIS fighter was hard to swallow.

The easier, more obvious choice was to do nothing. But that was fraught, too. Even if word about the dead kid never got out, which was unlikely given all the photos and videos, doing nothing was a choice that would be with guys for the rest of their lives. Everyone who did nothing would have to live with being Eddie's accomplice. Year in and year out the guys would grow older, make rank, and raise their children knowing they were complicit in a murder, knowing they had lied to cover up for a cold-blooded pirate. It also meant for the rest of their lives, Eddie would have something on them.

THAT NIGHT MILLER called the whole platoon together in the cramped family living room they had converted into their meeting room. He wasn't thinking at all yet about a year or ten years, or the cost of staying silent. He was thinking about something more immediate: If Eddie had murdered once, he would probably do it again, and Miller needed to keep that from happening. He also needed to keep the practice from spreading to the platoon. So he had to debrief the guys pronto, because Eddie was away at his nightly debrief with the SOTF, and Miller had a small window when he could tell everyone the plan. Once that was squared away, he could think about what to do next.

The guys filed in and filled the room's battered couches. Others stood along the wall. Only Squad 1 had been out that day. Squad 2 had been on a rest day, and most still had no clue what had happened. Miller got up in front of them, still in his dirty uniform. He had no idea how guys would respond to the news. There was a good chance some would be totally cool with Eddie killing an ISIS captive. He half-expected some to start clapping. For all he knew, guys like Byrne and Villanueva had helped. But he didn't have time to worry about it. He expected Eddie back any minute. He was going to brief them on the murder as if he was briefing them on a mission. Short, no nonsense.

"So, Eddie killed a prisoner today," he said in his sternest, most "Sheriff" voice. There was no clapping. Only silence. "No matter how you feel about it morally, this isn't who we are, and we are not going to do this. It doesn't do anything for us tactically, it doesn't do anything to support the mission. It puts all of us at risk. We're not going to let it happen again."

He looked around for reactions. No one was smiling. No one was giving him a dirty look. Dille and Tolbert locked eyes with him and nodded. They had his back. As lead petty officer it was Miller's job to lay out the plan of action. He cleared his throat. "From now on, we need to have a perimeter around Eddie," he said. "And if the Iraqis bring in another prisoner, we need to intercept it. We can't let him do something like this again."

Dille was leaning against the wall. Miller seemed to have said his piece, so the sniper stepped forward. He said he knew some of the younger guys had taken individual trophy shots. "You guys think you're so badass taking these pictures. You look like a bunch of fucking amateurs. You want to be a cool guy? Then maybe act like you've been here before."

The platoon started to mutter in agreement. What Eddie did was stupid, one said. Selfish, said another. They talked about how it could fuck everything they were doing and agreed to make sure it didn't happen again. Miller decided not to bring up whether they should report Eddie. He was afraid if he did he might lose the consensus he needed, but at that moment he breathed a sigh of relief; despite all Eddie was doing, Alpha was still united.

Just then, Eddie walked in. The room went silent. Thinking quickly, Miller pretended to be wrapping up a standard after-action briefing for the morning. He reminded the guys to check the fuel and oil in the trucks. Everyone tried to file out in a hurry. Eddie stopped Corey Scott by the door. "Hey, what were you guys talking about?" he asked.

The medic paused. He wanted to avoid Eddie, but he was also

pissed about what he had done. "Guys aren't okay with what happened today," he said.

Eddie's brow tightened. "*Who's* not okay with it?"

A lot of the guys in the platoon were afraid of Eddie. He was a chief with hundreds of connections in the Teams. He had a huge influence over their futures. Scott wasn't one of them. He had been diagnosed with kidney damage from a bacteria he had picked up in Afghanistan, and he knew he was getting medically discharged from the Navy after this deployment. In terms of his career, no one could hurt him.

"I'm not going to dime anyone out. As a platoon we're not okay with it," Scott said.

Eddie gave a sideways glance, almost an eye roll—a look that said he thought the guys in Alpha, instead of being warriors, were acting like a bunch of politically correct turds. He shrugged. As he walked off, he said to Scott, "Next time I'll do it when you're not around."

JOSH VRIENS WALKED into Alpha's tactical operations center after the meeting. The TOC was a room no bigger than a home office, packed with all the platoon's computers and communications equipment. It also held a red civilian laptop where everyone in the platoon dumped their photos and helmet cam footage at the end of the day into a communal folder, which they were using to compile footage of their most badass missions and their funniest downtime antics for an end-of-deployment platoon video.

Vriens was still weirded out over what Eddie had done. *Fuck ISIS,* he thought, he didn't care if the fighter died. But Miller was right, Eddie's actions would screw all of them. It was amateur, and for an aggressive guy like Vriens, who wanted to kill as many enemies as possible, it threatened to derail plans. As he walked into the TOC, one of the younger SEALs from Squad 2 had the laptop open and was looking at pictures from the day. Vriens stopped when he saw the screen. A skinny Iraqi kid in a black tank top was splayed out on the ground, covered in dust. His head was being held up by Iraqi soldiers. It was worse than Vriens thought: Someone had actually taken photos of this stuff. Eddie and Portier were in the TOC going over plans for the next day. Eddie looked over as Vriens walked in and saw him staring at the screen. Eddie knew Vriens liked him. Their wives were good friends, and Eddie said he saw the young sniper as a good dude with the proper attitude toward combat, so he didn't try to hide what he had done.

"Yeah, that's the dude I stabbed," Eddie told him. The kid was sedated, but could still feel everything, Eddie said. After stabbing him the first time, he said, "I lifted his head, I looked into his eyes, and stabbed him again."

Portier was sitting right next to Eddie. "That was freakin' sick," Vriens heard the lieutenant say. "I don't know why guys are pissed, that should be in the platoon video."

Vriens left with a sinking feeling. Eddie had clearly gone off the rails. And the lieutenant was acting like a fanboy. He didn't know what to do. For now, like Miller, he decided to go on as if nothing was wrong.

Later that night, when everyone was turning in, Miller was sitting on his bed in the room he shared with the snipers when Eddie walked in and sat down across from him. The chief had Copenhagen packed in his lip and a plastic cup in his hand for spitting. "Hey, what's going on?" Eddie said casually.

Eddie didn't usually hang out and make small talk in Miller's room. Miller knew what the visit was about. Eddie must have realized he had a problem on his hands and was probing to see how big it was. Miller could feel his anger vibrate in every muscle of his body. For months he had maintained an aura of polite professionalism with Eddie and tried to support him despite growing frustration. He had picked up the slack for the chief with no complaints. He was determined to maintain that respect. But he wasn't going to let this slide. Miller looked at Eddie and told him some guys were pissed about the prisoner.

"Who?" Eddie asked. He looked genuinely surprised and concerned.

Miller wasn't buying it. He had seen firsthand that Eddie was a master manipulator. Eddie could roar and threaten like a lion. But if he thought the frontal assault wouldn't work, he dropped any tone of menace and became serious and concerned, or playful and agreeable. Sometimes he reacted like a loving father listening to his child cry about a scraped knee. Sometimes he reacted like an annoyed big brother tired of hearing his kid brother whine. He could use this judo to throw guys off-balance, exploiting their insecurities and emotions. Younger SEALs were left to wonder if they were being weak or naïve or even cowardly. It made them question if *they* were the problem, not Eddie.

Eddie looked at Miller with an expression of concern, as if perplexed why the young SEALs were disturbed by the death of an enemy. "Who's not good with it?" he asked again.

Shit, Miller thought, *Eddie's doing that thing*. He could feel Eddie coaxing him toward naming guys he knew Eddie would then destroy. He didn't want to create a split with Eddie, but he didn't want to throw anyone else on the grenade.

"I'm not good with it," he said.

Eddie likely realized he had a problem. The Sheriff had the support of the men. It would be hard to marginalize or undercut him. The best way forward would be to keep Miller on his side. Eddie smiled. He looked away slightly and sighed, as if to say, "Give me a break."

Miller didn't fold. Killing the captive had put the mission and everyone in the platoon in jeopardy, he told Eddie. It was wrong, and Eddie couldn't do shit like that again.

Eddie nodded thoughtfully. He spit in his cup. You're right, he said. But relax, it was ISIS. They would do a lot worse to one of us. If anyone came to ask about what happened, he'd say he was working on the guy and he just died.

He spit in his cup again and got up to leave. For some reason, he turned and said, "And I'm going to get another one."

"Eddie!" Miller said, shocked.

Eddie smiled and hit Miller on the shoulder, then said, "Quit your worryin'."

Eddie made little effort to hide the killing. Besides Miller and Scott, he also talked to Dille and Tolbert. He tried to explain to them that killing the ISIS fighter was no big deal. He had done similar things before on other deployments to people who weren't even enemy fighters. Still, he appeared to know the guys were pissed, so he switched his approach and apologized. I thought you'd be cool with it, he said. He told them next time he would be more careful.

Eventually the chief walked down the hall to the room he shared with the platoon lieutenants.

"How'd it go?" Portier asked when Eddie walked in. He was sitting on his bed. MacNeil was on his own bed a few feet away.

"It was okay, they were upset with what happened today," Eddie said.

Talk went back and forth between Eddie and Portier about how the victim was just an ISIS fighter. Just as in Vietnam, the chief appeared convinced that if ISIS was going to fight dirty, he'd have to fight just as dirty.

"Imagine what they would have done if they had one of us," Portier said.

Eddie agreed. "Exactly."

CHAPTER 6

MAN DOWN

Josh Vriens ducked and crawled into a dark rat hole that had been pecked in a concrete wall by ISIS fighters. He was following a line of other SEALs from Squad 2 as they squeezed one by one through the passage. Their body armor bulged with extra ammunition and their rifles hung at their chests as they shoved backpacks full of sniper gear, then passed the long tube of a Javelin, then boxes of ammunition and missiles, then medical gear, then water, then more ammunition. They emerged on the other side in a sunny courtyard, stood up, walked a few paces, and crouched down to crawl through another hole.

It was May 25, 2017—nearly a month after the murder. That morning, Eddie had announced to the squad that he had a new plan. It was only later that members of Alpha started to suspect that the new plan was at least as twisted as what had happened with the captive. Maybe more so.

The SEALs had driven deep into the city. Through the truck window Vriens watched as they passed the shot-up compound on the edge of the city where Eddie had stabbed the kid, then passed shattered blocks of collapsed houses and burned cars. The noose was tightening. May had brought some of the hardest fighting in the war. Coalition jets pounded the city with hundreds of air strikes. Huge swaths of Mosul were cleared of ISIS but were often so damaged in the process that nothing was left. As the squad motored through the shattered blocks, they passed a steady stream of refugees flowing out: mothers carrying children, old people being pushed in wheelbarrows, gaunt-eyed men who had spent years as captives. The platoon finally parked in a dense urban neighborhood near the heart of Mosul.

Now Vriens and the rest of Squad 2 were making their way through the bowels of a city block to the site of Eddie's new plan. ISIS had tunneled through a half dozen town houses, knocking rat holes through rooms and courtyards to make a passage hidden from outside eyes. The enemy had been driven out of the block and fallen back into the next neighborhood, but Eddie had found their tunnel network. It led to a pink stucco house that had exactly what the chief was looking for: a high roof that stuck up above most of the neighborhood with a low wall surrounding the roof as cover. The top floor offered a sweeping view toward old Mosul that would give them dozens of angles to shoot into enemy territory. And it wasn't just closer than the one kilometer they were supposed to stay behind the front line, it was right on top of it. The house was a perfect hunting ground. Eddie told the SEALs to expect great things. Before they ducked into the rat-hole network, he told everyone to turn off their trackers. No one could know they were getting so close.

Vriens ducked down and squeezed through one of the holes, hunched under a bulging sniper backpack, and emerged into a room. Crawling through houses was in some ways spookier than facing enemy fire. ISIS had been in those tunnels just days before, and no one knew what kinds of traps they had left behind. But the prospect of getting right up on the enemy made it worth it to Vriens. All the action the platoon had seen was still not enough for him.

Vriens was following EOD tech St. John Mondragon-Knapp, whom everyone called "Dragon." He was a big, muscled man with a bristly walrus mustache and a score on the military aptitude tests near the top of the charts. At thirty-three, he was older than most of the men in the platoon but was on his first combat deployment. He had a bohemian twist and had to get a waiver when he joined the Navy for past marijuana use. In his free time he designed tattoos in a notebook and painted decorations on the wings of the Puma. His job as an EOD was to clear hidden explosives. He led the squad through each hole with his eyes scanning for wires or pressure plates and anything that seemed out of place—especially items that a SEAL might be tempted to move. The squad filed past a wheelbarrow propped against a gate that had a grenade fastened to it, primed to blow if anyone tried to go through. He led them past an AK-47 magazine laid out on a table, also attached to explosives, poised to blow if anyone picked it up. They pushed forward, watching every step and handhold, and ducked into another rat hole.

A MONTH AFTER the stabbing, some of the men in Alpha were resigned to live with what Eddie had done. Some were scared of him. Others were more scared of the Navy's response. But Craig Miller was determined to get Eddie relieved as chief. He had gone looking for Portier within twenty-four hours of the murder and found him at a computer in the TOC. He knew Portier already knew about the murder. It hadn't taken long for everybody in the platoon to learn what had happened. Eddie seemed proud of it. Portier seemed to have no problem, either. It was not that they went on as if nothing had happened. They went on as if something *had* happened— something awesome. Eddie went around carrying the murder weapon on his belt. About a week after the murder, a package arrived from Bito. Eddie's new knife and combat hatchet had finally come. Eddie showed off his new blades to the platoon like an enthusiastic kid. He texted thanks to Bito, saying the knife and hatchet were both "sick!" Eddie signed off by saying about one of Bito's knives, "I already used it, I'll send you a pic later."

Even if Portier already knew, it was Miller's job as the lead petty officer to report any concerns of the men to the chain of command, and he was going to make sure he did his job right. True, he had already told Portier about the killing minutes after it happened, but things were so confusing then, so chaotic, so emotional, that he wasn't sure he had made it clear. It was critical that the officer in charge had no doubt that the chief had murdered a prisoner of war.

Along with Miller's collection of old things—his battered Jeep, his windup Rolex Sub, his fruit trees and honeybees—he also maintained a classic sense of morality. The Sheriff didn't have any particular religious beliefs. He didn't believe in heaven or hell. He had read the Greek Stoics and believed the rewards of virtue were immediate and real. If the world was going to be a better place, it wouldn't be because of some divine being, but because of the daily effort of individuals. In real ways, the future of humanity was built by the small actions of millions of everyday folks, and it could be torn down the same way.

Part of the reason he became a SEAL was to try to be that force of good. But he knew that doing the right thing sometimes came with a cost. Early on in BUD/S, Miller was in a line of students on the beach, trembling as they struggled to hold themselves up in a push-up position for minutes on end. The instructors were walking up and down the sand, harassing the students. They stopped a few SEALs down from Miller, at a young officer who had been chosen as the student officer in charge of the entire BUD/S class. You might as well quit now, they told the officer. It's only going to get worse. You have no business here. You're a disgrace. You're a terrible leader. And worse, your men don't respect you. Look at your men, not one of them respects you.

Miller knew his officer was a decent guy who was trying his hardest.

"I respect you!" Miller shouted. He was staring down at the sand, his arms burning. It was his Spartacus moment. He did it without thinking. In the moments after, he half-hoped that others in the boat crew would shout that they respected the officer, too. But there was only silence.

"Who said that?" the chief in charge said. He was leaning against the hood of a pickup parked on the beach, dark sunglasses on. He marched over, pulled Miller to his feet, and pushed him back against the truck hard enough that he banged his head on the door. If Miller thought the officer was such a good leader, the chief said, then he could follow that loser. While the other students watched, the chief had Miller and the young officer do flutter kicks, sit-ups, and bear crawls in the sand until they collapsed. A few days later, the officer rang the bell, and for the rest of BUD/S, Miller was marked. Every day he got hammered. The instructors were twice as hard on him. There were points where he was in so much pain he seriously thought he might die. Eventually, it was over and he had a Trident, but he had learned a painful lesson: If you want to stick up for what you believe in, don't be surprised if you end up all alone, and expect to pay.

In the TOC, Miller laid it all out to Portier. He had seen Eddie stab the prisoner. So had Corey Scott. Maybe some other guys, too. The lieutenant needed to do something. Miller was pretty sure Portier was in Eddie's camp. Anything Miller said might get back to the chief. So he skipped the talk about setting up a perimeter to keep Eddie from getting other prisoners. Instead he framed his concerns in terms of the whole platoon. Eddie was not doing his job as chief. His actions were selfish and had endangered the mission. Portier needed to do something now before Eddie got the whole platoon pulled from Iraq. He was hoping the SEALs could just quietly pull Eddie out. The platoon could keep working. Eddie would be out of their way.

To Miller's surprise, Portier didn't argue. He listened and nodded. He seemed to take everything on board. Miller was right, the lieutenant said. He told Miller he knew he had to do something. He said he would handle it.

It's in the officers' realm now, Miller thought as he left. Portier would talk to the officer in charge of the troop, Lieutenant Commander Robert Breisch, who would probably report it to the commander in charge of Team 7. They'd know what to do. Miller could get back to his job of running the platoon. The fix was in the works; he would just have to sit tight. He walked out of the meeting feeling about fifty times lighter.

Then nothing happened. Over the next few weeks, Miller kept looking for signs Eddie was going to get removed, but the rhythms of Mosul continued unchanged. The SEALs went out almost every day at dawn with the ERD soldiers. Eddie told the guys to turn off their trackers and push up to the front lines. The chief spent nearly all of his time on the sniper rifle firing at shadows. The officer in charge seemed to do nothing to rein him in. The one thing Eddie and Portier did to address the stabbing was to order everyone to delete any photos or videos from that day. If Portier was working on a fix, he was being extremely stealthy about it.

SEALs started to notice Eddie going on missions with his new hatchet on his belt. Eddie had promised he would bury the hatchet in someone's skull. But his first experience with it hadn't exactly been the type of stuff he could brag to Bito about. He was trying to pull it out of its sheath to show other SEALS, when it slipped and the pointed end jabbed him in the belly, leaving a bloody gash. Eddie often talked about the benefits of having a Purple Heart. The ribbon given for combat wounds not only gave a SEAL cred in the Teams, it also came with lifetime financial benefits. With the cut on his abdomen, Eddie went to the platoon medic, T. C. Byrne, and asked for him to fill out the paperwork for a Purple Heart. It wasn't the first time Eddie had asked for the Purple Heart paperwork based on minor injuries. Byrne refused, so Eddie went to a medic in a neighboring unit. He told the medic a story that it was a shrapnel wound that had happened while out on a mission that day. The medic checked with Byrne, then checked the records at the SOTF. Sorry, he told Eddie, can't do it. That's not a combat wound, your platoon didn't even go out on a mission that day.

Portier started wearing a hatchet, too. All the guys knew the stories about ax swingers in Team 6. Most of them might have dismissed Eddie as a poseur trying to look like he was part of DEVGRU, but not after the murder. Now the hatchet posed the very real threat that the platoon would get dragged into another bloody mess.

Miller kept an eye on Eddie. He told the Iraqis to keep prisoners away from the chief. But at the end of May, Miller had to fly back to California. His wife was due with their first child, and it was standard for a SEAL to be there. As the day neared, Miller kept watching Portier, expecting Eddie would get removed before he left. It didn't happen. Miller flew home hoping it would be only a matter of days before Eddie was pulled.

———

By the time Vriens was pushing his sniper bag through the rat holes, Miller had been gone for more than a week, but Eddie was still there, his tracker turned off, leading the squad to a spot right on the FLOT where he promised they were sure to find good hunting. At the end of the line of rat holes, the squad finally emerged at a spacious ground floor of what had once been a comfortable urban family home. It was the perfect spot, Eddie told them. The inhabitants had fled, leaving with only what they could carry. The family car was still parked in a small courtyard, covered with a mattress. On the third floor, double glass doors opened onto a sunny patio that looked out on a sea of rooftops. The pink walls of the patio were covered with gray pocks from the machine gun fire of an earlier battle. Shards of stucco and broken tile littered the floor.

The patio was open to all of Mosul and the ten thousand potential enemy sniper positions that it hid. Not to worry, said Eddie, the neighborhoods facing the patio had been cleared of ISIS. They were safe. An open stairway with an ornate white railing led up from the patio to the roof. From the top they could look out on the other side of the city, which had not been cleared. That was where Eddie wanted to set up.

The squad ferried loads of gear up to the patio level. Corey Scott put his medical gear in a sitting room by the glass doors and went to help bring up weapons. The other medic, T. C. Byrne, was a few blocks away where the squad had parked the trucks, waiting to respond in case of emergency.

In the sitting room Portier was setting up a small command post. He talked with Eddie about the plan for the day. Eddie wanted to spend all day on the sniper rifle as usual.

Dragon went out the patio doors and up the stairs to the roof to blow loopholes for the snipers, followed by Corey Scott. Ivan Villanueva and a sniper named Chris Shumake, who was slightly senior to Vriens, were just behind. From the stairs they could see deep into the city. A tall minaret as slender and pointed as a pencil rose above the rooftops and haze. At the top of the stairs Dragon was about to turn a corner and walk onto the roof when he suddenly jerked to one side and took a funny step. It was as if a string had suddenly yanked the leg on a marionette. Half of his body jolted forward. His shoulders jolted back. A split second later they heard the crack of a rifle. Dragon had been shot.

The territory Eddie had vouched to the squad as being friendly was, in fact, all ISIS. It had become a running joke that Eddie didn't always know where the front line was. Suddenly it was no longer funny. Dragon had walked unknowingly up an exposed staircase in front of an entire enemy neighborhood. Now he was lying on the ground at the top of the stairs moaning. The guys who had been behind him dove down the stairs and crouched behind a wall. Enemy snipers knew where they were and probably had crosshairs dialed in on the stairs, just waiting for the rescue team. Next person to pop his head up would likely get drilled.

Scott shouted to the SEALs below that he was putting on a tourniquet and would need cover fire to get down the stairs. Villanueva got up on one knee, raised an MK-48 light machine gun, and started spraying bullets out over the waist-high wall of the patio to provide cover. Chris Shumake stepped in next to him and raised his M-4 rifle. But where was he supposed to fire? He had no idea where the shot had come from. He fixed on the tall minaret in the distance and squeezed off shots as fast as he could. Vriens came rushing out to help. Training kicked in. There was no thought about anything but getting Dragon to safety. His eyes scanned the city, and he fired at any window or roofline that looked like a possible target, squeezing off shots. Eddie stayed safely inside. By that time Dragon had tumbled down the stairs with the help of Scott and was on the ground. He half-crawled across the patio while Scott pulled him by his body armor. As they reached the patio doors, Eddie grabbed Dragon's shirt and helped drag the bleeding EOD tech the last few feet inside.

Eddie and Scott slid Dragon across the floor to the sitting room and laid him out by a couch. Dragon sat up and muttered that he was okay. Then he collapsed. Eddie was pulling off Dragon's body armor while Scott swept his hands down the EOD tech's ribs and belly looking for the wound. When his hands passed by Dragon's belt they came up red. He had been shot right where the hip meets the pelvis.

From a sniper's perspective it was a masterful shot. The bullet hit the most vulnerable part of the SEAL that was not protected by body armor. The main veins and arteries for the leg ran right through the hip. There was potential for a big bleed. Scott didn't see much blood yet, but it was an ugly wound because the blood could be pooling in the abdomen, which meant the medics wouldn't necessarily see it. There was no good way to wrap a tourniquet to stanch the bleeding so high up on the hip. Worse, Scott couldn't find an exit wound, which meant the bullet might have ricocheted through the pelvis, tearing up Dragon on the inside.

Vriens was at the door with his rifle still up. He glanced over and could see by the look on Scott's face that the wound was a problem.

Eddie and Portier saw an even bigger problem. It wasn't where Dragon had been shot on his body, it was where he'd been shot in the city. Dragon was hit on a roof where Alpha was not supposed to be, on a block where the SOTF had forbidden them to go, way too close to the FLOT on a morning when their trackers were not showing that they were there. Now Dragon needed urgent medical care and a helicopter evac. But if the platoon radioed for help at their location, they were busted. After months of sneaking forward, the platoon had worn down the SOTF commander's patience. He had warned them over and over not to go closer than about 1,000 meters. He even had them start doing regular check-ins with their location. This might be the last straw.

Vriens saw Eddie grab Dragon by the shirt and speak loudly into his face. *You're going to tell everyone that you got shot back at the trucks,* the chief said. *You did not get shot here.*

Portier paced the living room shouting at Eddie from across the room. If we call this in, they'll see us, he yelled. They'll know where we are. We have to get out of here.

Eddie tried to calm Portier down. No problem, he said, we'll just sneak Dragon out through the rat holes. Eddie turned to the guys. Grab all the gear and get it back to the trucks, he said, and get ready for a long carry.

Portier keyed his mic and radioed his second in command, Tom MacNeil, who was about five blocks away, waiting with the armored trucks.

"Someone's been shot," he said. Then he told MacNeil not to call for a helicopter.

MacNeil immediately radioed back. Who had been shot? What was the status? What was the plan? Portier never responded.

Vriens and Gio Kirylo began shuttling the weapons through the long chain of rat holes. When they got back for another load, Scott had his head down over the patient, tuning out everything but his work. He had immobilized Dragon with ketamine and was packing the wound. Eddie was clearly growing impatient. Vriens heard him shout at the medic to just slap a chest seal bandage over the wound so they could get moving.

Eddie and Scott dragged Dragon downstairs, his feet thumping on each step as they went. Dragon was a big man, over two hundred pounds. He was not going to be an easy carry through the tunnels. MacNeil kept coming over the radio asking for a status report. He had a second medic waiting, and the JTAC was ready to spin up a helicopter. They had a landing zone selected in a vacant field nearby. They just needed the go-ahead. There was no reply.

Down on the ground floor Vriens returned from his second supply run and found Scott and Eddie with Dragon, who was laid out on the floor. Vriens looked at the first rat hole he'd have to haul Dragon through, then the second, and the third. Getting him through the maze would take time—time he wasn't sure Dragon had. Scott agreed. They would have to risk carrying him through the streets. Scott pulled out a fabric litter that looked a bit like a hammock with handles and was getting ready to gather some SEALs to carry it out the front door. Before he had the litter spread out, Eddie lifted Dragon and threw him over his shoulder.

The SEALs watched, dumbfounded. It was something out of a bad action movie and definitely the wrong thing to do with a guy who'd been shot through the middle. Eddie jogged out the main door and into the street. He humped Dragon about two blocks to an intersection where one of the trucks had just pulled up. T. C. Byrne was waiting with his medical gear. The first thing Eddie said when he reached the trucks was not an update about the patient or anything about what had happened at the house. Instead he asked, Do they know where we were?

WHEN TOM MACNEIL heard the message on the radio telling him not to call the helicopters, he knew exactly why. Eddie had snuck out of bounds, was now afraid of getting caught, and a wounded teammate was going to pay the price.

Whatever respect MacNeil had once had for Eddie and Portier, there was not a shred left. A few weeks before Dragon was shot, MacNeil had seen something that suggested Miller's fears about Eddie trying to kill another captive were dead-on.

It happened on a quiet morning when the platoon was not scheduled to go out. ERD got in touch with Eddie and let him know they had another captive. If he would meet the Iraqis in the city, they would hand him over. It was supposed to be a rest day, but around noon, with little in the way of a heads-up, Eddie told Squad 2 to get the trucks ready; they were going into Mosul. Josh Vriens drove Eddie. MacNeil rode in a separate truck. At the time Eddie knew Miller and some of his boy scout buddies in Squad 1 were pissed about the stabbing, but Vriens had been careful to appear to be one of Eddie's allies. General al-Jubouri got another prisoner for me, Eddie told Vriens as they drove.

"Oh really?" Vriens said, trying to play cool. He had been excited when he heard the squad was going out. The battle for Mosul had been raging all week. ISIS was on the ropes. He was looking forward to another chance to bag some bad guys. Eddie's announcement was a big letdown. Apparently the plan was to spend all afternoon doing whatever he planned to do with a captive. As much as part of Vriens wanted to torture ISIS fighters, he saw no point. Better to go out and actually try to win the war. He looked at Eddie and thought, *What a fucking turd.*

The squad parked in a rubbled block within sight of what had been one of the main medical centers in the city, the Al-Jamhuri

Hospital. ISIS was holed up in the hospital's eleven-story tower, from which it sprayed gunfire at fleeing civilians and advancing Iraqi soldiers. Repeated air strikes had failed to dislodge the gunners. As the SEALs pulled up, ERD soldiers were gathered in groups, staging to go forward toward the front line. Iraqi officers in camouflage waved the SEALs' trucks into a secure area, and Eddie got out to talk to them. Vriens watched through the windshield, wishing he could get out and find a good sniper position.

Eddie radioed the guys with him that he wanted them to stay in the trucks. Only a few guys were coming with him. Eddie pulled out MacNeil. He also brought T. C. Byrne, the Marine Gio Kirylo, and an interpreter. For security, he added senior sniper Chris Shumake. Vriens had to stay in the truck. He watched with simmering rage as Eddie and the others walked half a block down and entered a small mosque.

An ERD Humvee pulled up. An Iraqi soldier got out and pulled out a captive dressed in a loose black shirt. The hands were bound, and the head was covered by a cloth sack. Vriens watched the soldier heft the captive over his shoulder like a sack of flour and jog past with the captive bouncing, then turn into the mosque.

Given what had happened a few weeks before, Vriens figured there was a good chance he would never see the hooded figure alive again. But he also knew there was an obstacle in Eddie's way that might keep him from doing something truly stupid, even if Miller wasn't around: The boss was there. The troop's commanding officer, Lieutenant Commander Robert Breisch, was with the platoon for a week. He had brought with him a senior aide. Both men were shadowing the platoon on every mission. Both had gone with Eddie into the mosque. Eddie may be off his rocker, Vriens figured, but there was no way he would murder a captive in front of a lieutenant commander.

Inside the mosque, the SEALs gathered in a back room that had been pummeled by fighting. The only light came from holes punched in the walls by explosions. The floor was scattered with dirty blankets and dried pools of blood from the wounded. The Iraqi soldier brought the captive in and set him in a chair near the center of the room.

MacNeil walked up and stood in front of him with a notebook and a bottle of water. One of the expectations of junior SEAL officers was to be able to question captives on the battlefield for immediate tactical intelligence. That's what MacNeil had been brought in to do. Maybe the SEALs could gain some info on the hospital for the ERD assault.

Someone in the group pulled the sack off the captive's head. There was a moment of pause. It was not a military fighter who looked up at them. It was an old man. He had white hair and a close-cropped white beard. He was gaunt, with bags under his eyes. The shape of his skull and the lines of his collarbones showed clearly through his thin skin. It appeared that he had not eaten well in a long time. He looked around without focusing, as if in the chaos he had lost his glasses. His voice was a husky rasp.

Undeterred, MacNeil started to question the prisoner. The guys from Alpha stood off to one side with their hands resting on their rifles. Breisch and his aide stood off to another. "What is your name?" MacNeil asked through the interpreter. "Where do you live? Who do you work for?" The man didn't answer immediately. Blood was smeared on his head. His left eye was swollen. He seemed dazed. It looked like ERD had already worked him over.

Eddie paced menacingly behind MacNeil, growing impatient. Ask if he's ISIS, Eddie barked at the interpreter. The man denied it. Eddie muttered and told the interpreter to ask again.

From his guard position, Byrne watched what was happening and looked over at Breisch, waiting for the troop commander to tell Eddie to cool off. Breisch made no move. *Shit*, Byrne thought, *here we go again.*

Shumake was standing next to him with his hand on his rifle. He glanced at Breisch, too, and wondered why he wasn't stepping in.

The platoon didn't know that Breisch had known Eddie longer than anyone else in Team 7. In 2009, when Breisch was a fresh junior-grade lieutenant in SEAL Team 1, he was put in charge of Eddie's platoon in Afghanistan after the original lieutenant got his legs blown off. He had little combat experience, so Eddie and the rest of the Good Old Boys took Breisch under their wing. That was the deployment when Eddie had served with Bito and Bito had gone out nearly naked in war paint to scare the locals. It was also the deployment when Eddie claimed he shot through a little girl. Breisch had been in charge for all of it.

After that deployment, Breisch became Eddie's direct supervisor again when both moved to BUD/S. He knew Eddie had issues there, too. Eddie got in hot water for telling the little girl story. He also got in trouble for striking a student. Rather than throw the book at him, the SEALs quietly moved Eddie. He was shuffled to other assignments in other places where his past could be concealed. Breisch knew, too, that Eddie had fought with a gate guard at Coronado and been arrested for assault. Yet after all those fuckups, Breisch stood behind Eddie. As troop commander, he had picked Eddie for the toughest assignment in Iraq, he later said, because "I had complete trust and confidence in him."

Breisch had been an enlisted SEAL before becoming an officer, which made him what the military calls a mustang. Often mustangs had extra credibility with troops because they had walked in their shoes. But Breisch sometimes wore his mustang pedigree on his sleeve. He was always reminding the SEALs that he was one of them. His senior enlisted advisor, Brian Alazzawi, thought he acted too much like one of the guys and didn't do his job as commander. It caused a rift. By the end of the Mosul deployment, Alazzawi and Breisch hated each other and were barely speaking.

The younger SEALs knew none of this as they watched Breisch stand by while Eddie yelled at the prisoner. The old man continued to mutter and give one-word answers. The interpreter kept asking him if he was ISIS. Eddie kept shouting. Then Eddie pulled out the hatchet Bito had sent him.

Shumake looked over at Breisch again. He saw no sign that the commander was going to step in. This was the guy Miller had been expecting to punish Eddie for the stabbing, and everything Shumake saw suggested that Eddie was about to hack the prisoner to death in front of him. Shumake felt he had no power to stop what was happening, but he sure as hell didn't want to get mixed up in it. He was thinking about edging toward the door when Eddie looked at Shumake and Byrne and told them to get the fuck out. Breisch's aide left, too.

That left only Eddie, MacNeil, Kirylo, and Breisch with an interpreter and a few Iraqi soldiers.

MacNeil looked at Eddie holding his hatchet—the hatchet Eddie had told Bito he would bury in someone's skull. This was really, really bad. Breisch wasn't doing anything to calm Eddie down. MacNeil had not reported Eddie for the stabbing outside of the platoon, believing that Portier and Breisch would take care of it. Now here was Breisch standing by, saying nothing. MacNeil decided it was up to him. He pulled Eddie aside. Look, we aren't getting anywhere with the yelling approach, he said, so let's try something different. Eddie grudgingly agreed.

MacNeil sat down across from the prisoner and gave him a bottle of water. The man sucked the whole bottle down. MacNeil ripped open the tough plastic package of an MRE and pulled out some food. He let the man eat. Slowly, he started asking questions again. This time, he got more answers. The man said he used to work at the hospital, which ISIS had taken over. He was an X-ray technician. He had been held by ISIS and forced to work. They gave him barely any food.

Tap.

MacNeil heard something metal knock against the concrete wall. He stopped and looked up. Eddie had walked around behind the prisoner and was leaning against the wall a few feet away. He had his hatchet out. *Tap.* He hit the hatchet against the wall. *Tap.* It was as if Eddie was saying, Time's up, they tried MacNeil's way, now it's Eddie's turn. *Tap.*

The interpreter, trying to defuse the situation, offered to throw his shoe at the old man—one of the ultimate signs of disrespect in Iraqi culture. *Tap.* Eddie looked right at MacNeil but said nothing. Breisch did not step in. *Tap.* MacNeil sensed that the situation was slipping out of control—Eddie might bury the hatchet in the man's skull at any moment. MacNeil stood up and called both Breisch and Eddie into a side room. Look, there's no point in killing this guy, he said. What's our objective? The objective is to get information. Killing him doesn't add anything to that. We need to tone it down and move forward. After a moment of silence, Breisch agreed. Perhaps realizing that the troop commander was no longer on board, Eddie's demeanor changed. He put his hatchet back in his belt.

Shumake and Byrne saw an Iraqi soldier carry the old man out of the mosque a few minutes later. They were surprised to see him still alive. Eddie came out with MacNeil and Breisch a while later. Eddie climbed into the truck where Vriens was waiting.

"So what happened?" Vriens asked.

Just some old man, Eddie said, he wasn't ISIS. He wasn't a threat.

Vriens thought he heard a note of irritation in the chief's voice.

After that day MacNeil was done with Eddie. He knew he could not trust him. So when he heard over the radio that someone at the pink house was shot and he should not call a helicopter, he had the SEALs with him call anyway.

T. C. BYRNE pulled one of the trucks up as close as possible to Dragon, stopping on the edge of a bomb crater that cut the road in half. He saw Eddie shuffling with Dragon over his shoulder and opened the door so they could pull him inside. Once Dragon was laid out in the back of the truck, Byrne straddled him like a saddle horse and started working while Corey Scott assisted. Another SEAL at the wheel raced through Mosul, leaning on the horn. It was a ten-mile drive back to their small forward operating base. MacNeil had alerted the helicopter crew to have a medevac waiting.

Dragon looked around the truck in a daze and moaned. His eyes rolled wildly.

"Dragon, you're all right," Byrne said as he ripped the wrapper off a syringe. "You're on ketamine. You're going to be okay, buddy." Byrne was worried, though. Dragon's vitals were slipping. His pulse wasn't right. Byrne suspected internal bleeding. Dragon needed a blood transfusion, but the medic had nothing to give him. Byrne had memorized everyone's blood type and knew there were no SEALs in the truck who had the right blood. Then Byrne remembered something: *He* had the right blood. As the truck bounced over the rubble in the road, Byrne pulled out an IV, stuck the needle into his forearm, filled a bag, and gave it to his platoon mate.

The helicopter MacNeil called was spun up and ready when they arrived at their forward operating base. It lifted off with Dragon and Byrne and soared to a hospital at a nearby American air base.

Dragon eventually made a full recovery and remained in the Navy. The wound to the platoon was not as easy to heal. Not everyone had been broken up about Eddie stabbing an ISIS fighter. But when Dragon got shot, it was different. Byrne, who had defended Eddie for months, could not believe the chief had chosen not to call for a medevac and tried to cover his own ass instead of saving a wounded EOD tech. If loyalty was the religion of brotherhood, Eddie had committed an unforgivable sin. The other EOD soldiers were so angry they almost pulled out of Mosul, leaving Alpha on its own.

Eddie went on as if nothing had happened. When the SOTF commander asked later that day how it was possible for a guy to get shot when the platoon was supposed to be a kilometer behind the front lines, Eddie and Portier made up a cover story. It was the partner force's fault, they said. Some idiot Iraqi soldier probably shot off his gun, not paying attention. The colonel didn't press the issue. Eddie and Portier never had to divulge their true location. They never had to explain how Eddie had sent Dragon up the stairs in full view of the enemy. They never had to account for not calling in the helicopter. The next day the platoon went back to running missions as if nothing had happened. If Dragon hadn't managed to dodge a bullet, Eddie and Portier had.

EDDIE'S SCREWUP ON the roof wasn't a one-off. Though he had a reputation as an elite badass warrior, it was built largely on his own stories. Beneath that SEAL veneer was a long history of disappointments and screwups that had dogged him for much of his life.

He had grown up the oldest of two boys of a West Point graduate and Army officer who was in many ways the opposite of Eddie. If there was a dangerous end of the Army, his father was at the opposite end. He was studious and fluent in Chinese. He was an understated Irish Catholic who took the boys to church every Sunday and liked to scuba dive on vacation. Eddie spent nearly all of his childhood shuttling between posts in Asia and stints at the Pentagon. Because the family moved often, Eddie became adept at fitting in. He would morph to fit each new neighborhood. He had a charm and good looks that made it easy to make friends. He liked to play soccer. But unlike his parents and his younger brother, he had a rebellious side and a knack for finding trouble.

As a kid, Eddie gravitated toward war movies and heavy metal. He struggled in school. When he was in middle school he was diagnosed with ADHD and dyslexia. He got put in classes for kids who had trouble learning and eventually fell in with a group of friends he later described as a "wild crowd."

In high school he started skipping class, smoking weed, and sneaking out of the house. He was also getting into fights. Freshman year he was knocked out by a senior. A couple of years later at a baseball practice he was pitching, got into an argument with a batter, and got dropped by a bat to the side of the head. Hoping to keep him out of trouble, his parents sent him to a private Catholic boarding school in Connecticut. He was soon kicked out for fighting.

Eddie graduated from high school—but barely. He tried community college but didn't last a semester. He got a job at a grocery store but was fired. He worked construction jobs, and at an animal shelter. He was hanging out with a bunch of directionless older guys. One night in 1999, at age nineteen, he was watching TV with them well past midnight, looked around at the sad scene, and decided he had to find something else. He drove to the first recruiting office he saw, which happened to be for the Navy, and waited the rest of the night for it to open. He enlisted that morning without telling his family.

In the Navy he also struggled. As a young medic he got into a drunken fight with the officer in charge of his platoon and punched him in the face. He was passed over for promotions. After five years in the Navy he had barely progressed in rank.

There's a saying in the SEALs that some men become SEALs

because they can do anything, and some become SEALs because they can't do anything else. Eddie tried over and over to get into the SEALs and kept getting denied. Besides the marks on his record for assaulting an officer, his test scores weren't good. His aptitude was only average in most of the categories tested by the military, and well below average in math. But finally he got lucky. As the wars in Iraq and Afghanistan grinded into their second and third years, the SEALs were expanding and unable to meet recruitment goals. Veterans faced with constant deployments were getting out. The Navy needed more men. And there was Eddie, already trained as a medic, raising his hand to go.

In the SEALs he struggled too. The Teams brought him in as a medic. He failed to make it through the SEALs combat medical training the first time, despite his years of experience. He was separated from his platoon in Afghanistan in 2009 over differences that remain unclear. As a BUD/S instructor he hit a student and was quietly reassigned. He was held back from a deployment to Iraq after trying to run over the gate guard. Through it all, Eddie always had a way of working things out. A lifetime of moving every few years had taught him how to read people and make allies. He knew how to tell what people wanted to hear. SEALs were always looking out for him. They liked him. They wanted to give him the benefit of the doubt.

But behind Eddie's friendly front was a darker, meaner human being. He quietly trashed many of the SEALs in his so-called brotherhood, saying negative things about several, especially guys he seemed worried he didn't measure up to. He bitched incessantly about his superiors. He was openly homophobic and talked about how transgender people should be taken out and dropped in the ocean. And he persistently made racist comments. Text messages he sent that he thought few others would see showed a simmering contempt for his fellow man that the guys in Alpha later recognized in Iraq. A few months before deployment, Eddie had texted his old platoon chief, who was now a warrant officer, to ask if he wanted to go to brunch. That day there was a demonstration in San Diego over the police killing of a mentally ill Black man.

The warrant officer joked that he couldn't go, saying, "I'll be busy at the riots."

"Are you going down there?" Eddie texted. Then, perhaps in jest, he added, "Run those niggers over."

THE MORNING AFTER Dragon was shot, Eddie called the guys together and made an announcement that showed how much he had learned from the miscalculation on the roof of the pink house. They were going into Mosul again, he said, and they were going right back to the same spot. Same squad, same rat holes, same stairs.

The guys were shocked but didn't say anything. No one wanted to look like a coward. They dutifully drove into the heart of the city and humped their gear back through the tunnels, but many privately thought the chief was going nuts. Going back to the same spot was, to say the least, bad tactics. SEALs are trained to strike unexpectedly, then disappear. Once the enemy knew where a sniper hide was, there was no point in going back. And if the only stairway in and out faced an enemy sniper skilled enough to hit a guy just below the body armor, there was *really* no point. But to object was close to treason. Eddie was the chief. All the SEAL emphasis on creativity and freedom only applied outside the platoon. Inside the platoon, the chief was God. It was his call. Any SEAL could say they weren't cool with it, but they'd be benched for sure and would probably have to turn in their Trident after the deployment for insubordination. They would never be a SEAL again.

Going back to the pink house made so little sense that as Vriens crawled through the rat holes again, he was forced to consider a hunch that he had repeatedly tried to dismiss: Maybe Eddie was hoping to get someone killed on the deployment as a way of building his own résumé. At a barbecue right before deployment, Eddie had told the sniper that it wouldn't be a real deployment unless a SEAL died. Early in the deployment Vriens had nearly been hit with an RPG and Eddie almost immediately ordered him to go back to the same spot. There was no tactical reason to do it, and Vriens had immediately seen it as an order designed to put him in danger to try to bait the enemy. Now they were going back to the staircase where Dragon had just been shot. If there was a good reason, Vriens would do it in a heartbeat, but he couldn't see any beyond Eddie wanting to get someone zapped. Vriens knew the Navy tended to throw medals at platoons with a bunch of casualties. Was that what this was all about? Did Eddie just want to tell a good story about a Purple Heart, or a knife kill, or the day he threw a SEAL over his shoulder and sprinted down the street? Did he want to be able to post photos of himself solemnly bent over a casket? As Vriens crawled through the rat holes, he shook his head and hoped he was being overly dramatic.

When the squad reached the pink house, they sprinted up the exposed staircase without incident. Eddie and the other snipers set up their rifles and spent several hours peering through loopholes, scanning the streets for fighters. Eddie, as usual, took his fair share of shots at targets no one else saw. After several hours, Eddie asked how many Carl G rockets they had with them. The guys said they thought they had about ten. Eddie had them launch the whole supply through a loophole, hitting random targets in the city. As they did, Eddie had the squad take photos of him smiling with the rocket launcher slung over his shoulder that he could share with friends back home. If ISIS didn't know the SEALs were back at the pink house at the beginning of the day, the rockets ensured they knew by the end. It was almost certain that if they went back again they would get hit.

The next morning Eddie brought everyone together to brief them on the plan. They were going back to the pink house for a third time. A few hours later, Shumake and Byrne were ferrying gear through the rat holes and both had the same thought: "Why the fuck are we doing this?" Now both shared the growing suspicion that the chief was trying to get someone killed to get a medal. Nothing else made sense. The two sprinted up the stairs and set up on the roof with Eddie and Ivan Villanueva. They had sniper rifles out, but there were no targets. The city was dead. Then a small off-the-shelf hobby drone flew over. It circled several times and buzzed away. The men watched it go with a feeling of dread—ISIS used toy drones to scout. The SEALs had almost certainly been spotted. A minute later, machine gun fire started slapping against the walls of the house. The SEALs hit the deck as bullets thwacked the low cinder block wall around the roof and shards of cement showered down around them. They had to get out of there before ISIS hit them with mortars or rocket-propelled grenades. But the only way out was the stairs where Dragon got shot. And those were getting pelted.

The squad couldn't call for a Hellfire strike or artillery mission for the same reason they hadn't been able to call for a medevac for Dragon: It would reveal that they were where they weren't supposed to be. Eddie hugged the ground, saying little. Shumake looked over at Byrne. Got any ideas? he asked. Byrne remembered that his med kit below in the sitting room had a smoke grenade for signaling helicopters. He yelled down for other SEALs in the sitting room to pop the grenade by the stairway to create a smoke screen.

Thick white smoke started to drift over the patio. Eddie looked at Byrne and shouted for Byrne and Shumake to go first while Eddie and Villanueva laid down cover fire. It was a noble gesture, Byrne thought. In seconds he was on his feet and sprinting down through the smoke. It only occurred to him halfway down that maybe Eddie let him go first to see if he'd get shot. As he ran, Eddie and Villanueva showered gunfire out over the city. As soon as Byrne and Shumake hit the patio below, they dropped behind a low wall and unloaded on the city to cover the chief. Eddie and Villanueva rushed down the stairs, leaving piles of rockets and Javelin missiles on the roof. Eddie later sent Iraqi soldiers back to fetch the gear.

There could easily have been another man down that day. Maybe two or three. The SEAL Teams naturally drew motivated go-getters who wanted to be in combat, and that was certainly true of Alpha. No one shied away from a gunfight. But there was a line between bravery and stupidity. There was no strategic objective at the pink house. They weren't furthering any mission. They hadn't even seen any targets. They had lost the element of surprise. They were sitting ducks. The only thing that kept sending them back was Eddie, and no one could quite figure out why.

The platoon's two squads rotated that night. That meant a few days off for Squad 2. Squad 1 would go out next. That night Eddie walked into the room of the senior Squad 1 members and sat down on the bed. As usual he had Copenhagen in his lip and a spit cup in his hand. Dylan Dille and Dalton Tolbert were there kicking back. Eddie pulled out his smartphone and zoomed in on a map of Mosul.

"Hey, this is where we're going tomorrow," he said.

He made no mention of anything that had happened with Squad 2, but on the map he pointed to the pink house.

Tolbert looked at the map. Even though Eddie was trying to hide it, Tolbert knew exactly what had gone down on the roof. The boys in Squad 2 had told him everything. He figured Eddie was hoping Squad 1 had no idea so he could send Tolbert or Dille to walk up the stairs. Then, *boom*. He wasn't going to play that game.

When Miller left for the birth of his child, Tolbert had taken over as lead petty officer. And while Miller had tried to be a diplomatic peacemaker who went through the proper channels, Tolbert had zero interest in that. His upbringing had taught him to call out a stupid idea when he saw one.

"That's where Dragon got shot, dude. No way we're going there," he told Eddie.

It was the first time anyone in the platoon had even remotely defied the chief. It was subtle. Any outsider might have missed it. But within the platoon, it was seismic. Someone had challenged Eddie's authority. Not even the officers had been willing to do that.

Eddie was silent. He could have blown up. He could have yelled. But he had a more effective approach: Make the other SEALs believe they're acting like cowards. He spit in his cup, then he gave Tolbert an annoyed big brother look that said he thought the sniper was being a bitch. "Don't worry about it, Dalton. Everything's going to be fine," he said.

"Well, someone has to worry about it," Tolbert shot back.

Eddie smiled warmly and said, "Hey, if it's too much for you to handle, that's cool. We'll leave you back at base." He spit in his cup again, got up, and walked out.

The next day, for reasons Eddie never explained, he did not make the squad go back to the pink house, but Tolbert didn't necessarily see it as a win. Eddie might just be holding his fire, waiting to do something to get back at him later. He might not send him up the pink house stairs, but there were plenty of other stairs, other windows, other rooftops. Tolbert joined the growing number of SEALs who were suspicious that Eddie might try to get them killed.

Under his cool demeanor, Eddie was furious. A few days later, Eddie texted his friend and fellow chief Stephen Snead in California. "When you were over here did you get the feeling that some of your guys were pussies and didn't want to go out? I am starting to get that feeling now and it's pissing me off!"

CHAPTER 7

THE TOWERS

Dylan Dille scanned the medieval maze of old Mosul through the black-rimmed eye of his scope. The senior sniper was hidden about 750 meters away in a pile of rubble across the Tigris River. As he searched the alleyways and street corners, he could feel his heart beat under his body armor and his brow go tense because he knew Eddie was hunting, too, and he would have to try to get the first shot.

It was June 2017, four months into the deployment. Eddie had given up on going back to the roof of the pink house and instead had settled on a new place that the SEALs in Alpha called the Towers. The site was two buildings on the east bank of the Tigris standing side by side across the green water from old Mosul. Around the Towers stood the ruins of a carnival grounds still filled with rides and a weed-choked park where locals once spent holidays. The Towers had high ceilings and curving staircases designed to host lavish celebrations. But the war had left the park waist-high with weeds and littered with unexploded shells, and the Towers were little more than bombed-out gray concrete bones.

At the base of the Towers a modern six-lane concrete bridge had once crossed the river, but it and every other bridge across the Tigris had been destroyed. The center lay broken in two by a massive air strike, as if snapped by a mighty karate chop. The pieces had fallen into the water, leaving two jagged stumps that jutted out over the river.

The battle for Mosul was in its last desperate weeks. Block by block the Iraqi Army had pushed ISIS into one corner of the old city with its back up against the river. Alpha had set up across the river to shoot the enemy in the back. The platoon spent day after day there, harassing ISIS from the rear while the Iraqi Army attacked from the front.

Old Mosul presented the SEALs with a tangle of civilians and enemy targets. They passed and intermingled on the street. Watching through his scope, Dille tried to hunt for details that distinguished the two. He could see the faded floral print on a woman's hijab as she stepped out of her house, too colorful to be the dress of ISIS. He spotted a man in an old bowling shirt who had been bent over the engine of his car on and off for days but had still not gotten it running. Just a local, he decided. Rarely did he see actual fighters with guns venture out. They were too smart for that. But he hunted for men who seemed out of place: the ones who crossed the street with too much purpose for a besieged city where there was nowhere to go. In his scope he could see the sweat on their faces, their darting looks. Some of them walked while gripping tightly the arm of a child, their clenched fingers around the small arm, showing that they were using a local boy as a shield. It was a confusing, complex tangle, but a sniper watching long enough could tease apart threads and find the targets.

Unfortunately, Dille quickly learned that his chief had no interest in taking the time to establish who was who. The first morning the snipers arrived at the Towers, the chief climbed up the curving stairway to the top floor of the north building and set up a tripod and a small folding chair in the middle of a room with a blown-out wall. He almost immediately started shooting one round after another. *Boom. Boom. Boom.* Dille scrambled to his own rifle and checked the chief's angle to try to line up his scope so he could see what Eddie was shooting at. He spotted a sandbank along the river where a narrow alley came down to the water. About fifty people had gathered to wash in the water. Dille saw the crowd scatter amid the shooting and sprint back into the city. Dille's angle didn't give him a full view of ground level on the riverbank, so he wasn't sure if Eddie had hit anyone, but about one thing he had no doubt: These people weren't legit targets.

At the same spot a few days later, Dille saw three women making their way along a path through deep reeds. He heard Eddie start firing and saw the women turn and disappear into the reeds. Had they been wounded or killed? Dille couldn't be sure, but he was increasingly sure his chief was shooting at anyone he saw, civilian or fighter, man or woman.

Dille realized his mission in Mosul would have to shift. He had come to the Towers to kill ISIS. Instead he was going to have to keep Eddie from killing civilians. He would do it by firing warning shots to scare people away before Eddie could spot them. The strategy came to him instinctively one morning a few days after Alpha had started operations in the Towers. Eddie had set up in a bathroom that offered a good view of the city from the north tower. Dille and Dalton Tolbert both wanted to stay as far away from Eddie as possible, so that day they set up in the south tower.

That morning Dille spotted a man coming down a road leading to the river with a boy. They were at a spot where Dille could see them for about a half block before they came into Eddie's view. Dille focused his scope on the pair. He noticed the man wasn't gripping the boy by the arm. Instead, it was the boy who was leading the man along, gently pulling him by the sleeve. It was a small detail that told everything: They were family, and almost certainly not enemy fighters. Dille had to do something before Eddie could get a shot. Knowing he had only seconds, he aimed a few meters in front of the pair and just a degree off to the side, hoping a bullet would hit the dirt in the road and scare them back. He squeezed the trigger. He saw a splash of dust and watched the pair scurry back the way they came. As they ran, he breathed a sigh of relief.

That night Dille told Tolbert what he had done. He was almost ashamed to admit it. He knew shooting warning shots was a quiet form of insurrection against Eddie and might even help ISIS, but he felt he had no choice. To his surprise, Tolbert smiled and said he had been doing the exact same thing. They agreed to keep doing it to try to buy time. When Craig Miller had left, he told them he had reported Eddie to Jake Portier and Portier vowed to take care of it, so a fix was in the works. Both snipers hoped they could limit the damage until Eddie was removed.

It was a high-stress operation. A warning shot had to hit close enough to scare off a target, but not so close that it accidentally killed. Snipers had to read the subtle clues to decide who deserved a warning and who didn't. But because Eddie shared much of the same field of fire as the other snipers, they often only had seconds to spot a person, make a decision, and line up a shot before Eddie got a chance to fire.

It was the opposite of what sniper work was supposed to be. Dille and Tolbert had gotten a small taste of what the real work was like before Eddie's constant shooting put them on a new mission. One morning, Dille was scanning the street life for targets when he spotted a man in a saffron-and-gold robe hustling down a side street amid the dusty locals. He had a long, bushy beard but no mustache and full, round cheeks that suggested he was not sharing in the besieged city's hunger. "Check this dude out," Dille called over to Tolbert, who was tucked behind some rubble a dozen feet away.

"Talk me on," Tolbert said. He traced his scope along the outlines of the city as Dille guided him verbally in a hopscotch of known landmarks until he was at the right street: the green mosque, then the grassy bank, side street to the north.

"Looks like homeboy is doing a little too good," Tolbert said.

They watched him. He hurried down the road and turned down a side alley. There he peered around furtively, then crawled through a rat hole pecked in the wall of a house. Dille swung his scope to the front of the house. It seemed normal enough. No fighters on the roof, no young men loitering outside. The two snipers waited and watched. They saw members of a family come in and out through the front door. The man in the robe was not one of them.

"Definitely something shady," Tolbert said.

The SEALs' rules of engagement didn't require a target to be armed. If snipers saw someone they reasonably thought was aiding

ISIS in any way, they could shoot. But both men were extremely careful, knowing every bad shot could galvanize the locals against them and build support for the enemy.

Tolbert and Dille kept their scopes trained on the house, figuring the man with the saffron robe would eventually emerge. Finally, they saw him crawl out of the hole. The snipers both instinctively slid their fingers to their triggers. No one would crawl from a rat hole like that instead of using the front door unless he was ISIS. As the man squeezed out of the rat hole, Dille centered him in his scope. So did Tolbert. Just as Tolbert was putting pressure on his trigger and exhaling to fire, Dille took the shot. Dille would later remember that shot as an example of what his work was supposed to be: Calm. Calculated. Considered. Justified. He wouldn't get many more like it.

Eddie's shooting forced a shift. Now the snipers had to race to keep people from getting murdered. Every day when Dille lay down behind his rifle, his heart would pound as he watched the street and searched for the next person to come around the corner, knowing he would have only a few seconds to decide whether to save or end a life. Karma was still the driving force of the platoon, but it had flipped. Instead of inflicting the cosmic payback on evildoers, Dille was now trying to protect the world from one. It was exhausting. The tension of being forced to fire at people to make them flee in terror without accidentally killing them left him covered in sweat. The pressure of spending hour after hour hunting, knowing he had lives in his hands, fried his nerves. By the end of each day he tottered down the winding stairs with his hands shaking, physically and emotionally drained. He wasn't sure how long he could keep it up.

EDDIE TOOK THE PLATOON back to the Towers day after day. Each morning Alpha would arrive and park the trucks behind the buildings, then ferry gear up the winding, burned-out stairs to the third floor. For the first few days, locals ventured out oblivious to the snipers, and the streets along the river teemed with targets. Eddie quickly took care of that.

The chief shot constantly. For most snipers, the work was about watching and waiting. On a busy day, good snipers might take three or four shots. Sometimes none. Not Eddie. He reliably shot ten or twenty times a day. Sometimes more. Occasionally in rapid succession. *Bang.* Slide the bolt to reload. *Bang.* Slide the bolt to reload. *Bang.* A box of .300 Win Mag sniper ammo came with twenty rounds. It was not unusual for him to send Ivan Villanueva back down to the truck at midday for another box.

After a few days of Eddie firing, the streets cleared like a scene in an old Western. Still, Eddie kept taking the platoon back to the Towers and at the end of the day boasting to the boys about his kills. Early in the deployment most of Alpha just rolled their eyes when Eddie bragged about kills. But after the ISIS prisoner, no one was laughing anymore. They had no doubt Eddie was inflating his numbers, but one by one, they witnessed things that convinced them that he was gunning down civilians.

Joe Arrington was in the same building as Eddie one morning, scanning north along the river with his scope when he heard a shot from Eddie's position. He swung his scope south and stopped on the same dirt road leading down to the river where days before Dille had scared away the boy holding the man's sleeve. Arrington spotted a man down on the ground. He was older, with gray hair. The man rocked in agony, unable to get up. Arrington was at a slightly different angle from Eddie, and a wall blocked part of his view. He could only see half of the man. But clearly to one side he could see the item the man had been carrying when the bullet dropped him. It was an empty plastic jug. The city had no running water. The man had probably been going to the river to get some.

Arrington watched the man writhe in pain for several minutes. No one was coming to help. The sniper decided to put him out of his misery. But because of the wall, he couldn't get a clear shot. He had to watch the man's struggle grow weaker and weaker over an agonizingly long stretch of time until finally he stopped moving. That night, Arrington told Dille and Tolbert what he had seen. He described the anguish of watching the old man suffer. The other snipers shook their heads and said they had witnessed similar shots.

Soon nearly the whole platoon was aware of the kinds of shots

Eddie was taking. No one had actually seen Eddie pull the trigger and kill a civilian, but his statements to the platoon left them little doubt. Chris Shumake, the senior sniper in Squad 2, later said Eddie told him shooting unarmed people was no different from shooting ISIS fighters because "if they are helping ISIS, they are ISIS." Ivan Villanueva said the chief told him, "If you're leaving your house for any reason," then you're ISIS. Corey Scott said Eddie would "make comments that he was okay with killing women and kids." Scott added, "You could tell he was perfectly okay with killing anybody that was moving." He said he saw Eddie shoot an old man in the back and said Eddie justified it by saying, "The man could've been going to get a gun."

One of the few things the people of Mosul had going for them was that Eddie was not a very good shot. He told his SEALs he had been trained at the Marines scout sniper course before becoming a SEAL. But, in fact, he had only been a medic at the course, not a sniper, and he never got a certificate. Records did not show he had been through formal SEAL sniper training, either, and his lack of knowledge showed. While other snipers tried to find protected hides where they could lie prone for a steady shot, Eddie often plopped down in the open on a folding camp chair, completely exposed to enemy snipers, and shot from a tall tripod that made his firing less accurate. He used an outdated scope and often didn't adjust when he switched ammunition, which had the potential to put his shots off by several feet. The other snipers never corrected him, hoping his sloppiness would save lives.

As the deployment wore on, Eddie grew reclusive and disturbing, even while not on missions. The platoon had set up a small outdoor gym with cinder blocks and sandbags at their house, and during the hour each day when Eddie was using it, no one else was allowed. Gym time, he told them, is my time. They also suspected him of stealing. First it was going through guys' closets scrounging for food and tobacco. Then the platoon noticed someone had taken the jar of money used to pay for energy drinks from the communal fridge.

Then Miller was missing a pair of sunglasses. When he mentioned they were missing, he saw Eddie surreptitiously put them back. It was just petty theft, but in a tribal culture based on trust and respect, it was toxic. Many guys were resigned to get through the two months they had left in Iraq with as little exposure to Eddie as possible.

On deployment Dille was reading a book called *On Killing* by a former Army Ranger named Dave Grossman. It explored the psychological toll on warfighters of taking a life. It also talked about how psychopaths enamored of killing sometimes gravitated to military service. Dille highlighted that passage. He highlighted passages about the long-term damage to troops forced to participate in atrocities. And he highlighted a passage that hit close to home because it so accurately captured how he felt about Eddie: "Those who commit atrocity have made a Faustian bargain with evil. They have sold their conscience, their future, and their peace of mind for a brief, fleeting, self-destructive advantage."

Sometimes when Dille and Tolbert were alone in the south tower or riding in the truck, they would talk about whether Eddie had been born a cold-blooded murderer or had become that way after years of deploying. Maybe he had done too many pumps in Iraq and Afghanistan. Maybe it was post-traumatic stress disorder or a brain injury. Maybe his humanity had been so worn down since 2001 that he just wanted to eradicate all Middle Easterners like lice. It was also possible he had just gravitated to a profession where he could not only act on his darkest impulses but get medals for it. Or maybe Eddie, who had moved constantly growing up and learned to fit in with each new crowd, was doing all this stuff just to be accepted by other pirates. In the discussions, the takeaway was always the same: It really made no difference whether Eddie was born bad or made that way. He was still killing innocent people, and they needed to do what they could to stop it, at least until the SEAL brass pulled Eddie from the platoon.

But as the weeks went by, Dille started to doubt that the leadership was going to act. Portier was as enamored of Eddie as ever. The lieutenant regularly set up in the same building as the snipers who were taking warning shots, often just steps away. One morning Portier looked up after Tolbert fired a shot and asked Tolbert if he had hit anything. Dille and Tolbert decided to level with him. They weren't shooting to kill, they said. They were shooting to keep people away from Eddie. Portier looked confused. Tolbert rolled his eyes and told him, "Jake, come on, you gotta know Eddie is killing civilians."

Portier seemed to stutter. He said it wasn't his job to second-guess the snipers in the platoon. He trusted individuals to make good decisions. He had to let them do their jobs.

"But Jake, we're telling you now, he's killing civilians," Dille said.

Miller had reported a crime. Now Dille was reporting a second.

Portier demurred. He repeated that he trusted Eddie. Dille and Tolbert were probably misinterpreting who he was shooting. Tolbert went back to his rifle thinking to himself, *Okay, I'm gonna show the lieutenant exactly who Eddie is shooting.*

Later that morning Dille and Tolbert were scanning through the neighborhood and stopped at a Y intersection that led down toward the river. Two old men were standing on a street corner talking. They wore flowing white ankle-length tunics and had long, wispy gray beards. They appeared to be doing nothing in particular, just talking like old men talk.

Oh shit, Dille thought. He knew the street corner was visible from Eddie's hide in the north tower. If Dille didn't act fast, Eddie would spot them. Dille had to take a warning shot, but were these guys really locals or were they combatants? He raced through a checklist of clues. No weapons. No supplies. Not doing anything to support the enemy. Not carrying—

A shot rang out. Both Dille and Tolbert heard it echo from Eddie's position in the north tower. Through his scope Dille saw the air warp as a bullet swam through the heat waves. He saw the loose cotton of one man's tunic ripple as a bullet hit him in the small of the back. The man stumbled forward. A spot of blood appeared on his back.

Both men ran around the corner, out of Eddie's line of sight but still in sight of Tolbert and Dille. The blood on the white fabric spread until it was the size of a dinner plate. The man collapsed against a piece of wreckage in the street.

"Yup, Eddie just shot an eighty-year-old man," Tolbert announced in a clear, loud voice, so the lieutenant could hear.

The man pushed himself up on his arms and tried to lurch a few steps forward, then stumbled and sprawled out on the dirt.

"Uhhh . . . he's down," Tolbert announced. Dille could hear him. He knew the lieutenant could too. "Oh . . . he's trying to get up again. No . . . no . . . he's down again. Definitely down. Yeah, he's probably going to die now."

After several seconds, the man struggled to his feet one more time and stumbled out of sight. The snipers never learned what happened to him, but with little medical care available, Dille guessed he was probably in for a slow, painful death.

Eddie called over the radio to report that he had taken the shot but thought he had missed. Dille and Tolbert didn't radio back to give him the satisfaction of knowing he had hit.

Dille felt his heart sag. The shooting almost felt like it was just as much his fault as Eddie's. He hadn't been fast enough. He'd have to do better next time. He wrote in his journal that night that he had been on the sniper rifle and had taken a few warning shots, then concluded: "Missed getting old man from getting shot."

That night Josh Graffam, one of Alpha's new guys, ran into Dille in the little kitchen in their house. Graffam had been Eddie's assistant that day in the north tower and had seen everything. Did you see the old man today? Eddie thought he missed, but he hit that guy, Graffam told Dille. He patted his lower back, right where the bullet had entered.

Dille nodded. He didn't want to be reminded.

In the chaos of the deployment, the old man was the only shooting where the date of the killing later stood out clearly in Dille's memory. It was June 18, Father's Day. He remembered calling his father that evening, and when he did, the image of the old man struggling on the ground came back to him. He told his dad what he had seen, then said, "I bet the guy was someone's father."

Dille wished the Sheriff were back with the platoon. He began to truly hate the chief. He hated how he had become complicit in Eddie's bullshit. He wished they could just do the job they had come to do. Every time Eddie set up his tripod in the middle of a blown-out room with no cover that was completely open to Mosul, Dille found himself hoping that Eddie would get shot.

WITH EACH PASSING DAY, Eddie seemed to become more unglued. Back at the house, he stayed away from the other SEALs and brooded in his room. Multiple times the SEALs were awakened in the tight quarters by the chief screaming in his sleep. He seemed to be going mad.

Eddie had a secret he had kept from the platoon. While he was supposed to be leading the team, he was struggling with an opioid addiction and other drug problems.

It had started years before. Eddie began taking a painkiller called tramadol to ease sore joints. Tramadol is a synthetic opioid and a cousin of oxycodone—the pill widely blamed for starting the opioid epidemic in the United States. Tramadol had been approved by the Food and Drug Administration in 1995 as a safer alternative to other opioids. Manufacturers claimed it offered the same pain relief without the risk of addiction and marketed it as safe enough for children and the elderly. It was considered so harmless that no prescription was required. For a long time few people used it, but between 2008 and 2013 the number of users nationwide soared to forty-four million.

The Navy handed out tramadol freely for minor aches and pains. Medics could dispense it with little oversight. At low doses the pills were relatively harmless, but taking more than the daily recommendation produced a euphoric high. A stressed-out SEAL on his fourth deployment could pop a couple with some beers and float on a cloud. Some guys started to chase that feeling. Eddie and a number of buddies he came up with through the Teams started doing tramadol regularly, referring to it by a number of pet names: *trammies, T bombs,* or simply *Ts.*

Eventually the Drug Enforcement Agency recognized that tramadol wasn't as safe as advertised, and in 2014 the agency cracked down, making tramadol a Schedule IV controlled substance. That meant Eddie now had to get a prescription. That wasn't a big deal, though. A high-tempo SEAL had any number of reasons for a pain-killer. A few weeks after the change Eddie visited a Navy doctor and left with a prescription for a thousand T bombs.

From that point on, he became a repeat customer at Navy doctors and pain clinics. He assured the medical staff he was using the pills "sparingly" to treat lower back pain, but he kept running out and asking for more.

Eddie got promoted. So did several of his friends who shared the habit. Some of them became senior chiefs and warrant officers. They were rising up in the SEAL hierarchy while quietly addicted. The problem went well beyond Eddie's social circle. By 2016 tramadol was the third-leading cause of opiate overdoses in the military. The SEALs were the elite of the elite, but when it came to opioid addiction, they had the same problem as the rest of the country.

The Navy tried to rein in the opioid crisis. Prescriptions got smaller and harder to get. In the summer of 2016, Eddie's SEAL Team got a new physician's assistant who tried to stop issuing tramadol entirely. Eddie was irate. One of Eddie's closest buddies had been his platoon chief when Eddie was the lead petty officer. They appeared to have developed the same opioid habit. The platoon chief went on to become a chief warrant officer, but they stayed in touch, including regular texts about tramadol. "I need to find a connection for t's. This new guy . . . just cut everyone off at the team for any prescriptions," Eddie texted his friend.

"What the fuck, did he say why?" the warrant officer replied.

"He is a complete fag! He said no one needs to be on meds," Eddie said.

Eddie went outside the Team to a Navy pain clinic and got a new prescription, but he also started looking for another supply. He found he could get trammies just over the border from San Diego in Tijuana without a doctor's script. Instead of going himself, in October 2016 he asked Ivan Villanueva, his gopher, to get his mom to buy some and bring it back for him.

The SEALs had mandatory random drug tests. But Tom MacNeil, the officer in charge of keeping the records, noticed Eddie started skipping the tests. And as was the case with so many other infractions before, he never got in trouble.

In December 2016, just weeks before Alpha deployed to Mosul, all SEAL Teams on the East Coast halted training for a safety stand-down to address widespread drug problems in the Teams. "I feel like I'm watching our foundation, our culture erode in front of our eyes," the commander of the East Coast SEALs said in an email to the force. That same month, the Navy prescribed Eddie one hundred trammies. By early January his supply was out. "Do you still have any more Mexican Ts leftover?" he texted his warrant officer friend. When his friend said no, Eddie replied, simply, "Fuck."

Eddie went back to Villanueva. He had smoothed over Villanueva's bar-fight arrest the week before. Now he told Villanueva that the pills his mother bought in Mexico were no good, and he needed him to get more. If the gopher could find good Ts, Eddie wanted "a bunch for deployment." Then the chief told him they should discuss Villanueva's career track as a SEAL.

Villanueva texted Eddie on a Sunday that his mom had purchased five hundred. Eddie said he was at church so couldn't do a handoff. "Just put it in the back of my truck," he said.

In Iraq, guys in Alpha started to notice the signs of a drug habit, even if no one fully realized the extent of the problem. Craig Miller would sometimes notice Eddie slipping pills into his mouth secretively. Dylan Dille could hear pill bottles rattling in Eddie's sniper bag as he walked up the stairs into the Towers. Josh Vriens saw empty blister packs scattered around Eddie's seat in the M-ATV.

Eddie had his own fully stocked medic's bag that included 150 tramadol pills. The records he was required to keep show he prescribed nearly all his trammies to two Iraqi interpreters, even though the platoon medics couldn't remember Eddie giving pills out to anyone.

As medics, Corey Scott and T. C. Byrne probably saw Eddie's addiction most clearly because he would come to them for supplies. When Eddie couldn't get what he wanted from Alpha medics, he tried the medics in other platoons. It got to the point where when a new medic showed up near the end of deployment, the others had to warn him that the chief would hit him up for drugs.

On the day Dille and Dalton saw the old man get shot in the back, Eddie's warrant officer friend texted from California. He asked, "What color were the good T's from Mexico???"

Pink, Eddie said.

The warrant officer replied, "Ready for a care package?"

Tramadol was not the only controlled substance Eddie used regularly. The medics had a supply of a stimulant called Provigil in case SEALs needed to stay awake on multi-day operations. Few in the platoon ever used it. But SEALs saw Eddie take it regularly. On missions, it showed. Vriens noticed Eddie would often be unusually "amped up." Dille said that Eddie was sometimes like "the Energizer Bunny."

Eddie was also injecting himself with testosterone. Early on in the deployment he texted his warrant officer friend, "I need to get some vitamin x. I've dropped a ton of weight and the workout situation here sucks." A short time later, Eddie got an Iraqi interpreter to buy him steroids at a local shop, then tried to stiff him for the cost. SEALs later found syringes all over his room.

Steroids, stimulants, and opioids. Even the SEALs who saw Eddie every day couldn't say for sure what effect the substances might have had on him, but each drug would have fundamentally changed the chemistry of Eddie's brain. Testosterone can increase aggression and erode moral decision-making. Provigil can leave people sleepless and agitated and in some cases cause mania and paranoid delusions. Tramadol slows the executive brain function of chronic abusers. And if the supply is interrupted, withdrawal symptoms can include psychosis, paranoia, even hallucinations. None of the drugs alone would explain why Eddie had become so fixated on killing. He may have harbored an inclination long before he joined the SEALs. He may have been conditioned by years spent in pirate circles where killing wasn't just accepted but was a path to status. That edge may have already been in Eddie's personality when he got to Mosul, but the drugs could have pushed him over.

The SEALs who heard Eddie scream at night thought he might also have been grappling with ghosts from earlier deployments. Brain injuries may have also warped Eddie's behavior. Eddie had never been hit by a blast big enough to officially land him on the Navy's wounded roster. No IEDs had apparently ever shredded a truck he was riding in; no mortars had ever blown him off his feet. But years of heavy machine gun fire, rockets, and blows to the head during training may have taken their toll. After Mosul, when he finally went to the Intrepid Center to get a clinical assessment, he complained of forgetting names and misplacing objects. When a doctor asked how many blasts he had been exposed to, he said probably four hundred. He did poorly on the center's visual and spatial memory tests. He didn't identify patterns or recall details of how they were arranged. In spatial cognition he scored almost at the bottom, in the sixteenth percentile. The neuropsychologist assessing him estimated that his total cognitive functioning had once been in the seventy-fifth percentile but, after years of traumatic brain injuries, had declined to the fiftieth. He had either become significantly impaired or was smart enough to try to make it look like he was.

If Eddie had indeed lost much of his ability to think straight by the time he was a chief, it came right at the point in his career when he most needed a clear head. He was in charge of more than a dozen SEALs in complex urban combat. Mosul was all about spotting complex spatial patterns: who belonged in the neighborhoods and who didn't, who showed the signs of being a combatant and who was just a civilian, who was maneuvering to attack the platoon, and how the platoon would shift to counterattack. But just when Eddie needed to be at his sharpest, the effects of drugs and years in the SEALs had likely worn him down.

EDDIE KEPT TAKING Alpha back to the Towers, day after day. It was like Captain Ahab and the whale, going further and further out toward what seemed to be self-destruction. A few of the more vocal guys, led by Tolbert, argued that they should move on from the Towers. Eddie wouldn't budge.

Josh Vriens was determined to make the best of it and stay focused on the mission. One morning, as the SEALs snuck into the Towers before sunrise and began setting up, he found a good place in the stairway of the southern building that offered a view north all the way to the blown-out bridge and south to the open intersection where Dille saw the old man get shot. Arrington was also set up on the sniper rifle that day. Portier and a handful of other SEALs were in the south tower to support the snipers. Eddie as usual had gone to the bathroom he liked to shoot from in the north building.

That morning, Vriens was trying not to let Eddie's bullshit get to him. Whatever dark sideshow was going on with the chief was not why he was in Mosul; he was there to wax bad dudes who needed to get waxed. Karma. As he set up his rifle, Vriens was looking forward to a productive morning. "I'm going to kill some motherfuckers today," he said to himself, "even if I have to stay on the glass all day."

The morning started off with promise. Vriens saw a few fighters sprinting across the intersection and squeezed off a few careful shots. Then things got quiet. The temperature climbed to over a hundred degrees. There was no foot traffic. The only movement was heat waves shimmering on the street. Vriens stayed on his scope, determined not to lose any chance.

He was scanning the rooftops along the river when he heard a shot from the north tower, then another. He got on the platoon radio. "What are you seeing, Eddie?" Vriens said. He was hoping to get in on the action.

Some by the bridge, Eddie said.

Vriens swung his scope north and spotted a group of figures. He focused in, but the only thing he saw was a group of four school-age girls. The girls were in pairs, making their way along the riverbank under the high jagged rim of the bombed-out bridge. One had on a blue dress. Another wore a gray dress and a hijab printed with bright flowers. Definitely not ISIS based on the way they were dressed, Vriens decided. Where were the fighters?

Vriens had no doubt some women in Mosul could be enemy fighters, and if they were armed he knew he might have to shoot them. But these girls were too young. Their clothes were too colorful.

They held nothing in their hands. There was no way they were enemies. If anything, they were probably trying to escape.

He was about to pan away and look for the real targets when he saw the girl with the flowered hijab clutch her stomach and go down. A shot echoed from the north tower. Two of the other girls ran. The girl's friend in blue looked across the river at the SEALs' position. Vriens could read the terror on her face. He watched through his scope as the girl in blue pulled the girl in the flowered hijab to her feet. She was doubled over, still clutching her stomach. The girl in blue pulled her along. They scrambled up over a dirt berm under the bridge, stumbled, and fell over the other side, out of sight.

Vriens was so shocked that he sat up from his rifle and stared out in a daze. Anger boiled up as he tried to make sense of what he had seen. He had heard a shot from the north tower, but that didn't make sense. Shooting an innocent child was so evil, so disgusting, that in his mind the only group capable of doing it was ISIS. That must be what happened, he told himself. He had seen ISIS shoot people trying to flee Mosul. He knew they didn't care whether they were shooting women or children. And it had just happened right in front of his eyes.

Jake Portier was in the room behind him, just off the stairwell. Vriens shouted back, "ISIS is shooting civilians again. I just saw them shoot a little girl." He got back behind his rifle and scanned for the gunmen. Who could be so heartless, so vile, that they would target a group of children? He wanted to find them and kill them. He savored the idea of drilling whatever fucker had done it. He stayed on his rifle for hours.

At the end of the day, back at the house, Vriens was still thinking about the look on the girl's face as he headed to his room to take off his gear. Right behind him was Arrington, lugging his sniper bag. As usual, they were doing an informal debrief on what had happened. "I saw ISIS shoot this little girl under the bridge today," Vriens told Arrington. It was right under the bridge. Flowered hijab. There were a group of them. "It was crazy, like, I watched it happen."

Arrington stopped walking. That wasn't ISIS, Arrington told him, that was Eddie. Eddie told me he took that shot. Vriens's mouth dropped open.

The bottom fell out. Vriens had joined the SEALs to protect the innocent. He had pushed for years to be aggressive and fearless so that when the real fighting came, he would crush whatever came. He had been one of Eddie's biggest disciples. He aspired to eventually become the same kind of battle-hardened frogman. Over the deployment Vriens had started to see Eddie's many flaws, but he had tried to put them aside and focus on the larger mission. Even when Eddie tried to send Vriens back out as bait in enemy fire after he was nearly hit by an RPG, Vriens justified it as Eddie trying to take the fight to the enemy. Now he realized Eddie *was* the enemy.

Vriens's whole image of Eddie suddenly reversed, like a photo negative. All those stories Eddie told about shooting people in Afghanistan had once seemed cool. Suddenly, they were chilling. Had the young girl in Afghanistan that Eddie boasted about shooting looked anything like the girls by the Tigris? Had the man carrying her really been a Taliban fighter, or was he just a farmer? How long had Eddie been murdering people?

The sniper knew he had to do something, but he realized he was trapped. It seemed clear after the stabbing of the ISIS prisoner that there was no point reporting things to Portier. More than likely, word would just get back to Eddie. If Eddie started to suspect Vriens wasn't down with what was going on, he'd bench him back at the safe house. If Vriens was benched, one of the more experienced guys in the squad would be missing, which would put other SEALs in danger. It would also expose the new guys to Eddie's pirate influence without an older guy to intervene. He reached a miserable conclusion: It was better just to say nothing. Eddie's platoon was like a gang. If you were good with what the boss was doing, he'd take care of you. If you made trouble, trouble might find you. Either way, there was no good way out.

The more Vriens thought about it, the more his whole perception of the SEAL Teams started to crumble. He didn't know if it was just Eddie that was all messed up, or if it went further. Was it just one platoon or platoons all over the Teams? For a long time Vriens had been planning to try out for DEVGRU after Mosul. Eddie encouraged it. He said Vriens would be perfect. After watching the girl get shot, Vriens was afraid he'd get there only to find more guys like Eddie. A few days after the girl was shot, Vriens told Eddie not to submit his paperwork, he didn't want to go to DEVGRU anymore.

THE SHERIFF RETURNED from California at the end of June, after being away from the unit for a month.

The guys in the platoon had kept everything from him while he was in San Diego so he could focus on his wife and newborn son. But within a day of getting back it was clear to him that things had gotten much worse. First of all, Eddie was still there. Portier seemed to have done nothing to alert the SEAL brass, the SOTF, or anyone else about the murder. Second, the relationship between the guys and the chief had grown poisonous. Guys were barely speaking to Eddie. Even guys like Vriens, Villanueva, and Byrne, who had been Eddie's biggest fans, skulked around like beaten dogs. When not on missions, Eddie spent much of his time shut up in his room or working out alone. Dalton Tolbert, who was the acting lead petty officer and should have been Eddie's right-hand man, looked ready to punch the chief in the face. As soon as Miller arrived and asked for a debrief, Tolbert told him, "I fuckin' hate that guy."

Soon after Craig Miller's return, Eddie invited him into his room and sat down across from Miller on a bed. Congratulations on the new baby, Eddie said. He pulled out the newest Half Face Blades knife Bito had sent him and presented it as a gift. You've been crushing it as an LPO. I'm really glad to have you back, Eddie told him. He said he'd been having problems with Tolbert and Dylan Dille. The snipers were afraid to go out on missions. They were being total pussies.

Eddie seemed noticeably different than when Miller had left. His voice had a ragged edge that Miller hadn't noticed before. His eyes danced around, both tired and anxious. Eddie seemed to have grown withdrawn and paranoid. He was convinced Tolbert was talking shit about him and turning the younger guys against him, trying to stir up a mutiny. He suspected Dille was in on it, too.

Miller tried not to show a reaction. His job as lead petty officer was to support Eddie. He had never criticized him or defied him in front of the men, even after the stabbing. Eddie still viewed him as an ally. Eddie knew Miller kept close tabs on the guys and probably had a better sense of what was smoldering in the platoon.

Who's against me? Eddie asked Miller abruptly. And what were they saying?

Miller looked at the knife in his hands. He suspected the gift came at a price. It appeared that Eddie was trying to buy loyalty. And information. But there was no way Miller was taking Eddie's side after seeing him murder a captive. He still hoped that any day now Portier and the troop commander would step in and remove Eddie for good. Even so, he owed Eddie the courtesy of being straight with him about what he was hearing from Tolbert and others.

"Guys are pissed at the decisions you're making," Miller said. Why are you going back to the Towers over and over, or that rooftop? It's not personal, Eddie. It's tactics. What you are doing doesn't make any sense.

Miller didn't bring up the ISIS prisoner. He worried that if Eddie knew he was intent on reporting the murder, the chief would find a way to kill him. But he wanted Eddie to know that the guys thought neglecting his responsibilities as chief and returning to the Towers every day was a bad deal.

Eddie pressed Miller. He wanted to know who specifically was complaining. Miller refused to say. He didn't want Eddie to come down on anyone. "Just talk to the guys. Sit down and listen to them," Miller said.

Eddie switched modes. He adopted his most understanding, paternal tone. He said Miller was right, he would try to listen better. He said he appreciated Miller talking with him. He hoped Miller enjoyed the new knife.

The next day the chief took the platoon back to the Towers.

CHAPTER 8

BAD TARGETS

THE MAIL ARRIVED at Alpha's combat house on the edge of Mosul and Eddie ripped open a box to discover another new knife he had ordered from Bito. He went back to his room and sent his friend a text to say thanks: "The knife came today. Looks nice. I'll sink it into someone in the next couple weeks."

Then Eddie noticed Tom MacNeil's phone sitting in the room that they shared. He picked it up. Over the months in Mosul, Eddie's opinion of MacNeil was starting to cool. MacNeil was not as pliable as Portier. He was always arguing about the rules of engagement. He would bitch to Portier about things Eddie did. He didn't always follow orders. When Eddie told him once to call in false coordinates so he could fire on a mosque, MacNeil refused. And he had stepped in when the Iraqis provided a second captive and Eddie had his hatchet out. Plus, MacNeil was friendly with the snipers that Eddie was sure were hatching mutiny.

Eddie picked up the phone and read the last text that MacNeil had sent: "How are the guys doing?"

It was July 7, 2017. MacNeil had texted Joe Arrington because he was worried about how Squad 1 was holding up going back to the Towers every day. As the assistant officer in charge, he was sick of how Eddie was acting and even more disgusted that every time he brought it up to Portier, he would say, "I'll take care of it," or "I'm working on it," but nothing ever seemed to change. MacNeil believed that SEALs should be creative, but he had always trusted that a war crime would be dealt with by the book. Instead, it looked like the SEAL Teams were trying to bury everything.

Arrington was the platoon's most experienced JTAC. As the prime bomb-dropper he probably could claim more kills than anyone, but it was not his style. He was a goofy, unassuming guy who didn't buy into all the pirate bravado and Punisher skulls. He liked to surf and mountain bike. Combat was his job but not his life.

By that point in the deployment, nearly everyone in the platoon just wanted to get out of Mosul alive. Despite Eddie, the past six months had been a clear success. Alpha accomplished their mission to support the ERD troops taking the city block by block. The platoon had pinpointed ISIS strongholds, pounded positions with hundreds of mortars, spotted car bombs and called in air strikes long before the suicide drivers reached their targets, and picked off enemy fighters at long range with sniper rifles. All of them were proud of what they had accomplished. At the same time, though, the chief had grown increasingly erratic. After his constant sniper fire had scared almost everyone out of the streets, he tried to drive people out into the open. He went on what he called "gun runs," driving one of the armored trucks up onto the blown-out bridge to empty the heavy machine gun into the city. He ordered the junior SEALs to fire rockets into the neighborhoods with no clear targets. He even hung up an American flag on one of the Towers, hoping to draw fighters out—a tactic lifted directly from the book *American Sniper*. The Towers got hit by heavier and heavier weapons. One night ISIS hit with a rocket attack powerful enough to knock down a whole portion of a building. The SEALs figured it was only a matter of time before someone was killed.

Eddie read over MacNeil's text. MacNeil asked how the guys were doing. Arrington's response: "The guys are fine, they're over working for Eddie, but they're fine."

Rage started to build as Eddie looked at the response. He had served with Arrington for longer than anyone in the platoon. He'd always thought Arrington was a bit of an oddball, but he never figured he would be a traitor. So ol' Bubbles was sick of him? He knew Dille and Tolbert were talking trash about him. They had probably convinced some of the new guys to join their little mutiny. Arrington, too. Eddie had to do something. Now.

That day the Iraqi prime minister, Haider al-Abadi, arrived in Mosul. He stood in the street in a black military uniform and declared victory over ISIS in the city. Crowds of celebrating soldiers and civilians thronged around him amid smoldering piles of rubble bristling with rebar, waving Iraqi flags and firing guns into the air. A few pockets of ISIS resistance still waited to the north, but the great Battle of Mosul was over.

Even as that fight was drawing to a close, though, the battle for Alpha platoon was about to explode. Eddie decided he couldn't have a turd like Arrington undermining him. Tolbert had been openly defying him. Miller was no longer on his side. Even the young guys were starting to question him. He didn't get it. Alpha was on a dream deployment with combat opportunities they might never see again. And all they did was whine and second-guess him. Now here was Bubbles trying to blame *him* for the problems. Time to put the hammer down.

Eddie found Portier and told him that this shit needed to end—he was kicking Arrington out of the platoon.

That day, Squad 1 had just started a rest rotation at the safe house an hour outside of the city. Arrington, Miller, Dille, and Tolbert were catching up on the things they couldn't do in Mosul—email, laundry, fixing gear. Miller was in the kitchen when a text message arrived from Portier. Tell Arrington to pack his stuff, it read, he's going to another platoon and we're getting a new JTAC to replace him.

"What the fuck is this shit?" Arrington said as soon as he heard. He stormed into the kitchen where Miller still had his phone in his hand. He didn't like Eddie and knew the feeling was mutual, but he didn't want to leave Alpha. The platoon had only about a month left in the deployment, and much of that would be taken up by packing and inventorying all their stuff. Effectively, the job was done. By the time a new JTAC arrived and learned the ropes it would be time to go home. This was just a way for Eddie to screw him.

Arrington hadn't done anything wrong. He was a top JTAC and had never complained about missions. He had even kept his mouth shut about going back to the Towers over and over. All the shit Eddie was doing, and Arrington was getting fired? Fuck that, he told Miller.

The other guys heard the commotion and gathered in the kitchen. Arrington was a respected guy who was good at his job. They all agreed trying to replace him seemed like a ridiculously bad move, even for Eddie. Miller texted Portier to try to get him to change his mind. The senior SEALs in the squad crowded around to hear Portier's response.

No dice, Miller told them, looking at his phone. I guess Eddie's really pissed.

The guys started to grumble, but the Sheriff quieted them down. He wanted to avoid an all-out insurrection. Look, I agree kicking Arrington out of the platoon is stupid, he said, but Eddie's the chief, it's his call. We can't just tell him no. Miller was trying to find a way to flank the chief but didn't see one.

Dalton Tolbert stiffened as he listened. His upbringing had made it easier to spot treachery disguised as the system.

"No," Tolbert said. "No way. Nope. Joe's not going anywhere. We have to fight this."

This is bigger than Arrington, he said. Eddie had straight-up murdered people. Portier wasn't doing shit about it. Tolbert believed Alpha could still bring Eddie to justice when they got home, but only if they stuck together. Let Arrington go and who would be next? Eddie would dismantle Alpha piece by piece. He would send them to new assignments and probably say bad things about them, quietly, to their new chiefs. He would make it look like a courtesy: Heads up, you have a real turd coming. He would say the guys had been afraid to fight in Mosul. As strangers in new platoons, they would have no credibility. Everyone would look at them like disgruntled cowards. The guys from Alpha would be alone, with no one around to vouch for them. At that point, if they tried to tell anyone that the great Eddie Gallagher was really a screwup and a murderer, who would believe them? Eddie would be free to bury the whole thing.

"If he divides us, we have no chance," Tolbert said. "We have to make a stand."

Dille agreed. He could almost hear Eddie in his head telling stories when he got home about how he had run through fire to save Dragon, about his incredible sniper shots that would put all of Chris Kyle's feats to shame. In order to build his own mythology, he would need to persuade everyone that the guys who said different were just a bunch of turds who couldn't handle Mosul. Arrington was the start, but he likely wasn't the end.

Tolbert's right, Dille said. Eddie has to be held accountable for what he's done, but it will take all of us standing together.

Miller hesitated. Even as everything was coming off the rails, he saw the rules as a refuge. No one wanted Eddie to face justice more than him, but refusing a lawful order from the chief was waving a red flag in front of the bull. He didn't see how it could solve any problems. Alpha could all lose their jobs over it. They could be court-martialed. Then Eddie would paint them as a bunch of lying, disgruntled cowards anyway. Miller wanted to stick up for Arrington, but he pushed the guys to make one more phone call to Eddie before they did anything they'd regret. Maybe they could smooth it over.

Okay, Tolbert said, but we have to do it on speakerphone so everyone can hear. He didn't want Eddie to work any of his manipulative jiujitsu on Arrington or Miller or anyone else. They were going to do this together.

Miller dialed and Portier picked up in Mosul. Miller told him they wanted to talk about Arrington. Tolbert leaned in and said, "Put Eddie on!"

There was a pause. Then Portier said Eddie wasn't going to take the phone.

"Well, we're not sending Arrington back," Tolbert said in a stern voice. "This is total bullshit and you know it. He's not going anywhere."

Eddie got on the phone and started swearing. The SEALs could hear the rage amping through the tiny speaker. Arrington was fuck-ing going, Eddie said. They were going to do what they were fucking told. He was coming to get Arrington the next day and it wasn't up for fucking discussion. And Arrington shouldn't be talking shit be-hind people's backs.

Arrington leaned over the phone and shot back, "That's funny coming from you. You're the master of it!"

"FUCK YOU!" Eddie shouted.

"NO, FUCK YOU!" Arrington said.

"NO, FUCK YOU!" Eddie shouted. He hung up.

The SEALs looked at each other wide-eyed. Miller was silent. They had definitely not managed to smooth things over. The chief was raving, and he was driving up in the morning to lay down the law. "This isn't good. What are we going to do?" Miller said. "What's Eddie going to do?"

"He's gonna be pissed, he might be ready to throw down," Dille said.

Tolbert was so revved up that all he could do was laugh. "I don't really care at this point," he said. It felt good to finally have the enemy out in the open. He looked at Dille and said, "I'm not afraid of Eddie. I mean, are you?"

Dille smiled, too. Even though he was quiet and never liked to beat his chest, he was a vicious boxer who used the same calculating patience with his fists that he did with a sniper rifle. Eddie was only five-foot-eight and had a short reach, plus he was impulsive. Dille savored the idea of knocking the chief out.

"No, man. Honestly, I'm not," Dille told his friend. Then he paused. Eddie had been acting so weird lately, he said, we don't know what he'll do. If Eddie wanted to start something, no problem, the four of them could beat his ass. They were younger and bigger. They had numbers on their side. "But what if he pulls his knife?" Dille said. "Or a gun?"

There was silence. No one spoke up to say they thought it was unlikely. The idea that Eddie might draw on another SEAL would have seemed crazy in a normal context, but they were a long way from normal. They believed Eddie had killed multiple people. He was looking at prison if they talked. He had gotten stranger and stranger over the months. He might do something desperate.

"We're going to need a guardian angel," Dille said, someone with a pistol whose sole job was to stand watch in case anything happened. There was no argument in the group. They decided that the guardian angel should be the fastest and best pistol shooter in SEAL Team 7: Craig Miller.

It was the last thing Miller wanted to hear, but he knew they were right. Since the day five months before when Miller arrived in Iraq with Eddie, the chief had grown more unhinged. It was totally reasonable to be ready with a gun. At the same time, it was insane to even talk about shooting another Navy SEAL. The SEALs were a brotherhood. Their training taught them to protect one another at all costs. Miller didn't want to kill Eddie. At the same time, he didn't want to put that responsibility on any of the other guys. He was their leader. It was on him. He grudgingly agreed. Just a few weeks before the end of what was billed as a dream deployment, he was prepared, if necessary, to shoot his own chief.

That night Miller called his parents in Texas and explained what was going on. There's a chance either I kill Eddie or Eddie kills me, he told his mother. He told her about the stabbing and had her write it down in her phone. That way, if things got really out of hand, at least there would be an outside witness who knew about the murder.

Miller's father got on the phone. Even though his father had been a frogman before him, he had never encountered anything like this. He urged caution and restraint. Don't act unless you are absolutely sure. Don't seek violence, try to find another way. But if there is a real threat to your friends and fellow SEALs, he said, I don't see what else you can do. Miller told his father he knew he was right, but even if he tried to do the right thing, it was almost certainly going to go really badly. There was a good chance Miller was going to get fired and kicked out of Iraq, and maybe kicked out of the Navy, he told him. He could even go to prison. He added, "I just hope Arrington's worth it."

The next morning the guys in Squad 1 started preparing for battle. Dille ran on a treadmill in the back room to warm up. Arrington started punching a heavy bag. If they needed to fight the chief, they wanted to be ready. Tolbert got a text from the SEALs in Mosul that Eddie and Portier were on their way in a white Ford pickup and would be there soon. Miller put on his uniform and slid a holster holding his 9mm pistol onto his belt.

The group kept tabs on the progress of the pickup through texts. Miller paced nervously in the main room. Chances were good that the storm now brewing would hit him the hardest. Try to avoid a fight, he told Arrington and Tolbert. Be ready to handle this civilly. We'll confront him together so he can't manipulate us, we won't back down, but the best thing to do now is try to work it out. That doesn't mean we can't turn him in when all this is done, but just try to make peace.

Arrington agreed. He wrote out a list of five complaints so when Eddie tried to change the subject or manipulate him he could remember why he was there. The first thing on the list was shooting civilians. No one thought the meeting was going to go well.

The truck pulled up with Eddie, Portier, and two other SEALs. There was a great room just inside the front door of the safe house, and the squad gathered there in a line. Dille, Tolbert, and Arrington all had their shirts off, ready to fight. Miller stood off to the side at an inconspicuous spot that offered a good angle on the room, with his pistol ready to fire.

Eddie was the first through the door. He had an M-4 assault rifle slung over his shoulder. Miller instinctively scanned for a threat. If a finger was on the trigger or the gun was pointed, he would shoot without waiting. His eyes found Eddie's hands. One was on the forward grip, but no hand was on the trigger.

As Eddie stepped inside and his eyes adjusted from the desert sun, he looked up and took a half step back. Three bare-chested snipers spread out in a line facing him. He glanced to the side and saw Miller with his hand hovering like an Old West gunslinger over his pistol. He half-opened his mouth to say something, then stopped. He put his rifle down. The guys could see a sudden physical change, his shoulders relaxed. He took a breath and nodded in a tacit recognition. He wasn't going to start throwing punches.

Miller's shooting hand went slack.

Eddie motioned to the computer room just off the main room. Come on, he said to Arrington, let's talk in here. They went in, and Eddie closed the door behind him.

Dille looked at Tolbert who looked at Miller.

"That was not supposed to happen. He shouldn't be in there alone," Dille hissed. He went to try the door. It was locked. He stood listening. He could hear the muffled tones of a calm conversation. No shouting. No breaking furniture. He thought about kicking the door down, but he decided to hold off.

Portier walked in from the truck. He saw the SEALs waiting and did the same surprised double take as Eddie. He stood awkwardly, as if acutely aware of what was happening, but not sure what to do.

"Jake, you have to do something. Just do something," Miller said.

Dille and Tolbert circled around the lieutenant and joined in. They weren't angry at Portier, just perplexed about why he didn't seem to see what Eddie was doing. Eddie's out of control, Tolbert told him. He tried to use short, clear sentences. Eddie's tactics are madness. Everything has gotten totally out of hand. You know it's true. Arrington shouldn't get in trouble for calling it out. No one is kicking him out of the platoon.

Portier's face was blank. He looked down at the floor as he responded. I'm not going to make any decisions yet, he said, I'll talk with my chief and we'll make a decision together.

This isn't about Arrington, it's about Eddie, and you know it, Miller said. He's not doing his job. He's stealing stuff. And he's making stupid decisions that put everyone at risk for no reason. He just sits on the sniper rifle killing civilians.

Tolbert jumped in and pointed a finger at the lieutenant: "And you're supposed to do something, and you're not!"

Portier raised his voice and told Tolbert not to point at him.

"Oh, I'm fucking pointing at you!" Tolbert shouted. What little deference and respect the SEALs did afford their officer was pretty much gone.

Guys are pissed and we're not going to stand by anymore, Miller said. If you aren't going to do anything and the troop leadership isn't going to do anything, we're going over your head to the command master chief of the team.

Portier snorted. He knew as well as they did that many of the enlisted guys up the chain were friends of Eddie. They'll crush you, Portier told them.

Miller looked squarely at Portier and tried to level with him. He tried always to see the good in people. He thought Portier was a decent guy who was just young and had become enthralled with all of Eddie's pirate stories. He knew Portier had been bullied and manipulated, but now the lieutenant needed to do the right thing before it was too late. Portier was legally required to report any suspected war crimes immediately or face criminal charges himself. The longer he waited, the worse it would turn out for him.

"If you side with Eddie," Miller told him, "this isn't going to end well."

Portier didn't respond. He refused to look at Miller.

Behind the locked door of the computer room, Eddie and Arrington were having a conversation that Arrington later described as "civil." The two sat down across a desk. Eddie didn't seem angry anymore. He leaned back in his chair ready to listen. Arrington started going through his list of five complaints. "It feels like we have to put the reins on you versus you putting the reins on us," he began.

Eddie nodded and listened. His whole demeanor had shifted. Just like in the talks with guys after the stabbing, he appeared empathetic and kind. He became a father figure, the wise old chief. He denied everything with a tone that made it sound like the whole thing was a big misunderstanding by Arrington. Eddie addressed the stealing first. He said he had grown up in platoons where everyone was like family and they shared everything. He was sorry if Arrington saw that as stealing. As for tactics, Eddie sighed and said he had been deploying a lot longer than Arrington and knew a little bit more about what good tactics looked like. Then he turned to putting guys' lives in danger. That was part of the job, he said. Other SEALs in Coronado were banging down the door trying to get a chance to fight in Mosul. They would give their left nut, and probably their right, for a piece of the action. If Arrington or anyone else couldn't handle his leadership style and wanted out, he was sorry, but he understood. They were free to leave anytime.

Arrington was silent. With a velvet glove, Eddie had slapped Arrington with the ultimate SEAL insult: If you can't handle it, coward, go ahead and ring the bell.

Guys could say what they wanted, Eddie continued, there are some guys in the platoon who are just against me. To them I can't do anything right. They get together and bitch and blow everything out of proportion. This kind of sewing circle gossip happens on every deployment. It's natural. You get to the end of deployment and guys are pissed off and want to go home and they have to blame it on someone. Look, Eddie said, Alpha has had an amazing deployment. You guys are kicking ass. There are only a few weeks to go. After that, if guys are still angry, they never have to speak to me again. But for now let's just put our differences aside, stick together, and bring everyone home safe.

Arrington was genuinely defused. Eddie was offering peace, and Arrington decided to take it. He later summed up the whole episode by saying, "We had a good talk."

The door opened, and Arrington and Eddie emerged. Eddie announced the platoon wasn't going to get rid of Arrington. Then he turned to Miller. Fellas, he said with a kind lilt, you're obviously upset, tell me what I'm doing wrong. The platoon brought up the same stealing and killing that they had with Portier. Eddie gave the same kinds of responses he had given Arrington. The young SEALs might not be able to understand what he was doing as a chief, but it was all good. If they weren't up for it, he could work with them to get them out of there. Eddie said he thought highly of the guys. They were awesome operators. I applaud you for confronting me, he said. That took guts, he said, I respect you for doing it.

Miller let his guard down. Even Dille and Tolbert were so perplexed by Eddie's response that they didn't know how to react. Eddie left as if nothing had happened.

Right afterward, Eddie texted his boss, Alazzawi, to assure him everything was fine. "The meeting went well," he said. "As always lesson learned for me is I have to be more sensitive to people's feelings."

To the warrant officer who had sent him a care package, he texted a very different take. "I think I've seen the worst of the teams this deployment, especially from the younger guys. Shit is definitely different now."

AFTER THE CONFRONTATION with Arrington, Eddie never really went out on another mission. Alpha still had about six weeks left in Iraq, but Eddie spent nearly all of it back at the spacious safe house in Kurdistan. He wrote platoon evaluations and awards for the deployment. Portier wrote up a nomination to get Eddie a Silver Star for saving Dragon and other suspect acts of heroism. Eddie was careful not to mention the nomination to the platoon. For the most part, he stayed in his room alone in a recliner watching movies and playing videogames.

"I'll tell you what," he texted his friend Stephen Snead, who had set up the house in Kurdistan before Alpha replaced his platoon in Iraq. "That Lazy Boy that you put in this room is the best piece of gear ever. I lounge in that thing all day."

After the fall of Mosul, ISIS still held territory along the Syrian border near the town of Tal Afar. While Eddie was at the safe house, the rest of Alpha went out on missions without the chief. They followed the same battle rhythm that they had in Mosul. Set up behind the FLOT to support the Iraqi soldiers on the ground. Dig in mortars, set up snipers, and launch the Puma and Switchblade drones to hunt for targets. Eddie just wasn't around.

On August 1, Squad 2 drove out to the outskirts of Tal Afar. Josh Vriens climbed onto the roof of a farmhouse with a pair of binoculars. Even though Eddie seemed to have checked out, Vriens was still eager to go after ISIS. A handful of Peshmerga fighters stood with Vriens on the roof. The Peshmerga pointed out an ISIS checkpoint in the distance and said they took fire from it daily. Vriens studied the checkpoint through binoculars and decided to hit it with mortars. The squad set up their mortar tubes and launched two rounds to register the mortar tube so they could walk hits in on the checkpoint. When the rounds hit, two men came out of a hut at the checkpoint and fired at the SEALs. Vriens smiled. Open, hostile action. He was free to engage. But before they were able to fire more mortars, the squad intercepted communications from enemy territory. An ISIS radio transmission said the Americans had arrived and told other fighters to send the truck bomb. The squad sent the Puma circling over enemy territory to see if they could spot the truck bomb. The drone soon came across a tractor pulling a tank of liquid and followed the tractor to a small warehouse where it spotted people loading barrels onto a truck. From the sky it looked like a group of ISIS fighters with homemade explosives. Vriens called over a Peshmerga leader to look at the grainy gray video footage. Yes, he said through an interpreter, that warehouse is a known ISIS supply point.

Vriens called down from the roof to the SEALs below. The tractor was the perfect target for the Switchblade.

A junior SEAL named Christian Mullan was at the controls of the Switchblade. He launched the drone from an upright tube like a mortar and it immediately unfolded four wings and buzzed away at 60 mph. As the Switchblade sped into the sky, Mullan held what looked like an oversized videogame controller with a small black-and-white screen in the middle. The camera on the Switchblade was even grainier than the one on the Puma. All throughout deployment the platoon had struggled to use the new weapon. Often the camera was so poor that the SEALs couldn't find targets that the Puma had spotted. The Switchblade could only circle and search for about fifteen minutes before running out of power, but once it was launched, there was no way to bring it back. If the pilot couldn't find a target, there was a self-destruct button that sent the little drone skyward to explode. Over the deployment the platoon had launched several but only ever managed to score one confirmed kill. The drone transmitted grainy gray photos of the last seconds of its dive. On that single successful run, the last frame was a bearded fighter with a rifle slung over his back, looking over his shoulder in terror as he ran for his life.

The squad hoped for a second hit that morning. Vriens watched the camera feed from the Puma and helped guide Mullan with the Switchblade. They spotted the warehouse and the truck full of barrels. The Switchblade made a circle around the target and Mullan set the coordinates for the dive bomb. Vriens came over to look at the screen. There was a grainy group of figures near the truck. They shuffled into a row with one figure standing a few feet out in front of them.

"Sweet," Vriens said, studying the video. "They're doing the martyr photo with the driver before he goes and blows himself up." It was the perfect time to get them all.

Vriens was on the roof with a junior-grade lieutenant named A. J. Hansen, who had only been in command a few times. Portier was down in the truck on the radio. Vriens and Hansen looked at the video and gave Mullan the green light. The pilot pressed a button that sent the Switchblade into a kill dive. The drone sped up into a streaking blur. As it dove it sent back a rapid succession of photos. The frames zoomed closer as it closed in on the warehouse. First the frame showed the whole yard and the building, then just the line of people and the truck, then just the people. The Switchblade was now too far into its dive to abort. The photos clicked closer and closer until for a split second the grainy feed showed the figures in detail: the cut of their clothes, the outlines of their faces. Then closer until the last frame showed the face of the person at the center of the Switchblade's target.

In the distance the SEALs heard the explosion. Normally they would have cheered a hit on ISIS, but no one said anything at all. They just stared at the last images on the little screen. There was a boy, maybe eight years old. There appeared to be two other boys on the edges of the frame.

Vriens looked at Mullan. He had seen it too. The group they had targeted was full of children.

Take a block of Swiss cheese, slice it up, and then stack up all the slices randomly, and one time in a million, the holes will all line up. That is how the troop commander, Lieutenant Commander Breisch, later explained the strike. A series of small failures—a clumsy translation, a new weapon, a junior leader, a grainy screen, a mistaken call about a truck, all lined up and led to something catastrophic. One of the biggest holes in the cheese was the absence of a chief with the experience and patience to know how battlefield mistakes can compound. That's why platoons had chiefs. At the same time, no one in the squad would have argued that Eddie might have made anything better.

An American Predator drone circling the area at the same time as the Switchblade spotted the strike, and its high-resolution camera captured the dead scattered on the ground. The drone pilot sent out a civilian casualties alert. Within an hour, the SOTF had been notified. Top commanders radioed the squad to shut down and return to base immediately. On the high-definition monitors back at the SOTF command center, the commander replayed the Predator footage of the strike. "Wow, that's fucking bad," Portier said when he saw it. But he insisted it was an honest mistake. What were clearly women and children on the big screen had "just looked like blobs" on the tiny Switchblade controller.

The whole platoon was put on lockdown and an investigation started. Alpha had four weeks left in its deployment, but for the rest of it, they were not allowed to leave the house. A mistake on the battlefield had managed to do what all Eddie's sniper shots and rocket strikes on civilians had not. Eddie was finally benched—officially.

Vriens tried not to think about the Switchblade. The whole deployment he had tried to keep his aggression focused. He had rejected Eddie's approach, which seemed to be about shooting everything that moved. He had been determined to be a professional, and he had totally failed. Thinking about the strike was more painful than remembering the girl getting shot down. The girl was on Eddie. The children hit by the Switchblade were on him.

ONE OF THE JOBS of a platoon chief was to greet the incoming chief of the platoon replacing him and show him the ropes. Stephen Snead had done it for Eddie. Now Eddie had to do it for a new chief. It meant staying after most of the platoon went home to ensure the new guys had all the best, most up-to-date intel to make the mission a success. Eddie had no plans to do it.

For most of July and August, Eddie had been counting down the days until he could get out of Iraq. The chief from a platoon in SEAL Team 3 was arriving at the very end of August. When Eddie learned the Team 3 chief would be a few days late, he complained about having to stay. "Fuck this place when there is nothing to do," he texted Snead. "Team 3 turds aren't even coming on the first flight or possibly the second flight."

Up on the roof of the safe house, Snead's platoon had built a bar. In the weeks Alpha was locked down, they made improvements, adding lights and music. They painted a sign behind the bar dedicating it to Snead's fallen EOD tech. Most nights the SEALs congregated on the roof to drink beer and take turns playing music. Drinking in Iraq was against the U.S. military regulations, but the rule had been regularly disobeyed by SEALs up and down the ranks for years. It was one of the many rank-and-file rules they felt didn't apply. As long as no one was on duty and nothing got rowdy, they didn't see a problem. The officers went to the rooftop with the enlisted guys. They weren't in a war zone, they had nothing to do. A few beers wasn't a big deal.

Eddie rarely went to the roof. Not because he didn't drink on deployment, but because he no longer wanted to look at anyone in the platoon. He had already started to craft the story of what had gone wrong. It wasn't about the stabbing or the shootings, it was that the younger guys were a bunch of whiners. "Bro this last month is dragging out," Eddie texted his warrant officer friend in mid-August. "I am glad I'm not doing another platoon next, I fucking hate this generation of team guys."

The feeling in the platoon was overwhelmingly mutual. At the bar on the rooftop, both squads were together for the first time without Eddie. Over beers they started to realize how messed up things had gotten. Eddie had intentionally split the platoon, then used the isolation to completely warp their views and keep them off-balance. He spent the whole deployment telling Squad 1 they were a bunch of fuckups and that Squad 2 was crushing it. And he did the same to Squad 2. Men began to doubt themselves and mistrust the other squad. Eddie was beating them down, making them feel inferior, keeping them isolated like some two-bit cult leader, even as he was feeding them accounts of the battlefield that built himself up to be a god.

Slowly, on the rooftop, the SEALs realized they were all dealing with the same crap. Joe Arrington talked about all the shit he had seen Eddie do. Ivan Villanueva told the guys it had started before Mosul, and shared that Eddie had sent his mother to buy drugs. Dylan Dille told the story of the old man shot in the back. Josh Vriens said he had seen the same kind of thing. He was both glad he was no longer alone in doubting Eddie and furious that the problem was much bigger than just one schoolgirl. Vriens stood up and said they had to do something.

"We already talked to Jake," Dille told Vriens. "I'm not too sure he's going to do anything."

"No way," Vriens said. "Eddie's already worked his magic on Jake."

They knew they had to report Eddie. They decided they should first get home safe, then something had to be done, and quickly. If they didn't speak up, Eddie would regale all of Coronado with his heroics. He'd be celebrated. He'd be promoted. He'd be given more responsibility and be put in charge of more SEALs, maybe a whole troop and eventually a whole Team. His pirate influence would spread to a whole new generation as he picked which guys climbed the ranks. To Vriens and Dille, Eddie was not just a psycho who had fucked up their deployment or killed innocent people, he was a cancer that had to be cut out of the SEAL Teams because there was no telling how far it would spread.

Eddie was determined to get on the first plane home, leaving behind his responsibilities and his men, but he was unable to get approval from above. Then, at the last minute, he reported a family emergency. He said his teenage stepdaughter had run away from home and he needed to get back ASAP to help. MacNeil told Eddie he needed him to stay for the turnover. Eddie took off anyway.

"Left a day early to deal with the family drama," Eddie texted Alazzawi at the end of August. "Bro I was happy to get away from my platoon, I was beginning to hate them all at the end."

Eddie sent several more texts to his friends as he made his way through stopovers on the way home to California. They seemed primarily focused on getting home in time for a big pay-per-view boxing match.

Back in Iraq, the rest of Alpha watched Eddie's family post photos on Facebook of him grilling and drinking beer at the warrant officer's house. The family was there, watching the fight. Some emergency. Someone found one of Eddie's uniform name tags and stuck it to a whiteboard in the main room of the safe house, then drew a giant arrow pointing toward it and wrote the word "Turd."

THE WHOLE PLATOON, minus Eddie, had to stop in Heidelberg, Germany, on the way home a few days later. One of the requirements of the layover was an individual session with a special operations psychologist to make sure there were no pressing issues from combat that had to be addressed before SEALs hit the States. Traditionally, SEALs treated the meeting with the shrink as a box to check as quickly as possible before going home. But some of the guys in the platoon saw it as the first chance to document what they had seen with someone outside the platoon. They set up a group chat so that they could keep tabs on one another while traveling. Someone texted that they should all tell the psych their concerns about Eddie. The SEALs started joking around because they had heard the psych was attractive.

"Seriously. Tell the truth," Dalton Tolbert urged the platoon. "It's only going to help us resolve this."

"Definitely telling the truth," Joe Arrington replied.

Germany was the first time Josh Vriens had allowed himself to reflect on what happened. Iraq had been too hectic, and his subconscious had put up defenses that kept him from dwelling on his inner thoughts. Now he was somewhere safe, and the thoughts were leaking out of every seam. That afternoon it was Vriens's turn to sit down with the psych. He decided not to hide anything. He needed to come clean. Part of him hoped he could drop everything that was burdening him like a duffel on a tarmac, so he wouldn't have to carry it home. He slumped into a chair. After a deep breath, he told the psychologist that his chief was killing civilians, and that he had seen him do it. He had seen a girl get shot and her friend look toward him in terror. There was more, he said. Other guys had seen other things. Old men and women. A teenage kid stabbed. It had gone on for months. Worst part was, Vriens had stood by and done nothing. It hurt even to say it.

Just then a SEAL from Golf platoon pounded on the door. He had been waiting out in the hall and Vriens was taking much longer than usual. The SEAL had been drinking and wanted to get the appointment over with. He stuck his head in, drink in hand.

"I'll be done in a minute, bro, just hold on," Vriens said. He knew there was still more he had to unload, but wasn't sure if he could do it, or if he should. He wanted to talk about the Switchblade. It was just a mistake, just an honest mistake, he said. He had tried his best. Guys were just trying to do their jobs, but children had died. He'd do anything to reverse it, but there was no way to bring those families back.

Vriens had been in the SEALs for seven years. They were years of almost total sacrifice with constant training, painful physical struggle, and a fair amount of danger. He'd deployed around the world. He'd worked hard to make his platoon the best. He had been picked for a dream deployment in Mosul that positioned him to write his own ticket in the SEALs. And then everything had collapsed. Vriens didn't know if he wanted to be a SEAL anymore. The whole squad was under investigation for the Switchblade. He could be court-martialed and be sent to prison. Vriens had young kids. And meanwhile Eddie—

The SEAL from Golf platoon banged on the door again and stuck his head in. He asked if Vriens was done yet. Vriens noticed the drink in his hand. All of the rage and frustration that had been building in Mosul suddenly hit like a Hellfire. Vriens jumped up from his seat, slapped the drink out of the SEAL's hand, knocked him to the floor, and started choking him.

CHAPTER 9

LOYALTY

WHAT THE HELL was wrong with Alpha? Back at the base in Coronado, Senior Chief Brian Alazzawi could tell something was up. After twenty years and eight stints overseas, he had been around the Teams long enough to know how things should go right after deployment. It was supposed to be a honeymoon. Other platoons were eating burritos with their shirts off at the beach and going home at noon to spend time with their families. Alpha had returned from a dream deployment and all of Team 7 was buzzing about how they were a total pack of studs. The official statistics from Mosul told the story of the kind of savage combat that the SEALs hadn't seen in years: 189 enemy positions obliterated, 13 vehicle-borne IEDs destroyed, 546 enemy fighters killed. Incredible. Career-making. Totally badass. But whenever the senior chief passed Alpha's high bay, he could sense the hate and discontent. The guys were moping around like they had shit their pants.

Alazzawi had a bushy mustache and dozens of black tattoos that made him look like he should be riding a Harley, but he liked to pedal around the small SEAL base on a beach cruiser. About a week after his platoons returned from Iraq, he was pedaling back to his office when he spotted Jake Portier and Eddie outside the Alpha high bay, talking by Eddie's pickup. It was early September 2017.

Alazzawi put on the brakes. This was his chance to figure out what was up.

He pulled up next to the tailgate and started some small talk with the chief: Good to be back, hope the wife and kids are doing well, congrats again on crushing ISIS. After a little back-and-forth, he got down to what he really wanted to know: "Hey, everything cool with Alpha? They seem a little off."

Eddie smiled like nothing was wrong. Yeah, they're fine, he said. Just venting. His tone was that of a dad dealing with his teenager's latest breakup. It was just petty drama, he said. Some guys got their feelings hurt.

"Yeah, I hear that. Well, let 'em vent. It's good for 'em," Alazzawi said. He knew how six months of living in shitty conditions with little rest or privacy could turn a platoon ugly. But usually they were hugging again as soon as they got home. This seemed more serious. If it's one or two bitching, that's to be expected, he told Eddie. If there are six or eight, something is wrong and you need to sit them down and figure it out.

Yeah, Eddie said. They're just being pussies. He said a few guys in the platoon had balked at going out on missions and Eddie had come down hard on them. Now they had their panties in a bunch.

As Eddie was talking, Alazzawi kept his eye on Eddie's young lieutenant, waiting for him to speak up. He probably had his own take on the problem. But Portier said nothing. Not a word. He just looked down and to the side. It struck Alazzawi as strange. It could be this was bigger than one or two guys with a grudge. As the senior enlisted SEAL in the troop, it was Alazzawi's job to make sure everything in the ranks ran smoothly. He was the fixer. If there was petty drama, he'd need to figure out the cause and find a way to make peace. If there was something bigger . . . well, he'd figure that out, too. He pedaled off without saying much more but made a mental note to ask around until he found out what was up.

It didn't take long for him to start hearing rumors. On the flight back from Iraq in a cavernous cargo jet, the guys in Alpha had not been shy about their gripes. They intentionally kept the killings quiet but told anyone who asked that, broadly speaking, Eddie was a disaster. His approach to warfare was idiotic. He was so clueless that he had almost gotten guys killed. He used guys as bait. He was making up stories to get medals. And he was stealing from the platoon.

It was the stealing that first caught Alazzawi's attention. Tactics were subjective. What a guy in his first deployment might see as reckless might just be another day at the rodeo for a seasoned chief. Besides, as the platoon chief, tactics were Eddie's call. Alazzawi didn't want to second-guess him. But stealing from his own platoon? That raised a flag. As soon as he heard, he pedaled off to find Eddie.

"Please tell me you're not fucking stealing, 'cause that's what your guys are saying about you," Alazzawi told Eddie when he found him.

Eddie looked confused, as if it was the first he was hearing about it. He took a moment to consider, then told the chief it was probably just a misunderstanding. He might have taken a snack bar here or there, or an energy drink, maybe even a can of Copenhagen when he really needed it, but he had been brought up like that in the Teams, sharing everything. Guess the millennial guys coming up are different, he said.

Alazzawi chuckled. He definitely had moments when he shared the chief's view that the latest generation was a little too in touch with their feelings. Still, he wanted this dealt with. "You need to call your guys in and hear them out," he said. There was no reason for high school gossip over PowerBars and Red Bulls. It could grow into something ugly that would impact the mission. For the good of everyone, he said, make peace.

After Alazzawi left, Eddie stalked off and found a few of the guys from Alpha cleaning weapons. He cornered one of the younger guys from Squad 2, Christian Mullan. Who's talking shit about me? asked Eddie. Mullan didn't answer. There was a pretty good roster of possibilities. Could have been anyone in the platoon. He told Eddie he didn't know. Well, tell them to tell it to my face like a man, Eddie said, so I can break their noses.

He walked off.

A short time later, a text from Dalton Tolbert pinged on the phones of all the senior SEALs in Alpha. They had set up a group chat at the end of deployment specifically to coordinate how to deal with Eddie. During the showdown in Mosul over kicking out Joe Arrington, Eddie had told the guys they were acting like a gossipy bunch of women in a sewing circle. In his honor, they named the group text the Sewing Circle. The Circle had decided they were going to report Eddie to the authorities but hadn't yet figured out how. The obvious way was to report to Portier, but they already had tried that, and it was a dead end. Breisch was the next step up, but they had suspicions about him, too. They weren't sure where to go from there, but Tolbert pinged them all to say it was time to figure it out.

"I know some of y'all just got back and don't want to hear this but I guess Eddie is out for blood. We need to talk to someone ASAP," the sniper told them. "Guess he's asking around who said he's stealing."

"Eddie talked to me in the high bay today," Corey Scott, the medic, replied. Eddie had warned him he was going to kill the motherfuckers who were talking behind his back and demanded to know who they were. "I told him if he wants to know what people are saying he can bring everybody in and ask. Not sure how to handle him but he is ready to fight or kill people so we do need to have this talk with leadership."

The others agreed that they were down to tell the leadership ASAP.

"Did he actually say 'kill'?" Tolbert asked.

"He was talking about fighting people, then mentioned he'd be down to kill someone as well," Scott replied.

Josh Vriens cracked a joke: "I've personally never seen him kill an able-bodied male, so I'm not sure how he intends to do that." He asked what the end goal was in talking to the leadership. Was it to pull Eddie's Trident and kick him out of the SEALs or just to make sure he wouldn't be in a leadership position again?

"That's their decision," Joe Arrington said. "We just need to give them the truth because we are concerned."

Craig Miller told everyone he would take care of it. He was the point man. But before he could speak to anyone up the chain of command, Eddie called a mandatory meeting in the high bay at 1300 hours.

Tom MacNeil saw the text about the meeting and was furious. What could Eddie possibly have to say to all of them after Mosul? The junior lieutenant went to confront Portier and found him talking with Miller in the parking lot just outside the high bay. "What's this Eddie meeting about?" MacNeil asked Portier. Don't give Eddie a forum to address the whole platoon. You've given him too many chances already. He just needs to go.

Eddie saw them in the parking lot and came over at a fast clip, catching the last few lines of the conversation. The junior officer he had once thought was a rising star was now clearly a liability. Eddie was not ready to back down. MacNeil had turned off the ATAKs just like everyone else. He had snuck around and lied to the SOTF; he had not reported the stabbing he knew had happened. He was in the group photo. He wasn't clean in all this. Eddie got in the young lieutenant's face and started yelling.

"I have shit on all of you," Eddie told him. "If you take me down, I will take all of you down."

MacNeil and Portier were silent. Miller saw the distant look on the officers' faces and worried that Eddie might be right.

The meeting started a few minutes later. SEALs gathered in a somber array around the ratty old couches in the back of the high bay. The devilish gaze of the mural of the Bad Karma Chick in her fire-red bustier stared down at them. No one really felt like the embodiment of karma anymore. The room was silent and downcast. The guys didn't want to be there. Most of them had been hoping they would never see Eddie again.

If Eddie was intimidated by the room, he didn't show it. He stood up in front of them all and stared down each man. There's a lot of chatter going around, he said, and I want to address it right now. I bring you in here as a sign of respect. I don't need to do this. I've been called a lot of things . . . but never a thief.

A silent shock wave went through the room. Eddie's announcement was almost funny. All the shit that went down, and Eddie wanted to talk about being called a thief? *We're calling you a lot worse than that,* thought Dille.

There was an incredulous silence. No one spoke for almost a minute.

"All right, ranks are off," Eddie said. "Tell me exactly what I stole from anybody. Come on, what did I do?"

Tolbert broke the silence, as usual. Eddie just wanted to discuss the little stuff? Fine, there was no shortage. Fuck it. They could still turn him in for murder tomorrow.

You took Red Bulls out of the fridge on deployment that weren't yours, Tolbert said. And the communal cash jar on top of the fridge that was used to buy more drinks, you took that too.

Eddie said he might have taken a Red Bull, he couldn't remember, then said sarcastically, "Please tell me there is something else."

The dam broke. Guys started jumping in. They had caught Eddie opening their care packages and rooting through to take what he wanted: food, beer, Copenhagen. It's not like the stuff was just left out somewhere. Eddie had gone into Dille's room, into his closet, dug through his stuff, and eaten a whole jar of Trader Joe's cookie butter.

"Hey, sorry," Eddie said. "When I grew up in the Teams it was more a family, we shared everything."

Eddie had tried to steal thousands of dollars' worth of gear on the way home. He had tried to stiff one of the interpreters who bought him testosterone. He had even tried to steal a commemorative shadow box in the safe house created to honor the EOD tech who died on the previous deployment.

Miller was growing angry. He had intentionally decided not to confront Eddie about the murders, but he wasn't going to let Eddie limit the conversation to Red Bulls and cookie butter. "You made Villanueva buy you drugs," he said. "That's really fucked up."

Eddie placed his hands out, palms down, as if telling the guys to calm down.

"And guys are pissed you're using them as bait," Vriens yelled.

"That's tactics. I'm not going to discuss tactics," Eddie shot back. "If I went back to Mosul again, I wouldn't do anything differently."

The guys kept hitting him with accusations. Any time anyone tried to bring up more serious stuff—firing rockets at nothing, lying about targets, shooting at civilians—Eddie refused to engage. He was there to talk about stealing and stealing only. The rest was tactics. When they were platoon chiefs, they could run things how they wanted.

After about twenty minutes the room went silent. The men were still seething, but there was no way they were going to talk it out.

Look, Eddie said, I know you guys don't like me, but you just need to get over it and move on with your careers. If you're willing to drop it, so am I. You guys did good in Mosul, don't fuck it up now.

Eddie walked out without saying more, pursued by the stares of more than a dozen angry men. The silence hid a standoff that both the chief and his men likely understood could not hold for long.

EDDIE TOLD FRIENDS he had taken care of the problem. He hadn't. The guys were still set on turning him in. The question was how. For all their special training, the SEALs knew next to nothing about the military criminal justice system or how to report a crime. And even if they did, as frogmen they didn't do things strictly by the books. It wouldn't be cool to go outside the Teams and, say, call the Naval Criminal Investigative Service hotline. It wasn't seen as right to take family business outside the family. Besides, the SEAL Teams were so anti-NCIS that most of the guys didn't even know there was a hotline. No one had ever told them.

Right after the meeting in the high bay, the whole troop went on a two-week post-deployment leave. Craig Miller was for the first time in months able to spend real time with his wife and new son. He allowed himself to put Eddie out of his mind. But right after the break, Miller was in a hallway on the third floor of Team 7's offices and ran into Alazzawi. The senior chief had been looking for him.

"We need to talk," Alazzawi said.

"Yeah, we do," Miller agreed. It was the chance he had been waiting for—the chance to report the crime without Portier there to bury it.

Alazzawi pulled him into an empty conference room.

"Dude, what happened to Alpha?" Alazzawi said as he slid into a chair and folded his big, tattooed arms on the table.

Miller sighed. He started with the small stuff: the repeated trips to the Towers, the bad tactics, the stealing. Eddie just wasn't a good chief.

Alazzawi started to play devil's advocate. What might seem like bad tactics to a younger guy might be totally fine to an experienced chief like Eddie. And he wasn't going to fry Eddie over a PowerBar or some beef jerky.

Miller stopped him. It was more than that, he said. Part of Miller wished he could get Eddie fired without telling anyone about the murders. It would be simpler just to make him go away without launching a full-blown investigation. Miller didn't even know what a full-blown investigation might look like. But Alazzawi seemed unmoved. Bad stuff happened in Iraq, Miller told him. Really bad stuff. Eddie was shooting at civilians and bragging about it. Guys had seen it. Women, old people, children. The guys had confronted Eddie on deployment. They had told Portier, but the officer did nothing.

Alazzawi shook his head in silence. As the senior enlisted guy in the troop, he was in charge of fixing things. How the fuck was he going to fix this? He didn't hate Eddie like many of the guys in Alpha did. He actually kind of liked him. But he had to do something before things got worse. He couldn't have guys going around talking about murder. It would cause an insurrection in Coronado and certainly get the attention of Big Navy. He let out a long breath.

Got any proof? he asked. If you come at a guy like Eddie Gallagher with murder accusations, you better have some helmet cam footage or something. Eddie is slippery as an eel. "It's gonna be your word against his, and it's going to be difficult to get anyone to believe you, based on his reputation," Alazzawi said. "So unless someone actually witnessed something—"

"I saw him stab a prisoner," Miller interjected.

Alazzawi stopped mid-sentence.

"Where the fuck'd he stab him at?" he asked.

On deployment Miller harbored some suspicion that both Breisch and Alazzawi knew about the captive and either didn't care or outright approved. Alazzawi's response made Miller believe the senior chief was hearing about it for the first time. Miller pointed to the base of his neck.

When? Alazzawi said.

About four months ago, Miller said.

Holy shit, Alazzawi thought. You'd be hard-pressed to find anyone on the base who really cared that an ISIS fighter was dead. But killing a prisoner of war? That was a different matter. If it was true, it was obviously murder. Cold-blooded. And four months had passed with no action. No matter what happened now, the frag radius was going to be huge. The young officers in the platoon might all be on the hook for failing to report. So might some of the enlisted guys. So might Miller. So what was the senior chief supposed to do now?

Alazzawi wasn't a pirate, but he had been raised in the Teams among pirates, getting the SEAL code of loyalty and brotherhood drilled into him. It wasn't expressly said anywhere in the SEAL ethos that every new SEAL memorized, but everyone knew the code of loyalty included silence. That was the dark side to loyalty. Being loyal to your brothers meant you would crawl into a burning helicopter to pull them out. It also meant you didn't fucking rat. You had your brother's back, no matter what. You shut up and dealt with things in the family. Eddie had put the platoon in a no-win situation. Come forward, you're a rat; don't come forward, you're a criminal. Rat on Eddie, you betray the brotherhood; don't rat on Eddie, you betray the rule of law that SEALs swear to uphold. Eddie had served them a real shit sandwich. Alazzawi could either be loyal to Eddie or loyal to Alpha—but not both. And no matter what happened, it was going to be ugly.

Listen, he told Miller, this is serious shit. Portier could go down, MacNeil could go down. Breisch could go down. So could guys in the platoon, if they had any part in it.

Miller nodded. He had the same look of pain and resignation that he had often worn while trying to limp through BUD/S with a broken foot. He had thought a lot about what to do, and he knew everyone might not come out clean. But pain or no pain, he couldn't ring out, he had to push forward. Maybe Eddie could just be fired or forced to retire. Maybe he could be put at a supply desk somewhere where he couldn't do any damage. But whatever happened, he couldn't be in charge of SEALs again.

"All right," Alazzawi said, "what do you think we should do?"

"I don't know," Miller said. "I just don't want other guys to burn because Eddie is a piece of shit."

Just then, Portier walked into the room looking for someone. The senior chief stood up and brushed his uniform down as if he and Miller were just wrapping up a friendly chat. Glad you're back, he told Miller. Enjoy being home.

Alazzawi walked down the hall to Breisch's office and immediately reported what he had heard. Breisch stuck his head out into the hall, called Portier into his office, and shut the door. Miller watched the lieutenant go in. *This is it,* he thought. *It's all done. No stopping it now.*

About an hour later, Portier walked into the high bay looking as if he'd just gotten a fatal diagnosis. He found Miller sorting gear by the storage shelves and said, "What did you tell Al?"

"I told him everything," Miller said grimly, almost apologizing.

Portier looked at the shelves and for a moment didn't say anything. Then he looked over at Miller and sighed as if the Sheriff had screwed up big-time. "Okay," he said. He started walking away. As he watched him go, Miller felt his skin prickle as pent-up anger from the deployment surfaced. He wasn't going to let Portier try to blame him.

"And I'm telling you again right now!" Miller yelled. Portier was still walking away. This fuckup was as much on Portier as it was on Eddie. If the lieutenant had only had an ounce of spine, it would have ended before Eddie killed anyone. Miller went around the shelves to catch Portier on the other side. Miller started to list all the things that happened—shooting civilians, the gun runs with the armored trucks. His voice grew louder and louder as Portier walked away. All those stupid missiles and rockets. He was almost shouting by the time he got to photos over the murdered prisoner, half-hoping that someone else in neighboring high bays would hear.

The door slammed shut. The lieutenant was gone.

A FEW DAYS after the meeting in the high bay, Eddie went to the doctor complaining of a traumatic brain injury. He said it had been caused by a blast in Mosul that had left him unconscious for nearly a minute—a blast the chief had never mentioned to the medics or Alpha's squad leaders. He told the doctor he was increasingly irritable, had difficulty finishing sentences, couldn't focus, and was too wound-up to sleep. When the guys from Alpha heard later that he was claiming an injury again, they just shook their heads.

Eddie asked for a referral to go to the traumatic brain injury clinic at the National Intrepid Center of Excellence. His visit to the doctor may have been for a real combat injury that the platoon medics were not aware of, but if Eddie was concerned that some guys in the platoon were maneuvering against him, a traumatic brain injury diagnosis would provide a handy way to get out of the SEALs quickly, and with benefits.

There were signs Eddie knew the high bay meeting hadn't put things to rest with Alpha. After the meeting, he had several closed-door discussions with Portier, Alazzawi, and Breisch. At times Tom MacNeil was doing paperwork in the office they wanted to use and they would just tell him "Get the fuck out."

Eddie wasn't eligible for retirement until 2019. If he wanted to get out with a pension before that, he would have to get a medical discharge. At the traumatic brain injury clinic he could get formal documentation for all the minor combat injuries and psychological issues that he'd downplayed for years. Even without a Purple Heart or other formal documentation of previous injuries, it wasn't hard for a SEAL chief with several deployments to present enough scrapes and dings to leave the clinic with a medical discharge and a pension. In addition, regulations written to protect troops with brain injuries and PTSD made it difficult for the Navy to discipline sailors for misconduct once they started the medical evaluation process. If things started to go sideways with Alpha and Eddie needed a quick exit from the Navy, the TBI clinic was the best route.

As a bonus, Eddie also left the doctor's office with a new tramadol prescription.

"I got a script for some trammies, picking it up tomorrow," he texted the warrant officer friend who had sent him a care package in Iraq.

"Gettin back on the T-train?" the warrant officer wrote back.

"Yup, they are being super cool now that they think I have TBI haha," Eddie said.

Later that day, after he had gotten out of the doctor's office, Eddie got news that appeared to make him reconsider going the TBI route. Leaders in the SEALs above the level of Breisch and Alazzawi were impressed with his work in Mosul. They had decided to give him a plum new assignment. He was going to work at the SEALs Special Operations Urban Combat training. It was where all SEAL platoons went to learn how to fight door-to-door and rooftop-to-rooftop in urban areas. What Eddie had done in Mosul, the Navy now wanted him to teach to every SEAL on the West Coast. It was exactly what Alpha had feared: Instead of getting pushed out of the SEALs, Eddie was getting pushed up.

THE CONFRONTATION IN the high bay was the last time the platoon ever gathered together. The two-year training and deployment cycle had come to an end. The new guys moved up in Alpha and welcomed a fresh batch of new guys. The senior guys left for new assignments. Craig Miller, Josh Vriens, Corey Scott, and a handful of others were tapped to become instructors at BUD/S. Joe Arrington became a JTAC instructor. Eddie's gopher, Ivan Villanueva, went to sniper school. T. C. Byrne and Dalton Tolbert were selected for a punishing six-month ordeal called Green Team in Virginia, where they could try out to join DEVGRU. And after a smashingly successful deployment, Jake Portier was picked to teach up-and-coming platoon lieutenants the art of being a commander in urban ground warfare.

Dylan Dille could have easily moved up, too, but he realized after a few weeks home that he didn't want it anymore. He had spent years training to become one of the top snipers in the SEALs and now had six months of urban combat experience that would allow him to write his ticket almost anywhere in the Teams. It should have been the height of his career. But he had joined the SEALs to try to make the world a better place, and after Mosul, he no longer thought it was possible to make the world a better place by looking through a sniper scope. It wasn't just that Eddie had tainted everything he admired about the SEALs. It was something more fundamental. In Mosul, Dille had been given the freedom to kill and the responsibility to decide who lived and died. It didn't take him long to realize that he wasn't worthy of that kind of godlike authority. He couldn't ever quite shake the nagging belief that whatever mix of problems created ISIS, it was foolish to think anyone could kill their way out of them. He wasn't really sure karma worked like that. He decided to leave the Navy behind. He didn't know what he planned to do long-term, but he definitely didn't want to be a shooter anymore.

Miller kept the scattered members of the Sewing Circle up to date with texts and phone calls. He told all the guys about his meeting with Alazzawi and how Al had talked to Breisch. The gears of justice were turning, he assured them, and it was only a matter of time before Eddie was nailed. They could go off to their new assignments knowing they had done their duty. Miller was proud that the platoon had stayed unified and done the right thing. He had a new baby, and his wife was now pregnant with another. With a job as an instructor he'd actually have regular hours so he could focus on being a father. It was a weight off his mind to not have to worry about Eddie.

Eddie spent much of the fall of 2017 chilling out. He had saved up a lot of leave time. His job as platoon chief was pretty much done, but his new Special Operations Urban Combat assignment wouldn't start till the new year. His wife, Andrea, bought him a devil-red Harley-Davidson and he took classes to learn to ride. He took her out to dinner and went with the kids to the movies. He met up with his buddies for beers and watched the UFC fights. Eddie and Andrea had dinner with Portier and his fiancée, and Eddie gave the lieutenant a respectable bottle of bourbon as a post-deployment gift. He made a number of visits to his buddy Bito's knife-making workshop to check out new blades. He reminded Portier to put in the paperwork for Eddie's Purple Heart.

Eddie also tried to find ways to supplement his tramadol prescription without tipping off his wife. "I found a way to order trammies online," he texted the warrant officer. "You'll have to order it, Andrea will get in my shit if she finds out. I'll give you the money. It's expensive."

In late November, perhaps believing the drama of Alpha platoon was behind him, Eddie reached out to Alazzawi. If he was going to stay in the Navy, he would need allies. "I realized I didn't tell you what an honor it was working with you," Eddie said in a text. "I know I was a pain in the ass at times but I am sure you were too when you were a platoon chief so I won't apologize."

The platoon believed Alazzawi was quietly working behind the scenes to nail Eddie for murder, but if he was, he held his cards close. "Congrats on a very successful Platoon Chief run," he replied. "U Should be very proud of what you did. I appreciate the hard work you put in with the little, if any oversight needed to get it done right. Made my life a lot easier."

In December, in a gesture of reconciliation to the platoon, Eddie designed a plaque to commemorate Alpha's deployment. It was a traditional SEAL keepsake made of wood with the image of the Bad Karma Chick engraved at the top. Eddie already had a few like it from previous deployments with the Good Old Boys. This was the first one he had designed himself. There was a spot in the middle where each guy could add a photo from deployment, and the plaque had everyone's name, arranged by rank.

When the platoon saw the design, they could hardly contain their disgust. It was riddled with typos. Instead of putting Lieutenant Jake Portier's name in the top spot, Eddie had put his own. And underneath the photo, in a spot where a platoon motto would normally go, Eddie had written, "KILL 'EM ALL!"

"Names missing, names misspelled," Ivan Villanueva said in a text to the rest of the platoon when he saw it.

"Can I spell my name correctly, or is that extra?" Tolbert replied. He added, "To be fair, I'm surprised it doesn't just say his name only."

"Trash," said one of the mortarmen, Michael Stoner. "Was 'KILL 'EM ALL' ever a thing?"

"For some people," Tolbert said, "it was the only thing."

"LOL," said Arrington. Then after a second of consideration, he responded to his own text. "Actually, that's not funny."

A MONTH LATER, Craig Miller cut across the sun-bleached concrete courtyard at the center of the BUD/S training area, where so many generations of SEALs had suffered through endless push-ups and sit-ups that everyone called the space "the Grinder." Miller marched through the yard, determined to find out what the deal was with Eddie.

It was January 2018, seven months after Miller first reported the stabbing to his platoon commander, Jake Portier, and more than three months after he had reported it to Senior Chief Alazzawi. During those months, Miller thought the SEALs were doing something to force Eddie out of the Teams. Not anymore. He had heard from a friend working in headquarters that Eddie not only was still in the SEALs but had been given a high-profile gig at Special Operations Urban Combat training and was going to be awarded the Silver Star.

Miller was furious. He had assured the other guys in the platoon that things were getting done. The Sheriff always kept his word. He knew that a lot of guys might have let what happened in Iraq slide. After all, little good could come from turning in your chief. Eddie had friends all over Teams on both coasts. They wouldn't forget. Pirates dealt harshly with rats. No one would call the guys rats to their faces, probably, but over time they'd be quietly ostracized, undercut, passed over, and pushed into more and more marginal assignments until they finally got the message and left the Navy. If the pirates had their way, Miller could say goodbye to the career he'd been working toward his whole life. He might as well just pull off his Trident pin and walk away.

Staying silent was safer. If Miller and the rest of Alpha just kept their heads down, they could continue to coast on the fiction Eddie had created about their awesome feats in Mosul. It was a path to choice assignments. Eddie would almost certainly continue to work his way higher in the ranks. He would reward the platoon for its loyalty. There would be favors, hookups, promotions. The only downside was that Miller would have to live with himself. His son was starting to crawl. One day he would stand up and walk, and eventually he would be old enough to read about the Battle of Mosul and ask about it. Miller wanted to be able to look his son in the eye on that day.

Even so, Miller went back and forth. Sometimes he felt Eddie just needed to be put at a desk where he couldn't harm any more people. Let him retire. Force him out of the way. That would save the trouble and guilt of sending a SEAL to prison in a public trial that would give the Teams a black eye. But other times, Miller would lie awake in the middle of the night next to his wife and picture what he saw in that dusty yard in Mosul and say to himself that a desk job wasn't enough. It wasn't justice.

Eddie had sworn an oath to uphold the Constitution over the body of a man he had murdered. Eddie obviously didn't believe those words, but Miller did. There was no way to serve the SEALs or the Constitution if guys like the Sheriff weren't willing to stand up and face the fire. If it sounded a little dramatic, it was also true. Take away willingness to fight for virtue, and the SEALs would eventually just be a well-equipped murder squad.

As new BUD/S instructors, Miller and Josh Vriens had to go through a three-week ethics and leadership course in January 2018. As part of the course, veteran frogmen from every era came to talk about case studies. It was a relatively new requirement that Eddie didn't have to meet as a new instructor in 2010. It had been put in place because the brass was concerned about the growing influence of pirates and what they called "ethical drift." For some years, top leaders in the SEALs had known that the Teams were drifting off course. Maybe only a few degrees off true north, but they knew over time it could carry guys into dark waters. Out there, violence was no longer a tool to reach an end, it was the end.

One of the speakers at the class was a white-haired frogman who addressed the mistakes of the Vietnam era. He had served in Senator Bob Kerrey's platoon when a clandestine kidnapping mission went off the rails and SEALs ended up killing twenty-one unarmed villagers. The old frogman talked about how things had gone wrong and how they had covered it up instead of owning up to the mistake. Over the years it had destroyed some of them.

Vriens came up to Miller after the talk and Miller could see the big sniper was weighed down by worry. Vriens had taken the deployment harder than almost anybody. Once the most gung-ho gunslinger in the platoon, he had grown sullen and silent. He had a toddler at home and another baby on the way but spent most of his time so distracted and angry that his wife started wondering if he had sustained a brain injury in Iraq. At church each week his mind wandered and he barely heard what the pastor was saying. He had once believed the values spelled out in the SEAL ethos were *his* values: Defend the defenseless, live with honor and integrity, accept the extraordinary risks of the work, be humble and fade away when the work is done. But after Mosul he began wondering if the SEAL ethos was a fig leaf covering a darker set of values: violence and selfishness, silence and loyalty, the creed of every gang.

On top of everything else, Vriens was carrying the weight of the Switchblade strike. The strike had been ruled an accident, and he managed to avoid formal punishment, but he couldn't deny what had happened. Before Mosul his view of Christianity was basically that if you lived right and did good, you would be rewarded. But now it felt like he was living through some Old Testament ordeal with God repeatedly visiting him with misfortune. He had spent years thinking he was the good guy. He believed the SEALs were good guys. That had been taken from him. He was having nightmares. Even when he was awake, he was tumbling through dark thoughts. He never said the word *suicide* to himself, but he wasn't sure he deserved to live.

"Craig, dude, I am not sleeping. I have not been sleeping for a long time," he said after the class on Vietnam. "We need to do something. I mean, fuck, we could easily be one of these case studies."

This thing is going to get buried unless we push it, Vriens said. Corey Scott and Michael Stoner were in the same training course, and Miller knew they had the same concern. Vriens had decided to leave the Navy. After a deployment with Eddie he didn't want to be a SEAL anymore. "Look, I'll be the fall guy, I'll put my name on the report," he said. Other SEALs could call him a rat or a traitor. It wouldn't matter, he'd be out.

Miller briefly considered it. But having just one guy come forward wouldn't work. Eddie would tear that guy apart. His support in the Teams was too deep. Alpha had to stay united. That was the key. Miller was sure he could get the commanders to do the right thing. Just hold on, he told Vriens, let me work this out.

That's why he was crossing the Grinder. Miller had called his former troop commander to see where the investigation was headed, and Breisch had told him to meet in his office. Miller reached the office and pushed open the door.

"Is Eddie really getting a Silver Star?" Miller asked before he even sat down. He knew Alazzawi had already told Breisch about the stabbing, so he couldn't get his head around why Eddie was going to get a big medal for heroism.

Breisch, like nearly every other SEAL around the Grinder, was fit and slender. He had a frogman's confident gaze. He smiled. He didn't seem to want a conflict with Miller.

It looks that way, he told Miller. Does that surprise you?

Yeah, the Sheriff said emphatically. Half the things in the award had never happened, he said, and the other half are things other guys did. "Look, I need to make sure you're tracking some things," Miller told Breisch. He wanted to give the commander the benefit of the doubt. Maybe Alazzawi hadn't told him everything. Maybe he was still in the dark. Miller went through everything about Mosul: Eddie's random sniper shots, a girl and an old man shot, and a prisoner executed with a hunting knife. Breisch listened with all the reaction of a statue. There was a long pause.

Regulations required Breisch to report even the suspicion of a violation of the laws of armed conflict as soon as he heard them. Miller understood that the SEAL leadership might try some frogman fix that quietly circumvented official channels. By January, though, it was clear they weren't even doing that.

I need to think about this, Breisch said. He nodded and smiled. He thanked Miller for coming forward and said he would take care of it. He said he had to talk to some people.

Even though it was the third time Miller had reported the murder, he got up to leave feeling encouraged. At least Breisch had listened. He hadn't argued. He hadn't kicked Miller out of his office. He hadn't stuck up for Eddie. Maybe Breisch was finally starting to see Eddie for who he really was. But before Miller could leave, Breisch stopped him.

Besides all the stuff that happened in Mosul, Breisch said, would you feel comfortable letting your son deploy with Eddie?

In a moment, all Miller's hopes that the commander was starting to understand exploded like a grenade. "Absolutely not!" he said.

Okay, Breisch said, nodding in thought. What about other people's sons?

"Fuck it," Vriens said after Miller had told him about the meeting with Breisch. It was a few days later and they were sitting through another class on leadership. Vriens wanted to blow things up and didn't care what the collateral damage was. "If they want to be shady and try to pretend nothing ever happened," he told Miller, "we should just go straight to the commodore's office. And if he doesn't do anything, we can go to Fox News."

Miller went to confront Alazzawi, who had been promoted to master chief. Miller still loved the SEAL Teams and wanted to give the system a chance to work. "Guys are running out of patience," he told Alazzawi. "If you don't do something, there's a chance they'll go to the media."

Alazzawi snapped to attention. Don't do that, don't do that, he said. Frogmen were supposed to be covert. No need to come out in the open. There had to be another way that made everyone happy that didn't involve a full-blown war crimes investigation. He would figure out a way. Look, make me a deal, he told Miller. Just hold off. I promise I'll work this out.

Alazzawi talked to some of the top-ranking chiefs. A few days later, at the end of January, the SEAL command pulled Eddie from his job at Special Operations Urban Combat. Eddie was not amused. He went and found Alazzawi at the base in Coronado.

Why am I not working? he asked. Eddie had been talking about his badass combat deployment to whoever at Coronado would listen. When anyone mentioned the bad blood with Alpha, he dismissed it as just a bunch of whiny turds who couldn't handle Gallagher-style warfare. If the other SEALs saw him suddenly get benched over Mosul, it wouldn't look good.

Alazzawi tried to be direct. Look, he said, guys from Alpha are raising some disturbing accusations about deployment. It isn't a good time for you to be an instructor in front of students.

That's all bullshit, Eddie shot back. Whatever they're saying, I can clear it.

"This isn't about tactics. Guys are saying some serious shit about you. Like about a prisoner," Alazzawi said.

Eddie let out a half laugh, as if to say, *Is that it?* He knew what they were referring to, he said, and that was bullshit, too. Eddie said he had been working on an ISIS captive and the guy had grabbed for his belt near his gun, so he had fucked him up.

There it was. Even if Eddie was saying it was self-defense, Eddie had just admitted he had killed the captive. Now Alazzawi had confirmation. And a confession. Eddie would have to be dealt with. Alazzawi got up to leave and said, "Hey, man, it's your story, be able to tell it. Because at the end of the day that's the allegation coming out on you."

It's all good, Eddie said. Don't worry, I can clear it.

Later, when he texted a SEAL chief and longtime friend he sometimes talked trammies with, he was much less confident.

"I am dealing with some shit, I'll have to tell you on Monday. It's fucked," he said.

"Geez, bro, you good?" the chief asked.

"No," Eddie said.

Eddie was never one to give up, and he wasn't going to now. He wanted his sweet Special Operations Urban Combat training assignment back. He wanted his medals. He talked with Alazzawi and Breisch and tried to smooth things over. He went up the chain to the top enlisted SEAL master chief at Coronado, hoping to figure out how to make Alpha go away. It didn't go well. "Nothing can be done with these turds," Eddie texted his chief friend after the meeting. He said the command master chief was worried that if an official investigation started, no one could stop it. Best thing to do is just lay low and see what happens. Maybe it would just simmer down and go away.

"So I'm chilling here for a while," Eddie texted. But he wasn't just going to sit there and take it, he told the chief. "I am just going to let everyone know who these fucks are and what they are about."

He was pretty sure he knew which turds were talking shit: Craig Miller and the sniper twins, Dalton Tolbert and Dylan Dille, who had second-guessed Eddie all deployment.

Eddie didn't know what they had on him. If it was just their word, then he could probably survive it. He had been through investigations before and had always emerged intact. But if it was more, it could be a problem. There were a lot of photos and videos taken the day of the stabbing. Who knew where they all ended up? Eddie started reaching out to guys he thought he could trust. T. C. Byrne was the medic he had hand-selected to come to Alpha platoon. Eddie had given Byrne a glowing recommendation for Green Team, and they had parted on good terms. He tracked him down to find out what he knew.

Eddie didn't know he was part of the Sewing Circle.

"Had an awkward run-in with Eddie in the parking lot behind the team," Byrne texted the group. It was mid-February, a few weeks after Eddie learned some guys in Alpha were pushing an investigation. "He asked about Green Team, then he immediately said he's getting forced out and he's moving on. He mentioned the video of him is the reason. He was being very vague."

"Vague about what though?" Michael Stoner asked. "I feel like he's more than likely already been notified that we all reported it up and what we reported up."

"He is trying to figure out if there is a video," Miller guessed. "If there isn't a video, he may try to force an investigation to clear himself. If he thinks there is, he will accept his fate. He is just probing."

What both Alpha and Eddie didn't know was that nothing had been officially reported up. A handful of senior enlisted frogmen, led by Alazzawi, were thinking about shoving Eddie into a new assignment in a quiet corner where perhaps he would eventually get the message and leave the SEALs, but Breisch had not alerted the chain of command, so no criminal investigation had started, and chain of command at Coronado still had no clue. Neither did the larger Navy or the Naval Criminal Investigative Service.

The frogman plan to get Eddie to disappear quietly might have worked if the guys in Alpha had been on board. But they weren't. In fact, they were doing the opposite of keeping it quiet. To anyone in the Teams who asked, they would say that Eddie was a lying, thieving psycho who had no business being in the SEALs. Ask for details, they were happy to provide them, war crimes and all. Golf platoon was talking too.

Gossip about Eddie was getting so widespread by March 2018 that Breisch and Alazzawi decided they needed to call Alpha together and give them an ultimatum: Either report Eddie Gallagher for war crimes or shut the fuck up. They told the platoon to meet with them.

Miller texted the guys and asked if they were willing to talk to their old command team. Their quick replies left no doubt.

Dylan Dille was in.

Michael Stoner: "In."

Josh Vriens: "Down."

Corey Scott: "Fine with me."

Joe Arrington: "Yup."

Ivan Villanueva: "Send it."

A. J. Hansen: "Check."

Dalton Tolbert and T. C. Byrne had just left for Green Team.

Tom MacNeil had moved to the Naval Postgraduate School in Monterey as he climbed the officer ladder. David Shaw the JTAC was on his way out of the Navy. None of them could be there, but all told Miller they were behind him. That was the vast majority of Alpha. As far as Miller knew, there was no one in the platoon that didn't want Eddie dealt with.

Alazzawi told the SEALs to meet at a lecture hall called the Donnell Classroom, not far from the Grinder. It would be big enough to hold all of them but private enough to have a real discussion. At the very end of March 2018, seven SEALs from Alpha wearing green camouflage uniforms filed into the room a few minutes before 11 A.M. Nearly all of the senior SEALs were there: Miller, the lead petty officer; the snipers, Vriens and Dille; and Scott, the medic who had witnessed the stabbing.

Breisch took his place at the front and told them he was tired of the trash talk. It was time either to report Eddie to the authorities or to drop it. The gauntlet was thrown down. The former enlisted SEAL turned troop commander apparently was not going to betray the code of loyalty, even though regulations required it. He was putting it on the junior SEALs, almost daring them to act: You want to rat on Eddie? Then you do it.

Miller was starting to think the boss would back Eddie no matter what. He knew Breisch and Eddie had come up through the Teams together and Breisch had stood by Eddie at every turn. Now Eddie was the star of the Battle of Mosul and Breisch's highest-profile SEAL. If he was suddenly revealed as a war criminal, it would tarnish everything the troop commander had accomplished. People might start asking what kind of officer Breisch was.

Breisch warned the platoon that if a bunch of relatively low-ranking guys reported a chief like Eddie, they might end up looking like fools. Unless they had photos or video or something hard, forget it. The SEAL Teams would not look kindly on it, and the accusers would all get their Tridents pulled and be tossed out of the Navy. It was up to them, he said.

None of the SEALs had ever been taught that under Navy regulations, it was not up to them. Officers were not supposed to ask the troops whether they wanted to report a crime. Crimes were not reported after taking a vote. And it was not the job of the commander to try to weigh the facts and decide whether an investigation was really warranted. That was what the investigation was for. Everyone was supposed to report up the chain of command and move on. Other authorities would order the independent fact-finding and decide what to do.

Alazzawi got up in front of the men and said what they all knew. "Fellas, the frag radius of something like this is going to be fucking major." The master chief was a year older than Breisch and had deployed more. He was supposed to be the mature one in the room, the leader, but he seemed to argue both sides, as if he was himself unsure what to do.

Alazzawi had zero love for those "KILL 'EM ALL" crusaders in the Teams. His full name was Brian Hussein Alazzawi. His father had immigrated from Iraq in the 1970s. A lot of his family still lived there. On deployments he'd seen SEALs trash houses and rough people up, smash things for no reason, and dismiss it by saying, "Fuck the towelheads." He was always one to push back. The war was not with the Iraqi people; it was with the criminals and jihadists. There was a difference between being an operator and being a pirate. If Eddie couldn't distinguish between doing the job and making war on an entire culture, then fuck him.

At the same time he worried that the investigation might take down a lot of good SEALs. He suspected other stuff had happened on deployment and it would all come out if NCIS got involved. The SEAL Teams had long existed on the edge of what was acceptable. They had to. They were doing the nation's dirty work, not teaching kindergarten. And the guys willing to do it were always going to be a bit fringe. The line between the Navy's trained killers and criminals was clear, but it wasn't always very wide. Messed-up things happened in combat, and Alazzawi knew that if SEALs didn't stand together, if they let a bunch of rear-echelon desk pilots pick them apart after the fact, everyone might end up behind bars.

Then there was the problem of Eddie. Alazzawi had supervised him for three years. He knew Eddie was a hard dude. Attack him head-on, he wasn't going to back down. "Eddie's like a cornered rat. If you come at him, he's going to fight," he told the platoon. He'll pull out everything. He'll try to take you down. So don't come at him unless you have something real and you are ready.

Some guys in the room asked if there was a middle way. They didn't want to blow things up with a criminal investigation; they just wanted Eddie out of the SEALs.

Alazzawi shook his head. It doesn't look that way, gents, he said. Right now, Eddie Gallagher looks great on paper. Best chief in the team. Top marks. Medal for valor. Even if they got him moved out of his Special Operations Urban Combat assignment, he'd get a new assignment and probably do pretty well there. He always does. People like him. He'll become a senior chief. He'll probably even become a master chief. He'll almost certainly be back out there eventually leading SEALs.

"So that's it?" Josh Vriens said, his eyes throwing daggers at the leaders. "Eddie gets to just go on with his life? He said he's gonna kill us."

Do you really think he's going to kill you? Breisch said. He raised an eyebrow.

"I saw him shoot a little girl," Vriens fired back.

"And I saw him stab a guy," Corey Scott said.

Breisch stopped them. It was as if he specifically didn't want to hear about any crimes. If he insulated himself, there would be deniability, a chance he could stay clear of the blast. If you saw anything criminal, report it, he said. If not, shut up. Up to you what you want to do.

Both Breisch and Alazzawi left the room to let them confer.

Dylan Dille was the first to speak. They had been kept separated by squad in Mosul, and he still didn't have a full understanding of who had seen what there. If they were going to report Eddie, he wanted it to be clear. "So who actually, no shit, with their own eyes saw Eddie commit a war crime?" he asked.

"I saw him stab the guy," Scott said. He said that Villanueva, who had been unable to attend the meeting because of training, had seen it, too.

"Me too," said Miller.

Vriens spoke up about the girl.

Dille said he had seen Eddie shoot multiple times at civilians but was only sure the chief had hit the old man on Father's Day. Dille said Tolbert had seen it. Josh Graffam, too.

"So what do you guys think we should do?" the Sheriff asked, looking around.

Vriens spoke up. He was getting out, so he didn't care about himself, but his instinct was to protect his friends. Eddie said he has shit on all of us, and he probably does, he said. There were guys who posed for the photo. Guys who took their own photos with the body, guys involved in the Switchblade strike. He knew there were guys who took sniper shots they regretted. "Look, we do this, that's all going to come out," he said. "A lot of us are going to take it on the chin. We could all end up getting fired. Are you good with that?"

There was a moment of silence.

To everyone's surprise, Corey Scott, who very rarely had much to say, spoke first. The Ghost was slated to get out of the Navy, but for now he was an instructor at BUD/S with Miller and Vriens. He turned to them. "Eddie's going to be leading SEALs," he said. "If Eddie gets one of our students killed on a deployment, how are we going to look their parents in the eyes knowing we could have stopped him?"

There was a long silence.

"Okay, let's take a vote," Miller said. "Who thinks we should report—"

Before he had finished, Scott put up his hand.

Vriens was surprised. He considered Scott a guy who showed up late, left early, and only did what was expected. He wasn't exactly a man who charged ahead with the SEAL ethos on his sleeve. If Scott was that adamant about reporting Eddie, then Vriens was one hundred percent behind him. He raised his hand.

Dille felt the same way. He knew the weight of the investigation would fall most heavily on the witnesses to the stabbing. He wasn't going to vote yes unless they were on board. Scott was the one who had seen it most clearly. If Scott was in, Dille was in. He raised his hand. One by one, so did everyone else.

Breisch popped his head back in the door of the classroom. "So you want to report something?" he asked. Okay, he said, no problem, I'll take care of it. But for the record, he said, this was the first time he had heard about anything criminal.

Miller felt they had no choice but to trust Breisch. It was Friday. The team had Monday off for Easter. Breisch said he would make the report to the Team 7 commander first thing Tuesday.

Tuesday morning, Breisch, Portier, and Alazzawi went to the Team 7 commander's office. They sat down to tell the commander in charge about the murder allegations, but then Breisch and Portier talked in circles. They brought up problems with rumors and petty stealing in Alpha and complaints of bad tactics. They talked about bad blood between disgruntled SEALs. No war crimes were mentioned.

That afternoon, Alazzawi found Miller. "They bitched out," he said. "They didn't fucking do it. It's on you now."

ALMOST EXACTLY FIFTY years before Alpha met their leadership in a classroom at Naval Base Coronado, a company of about 150 Army soldiers in Vietnam poured out of helicopters and began raking a small village with gunfire. The troops encountered no resistance but continued shooting anyway. They went on a rampage, setting huts on fire, stabbing old men, raping women, and taking scalps as trophies. That morning became known years later as the My Lai Massacre and was eventually recognized as the most notorious atrocity of the Vietnam War. But on that day and for several years after, the Army proclaimed it a decisive victory. Newspapers across the United States carried news of a sweeping triumph. No Viet Cong fighters had been seen in the village, but *The New York Times* declared on the front page: "G.I.'s, in Pincer Move, Kill 128 in a Daylong Battle."

Some soldiers on the ground had witnessed what really happened and immediately sounded the alarm, but they were repeatedly ignored, sidelined, and silenced. No investigation started. No soldiers were questioned. No one went to the village to document the bodies. Instead, the colonel in charge issued commendation letters for a job well done.

The witnesses kept pressing authorities to do something, but by that point the whole chain of command was exposed. Admitting to a massacre and a cover-up would make the Army look bad. It wasn't just the soldiers who did the killing, it was the commanders, and the commanders' commanders, and the Army as a whole. Careers and promotions were on the line. Support for the war could be poisoned. The Army began a systematic effort to investigate the massacre out of existence and deny that it had ever occurred. A few months later, the Army issued a report that found that "the allegation that U.S. Forces shot and killed 450 to 500 civilians is obviously a Viet Cong propaganda move to discredit the United States" and took no further action.

Witnesses refused to give up and eventually took their allegations to Congress. Two years after the massacre, the Army charged eleven soldiers and officers with murder and rape and another fourteen officers with the cover-up. Then everyone involved tried to put the blame on someone else. The low-ranking soldiers said they were just following officers' orders. Officers said they had never ordered anything. Ultimately, in the systematic massacre of hundreds of people, only one junior officer named Lieutenant William Calley Jr. was ever convicted.

Craig Miller now found himself in a situation that, if not nearly as horrific as My Lai, had managed to exploit all the same weaknesses in the military. He had witnessed a murder. He had reported Eddie in Iraq. He had reported Eddie when he got home to Coronado. He had reported Eddie across the desk from the troop commander. He'd brought all the guys together to issue a united decision to report Eddie. Every time, nothing happened. The SEAL Teams seemed set on burying it.

No one along the way had ever told Miller to fuck off—at least not explicitly. Instead Miller got a soft, bureaucratic "Thank you for coming forward and sharing your concerns." But after nearly a year of hearing that, he now had little doubt that "thank you for coming forward" and "fuck off" were effectively the same thing. He had been raised to trust the SEALs, to see the frogmen as a true brotherhood, but he began to wonder if the whole thing was tainted by pirates.

Miller wasn't willing to become one of Eddie's accomplices. He didn't want to be that white-haired frogman the SEAL Teams invited back fifty years later to turn his regret into a lesson. No more wasting time. Alazzawi was right: It was on Miller now. On April 6, 2018, just a day after hearing that Breisch had bitched out in his meeting with the Team 7 commander, Miller went into Breisch's office with an iron look on his face. He found him at his desk and Portier sitting on a couch across the room. Both looked startled when the Sheriff came in.

"We're going to report it right now. Right now," Miller said.

Okay. No problem, Breisch told him. His voice danced with the nervous compliance of someone asking a bank robber to put down a gun. He nodded his head while he gathered his thoughts. Sure, we can do it right now, he said, but hang on a sec. Okay. Now. He paused and turned to Miller. Now, what are we talking about? What do you want to report?

Miller looked at the lieutenant commander like he had lost his mind.

"Eddie," Miller stammered. "Eddie and the prisoner."

Breisch scrunched his brow in an expression of confusion and waited, mouth half-open.

"The ISIS prisoner Eddie killed in Mosul?" Miller said.

Breisch held up his hand. Wait a minute, he said, you're telling me Eddie Gallagher killed an ISIS prisoner on deployment?

Miller looked around the room. It was so ridiculous it had to be a prank. He started to wonder if it was all being recorded. Then he regained his bearings. Whatever shit was going on, it didn't matter. He crossed his arms on his six-foot-two frame, his feet planted firmly in the middle of the office, his frogman watch on his wrist. If Breisch was recording, Miller wanted to say exactly what had happened.

"You knew about it. This isn't the first time we've talked about it. I have witnesses," Miller said. He looked at Portier. "Jake, the first time I talked to you about it was the night it happened."

Portier looked down. He mumbled that, actually, he didn't learn about it until near the end of the deployment.

"Whatever," Miller said. "Let's do it right now. How do we get this started?"

Breisch acted like he'd been asked how to repair a nuclear submarine. I'm not sure, he said. I guess we could send an email to one of the legal people? He turned back to his computer. He started typing and narrated as he did. Okay, so, Special Operator First Class Miller witnessed Eddie Gallagher stab . . . a prisoner?

"Yeah, in the neck. And Corey Scott witnessed it too," Miller said. "He's already mentioned it to you several times. He needs to be on there."

Breisch nodded and typed. It was no more than three sentences. Miller's trust in Breisch had grown so thin that he stepped around the desk to make sure the email was actually there and stood watching until Breisch clicked Send.

Breisch looked up at Miller. "Okay," he said. "It's done."

Within hours the Team 7 commander and the commodore in charge of all SEALs on the West Coast had read the allegations. By the end of the day, they had notified the Navy's version of the FBI, the Naval Criminal Investigative Service.

A few days later, Portier submitted his papers to resign from the Navy.

MILLER WALKED OUT of the room more angry than relieved. He didn't understand why the SEALs made it so difficult to do the right thing. But at least now the report had left the pirate ship. Outsiders had it. Professionals. They would know what to do.

Miller was proud of Alpha. The investigation might turn out to be a hard fight, but they were all stacked up and going through the door together. Eddie wasn't going to split them. Miller wasn't sure how it would turn out. He'd never dealt with the Naval Criminal Investigative Service before. But at least his brothers were with him.

He was still savoring that new feeling of lightness at home that night on the couch with his wife as they watched their son crawl around the living room when his phone rang. He recognized the area code from his hometown in Texas and picked up. On the other end was a strange voice, a guy speaking with a fast West Texas twang. He introduced himself as Jake Portier's lawyer, then said, You're in way over your head on this, my friend.

Before Miller had a chance to say much, the man fired a barrage of declaratives: This NCIS deal isn't going to end well. I know you think you've thought it through, but you haven't. They're going to search your house. What are they going to find? Any unregistered firearms? Any gear you're not supposed to have? What about those photos you guys were in? Everyone's going to lie to protect their buddies, and then NCIS will charge all of you for it. Half of your boys are probably going to get kicked out of the Navy over it. Some might even go to jail.

Miller could feel tension balling up in his chest. He hadn't even caught the lawyer's name, but the guy already seemed to know everything about the case. Miller looked over at his wife, then at his son on the floor. He started to respond, but the man cut him off.

Guys get screwed over all the time because they think they can trust NCIS. Bad idea, the man said. Not your fault, you didn't know, but NCIS is not your friend. Now you need to protect yourself. You need to protect your friends. First, don't talk to the cops. Period. Then get a lawyer. I can represent you if you want. I'll do it for free. Everyone will be fine if guys just shut up, now. No point in being a hero. There isn't enough evidence to convict, anyway. It's just a he-said-she-said case. Eddie is going to walk. Hell, he'll probably get a book deal out of it. And all you'll get is screwed.

CHAPTER 10

SPECIAL AGENTS

"WITH AS MANY details as you can, just tell me the story."

Craig Miller was sitting at a tiny table in a small windowless interrogation room with blank white walls. Just a block away, huge gray warships stood in rows along the pier of Naval Base San Diego, and the sun glinted off the Pacific. But Miller was deep inside the offices of the Naval Criminal Investigative Service. All he could see were four blank walls, three cheap office chairs, a box of tissues on the table, and two agents in plain clothes staring at him.

Miller was wearing a plain gray T-shirt and jeans to try to be inconspicuous, but his frogman Rolex Sub was still on his wrist. His big frame hunched uncomfortably forward. He had his arms between his knees. He was nervous, tense, already upset, though he had been trying to keep himself calm.

The lead agent tossed a notebook on the little table. His name was Special Agent Joseph Warpinski. Nothing seemed particularly Navy or police about him to Miller. He was tall and slender and wore jeans and a plaid flannel shirt. He had a full, thick beard and the low-key, confident way of speaking that one might hear from an especially discerning barista at a hipster espresso bar. He wasn't scribbling notes. His hands rested in his lap like he was settling in for a long conversation. And he didn't talk like a cop.

"With as many details as you can, just tell me the story," Warpinski said gently. Then he sat back patiently, letting quiet flood the tiny room. Miller had decided to ignore the mysterious lawyer and meet with NCIS without representation. He hoped it wasn't a mistake. Sitting in that tiny room, he realized that he had never told the whole story, start to finish, to anyone. He had mentioned bits and pieces to his wife and parents, mostly in bursts of frustration. He'd talked over what to do with the guys, but just to learn who knew what. He'd tried to tell the story to Breisch and Alazzawi, but those conversations had felt more like sparring matches. Miller wasn't sure if he had ever even fully told the story to himself.

Now he had the time and space to tell it, and someone who mattered waiting to hear it. That, in itself, made him hesitate. He hadn't been able to shake the conversation with that bizarre lawyer from the night before. He had stayed awake all night in bed wondering if he'd be locked up for the act of trying to report a crime. When he left home that morning, he hugged his wife tightly and told her he was unsure if he would ever come home. Now he had agents listening, and he wasn't sure if they were waiting to spring a trap.

"Okay." Miller let out a long breath and fumbled with a pad of paper. "I brought my notes . . . just stuff I jotted down this morning, 'cause I didn't know . . ." He glanced at what he had written and shook his head. He cleared his throat. He pressed his hand up to his temple. And in halting half sentences, he began.

In early May 2017, he said, his platoon was on the edge of Mosul. They were firing mortars and calling in air strikes on ISIS. They were there to support the Iraqi Army. And then a bunch of Iraqi soldiers arrived at their position with a wounded ISIS guy across the hood of a Humvee. "Probably like a sixteen-year-old or whatever, and I look over, and Eddie is there," Miller said. "I thought that was weird. Because Eddie was supposed to be with the forward element, and I couldn't understand why he was there."

Warpinski listened and nodded.

Miller said he watched for a while, then went to get some food and came back. "I was walking behind the Humvee and around it," Miller said. His voice quivered. "And then I looked down and I see this person laying there and he had, like, bandages on his leg, or whatever, and I see Eddie laying over him with the knife, sticking it into his neck."

As Miller said it, he saw it all happen again. He paused and took several breaths. He shook his head and swallowed hard. Warpinski didn't say a word. He waited, his hands not moving from his lap.

Miller took another breath. Recalling that morning was harder than he was prepared for. He shifted uncomfortably in his chair and willed himself to go on. "Corey Scott was right there," he stammered. "He was, like, pretty shocked by the whole thing. I could tell Corey was, like, freaking out a little bit with what he just did. There was nothing I could do at this point so I left that scene and just tried to catch my breath and just think about what I just saw."

Miller told Warpinski that he immediately went to find the lieutenant in charge and told him what had happened with Eddie, then said the situation was getting out of hand and the platoon needed to leave. He went to pack up and came back to find Jake Portier doing a reenlistment ceremony for Eddie over the body. "And I was just thinking like this is the most disgraceful thing I've ever seen in my life," Miller said.

Warpinski interrupted for the first time. "They do it with the body right there and everything?" he asked.

"Yeah, the body was right there," Miller said, catching his breath and nodding. "I just remember, like, this is so bad." Saying it out loud broke down a wall Miller had built around the murder in his mind so he could focus on the deployment. For the first time he saw the full tragedy of the day, not just the murder but the knife Eddie had shoved into every life in the platoon. He thought about going to jail instead of going home to see his wife and baby. His eyes got hot and looked toward the wall. The Sheriff was on the verge of tears.

Miller described how he feared that Eddie might know he had witnessed the execution, so he felt forced to get in the picture Portier was taking.

"I think Jake is like a good person, you know," he said. "I think Eddie was proud of it, and it was like part of things for him. The guy's freakin' evil, man."

Warpinski asked about the photos and Miller said he didn't know where NCIS might find them. He knew there was a good chance they were all deleted.

Miller went into the weeks at the Towers, where Eddie started targeting civilians. "The snipers told me they had stopped going after ISIS and were trying to shoot warning shots to get civilians away from Eddie," Miller said. "And I talked to Tom and Jake about this and . . ." His voice cracked. He stopped to wipe his eyes. He was a SEAL with a reputation as a hardass; he had not cried because he was upset since he was a boy. But he was overwhelmed. It hurt to know that telling the truth might somehow be seen as a betrayal. He regretted that it might end up with the lieutenants being charged with crimes. He didn't want to go to jail. And if he was being honest, he was scared that Eddie would find out and try to kill his wife and baby boy.

"Hey, if you need to take a break at any point, man, you can," Warpinski said. "Obviously this is some big shit, so take your time."

"Sorry, first time," Miller said, sniffing.

He said he was pretty sure the chain of command knew about the stabbing for months but didn't seem to do anything. Then he interrupted himself to mention that Eddie had told guys in the platoon he would kill anyone who was talking shit.

"That's something you should be aware of," Miller said, choking up again. "Because, I don't know, it's one thing to come back at me, but my family, you know?"

Warpinski glanced at Miller's notepad and saw there was a bullet point about whether Miller would be charged with a crime. Warpinski told him not to worry. If he had even the slightest suspicion Miller had committed a crime, he was required to give Miller formal notification of Miller's rights. "Right now," he said, "you are one hundred percent here as a witness."

Miller walked out of the office two hours later a free man. Though he was completely drained and exhausted, he immediately called some of the senior guys in Alpha. He told them he thought it was going to be okay. The agent had listened. He seemed cool. Miller didn't think any of them were going to jail.

WARPINSKI LEFT THE INTERVIEW with his mind blown. The agent was thirty-two years old. He had done a little over two years with NCIS and seven with the U.S. Border Patrol before that. He had never worked a war crimes case. And he had definitely never worked a case involving a bunch of SEALs making accusations against their chain of command.

The case had dropped when Warpinski came to work Monday morning. Waiting for him was an email saying two SEALs had witnessed their platoon chief murder a prisoner. That in itself, even before the details came out, was a meteor impact. NCIS, despite the high drama of the top-rated TV series by the same name, was typically a pretty sleepy affair. Most of the cases were low-level drug busts and sexual assaults, with some theft here and there. Most crimes involving sailors occurred off base and were handled by civilian authorities. NCIS rarely investigated a murder. And after fewer than twenty-four hours on the case, it was clear that this wasn't just a simple murder. An eyewitness said Eddie Gallagher had stabbed a detainee, but there were also rumors of his shooting multiple civilians. There might be a photo of the whole platoon around the dead body. Even more bizarre, the witness said the platoon commander had arranged the photo. And it sounded like there was also a concerted effort by the leadership at multiple levels to keep the crime from seeing the light of day. If even half of that was true, this could end up being the biggest case of Warpinski's life.

Warpinski already had suspicions about the officers involved. Even before talking to Miller, he had tried to contact Portier, but the lieutenant refused to talk. He referred the agent to his lawyer. That was his right, Warpinski knew, but of course it made him wonder what the lieutenant was trying to hide. After talking to Miller, he had a better idea.

The agent needed to act fast, before any more of Alpha circled the wagons. That afternoon he called Corey Scott, the medic who had supposedly also witnessed the stabbing. He got him to come down to the headquarters the next day.

The Ghost sat down at the interrogation table in a black T-shirt that showed his broad shoulders. He was shaved bald, and his heavy brow and big arms made him look like hired muscle. Warpinski showed him his badge, took down his personal information, then closed his notebook and said, "Why do you think you're here?"

Scott didn't hesitate. "Probably for the prisoner stabbing incident," he said casually. "I was there, Eddie was there, T. C. Byrne, and then Ivan Villanueva."

Scott leaned back in his chair and started telling the story without any prodding. He seemed relaxed, unemotional—the opposite of Miller. He described how a wounded kid had come in. Eddie and the other medic, Byrne, were working on him, and one of the new guys, Villanueva, was helping. There were a bunch of Iraqis around. Scott came in late and knelt by the head to monitor vitals. As Scott talked, he picked a lash out of his eye and inspected it on the tip of his finger, as if not only at ease but a little bored.

"And then anyways, they kind of had everything under control, so I was kind of at the patient's head while they were working with him. And then all of a sudden Eddie just starts stabbin' the dude."

Warpinski broke in. "Just while everyone was just there working on him?"

"Yeah," Scott said. "I was at the head. Like, all of a sudden, Eddie's, like, stabbing this dude in the neck."

"Did he say anything about it or just start stabbing him just because?" Warpinski asked.

"No. I was kind of shocked, 'cause, like, there was a whole bunch of partner force around, so I was, like—it was a holy shit moment, no idea what to do."

The SEAL stopped himself and leaned forward. He started talking using his hands to make a point. "To preface all this," he said, "at the time Eddie was like a very respected chief. Our minds, we weren't on the lookout, like, 'Hey, keep an eye on this guy.' We respected him at the time and didn't really question anything yet. Had this happened later on in deployment, we would have all been watching him."

Warpinski asked how close Scott was to the stabbing.

"Like, a foot," Scott said.

"Did Eddie say anything or just pull out a knife and start stabbing him?" the agent asked.

"He just pulled out a knife and started stabbing him."

Any chance it was in self-defense? the agent asked.

Scott didn't hesitate. No.

Warpinski asked if the patient had been stable before the stabbing. Scott said yes. Then Warpinski asked if the patient would have been cared for by the Iraqi Army. Scott nearly snorted. Without going into detail about hearing ERD's torture captives, he said, "If the Iraqis got him, he probably would have died."

Warpinski asked what happened after the stabbing.

"I was kind of shocked at first. I kind of looked around. I was like, *Who else is seeing this?*" Scott said. "And then, like, I kind of stayed at the dude's head and—like, for a few minutes until he died."

There was a second of silence. Warpinski didn't want to interrupt any other details about the death. Scott said nothing.

"You said he stabbed him, one time, multiple times?" Warpinski said.

"It was probably two or three times," Scott said. He pointed his hand down into the base of his own neck, just above the right collarbone. "It was just like a stab like right here," he said. "In a few times."

Scott was straightforward until the agent started asking about the photos that Scott knew he appeared in. Suddenly the medic leaned back and folded his arms and his memory seemed to lapse. His answers became vague. Sometimes only one word. Any idea who was in the photos? No. Any idea who took the photo? No. Any idea who might have the photo? No.

Scott said he wasn't sure there even was a photo.

A DAY LATER, Warpinski had interviews with two snipers in the bag: Dylan Dille and Josh Vriens. The agent had tried to work fast and quiet. He planned to start with the senior guys who had come forward willingly—the Sewing Circle—and then work out from there.

Dille arrived in a long-sleeve plaid flannel shirt and a ball cap pulled low over his eyes. Right away, without any hesitation or much emotion, he started laying out what happened as if he was briefing for a sniper mission. "Eddie . . . to speak in layman's terms, he shot at a shit ton of people," he told Warpinski. In Mosul, Eddie would shoot at just about anyone moving—old men, women, kids. Dille saw the chief fire into crowds by the river. Dille estimated Eddie shot twenty to fifty people, and maybe five of them were legitimate targets. But the sniper was forthright about what he didn't know. He didn't know a lot of dates. He didn't know what had happened to the people Eddie shot at. The only one he really had a date and corroborating witnesses for was an old man Eddie shot in the back on Father's Day.

"I was, like, just praying for this guy," Dille said as he described watching the man struggle to get up and lurch away. "I don't know if you guys are like that, but I, you know, was just praying for him. And he got up and then walked away, and I don't—you know, I don't know if he made it."

What about the captive? Warpinski asked.

Dille said he hadn't seen the stabbing. He was there right before and right after. But it was his understanding that Eddie had used a custom fixed blade that he always wore in a black leather sheath across the small of his back. Warpinski pressed him for details about the knife. Dille started to describe it, then interrupted himself. You know what, he volunteered, Eddie is genius at manipulating people, but in other ways he's surprisingly stupid. Eddie had probably never bothered to get rid of the murder weapon. "I wouldn't doubt at all if he didn't wash the knife and it's still sitting in his op box."

Josh Vriens was just as open as Dille but more emotional. As soon as Warpinski asked the big sniper why he thought NCIS wanted to talk to him, Vriens said, "Yeah, my chief Eddie Gallagher." He looked around as if trying to decide where to start. "The biggest thing I guess . . ." He paused to think. "I can give you hours of instances."

Vriens said he hadn't seen the stabbing. He wasn't there that day, but he had heard Eddie admit to it that night. Everyone in the platoon knew. And, he said, "I saw a fourteen-, fifteen-year-old girl get shot in the stomach." He described the group of girls moving down by the river, then seeing one in a flower hijab get shot and collapse. At first he thought ISIS had shot her, he said, but another sniper, Joe Arrington, told him later that day Eddie had told him he had taken the shot.

"Is there anything you saw that those girls were doing, anything at all that could have justified that shot?" Warpinski asked.

"No," Vriens said quickly.

"Not a single thing?" he pressed

Vriens paused for several seconds. He rubbed his hand over his scalp as he pictured the scene on the riverbank. "No, I'll tell you right now, I one hundred percent would not have taken that shot. I don't know any Navy SEAL sniper that would have."

Vriens spent most of the interview trying to explain all the toxic behavior that wasn't exactly criminal. To him the lack of professionalism was vital to understanding the murders. Eddie was completely incompetent at tactics. He didn't know where the enemy was half the time. One guy got shot. Eddie had almost gotten Vriens killed using him as bait. It seemed like he was trying to get medals. And if you spoke out against him, he'd bench guys. Eddie had the whole command backing him, too. The platoon tried to tell Portier, Vriens said, but he wouldn't do anything. "He wanted to love the abusive father, I guess."

As Vriens spoke, he started to realize just how sinister the situation had been, and he could feel his anger rising. "The guy was toxic," he said. "We would freaking avoid him because the guy was so toxic."

Vriens knew he had to explain to NCIS why he had not reported Eddie sooner. That was the big question, right? Why had the sniper stayed silent all through Iraq? Why hadn't he spoken out? Why had he not done anything? He started to lay out how Eddie had put him in an impossible situation because the chief would bench anyone who said a word against him, and other SEALs were counting on him. So he kept quiet. "You shut up and you go out and you deal with it, or you speak up and you get benched," he said. "And I know for me . . ." He paused, overcome by the implications of his choice. He looked down and away, trying to hide his tears.

"Guys shot, nearly blown up." He stopped again, pushed his fists against his brow and cracked his knuckles as tears flowed out of his eyes. He took a breath and tried to continue. "It was like, all right, cool, I can speak up, stand my ground, I'll get benched and get sent back to the house, and he'll just do this to a new guy he can manipulate. So I was like, I'm going to be his right-hand man so no one else gets hurt." He shook his head at his decision, clenched his fists on his forehead, and took several deep breaths as Warpinski watched and waited.

"So I worked for him," Vriens finally said. "And kept my mouth shut."

WARPINSKI WAS CAUTIOUSLY encouraged by his progress. In the span of a little more than a week, NCIS had interviewed Miller, Scott, Dille, and Vriens. He had also gotten Eddie's gopher, Ivan Villanueva, who volunteered right away that he saw Eddie stab the prisoner in the rib. Agents had also interviewed the two guys on the East Coast trying out for DEVGRU, T. C. Byrne and Dalton Tolbert. NCIS had three eyewitnesses to the stabbing: Miller, Scott, and Villanueva. They also had at least two other potential murders to pursue: the old man Dille and Tolbert said Eddie shot in the back and the little girl Vriens said Eddie shot in the stomach. Warpinski had at least two more witnesses to track down who apparently knew about those shootings: Josh Graffam and Joe Arrington. Dille texted Warpinski a few days after his interview to let him know he had gone back through some photos and videos from deployment and found close-ups of the knife Eddie used in the murder. It showed a black leather sheath across his back. "That's awesome and exactly what I needed," Warpinski replied.

The case was off to a good start.

But having multiple eyewitnesses and a photo of a knife were anything but a slam dunk. NCIS still had no physical evidence that any crimes had taken place: no DNA, no photos of the stabbing, no video, no murder weapon, no blood spatter patterns, no body. They didn't even know the stabbing victim's name. Warpinski had no reason to doubt the SEALs who had come forward, but if they testified and Eddie denied everything, there was no physical evidence to back them up. A jury would have plenty of reasonable doubt to acquit.

If the investigation was going to get anywhere, Warpinski needed more. But he knew he probably wasn't going to get it. The crime scene was already a year old and located in a war zone about 7,000 miles from San Diego. He wasn't confident they'd find the body or a name. Put up a missing poster of a teenager like that in Mosul and you might hear from hundreds of families. But maybe Dille was right. Maybe Eddie was stupid enough that there was still physical evidence sitting around. If so, the first thing Warpinski would need to do was keep the investigation extremely quiet. If Eddie found out, he might destroy anything that remained. Then it would be over.

EDDIE ALREADY KNEW. In fact, he had likely learned about the investigation before Warpinski had. Craig Miller forced Breisch and Portier to report the Law of Armed Conflict violation on Friday, April 6, 2018. Warpinski didn't get the case until the following Monday. Eddie and his friends were already texting about it on Saturday. And Eddie immediately started working his sources in the Teams.

"So what did you hear?" he texted one of his buddies, a former SEAL named Kenneth Sheard.

"That they were holding it over you . . . but the ball dropped and a bunch of the new guys are coming after you . . . with HARD evidence. Threatening anyone who doesn't jump on board with collusion," Sheard replied.

Eddie replied that three senior guys in the platoon were saying they had video from one of their helmet cams. He added: "It is so fucked. I don't know, this whole thing has me stressed. I just want to get out with no trouble."

"Good copy . . . you seeing a psych?" Sheard asked. "Start going to psych . . . say you have ptsd blackout rage . . . some of it will be true, but go big bro. Honestly . . . they are coming hard it sounds like."

Rules designed to protect troops with post-traumatic stress dis-

SPECIAL AGENTS | 229

order could reduce the Navy's appetite to punish a SEAL, cut his sentence, or maybe kill the case entirely. Sheard urged Eddie to get his wife to say he was having blackout rage and sometimes hitting her. He said Eddie could then quietly retire, get disability, and he'd win. Eddie gave Sheard the names of the accusers. "Get the fuck out," Sheard concluded, "and some day we will just kill them."

Sheard said he had been through a criminal investigation. He gave Eddie a stern warning. "No TEXTING dude. Wipe all your shit. Smash your phone. Bury Hard drive bro. Like don't fuck around."

EDDIE'S FRIENDS IMMEDIATELY started to spread the word that a big investigation was brewing and that guys needed to keep quiet. One texted a member of Alpha platoon on Saturday: "It sounds like NCIS may want to talk to folks about a Law of Armed Conflict case. Here is what a JAG said about talking to NCIS or making a statement," he said, using the nickname for a military Judge Advocate General lawyer. He included a YouTube video titled "Don't Talk to the Police."

The link came from the same mysterious civilian lawyer who had called Craig Miller a few hours after Eddie was reported. He was known in Eddie's circle at Coronado because he had represented a number of SEALs pro bono in misconduct cases over the years, including a friend of Eddie's who'd recently been caught with a fake penis used to beat drug tests, called the Whizzinator. That friend had given the lawyer's name to Eddie just weeks before the investigation launched. Hours after Jake Portier watched Miller force Breisch to report Eddie, the lawyer got a call out of the blue from Portier, asking for help.

The lawyer's name was Brian Ferguson. He had no direct ties to the Navy or anyone involved, but he quickly became a central force in the case. He was thirty-nine, thin, balding, and a unique model of eccentric. He wore the same pair of worn jeans and faded blue Patagonia polo shirt almost every day—a low-key uniform that seemed half homage to Apple founder Steve Jobs and half homage to people who slept in their cars. He had grown up in West Texas oil country and would sometimes mention that he never had to worry about money, but he was vague about what he did for a living.

He was licensed as both an accountant and a lawyer in Texas and had no office or website but ran several limited liability corporations in his name out of a P.O. box that traced the path of some earlier passions. One LLC was set up to explore bringing high-speed rail to Texas; another was a company for single-fin surfboards. He was also a part-time lawyer in the Air Force Reserve. His civilian work? Ferguson would only tell people that it was not exciting. He moved things between corporations. He knew taxes. His letterhead had an oil derrick at the top. His real passion was representing military clients.

Ferguson was a registered Democrat and a longtime critic of the wars in Iraq and Afghanistan. It angered him that for years top officers had been able not only to walk away from the chaos they'd made in the Middle East but to get promoted for it. Meanwhile, the little guys at the bottom who did the killing too often got killed, maimed, or drummed out of the service for misconduct after several combat tours. He liked to joke that the military always did the right thing, but only after every other course of action had been exhausted. His act of civil disobedience and public charity in response to the endless wars in the Middle East was to represent the little guys for free. It began by helping out a college friend who went into the Army, then that friend referred him to someone else. He loved to surf and started meeting SEALs on the beach in Coronado. By 2018 much of the pro bono work he was doing was with frogmen.

SEALs who met Ferguson often later described him as a weird dude. He maneuvered with a confident West Texas swagger, but underneath was a jumpiness, as if he were having several thoughts at once. One of the first things SEALs often noticed about him was that he had a habit of revealing in vivid asides that he was gay—not something many people did in the hyper-hetero male world of the SEALs. "Yeah, I know him," he might say casually of a mutual acquaintance. "In fact, I used to blow him."

Ferguson had a history of insurgent efforts trying to upend order. As a student at the University of Texas in Austin, he twice ran rabble-rousing campaigns to be elected editor of the university's newspaper, even though he had never worked at the paper, had almost no journalism experience, and was loathed by much of the staff. A few weeks after he lost his second bid, a short-lived rival right-leaning student weekly paper launched. Ferguson insisted that he had no involvement. Then a few weeks after the launch, he showed up as one of the editors. After graduation Ferguson wooed investors and tried to get control of several major newspapers, including the *Austin American-Statesman* and the *Rocky Mountain News*. He assured investors he could reinvent the stodgy news business. Nearly all of those efforts fell flat.

Ferguson made no claims of being a good defense lawyer. In fact, he sometimes said he was barely qualified and had skipped most of his classes at the University of Texas Law School. If you get charged with a real crime, he would tell SEALs, I'll turn you over to a real lawyer. Mostly he just advised guys who were in administrative trouble, facing, at worst, discharge from the military. The most common advice he gave was to keep quiet. The cops are not your friends; they don't want to help you. When you talk to them, you will probably try to lie to protect your buddies. Then you're on the hook for making false statements. Better to lawyer up and stay safe.

The Gallagher case was the biggest thing he had ever gotten mixed up in. When Portier called him, he whipped into action, reaching out to as many people in the platoon as he could as fast as he could. He knew a lot of SEALs. His gut told him that whatever had happened in the platoon, everyone probably had something to hide. He told Alpha he didn't care if Eddie went to prison or not; he just wanted to make sure they were protected.

Three days after the crime was reported, Ferguson had notified NCIS that he was representing Portier, and Portier wasn't going to talk. For NCIS, that was a huge blow to the case. The lieutenant was at the center of the whole mess. He not only knew about the stabbing, but he also knew what Lieutenant Commander Robert Breisch knew and when. Despite repeated negotiations, Portier never said a word to NCIS.

Ferguson reached out to nearly everyone in the platoon. He said Big Navy was going to go nuclear over this case. It would fry the platoon to make itself look good. It was going to be an international diplomatic fiasco. The guys might even be sent to a war crimes tribunal in Baghdad to save face.

None of the SEALs knew much about the legal process, and several got scared. NCIS started getting letters of representation from Ferguson for guys Warpinski had not even contacted. The three EOD technicians were some of the first. That surprised the snipers in the platoon, because even before Dragon got shot, those guys seemed to hate Eddie, and Dragon had been around the captive with the medics and in the photo when Eddie did the ceremony. He would have been a helpful witness. Next came Josh Graffam, the new guy. He had often served as a spotter for Eddie. Dille said Graffam had seen the Father's Day shooting of the old man, and they had talked about it. He was another key witness. But he was invoking his right to remain silent.

As Warpinski raced to collect interviews, more and more doors started slamming. Guys didn't want to talk. Guys said they had an attorney NCIS would have to go through. Eventually Ferguson, the self-described terrible lawyer, represented thirteen of the twenty-one men who had deployed together to Mosul.

JOSH VRIENS NEEDED to blow off steam, so he decided to take his dog to the beach. It was the summer of 2018, and the investigation was in full swing. Like most of the guys, he had gotten the hard sell from Brian Ferguson. Unlike most of them, he had told the lawyer to get lost. Vriens wasn't worried about getting in trouble for telling the truth. He was the most overtly religious guy in Alpha, and he felt like he was being tested by God. He was trying to prove himself worthy. Still, the idea of getting fired or put in jail had him stressed. So did Eddie.

Eddie lived fewer than a dozen houses away in their neighborhood of San Diego. Before the investigation, Vriens had never seen Eddie walk past his house. But when the platoon went to NCIS, Eddie started walking his two French bulldogs down his sidewalk almost daily. Vriens would see him through the window, walking slowly, his stare fixed on the house. Vriens didn't say anything because he didn't want to upset his wife. But soon she noticed, too. Vriens took the walk-bys as a message. Eddie knew where he was vulnerable. Vriens and his wife started talking about moving.

That morning Vriens decided to go to the beach to decompress, figuring a few hours playing with his dog in the waves would clear his head. He stepped out his front door and headed out to his car with his eighteen-month-old son in one hand, his dog on a leash in the other, and a diaper bag under his arm. As he opened the car door, he looked up. At the end of the driveway was Eddie. He was staring at Vriens with a tight smirk.

Vriens straightened up and looked at him. Eddie stared back without saying a word.

Vriens could feel the heat rising. If this was Eddie's way of trying to intimidate him, he wasn't going to back down. Eddie had done too much bad stuff. It wasn't just the unshakable image of the girl in the flowered hijab gripping her stomach, it was how Eddie had smashed Vriens's view of the world. Eddie had taken the SEALs from him. And he wanted to make Eddie pay. He could feel the muscles tighten in his shoulders. If Eddie thought he was so badass, let him try going up against someone besides children and old people. Maybe the chief should learn what it felt like to tangle with someone bigger. Vriens wanted to send him sprawling into the street, then stand over him and tell him how disgusted he was, how for all his boasting and bragging, Eddie was nothing but a stain on the brotherhood and the worst kind of turd.

But Vriens knew instinctively that neither he nor the chief were likely to stop after getting punched. They were trained to go at opponents until someone was dead. Under those circumstances, even if Vriens won, he'd lose. He'd be in prison for years. Eddie would turn into some pathetic kind of martyr. He looked at the toddler in the back seat and the dog gazing up at him. His wife and infant daughter were just inside. His heart was pounding, his fists were clenched. But he realized how much was at stake. He took a deep breath, picked up his son, took the dog, and went inside. Later that afternoon, he started making arrangements to move.

Vriens was not the only guy who feared what Eddie might do. As Alazzawi had warned, Eddie was like a cornered rat. Come at him, he's going to fight. And the guys expected him to fight dirty. In the civilian world, most threats of violence are only threats, but not in Alpha. Everyone there was, quite literally, a trained killer. They knew how easy it was to slip in, do it, and slip out. They had practiced it. So every threat of violence was serious, and SEALs prepared for war. Craig Miller got a concealed weapons permit. Dylan Dille bought a shotgun to keep near his bed.

By then Dalton Tolbert and T. C. Byrne were far away from the Southern California drama. Both had packed up with their wives and moved to the SEALs' East Coast home in Virginia Beach to screen for DEVGRU. The Green Team selection course was like BUD/S in hyperdrive. Only two hundred SEALs even got the chance to try out, and the competition just to show up was fierce. Most guys who tried out for DEVGRU didn't make it. Years before, Eddie had tried and failed to make it. The screening week cut the pool of applicants from two hundred down to seventy. Both Byrne and Tolbert made the cut. But the challenge didn't stop there. Of that seventy, only about thirty would get into DEVGRU.

For both men, even getting to screen was almost a miracle, considering what they had gone through. For Tolbert, Green Team was the accomplishment he'd been struggling toward for a decade. His childhood hadn't stopped him. A coma had not stopped him. Eddie wouldn't either. Arriving at Green Team was his proof to the world that a nobody, frog-catching kid from the Ozarks who'd grown up with nothing could achieve anything he wanted.

Byrne was not as certain. He had been thrown against a truck by an RPG blast and been knocked out cold. Back home he struggled to keep his head straight. He kept forgetting where he had put his keys and wallet. The smallest things would send him into a rage. He didn't know if it was the stress of everything with Eddie or the lingering effects of the blast. The Navy diagnosed Byrne with a traumatic brain injury, but he wanted to keep going. He tried to put all his problems and doubts in a mental box, seal it up, and leave it behind in San Diego. Making the cut for Green Team was a sign he was back on track. But the case started to weigh on him. He was distraught that the platoon was splitting apart. Gio Kirylo had been one of his closest friends in Iraq, but refused to talk to NCIS. Then there was Dragon. Byrne couldn't help but remember that he had given Dragon his own blood, and now Dragon had lawyered up and was not standing with Alpha.

Tolbert and Byrne would have loved to forget the criminal investigation. But if they walked away, they would let their brothers down. If Eddie succeeded in dividing them, he had a chance at beating them. Both men had that thought in mind when they got random calls from a Texas number, a lawyer who introduced himself as Brian Ferguson and started warning them that Craig Miller was way out of his league, and if they wanted to save themselves they should keep quiet. Both SEALs politely told the lawyer to fuck off.

Tolbert and Byrne were thrown into months of high-velocity Green Team training and testing. The SEALs had to show they could shoot, jump, dive, run, and fight better and faster than anyone else in the Teams. They had to go through close-quarters combat drills twice as fast as they had at Team 7, with live ammunition and no room for mistakes. The instructors watched every move and could cut a SEAL for any reason.

And they had an extra hurdle. Eddie knew where they were and knew that they were vulnerable, and he appeared to be trying to rat-fuck them. Eddie talked often about brotherhood and loyalty, but he started reaching out through the extensive network of SEALs he knew to sink their chances at DEVGRU. He was especially angry about Tolbert, who had defied him in Mosul. He got his SEAL friends to reach out to the instructors. He told one he wanted them all to know "what a rat that faggot is."

Eddie reached out to another SEAL chief with connections at Green Team and told him, "We can't let this fucker make it through."

THE NAVY MOVED Eddie to a job in a logistics and supply unit where he was basically expected to babysit a desk until the investigation was over. As he sat there, he seemed to grow confident he would beat the rap. His sources said there was no real evidence—no photos, no video. He didn't go "hardcore PTSD," as a friend had suggested. He didn't try to get out of the Navy as soon as possible. He didn't even stop using drugs. Throughout the summer of 2018, he hung out with his family, went and had drinks with his buddies, and continued to order trammies online through a friend. He sent a few texts that even suggested he was smoking weed here and there. On June 7 he sent a text to his wife saying, "I love you, I just took a piss test, pray that it's clean."

Agent Joe Warpinski had been working the case hard, but he still didn't have any physical evidence, let alone a smoking gun. And he wasn't having a lot of luck.

He interviewed Lieutenant Commander Robert Breisch and Master Chief Brian Alazzawi, but both not only contradicted Craig Miller, they contradicted each other. Both said they knew nothing about the allegations of war crimes while they were in Iraq. Alazzawi said they learned about it four months later, around Christmas. Breisch said it was eight months later, days before the formal report was made. During the deployment, Breisch said, he had only heard that some photos were taken with a body. It was nothing criminal, he said, just "poor taste." And the photos had been deleted. It was no big surprise to Warpinski that both men seemed less than forthright. Admitting they knew too much too early could get them fired. But they didn't help the investigation.

Alazzawi did say one thing that caught the agent's interest: Eddie had admitted the killing to him. Before the investigation started, Eddie told him he had been working on the captive when the captive reached for his gun, and Eddie said, "I fucked him up." That was essentially a confession. It could be very useful.

Warpinski managed to track down platoon JTAC Joe Arrington for an interview, but Arrington had recently talked to Brian Ferguson, and he seemed hesitant. Even though Arrington had earlier confronted Eddie in Iraq about killing civilians and texted the whole platoon in September that they "gotta be honest" about what happened, with NCIS he was halting and vague. He talked about how he saw Eddie as "a selfish dick for years" and watched the chief's mental state deteriorate over the course of the deployment. But he didn't volunteer many specifics, especially about crimes. He said he saw Eddie shoot a man carrying a water jug who he thought was probably a civilian. It could have been the man Dille and Dalton saw, but he wasn't sure. It was possible, he said, that the man was a legal target. Vriens had told Warpinski that Eddie had told Arrington he had shot the little girl. Arrington didn't mention it to NCIS. He also didn't mention that he had been in any photos. At one point he asked Warpinski if he would actually have to testify. People might take it the wrong way, he said. It could make "everybody look like a bunch of rats."

Agent Warpinski's hopes rose when he learned that T. C. Byrne not only still had the red laptop that everyone had dumped photos on during deployment but also was willing to turn it over without a fight. NCIS ran it through a forensic analysis. But nearly everything on the laptop had been irrevocably deleted. Agents found nothing but traces of a folder called "Eddie's reenlist day" that had once contained photo and video files from the day of the murder.

Warpinski recovered a few of Byrne's helmet cam videos that showed Eddie arriving to intercept the captive and saying to the Iraqis, "Is he ISIS? I got him." But the camera clicked off right as Eddie started giving medical aid. There was another video from Byrne's cam, recorded a few hours later, showing Eddie flying a drone over the body. But the file numbers showed there were five files in between—videos recorded during the time of the murder and the reenlistment. Those five files were completely gone. Portier and Eddie had ordered the platoon to get rid of the photos, and someone had erased them in a way not even NCIS could undo.

Most murders started with a body but no suspect. This one started with a suspect but no body. And NCIS didn't even know the name of the victim. Other than the statements from a few SEALs, there was still no evidence a murder had even taken place: no DNA, no blood, no murder weapon.

NCIS sent a crime scene investigator to Mosul to hunt for the body and other evidence. The investigator located the blown-out Towers that the platoon had returned to over and over, still standing on the edge of the Tigris River. Inside, up the crumbling stairs, he found dozens of spent rounds from rockets and hundreds of sniper rifle shells. It was all consistent with what the witnesses described, but none of it proved there had been a crime.

Mosul was still far from safe. The investigator had to rely on an armed escort to get around. He drove out to the abandoned compound where the prisoner had been killed. It had been repaired and was now a base for Iraqi soldiers. The investigator found an English-speaking Iraqi colonel and explained what he was looking for. The colonel said he knew nothing about it.

The investigator made a quick search of the yard where the ISIS fighter had been killed and found a blue glove like the ones the medics had worn and what looked like a piece of skin and a bit of hair in a drain near where the SEALs said the body was stabbed. In another case, NCIS might have been able to use the skin to match the DNA of the victim. In this case, they had no idea who the victim was. They had no family they could use to match the DNA. The investigator asked if the colonel knew of any bodies buried around the compound. The colonel smirked as if to say, *You've got to be kidding me.* "This is war," the colonel said. "Bodies were all over the streets," he said. Twenty Assyrians were buried just outside the gate. The whole place, he said, was "like the horror movie *Chucky* with dead people everywhere."

NCIS was near a dead end. There wasn't much left to do but haul Eddie in and hope he would talk.

JUNE 20, 2018, was a Wednesday. As usual, Eddie had nothing much planned at his logistics job, but that morning the commander called and said he needed to meet with Eddie at 9:30. Eddie put on a uniform and knocked on the commander's door. When the officer opened the door, Joe Warpinski and a handful of other NCIS agents were waiting. They told him he was under arrest. They emptied his pockets, which held some nicotine gum, his keys, and an iPhone. Warpinski picked up the phone. Of course he wanted to see what it held.

You're in a secure area, phones aren't allowed in here, Warpinski told him. He told Eddie he was going to have to take it. Do you need to call anyone first? he asked. Warpinski watched over Eddie's shoulder. iPhones were hard to crack, but not if a suspect was careless enough to give away his code. Warpinski watched Eddie's thumb punch in four numbers and committed them to memory.

The agents drove Eddie to Naval Base San Diego and put him in one of the cramped, blank interrogation rooms that had hosted so many members of Alpha. Warpinski took off the cuffs and let Eddie stew there for a while before coming in to talk to him. He knew there was a good chance Eddie would talk. In years of law enforcement, Warpinski had learned one constant was that most suspects were too dumb to keep quiet. Get them to believe that telling the truth would make things go easier for them, and they would often spill their guts. He had worked a case right before Eddie's in which a low-ranking sailor on a destroyer stole a crate of grenades. Of course the kid had denied it, even when a state trooper found some of the grenades on the side of a desert highway in a Navy backpack with the kid's name on it. During the interrogation, Warpinski told the kid that investigators had found his fingerprints and DNA all over the grenades. It was a lie, but sometimes agents told lies to get the truth. The sailor invoked his right to remain silent. No problem, Warpinski and his partner told him, we have the case in the bag anyway. We'll write up our reports, but those reports will reflect whether you cooperated or not. It didn't take long for the kid to change his mind.

Warpinski came in and sat down across from Eddie. He explained that Eddie was being accused of war crimes, including murder. There was a ton of evidence. They had talked to all sorts of witnesses. "We just want to hear your side of the story," he said.

Eddie refused. He had seen friends go through criminal cases. He knew better than to say a word. He had been through interrogation training. No matter what, he'd learned, keep denying. Even if you think they have you, don't give a shred of validation. Even if there are eyewitnesses. Even if they say they have video. Deny, deny, deny.

Eddie said he wasn't talking. He gave Warpinski the number of a lawyer named Colby Vokey who was representing him. Then he kept quiet. Warpinski took the number and said he would be back soon. Eddie sat in the room for another six hours.

While Eddie was locked up at NCIS, twenty agents with tactical gear and a search warrant were raiding his house. They crossed the small yard in bulletproof vests, some with their guns drawn. Eddie's eighteen-year-old stepson came to the door with Eddie's nine-year-old son. Agents pulled both out into the yard with guns drawn and put them into a van. Eddie's wife, Andrea, wasn't home. His stepdaughter was visiting her father in Ohio. With the house empty, agents filed in looking for anything that might be involved in the crime: knives, guns, drugs, and any phones or computers that might have videos or photos from Iraq.

Eddie lived in a narrow stucco town house owned by the Navy. Nearly all the decorating had been done by Andrea. Little showed that Eddie lived there. Between training and deployment he was gone so often that he was almost a visitor in his own house. Eddie's few additions included a bench press and weights in the garage and a small alcove near the back door where his military plaques and awards hung. The agents rifled through drawers and boxes and seized a pile of old phones and iPads. They found a variety of knives, but none of them matched the description of the custom-made hunting blade in a black leather sheath. In the garage they found a medic's kit, a box of ammunition, and some breaching saws, all stolen from the Navy. They found bottles of testosterone and tramadol. It was all contraband, and any of it could get Eddie kicked out of the SEALs, but none of it helped with the murder case. With Eddie refusing to talk, Warpinski had to either turn up some evidence fast or drop the whole thing.

While one NCIS team was searching Eddie's house, another was searching his operator's cage. Eddie's cage had once been in the Alpha high bay, but he moved it when he started working at Special Operations Urban Combat. However, a lot of his old stuff from Mosul was still there. Inside Eddie's cage, amid the backpacks, duffel bags, and camouflage uniforms, NCIS found a black plastic Pelican case about the size of a cooler: his operator's box. The outside was decorated with a sticker of a Punisher skull that said, "ISIS hunting permit." There was a tag on the handle that read "Gallagher." An agent opened the box to reveal a rat's nest of gear. Sitting right on top were the Half Face Blades knife and hatchet Eddie had promised his friend Bito he would bury in someone's skull. Neither matched the description of a small custom blade in a black leather sheath. Next to them were Eddie's body armor. Below was a slew of smaller gear: a water bottle, a flashlight, rifle magazines, nicotine gum, a stack of patches from ERD, some batteries. The agent lifted it piece by piece. He picked up a radio headset, and there it was: a custom hunting knife in a black sheath. The blade was about three and a half inches long. The handle was mottled gray. It matched photos from the deployment exactly.

Dylan Dille had been right: Eddie had, indeed, been dumb enough to hold on to the murder weapon.

NCIS HAD A SECOND lucky break that day, but Warpinski wouldn't realize it for more than a month. Eddie's friend had warned him weeks earlier: "Wipe all your shit. Smash your phone." But Eddie had been as careless with his tactics with NCIS as he had in Mosul. In a drawer in his laundry room, NCIS found the iPhone 6 he had been using on the deployment. A few weeks later, when they pulled all the photos and texts off, Warpinski was stunned.

SEALs in the platoon told Warpinski that SEALs had taken all kinds of photos the day of the stabbing, but Eddie and Portier told everyone to delete them. As far as the SEALs knew, they were all gone forever. Eddie, however, had not been as careful with his own phone. When NCIS finally dumped the data from the seized phone, there was Eddie posing with the dead kid's head in one hand and his hunting knife in the other. They also found the group photo the SEALs had described, with Eddie kneeling at the center like the captain of a high school soccer team and a dirty, dead, nameless teenager splayed out in front. Just as he had held on to the murder weapon, he seemed unable to part with his trophy photos.

It was a huge leap forward. Before the raid, the only evidence NCIS had was the word of a few SEALs. Now it had not only the knife but also photos of the killer holding the victim in one hand and the knife in the other.

Warpinski knew a trophy photo when he saw one. In his seven years at the U.S. Border Patrol, he'd taken a few with drug runners he'd caught. He knew how guys wanted to celebrate a job well done. But this was something different, something darker—the ritual murder of a kid. It was enough to give anyone chills.

The evidence from the phone Eddie had so casually tossed into the laundry room drawer didn't stop at photos. Warpinski started going through thousands of texts and found evidence that the guys in the platoon never even knew existed. Nine days after Eddie posed for the trophy pic with the murder victim, he texted the photo to a friend back in California—the warrant officer he liked to talk trammies with. Along with the trophy pic he sent a message: "Good story behind this, got him with my hunting knife."

The warrant officer had been Gallagher's chief on an earlier deployment, and Eddie considered him a mentor. Throughout deployment Eddie had sent him photos and videos of rockets launching and combat in Mosul. It was almost as if he was trying to measure up. The knife kill was just one in a line of boasts.

"Nice," the warrant officer replied. "Be careful with pics."

"Yeah, that's the only one and I only trust you," Eddie said.

But it wasn't the only message. Eddie had also texted Stephen Snead, his friend and fellow chief, to whom he seemed eager to prove himself. "I got a cool story for you when I get back. I got my knife skills on," Eddie said.

"Haha fuck yeah," Snead replied.

Warpinski had struck pay dirt. Not only did NCIS now have a photo of the dead victim with wounds matching what witnesses described, but the killer was right there, kneeling over the victim, holding the murder weapon. That in itself was such an unlikely Hollywood turn of events that it seemed like it was right out of an episode of the *NCIS* TV series. And if that wasn't enough, the murder suspect also had texted the photo to a friend, saying he had done it.

Eddie had refused to talk, but here was his confession. If there were any doubt that Miller and the others were making up a story, this erased it. After all, how could a group of SEALs concoct a lie that perfectly matched a confession they never knew existed?

NCIS finally had enough evidence to charge the chief with murder.

AFTER THE RAID on his house, NCIS released Eddie. Putting him in jail would start the clock on his right to a speedy trial, and investigators needed more time. They knew where he was. They figured they could come for him when they were ready.

Eddie tried to brace for whatever was coming next from NCIS. He felt relieved that they had not held him in June. Maybe they didn't have anything solid. Even so, as June rolled into July and August, Eddie started to get things in order for his defense.

The warrant NCIS used to search Eddie's house and cage had given Eddie a bit more insight. It included the names of the accusers—just initials, actually, but he now knew who the traitors were: Craig Miller, Dylan Dille, Corey Scott, Dalton Tolbert, Joe Arrington, and Josh Vriens. The SEALs had their own loyalty code, and these guys had violated it. The brotherhood could protect guys it liked, but it could also do the opposite: target snitches, punish them, and drive them out. Eddie started working with friends—especially his old pal the knife maker, Andrew Arrabito—to get the word out about the rats.

Bito had grown his hair long after the Navy and gotten some bit parts and stunt work in Hollywood. He was doing some modeling work for men's brands that needed a menacing hombre with a big knife. He was also expanding his knife business and had started selling a new line of "pneumo spike" shivs designed specifically for stabbing lungs. Since Bito was out of the Navy and not a target of the investigation, he could help get back at the platoon while insulating Eddie.

The SEALs had a private Facebook group called 5326, named after the four-digit Navy enlistment code for combat swimmers. Only verified active-duty SEALs and SEAL veterans were allowed. There were thousands of guys from every era. Eddie told Bito they needed to use the group to make sure the snitches were put in their place. He gave Bito the names and added, "These guys are pieces of shit and cowards plus trying to make shit up about myself and other team guys."

Bito and Eddie went back and forth on how to spread the word without divulging too much and possibly getting into trouble. Eddie pushed Bito to do it soon: "I think we have enough facts to put out right now. Also add in they are working with NCIS currently so they cannot be trusted."

Bito dragged his feet. A week went by and Eddie grew impatient. He wanted the snitches to pay. He wanted the investigation to go away. He was totally stressed out. On top of everything else, he was out of tramadol. He texted a SEAL chief friend to see if he could bum some, but the chief only had a few packs left and was unwilling to share. He tried to get another friend to order trammies online so it wouldn't show up on the family credit card. He vowed to pay him back with cash. The friend said no.

At the end of August, Eddie was starting the intensive traumatic brain injury program at the National Intrepid Center of Excellence. He seemed to be pressing for action so he could go into the program knowing the ball was rolling on blacklisting the snitches. He texted Bito again to push him. Bito said he would post the names, but another week went by with nothing. "Are you going to put those names out this week?" Eddie pressed a third time.

Bito said he was worried that dumping active-duty SEAL names on the Web might hurt his knife business. He seemed willing to betray his fellow SEALs—he just didn't want the blowback. "I wish there was a way to drop them anonymously," he texted Eddie. "I may be able to like put a fake document up saying I was sent this by an active-duty guy saying not to trust these guys."

He created an image of a document that read: "The names of the Team guys that are and have been speaking to NCIS about other guys, other teams and past platoon deployments are as follows. I do believe there are a few more but these are the names for sure to start with. Please let others know as these dudes have taken it upon themselves to work with NCIS against the Teams both West and East coast. Lying and telling stories of what they 'heard' has happened, causing a huge investigation on hearsay." It listed four SEALs from Alpha, then concluded, "More to follow."

There was still time for Eddie to get the guys in Alpha before they got him.

"THIS IS NOT just bad, it's getting worse," Matt Rosenbloom said.

Rosenbloom was a Navy captain and the commodore of Group 1, the commanding officer who oversaw all SEALs on the West Coast. He had been watching the NCIS investigation since the day it started. As evidence mounted, he became increasingly convinced that Eddie was not just an operator mixed up in a murder case but a criminal with a long, dark history, scuttling around under cover of being a SEAL, and he needed to be crushed. Unfortunately for Rosenbloom, the Navy didn't seem to want to let him do it. And it was pissing him off.

So in early September, just as Eddie was taking meditation classes at the Intrepid Center, Rosenbloom went to the office of the Navy admiral in charge of the entire SEAL Teams, set a fat file on Special Operations Chief Edward Gallagher down on the table, and said something had to be done. Across from him sat two high-ranking and respected SEALs, Vice Admiral Tim Symanski, the current commander of all of Navy Special Warfare, and his replacement who would be taking over in a few weeks, Rear Admiral Collin Green.

It was getting worse, Rosenbloom said, because not only did the Navy have a big murder case on its hands, but the suspect appeared to be trying to silence and intimidate witnesses. The Navy had to act. Rosenbloom opened the file and started to brief the admirals.

Rosenbloom had actually started out on Eddie's side but steadily realized that Eddie wasn't just a turd but a weaponized version of the pirate ethos.

Like the SEALs he commanded, Rosenbloom was tall and fit, with a surfer's physique and pale eyes that over the years had shifted from blue to green. He'd gone through BUD/S when Eddie was still in grade school. In twenty-seven years in the SEALs, he had deployed more than a dozen times, including nine tours in Iraq and Afghanistan and a few where the location was still classified. After the invasion of Iraq in 2003, he'd overseen almost nightly raids and takedowns of insurgents. He commanded platoons, then troops, then rose to become commander of Team 7 and eventually a task force commander overseeing all of the special operations missions in northern Iraq. He was a seasoned operator who had watched the SEALs transform since 2001. He knew years of endless war had been hard on the Teams. They were in the hangover phase now, trying to recover and rebuild.

Yet when his staff lawyer knocked on his office door in May and told him they were looking at a court-martial that involved not only multiple murders but also a decorated platoon chief, Rosenbloom looked at him as if he had said Santa Claus was waiting outside his office. His instinct was to not believe it. There must be a misunderstanding. All manner of fucked-up things happen in war, he knew, but that didn't make them crimes. In his decades as an officer he had seen well-intentioned shots that ended in horrible outcomes. He believed the fog of war could make good dudes unwittingly do bad things. He knew too often the rules of engagement were written thousands of miles away by people who didn't understand the reality on the ground. He reflexively distrusted any report that a SEAL had committed cold-blooded murder in Iraq. There had to be another explanation.

The incident seemed at first to be fairly contained. It was a report of the death of a single detainee—maybe intentional, maybe not. Bad, but manageable. NCIS would take on the investigation and the SEALs would see what they came up with. Maybe it would turn out to be nothing. As the commodore, Rosenbloom was the convening authority on the case—it was his job to initiate the court-martial and oversee the trial—but his main responsibility was to stay completely out of it. There were Navy lawyers to handle the prosecution and the defense. There was a Navy judge to run the trial. As the commander, Rosenbloom was expected to avoid taking any actions that might tip the scales of justice. That included making statements that might hint at his opinion and might shape how lower-ranking members of the Navy would handle the case. Any statement or action could be deemed "unlawful command influence." And unlawful command influence could lead to charges being thrown out. If Rosenbloom wanted a fair court-martial, he had to keep his mouth shut.

In late summer NCIS submitted Warpinski's investigation report to the command. Rosenbloom flipped through the pages, reading summaries of what the SEALs had told Warpinski, and quickly realized the case was not what he had assumed. It read like something out of *Apocalypse Now*. Chief Gallagher appeared to have gone way upriver, shooting children and old men, firing rockets and machine guns into neighborhoods, doing drugs, stabbing a wounded prisoner of war to death. Rosenbloom, who was inclined to give every benefit of the doubt to his SEALs, found himself repeatedly muttering, *What the fuck?*

It didn't seem to be a case about combat. It wasn't a bad call under fire or rage over the loss of a comrade. It was just murder. Seemingly done just so the chief could tell his friends back home he had gotten a knife kill. Fucking pirates.

Rosenbloom kept reading. He had gotten his start in the SEALs in the 1990s, when the SEALs had not seen much combat for a generation, Demo Dick had been sent to prison, and the pirate culture was at low ebb. He knew things had changed after 2001. The SEALs had always had a lot of freedom to be creative. They trained operators to be fast and aggressive, to see overwhelming violence as a tool. Those were all critical parts of making warfighters. But they all relied on a foundation of character. And with the constant deployments there had been little time to cultivate character. Some platoons far from oversight had rekindled old pirate traditions.

It wasn't just Eddie. There had been a series of other incidents: Two SEALs were arrested for the death of an Army Special Forces soldier in Mali during a brutal hazing. Both of them were chiefs in Eddie's generation. There had been a number of drug use cases on the East Coast; a lot of those guys were chiefs, too. It all suggested a bigger problem lurking in the Teams. Pirates who had started as low-ranking shooters in the early days of the wars had worked their way up. And if something wasn't done, guys like Eddie would keep moving up until they ran the Teams.

Looking over the report, Rosenbloom pieced together that there appeared to be a multilayered cover-up involving the lieutenant in charge of the platoon and the lieutenant commander in charge of the troop. Rosenbloom had held both positions in his career. When he read through the information, he immediately came to the conclusion that both Jake Portier and Robert Breisch were lying to cover their asses. He didn't know either personally, but figured the only way they couldn't know about Eddie was if they were total morons. Portier had put in his papers to resign his commission, but he still had a job teaching new officers to be platoon commanders. *No way that's going to continue,* Rosenbloom thought to himself. Portier was pulled and stuck at a desk where he couldn't have any influence.

If Eddie was guilty, it was important that he was tried publicly. There had to be real consequences that everyone could see. If the Teams were going to get back on course, every SEAL had to know how the Navy dealt with pirates.

In the meantime, though, Rosenbloom wanted to take action. He decided he would pull Eddie's Trident. As commodore, he had total authority over who wore the pin. He could take it from anyone for any reason. There were a lot of rumors flying around Coronado about the case. Rosenbloom needed to send a message that the command was standing with Alpha. Let the courts decide if Eddie was guilty, but the commodore had already decided he didn't deserve to be in the brotherhood. Neither did Portier. Independent of any crime, they had failed in their professional duties. Their birds were gone.

Before the commodore could act, though, his staff talked him down. Take that large golden eagle away and a jury will notice it is not on Eddie's uniform in trial. Maybe it would sway their votes, maybe it wouldn't, but any good defense lawyer would argue unlawful command influence and try to get the case thrown out. The commodore had to hold his fire. It drove Rosenbloom crazy. He had always been blunt. It was part of what made him a good leader. He wanted to get up in front of his SEALs and tell them about the evidence he had seen, so the ranks would know who Eddie was. But he couldn't. It was one of only a few times in his career as a leader when he had to stay silent.

Even though Rosenbloom couldn't talk publicly, he felt he needed to act to protect the guys in Alpha. The report included highlights from Eddie's seized cellphones. Rosenbloom read the conversations where Eddie said he wanted to "bury" guys trying out for DEVGRU and spread the witnesses' names to thousands of SEALs on Facebook. He read the NCIS report about Eddie standing outside the house of Josh Vriens. The murders were an issue for a court trial, but what Eddie was doing to intimidate witnesses was an immediate issue for the commander. Already Rosenbloom knew some guys in the platoon were refusing to talk. He felt he had to stop Eddie before the whole case was sunk.

He called a meeting with the top admirals.

"We can't let this go on," he said as Szymanski and Green leafed through the reports.

The commodore said the only option was to lock Eddie up pending trial. It was a rare move in the Navy, but in the most serious cases where the authorities have reason to believe someone might turn violent or intimidate witnesses, it was allowed. The admirals agreed; the evidence seemed to justify it. But it also came with risk. As soon as they did it, they knew that they would have to charge Eddie. The case would go public. A media shitstorm would follow. Forget Eddie—it would look bad for every SEAL. But all three men agreed they had no choice.

A few days later, on September 9, 2018, Rosenbloom authorized the confinement order. Two days after that, on September 11, Eddie was in meditation therapy at the Intrepid Center when someone on the staff tapped on his shoulder and told him that Master Chief Brian Alazzawi was there to see him. Eddie walked out into the hall to find his fellow frogman from Mosul. He was waiting with two officers, who led Eddie away in cuffs.

CHAPTER 11

IMMUNITY

"Got a big one for you," Agent Joe Warpinski said. He sat down at a table in the Naval Base San Diego's legal office. On the other side was the base's brand-new lead prosecutor, a forty-year-old commander in Navy whites named Chris Czaplak. Warpinski had come over to introduce himself bearing a thick case file that he tossed across the table. "Murder case, multiple victims, Navy SEAL."

It was September 2018, a few days before Eddie was arrested.

Commander Czaplak raised his eyebrows. He was the most experienced Navy prosecutor on the West Coast. A Naval Academy grad who had done a number of years on a submarine crew before going to law school, Czaplak had been trying Navy cases for ten years, both as a prosecutor and as a defense attorney. In the civilian world it was exceptionally rare for defense attorneys to become prosecutors, but in the military it was standard, and Czaplak liked it that way. It gave Navy prosecutors something that their civilian counterparts sometimes lacked: an understanding and respect for both sides. Czaplak was confident but easygoing, a man who loved the law. He was completely bald and a bit round, with dark eyebrows and a ready laugh. His last name was pronounced *chap-lack,* but other legal staff who worked with him called him "Chappy." He had worked on a number of high-profile cases, including a few murders, though only from the defense side. Warpinski, as an NCIS agent, was in charge of investigating the crime. Czaplak would have to argue the case in court.

Czaplak leafed through the evidence spread out before him: A Navy SEAL chief overseas. Multiple witnesses. Photos. He stopped and read the text message that seemed to claim credit for the murder. Interesting. He kept going. There was no body, no autopsy, no smoking gun. If a slam-dunk case was a ten, this was maybe a seven. There was a lot to work with. But there was also still a lot of work to do.

Eddie had not entered a plea yet, but to his family and friends he had denied everything. There were no murders, no shootings, no nothing. It was all being made up by the platoon.

Any concern about the honesty of the witnesses? Czaplak asked. Warpinski said he didn't think so. There were guys in the platoon who weren't talking, but no one was contradicting what Craig Miller and the others were saying. NCIS had run background checks on all the guys. As far as he could tell, they were good.

Czaplak knew unless video evidence suddenly dropped in their laps, everything would come down to the witnesses, and that was a little scary. When it came to the SEALs, *tribal* was an understatement. The Navy was tribal. The SEALs were more like a cult. Witnesses would be under tremendous pressure to keep quiet. He was surprised anyone had come forward at all. They must have really hated the chief. NCIS and the prosecutors would have to hope the witnesses held together. At least Eddie was going to the brig so he couldn't get to them.

Warpinski and Czaplak started to quietly grind through the evidence. Eddie would go to trial in June 2019. In the meantime, they would hunt down leads and try to find new physical evidence that might strengthen the case.

Czaplak was joined by an assistant attorney named Lieutenant Brian John. He had a blond crew cut and pink cheeks that made him look much younger than his thirty-five years. He had been practicing as a Navy JAG for seven years, but this was his first murder. Before the Navy, John had been a high school civics teacher, and he still retained a lot of the textbook beliefs about how the United States should work. That was in part why he raised his hand to serve. Military lawyers got very little attention and next to no adoration. The public venerated the Navy SEALs as heroes. The Navy lawyers? The public barely thought of them at all. But John believed that respect for due process and the law was as critical to the Navy as its special operators or its aircraft carriers. You needed law and order to make everything work. Without it, what were they fighting for? But prosecuting a guy like Eddie wasn't going to be easy. No one around the base seemed to like it. He would sometimes hear sailors grumbling about Eddie being punished just for doing his job. After looking at the evidence, John knew that wasn't the case, but that's why the Navy needed lawyers: There had to be a fair and public hearing. Let a jury look at everything and decide.

At one point, John was interviewing Dylan Dille. The sniper was struggling with his decision to come forward. He was getting beaten up on Facebook and called a traitor. Sometimes he got so lost in thinking about the trial that he would spend all day in his pajamas. "You know, us coming to you, us doing this, isn't exactly popular," he told John. John replied, "It's not popular with us either. I don't give a shit, we don't murder prisoners."

Both Czaplak and John still had full caseloads, but the Gallagher case immediately took priority. It was the biggest case in the Navy—by far. Czaplak soon noted that his junior co-counsel was good under pressure. Right when they started working on the case in the fall of 2018, John's hometown, Paradise, California, was almost completely destroyed by a massive wildfire. His parents' house had been spared, but nearly everything else was gone. Neighbors and friends died in the flames. John's father had been a fire prevention coordinator. His mother, in her capacity as superintendent of schools, had lost five of nine schools. Nearly everything John knew from his childhood had been reduced to ash. The stress was clear on his face, but he kept going with his work, interviewing the key witnesses repeatedly, and trying to confirm critical details without ever letting his personal issues interfere with his professional duties.

Meanwhile, Agent Warpinski kept digging on the case, slowly

bringing more to light. Warpinski was able to track down one of Alpha's interpreters, the middle-aged Iraqi named Phil. Phil said he didn't witness the stabbing but mentioned that an Iraqi journalist had interviewed the victim just minutes before he was brought to the SEALs. Phil sent the agent a link to a video on YouTube. In the video, a journalist from Al Iraqiya, one of Iraq's leading news organizations, with "PRESS" printed in yellow on his body armor, got down on his knees and stuck a big microphone with a blue foam top just inches from a kid's face. The victim was lying in the dirt, unable to lift his head, speaking only in mumbling bursts. "Speak up," the reporter said in Arabic.

"I joined ISIS before Ramadan month," the kid said. Warpinski could tell it was the same kid from Eddie's photos: Same shaggy hair, same delicate shoulders and black tank top. Same face. The striking difference was that there were no bandages and no blood. His neck was completely smooth. Not even a scratch. Warpinski could see the reporter's watch. It said 9:00 A.M.

"Why did you join ISIS?" the reporter asked.

"My dad was beating me, and telling me we do not go with ISIS," the kid said.

"So why did you join them if your dad didn't want you to?"

"So they could tell me, 'Good job.'"

"That's it? So they would say, 'Good job'?"

The reporter turned to the camera. "Dear viewers, here is a young man, about seventeen years old—ISIS fooled him to join them."

Why did the Iraqis take the prisoner to Eddie instead of to an Iraqi medic? Warpinski had no idea. Were they really planning to give him medical attention? The video left a lot of questions unanswered. Warpinski still didn't know the victim's name. He didn't know where the body was. But at least he knew at 9 A.M. the kid was conscious and breathing, was able to speak, and had no visible wounds to his neck. And an hour or so later he was dead in a pool of blood at Eddie's feet. The video would keep Eddie from arguing the kid was bleeding out and almost dead when he arrived.

Another video came to Warpinski's desk. This one was on a disc mailed from Iraq, and it contained a statement submitted out of the blue from General Abbas al-Jubouri, the Iraqi officer who had part-nered with Eddie throughout the entire deployment. He said Eddie was innocent.

NCIS interviewed al-Jubouri several weeks later, but the inter-view produced as many questions as it answered. Al-Jubouri said he knew "Chief Ed" well. They had worked together almost daily for several months, along with a SEAL lieutenant whose name the gen-eral couldn't remember. He remembered the day the ISIS fighter was brought in. The boy was shot several times, including a bullet through the right leg that had hit an artery; he was "bleeding very badly." The SEALs tried to help the captive, but it was no use, the captive died.

The agent asked if the general had seen Eddie stab the prisoner. Al-Jubouri shook his head and clicked his tongue. "No—why would he do this? There was no need for this. No—he died from gunshot wounds. If I wanted to kill someone, I wouldn't do it in front of wit-nesses. There were twenty-plus people out there, including several Iraqi officers. He would never do that."

There were some things al-Jubouri clearly had wrong. The kid hadn't been shot several times, only once. And he'd been shot in the left leg, not the right. The video showed that the wound wasn't gush-ing blood. If the kid bled to death, photos suggested it was because someone had cut open his neck.

The bigger problem was not whether to believe al-Jubouri, it was what to do about the scarcity of physical evidence. Besides the pho-tos and texts and a few videos, there was nothing to tie Eddie to the murder. Then NCIS caught a break. They had sent Eddie's hunting knife to a lab for testing, and the results had finally come back. The murder weapon had been in Eddie's possession for more than a year. He had plenty of time to clean it, but the lab found two distinct forms of DNA on the knife. The first matched Eddie. The second was from an individual whose identity was unknown, but the test revealed two things: The DNA was from a man, and that man was Middle Eastern.

There was not enough DNA to tell if it had come from blood or just another person handling the knife. On its own, the new evidence was hardly a smoking gun. But together with the videos of the victim alive with Eddie, the photo of the victim dead with Eddie, with the bandage on his neck and blood on the ground, the three eyewitnesses, and the text Eddie sent bragging that he "Got him with my hunting knife," NCIS was getting close.

AN EMAIL ARRIVED from the FBI. Warpinski clicked it and started reading. It was not what he was expecting. There were new allegations against Eddie. Murder allegations. This time they were from Afghanistan.

Afghanistan had come up again and again in Warpinski's interviews with SEALs. Nearly everyone the agent talked to said they had heard Eddie tell the story of shooting a little girl to kill a Taliban. Eddie told it as a BUD/S instructor and again as the new chief of Alpha. Lieutenant Commander Robert Breisch knew the story, too. He told Warpinski he had been Eddie's platoon leader in 2010 when the girl was shot. Eddie was in another part of the country, embedded with an Army Special Forces team when it happened. In Breisch's telling, the Special Forces soldiers demanded an investigation, and Eddie was absolved of any wrongdoing.

Josh Vriens told the agent he had heard Eddie tell another story about that tour, in which Eddie saw a goat herder walking through a field and dropped him with a sniper rifle.

To Warpinski the Afghanistan stories were intriguing because they established a pattern, but NCIS had no plan to pursue them. Why chase leads on a nearly decade-old case when they would only take focus away from the stabbing? The best way to put Eddie behind bars was to stay locked on the one murder where they actually had some evidence.

But now there was this message from the FBI. He picked up the phone and dialed. The agent on the other end laid out the situation. The FBI had arrested an Army Special Forces soldier named John Rindt a few months before on child pornography charges. Rindt eventually agreed to plead guilty, and told the FBI he had seen something else the FBI should know about. When Eddie was arrested, his photo had been on the news. Rindt told agents he recognized the

SEAL and saw him shoot an unarmed farmer in a field in Afghanistan. It was in Helmand Province, Rindt said, 2010, in a rural town called Marjah.

Marjah at the time was a Taliban stronghold. The U.S. troop surge in Afghanistan was at its height, and commanders were determined to go in and clear the enemy out for good. The Marines would hold the ground, but Army Special Forces would strike first by helicopter and seize a few key strongpoints where they could set up snipers and machine guns to cover the Marines. One of those strongpoints was a two-story building at a rural crossroads that the troops nicknamed the Thunderdome.

The Special Forces guys were getting ready for the mission at the big American forward operating base when a random Navy SEAL sniper offered to come along to help.

The day after they landed, Rindt said, the SEAL and a handful of soldiers watched an Afghan peasant walk into the field. They noted that he was unarmed. Then the SEAL shot him for no reason.

"What did you just do? That man was unarmed!" the soldiers yelled at the SEAL.

"Well, they're all bad," Rindt recalled the SEAL saying.

Rindt and the other soldiers reported the killing to the Army commander, but Rindt said he was told to drop it.

In the FBI interview room, investigators spread out a series of photos of various SEALs and asked Rindt to pick the SEAL out of a lineup. He scanned them, trying to find a familiar face, but it had been nine years. The SEAL in Afghanistan had been wearing sunglasses, a helmet, and a beard. Rindt knew the SEAL had blond hair and blue eyes, but he had only been with the soldiers for about a day. Rindt failed to pick him out.

The FBI had an admitted child pornographer telling a story right before he was sentenced about a guy he had seen on the news. He had no evidence to back it up and had just flubbed the identification. That was pretty terrible evidence. Warpinski contacted a few other soldiers who had been at the Thunderdome, but they all refused to talk. For NCIS it was a dead end. Warpinski let it drop. It wasn't that he doubted the story; it was just that the juice wasn't worth the squeeze.

What Warpinski did not know was that two other soldiers from the Special Forces team also saw Eddie on the news and independently came to the identical conclusion as Rindt: *That's the same guy.* They remembered the scene from the Thunderdome clearly. It was February 15, 2010. Soldiers from the Army's 3rd Special Forces Operational Detachment Alpha 3121 were getting ready to board helicopters for the flight to take over the Thunderdome. At the last minute, a SEAL sniper signed on with them. His blond hair and reddish-blond beard were consistent with photos of Eddie from the time.

Right away, the SEAL started running his mouth, complaining about how the Special Forces weren't aggressive enough. But it quickly became obvious to everyone, the soldiers recalled, that the SEAL had no idea what he was doing. He claimed to be a sniper, but he shot too often and sometimes in the wrong direction. The snipers set up on a roof of the Thunderdome. Within hours, the SEAL fired recklessly at a convoy of Afghan partner forces, barely missing an Afghan driver with a bullet that buried itself in the dashboard.

The team held their position at the intersection all of the next day. Taliban forces fired several times from the distant tree line and soldiers returned fire, but for hours on end quiet pervaded the patchwork of farm fields around the Thunderdome. During one of those long lulls, the SEAL was behind his sniper rifle on a rooftop with two Special Forces soldiers acting as his spotters. Rindt was there, too. They watched an unarmed man walk out into a field to work the spring earth. The spotters called out that they saw a man with no weapon. Without warning, the SEAL fired, and the man fell dead.

"You just smoked that dude," a young spotter stammered. The soldiers immediately left the roof and reported what had just happened to their commander.

To the soldiers at the Thunderdome, the shooting was a massive fuckup. They were in the midst of a major offensive. If they reported the murder, they might be pulled back to the base and would not be there to provide overwatch to the Marines. Guys could die. Ignoring a murder was obviously wrong, but an investigation that would potentially cost American lives seemed worse. Just like with Mosul, it was a shit sandwich.

The officer in charge of the Special Forces team decided the best thing to do was just quietly get the SEAL out of there. He was put on the next helicopter to base with a curt *Thank you very much, never come back.*

The two soldiers besides Rindt who had seen everything never reached out to law enforcement and law enforcement never reached out to them. They didn't want the blowback they might get. And like Rindt, nine years on, they couldn't say for certain that the SEAL who had been with them for only one day was Eddie Gallagher. *The San Diego Union-Tribune* got hold of the FBI report and published a story. Through his lawyer, Eddie denied everything. The lawyer said Eddie had been investigated and cleared by the Army for accidentally shooting a little girl while aiming for the Taliban commander holding her. As for the man in the field in Marjah, the lawyer said it was impossible. Eddie couldn't have shot a farmer in Marjah, he said, because Eddie was never in Marjah and had never worked with Army Special Forces.

Navy records suggest the soldiers were right and the lawyer was wrong. Eddie's records show that, in fact, Eddie *was* in Marjah with Special Forces. In 2010 his platoon was assigned to another province in the western part of the country, but they had been given a village stability mission, living with locals, trying to make friends. To say the least, this was not Eddie's style. He wanted to fight. So he started volunteering for other missions. Eddie's performance evaluation right after the deployment, signed by Robert Breisch, said Eddie had "planned and coordinated combined sniper overwatch missions with Army Special Forces . . . in effective support of offensive operations in Marjah Province, Afghanistan."

Eddie was there at the right time and met the description of the guy who pulled the trigger. The soldiers' accounts matched what Vriens heard Eddie say about dropping a goat herder. There were other people still serving in the Army who knew about the whole ordeal. Fortunately for Eddie, the Navy had decided to drop it.

BRIAN FERGUSON TEXTED Craig Miller in November, a few months after Eddie was locked up, and warned that the investigation was growing more dire every day. It threatened to suck everyone in. The lawyer had already warned Ivan Villanueva that he was probably going to go to jail for buying trammies for Eddie in Mexico. He said Miller was at risk because he was in the photo with Eddie. Best-case scenario, Ferguson warned, everybody involved was going to get thrown out of the Navy. This is serious, and you are all going down if you don't get smart. Ferguson texted Miller the names of the crowd of guys from the platoon he was already representing and urged Miller to join.

"Those are good guys, don't screw it up," Miller responded. He still couldn't figure out what the deal was with this guy and why he was handing out free legal advice. Miller trusted Agent Warpinski. He trusted the prosecutors. He trusted the Navy. He didn't see any reason to trust a dude who showed up out of nowhere and suddenly seemed to know everything about a platoon he had no business with. Miller always tried to see the good in people, but he did not get a good vibe.

Ferguson told Miller it was important to get everyone to refuse to cooperate with NCIS. That would give the lawyer leverage to get total immunity for the whole platoon so nothing they said to NCIS or in court could hurt them. There was a good chance the higher-ranking SEALs like Breisch and Alazzawi were getting sucked into the investigation, and it might even go higher than that, he warned. If the brass felt threatened, they could easily turn on little guys like Miller and hang them out to dry. They needed protection.

Miller brushed him off. "I'm going to do the right thing. Let the chips fall where they fall. I tell every one of my guys, whatever you do, you have to tell the truth."

That was the last time they had any conversation of substance.

But Ferguson kept giving the same hard sell to just about every hold-out in the platoon. One by one more came over to his side. So many were eventually represented by him that the investigators and prosecutors started using his name as a verb. *Ferguson*, v., to lawyer up and refuse to cooperate with NCIS.

Joe Arrington, the JTAC who had almost come to blows with Eddie in Mosul and urged everyone to tell the truth when they came home, Fergusoned on November 19, 2018. Stephen Snead, the SEAL chief Eddie had texted all through deployment, Fergusoned on November 24. Ivan Villanueva, who had seen Eddie stab the ISIS captive, Fergusoned on December 4. And Corey Scott, the medic who was inches away when Eddie stabbed the kid in the neck, Fergusoned on December 5.

Each time a SEAL Fergusoned, a letter with Ferguson's oil derrick letterhead arrived in the Navy's legal office stating that NCIS and the prosecutors were no longer allowed to communicate with the witness without Ferguson present. The Navy couldn't figure out what the lawyer was up to. Was he just some freelance nutjob, or was he somehow in cahoots with Eddie? Warpinski asked Dylan Dille if the guys were getting skittish about coming forward. Dille replied, "Brian Ferguson has put the fear of God into everyone."

Ferguson always told people he had nothing to do with Eddie. Yes, he was speaking to Eddie's lawyers. And, yes, he even met a few times with Eddie, but just to help his own clients. The lawyer insisted he was involved just to keep the little guys from getting crushed by the system. He didn't want them to do the right thing only to take the fall for a bunch of officers who for years had ignored warning signs, promoted Eddie, partnered him with a bunch of war criminals in ERD, and created the whole fiasco. All the maneuvering over immunity was serving his clients. If it also helped Eddie, that wasn't Ferguson's problem.

Guys that signed with Ferguson described it to others in the platoon as a simple precaution: Better to be safe. As Miller watched one guy after another Ferguson, he heard them talk about being smart or careful or protected. Miller didn't buy it at all. He started to view the trial like a combat mission. There were plenty of ops the platoon had gone on where odds of getting shot were steep. It was one thing to take precautions, but that didn't mean you didn't go out. Guys were simply refusing to face the fire. To Miller that wasn't being smart, it was being a coward. He expected better from his men. He was mystified that a bunch of warfighters who had spent months fighting ISIS were suddenly afraid of a courtroom.

As Ferguson predicted, the fallout from the case did start to widen. Not long after Eddie was arrested, Alpha's officer in charge, Lieutenant Jake Portier, was charged for failing to report Eddie, conducting a reenlistment ceremony over the body, making false statements, dereliction of duty, and conduct unbecoming an officer and a gentleman. He denied all charges. Breisch was next. The Navy sent him a letter saying he was under criminal investigation.

In the commodore's command suite at Coronado, Captain Matt Rosenbloom looked at Portier's case from his perspective as a SEAL who had twice been in the same position leading platoons and tried to give the young lieutenant the benefit of the doubt. What if Portier had done his duty and had immediately reported the crimes to troop commander Robert Breisch, but Breisch, a longtime ally of Eddie who had deployed with the Good Old Boys, had told him to keep his mouth shut? It wasn't far-fetched. Maybe when the men in Alpha kept pressing Portier to act, he demurred because he knew it was no use. But Rosenbloom wasn't ready to cut Portier that much slack. Even if his troop commander had refused to act, Portier could have circumvented him. He could have handled Eddie, and had chosen not to. Rosenbloom had no say in who got charged, but he believed Portier should get what he deserved.

But what about Breisch? Rosenbloom had never understood why the troop commander seemed to have repeatedly stood by Eddie and tried to bury the investigation. The commodore wondered if maybe it had to do with what Eddie had yelled at Tom MacNeil in the parking lot by the high bay: *I have shit on all of you. If you take me down, I will take all of you down.*

Breisch had been on deployment with Eddie in Afghanistan in 2010 when Eddie said he shot the little girl and when Eddie was with the Special Forces in Marjah. He had been there when Eddie was quietly moved out of BUD/S for striking a student and when he was arrested for assaulting a gate guard. What if there were things Eddie knew about Breisch's past that kept Breisch silent? Rosenbloom wished he could have it out with Breisch and Portier frogman to frogman and find out what happened. But he couldn't. The legal rules tied his hands.

As Eddie sat in jail, Ferguson worked feverishly to deploy an immunity for his clients. He already had three key witnesses: Arrington, Villanueva, and Scott. He tried the hard sell on Dille and Tolbert but couldn't get them on board. T. C. Byrne was so weirded out by Ferguson that he told him to leave him alone and got his own lawyer. David Shaw, the JTAC, ignored attempts by Ferguson to reach him and willingly talked to NCIS without a lawyer. Miller did, too. He just wasn't afraid. He knew he was in the group photo, but he wasn't going to tap out just because he might end up having to answer for what he had done.

That really only left Josh Vriens. Ferguson pushed hard on the sniper. For weeks Vriens didn't respond to his texts, but eventually, Ferguson had Scott act as an envoy and Vriens agreed to a phone call. Immediately Ferguson pushed Vriens to get on board with the other guys. He didn't sound like a lawyer to Vriens, he sounded like a used car salesman. "I don't feel like I need a lawyer," Vriens told Ferguson. He hadn't been in any photos; he hadn't done anything wrong. He had already been investigated for the Switchblade.

That's what you think, Ferguson shot back. He asked why it had taken Vriens months to report the girl he had seen shot. "I did the best I could," Vriens said. He said he reported what he had seen to the chain of command. "I guess I didn't do more because I was desensitized to killing after so long in the SEALs."

See, you just implicated yourself in murder, Ferguson told him. Defense attorneys are gonna tear you apart on the stand, and you're gonna implicate yourself in a crime. A lot of guys just want the whole thing to go away. The case against Eddie is going to be weak, don't get caught on the wrong side of it.

Ferguson warned Vriens that he was in way over his head, but if anyone was in over his head, it was probably Ferguson. He openly told SEALs he represented that his limited legal expertise meant he could only handle small stuff. If they were ever charged with a crime, he said, they should call a real lawyer. When it looked like Jake Portier was going to get charged, Ferguson referred him to another lawyer. Even so, based on a cold call from Portier, Ferguson had gone on a mission to represent all of the platoon. The guys who didn't go with Ferguson suspected him of sinister motives. Some even thought he was working for Eddie. More likely he was simply recklessly naïve. It was just like running for editor of the student paper without ever working there. Experienced lawyers watching the case just shook their heads. Representing so many SEALs with so many potentially competing interests was a raging ethical conflict. Ferguson had all his clients sign a waiver acknowledging the conflict of interest, but what did that really mean? It wasn't clear where his allegiance actually resided.

On the phone, Ferguson warned Vriens that the Navy was going to pull his Trident.

"At this point, I don't give a fuck," Vriens told him. He was done with the SEALs. He was walking away. "They want my Trident, I'll put it right on their desk." Whatever Ferguson was selling, Vriens wasn't buying. He hung up and never talked to the lawyer again.

Ferguson stuck to his original plan to demand immunity. From the outside it seemed like a simple and reasonable request, but for prosecutors it came packed with risk. Chris Czaplak had been around enough criminal cases to know immunity could be twisted so that something intended to protect the witnesses could actually protect criminals. He laid out his concerns to his junior attorney, Brian John. The risk was not that SEALs with immunity would get away with whatever minor misconduct or even major misconduct happened on deployment, the risk was that they would go into court and take the fall for Eddie's crimes. It was an old mob trick. One guy agrees to sing, gets immunity, and then on the stand claims he committed all the crimes. If that happened, it would torpedo the case, and it would be almost impossible to prosecute the SEAL who took the rap because of the immunity. In other words, immunity was dangerous, especially if there was any doubt about the trustworthiness of the witnesses.

John listened to Czaplak's warnings reluctantly. He hadn't dealt much with immunity. He had never tried a murder case, and he had certainly never tried a case as complex as Eddie's, where half the platoon was lawyered up and not talking. Ultimately, he wanted to make sure he knew the truth. As a prosecutor, he was dying to hear what that half had to say. Maybe what Eddie was claiming was true. Maybe the guys in the Sewing Circle were all lying. John doubted it, but he'd feel more confident if he could hear from everyone. Wouldn't it be better, he suggested to Czaplak, to just grant everyone immunity and hear them out?

Too risky, Czaplak responded. The SEALs were a tribe, and some of them were probably willing to take a bullet for Eddie.

Maybe we get a prosecutor in from L.A. who's an expert at gang cases, John joked. That's what this is starting to feel like.

Seriously, Czaplak said. He was in a tough position. He wasn't going to hand out immunity to everyone, but it looked like Ferguson had forced the Navy's hand on at least two key guys: Corey Scott and Ivan Villanueva. Without them, there was only one witness to the stabbing—Miller, who only saw it from a distance. With only Miller the case was in big trouble.

Grudgingly, Czaplak emailed Ferguson. He drew up agreements to give Scott, Villanueva, and a handful of other SEALs what they wanted. He hoped it wouldn't blow up in his face.

CHAPTER 12

ANDREA'S WAR

Andrea Gallagher checked her makeup one last time and sat down in front of a green screen in a small TV studio. Her lips were a bold, glossy fuchsia, her eyelids shimmered like mother of pearl. Her highlighted blond hair was carefully styled so that it just brushed against her cheekbone. She wore a glittering necklace of gold shards that formed a collar over a fitted white dress. She was going on Fox News. And she had dressed for battle.

Andrea had conventional Fox News good looks, a conservative Christian heartland worldview, a fierce sense of loyalty to her husband, and a killer instinct. The green screen behind her appeared on camera as the skyline of Indianapolis—the capital of her home state. In front of her the silent, unblinking eye of a video camera gazed at her from a few feet away. It was December 2018. Eddie had been in prison for just over two months. She waited silently as a voice in her ear gave her a countdown. She took a breath. It was almost her time.

She heard the smooth voice of a TV host, the same voice millions of Americans were hearing at that moment as they tuned into Fox News: "From *war heroes* to alleged *war criminals.* Servicemen, warfighters under fire from the *very government* they agreed to serve."

An Army veteran turned professional conservative named Pete Hegseth was live in the Fox News studios in New York City with the outrageous story of what had happened to Edward Gallagher. He had invited Andrea to appear to tell the story on *Fox & Friends* and show the public the searing injustice of her husband being locked up for crimes he didn't commit.

The camera panned in on Hegseth in a sharp blue suit, white shirt, and Betsy Ross–red tie in front of a backdrop of the Stars and Stripes, his hair slicked back in a glossy wave. He was wearing a 101st Airborne Division pin. That morning he was waging his latest offensive in a personal campaign to defend troops accused of war crimes.

It was a battle he'd been fighting for months. Before officially joining the Fox News staff, he had served as an Army officer, and now he was the network's in-house blunt-talking grunt, there to vet-splain the complexities of war to the public. "I was a platoon leader in Iraq, I stood over wounded members of the enemy," he told viewers at one point while explaining Eddie's case. "I'm at the point I'd rather get the information from that guy, 'cause I don't really care if he dies."

Despite his frank talk, Hegseth was more Ivy League than G.I. Joe. He spent four years at Princeton University. Instead of ROTC, he was deeply involved in a conservative publication called *The Princeton Tory*, where he penned columns on conservative talking points like support of the invasion of Iraq or how the "homosexual lifestyle" was "abnormal and immoral." After graduating he worked at an investment bank before joining the Army Reserve. He did tours in Iraq and Afghanistan, but despite his brash declarations on camera, nothing in his military record suggested he saw much combat. In Iraq he was a civil affairs officer working with local officials to restore infrastructure. In Afghanistan he taught counterinsurgency classes for Afghan officers and left the deployment early to run unsuccessfully for Senate. Despite his relatively limited military career, Hegseth had used his penchant for the conservative spotlight and ties with Fox News to become one of Donald Trump's go-to advisors on veterans' issues.

On *Fox & Friends* that morning, Hegseth wanted to probe the absurdity of charging warfighters like Eddie for killing what he called "an ISIS dirtbag."

"Andrea, I want to go to you, wife of Navy SEAL Edward Gallagher. Talk to us about his situation and what you're facing," Hegseth said.

Andrea took a deep breath to respond. But before she had even said a word, Hegseth had told the audience volumes with his brief introduction: wife of Navy SEAL. Nearly nine years earlier, two black helicopters had descended on a sleeping compound in Pakistan and killed Osama bin Laden. After nearly a decade of searching and tens of thousands of deaths in Iraq and Afghanistan, one small group of special operators had brought the nation not just a welcome victory but vengeance. The killing launched a national love affair with the SEALs that was still going strong years later. What had once been an obscure Navy commando unit was suddenly a beloved symbol of America.

SEALs were a refreshing tonic to the never-ending wars. After years of stalemate, the American public no longer trusted its leaders when it came to the so-called war on terror. But the SEALs were different. SEALs never talked exit strategies or timetables. They just got stuff done. They were what was still admirable in America—a twenty-first-century update on the mythic cowboy hero, the nameless stranger riding in to save the day, then heading off into the sunset.

A flurry of publicity followed the bin Laden killing. Three different accounts of the mission hit the shelves. Chris Kyle's memoir *American Sniper* became an instant bestseller. There were SEAL guides to fitness, diet, and even parenting. Hollywood cranked out top-grossing SEAL movies in quick succession. SEALs endorsed workout equipment and charged top dollar for executive team-building camps. They graced the covers of dozens of romance novels. America's SEAL crush was so bad that the satirical news website *Duffelblog*—the military equivalent of *The Onion*—in 2017 ran the headline "High-Value Target Disappointed to Be Raided by Rangers Instead of Navy SEALs."

Andrea appeared on *Fox & Friends* amidst this flurry of Navy SEAL worship. Before even opening her mouth she already had the advantage of one of the nation's most beloved and trusted brands. Viewers simply had to hear she was the wife of a Navy SEAL to know that her husband was a hero.

This was not lost on Andrea. She worked as a portrait photographer, doing weddings and senior portraits, and had a side business teaching small business owners to turn their personal story into their brand. She knew she could use the power of image and story to help Eddie. She looked into the camera.

Hegseth asked how she and her SEAL husband were doing. She wanted them to know that the same corrupt establishment that had kept the nation in endless wars was now after her husband. "Our situation has been very, very dire," she said. "My husband had been accused by malcontents in his platoon that he had done an alleged act on a dying ISIS fighter. And that opportunity was grabbed by NCIS and jumped upon to try to bag a Navy SEAL."

ANDREA'S CAMPAIGN HAD started as a humble website called JusticeforEddie.com that she set up after Eddie was arrested. It was a way for Andrea to feel less helpless when Eddie was locked in the brig and she was thousands of miles away with three kids in Florida. She designed it herself, with a huge photo of Eddie standing at attention in the khaki service uniform of a chief, his right hand in a stiff salute above his sparkling blue eyes, the red-and-white stripes of a room-sized American flag behind him. She included a quote that reminded her of her husband: "We sleep safe in our beds because rough men stand ready in the night to visit violence on those who would do us harm." Then she added a link for donations. She must have had a hunch how incendiary the story might be. The SEALs were already a powerful brand. Her husband's story of a good man wronged by the system was incredible. Put together his SEAL good looks with social media's thirst for outrage, and how could people not take notice? She soon had fifty thousand followers on Facebook.

"Chief Gallagher has been charged with mistreating an ISIS terrorist during combat operations!" she typed in a typical update on the case. "On Patriot's Day, Sept 11th, 2018, NCIS snatched Chief Gallagher in the midst of TBI treatment, shackled him, kept him shackled in solitary confinement for 72 hrs. Chief Gallagher has been Indefinitely Detained, repeatedly denied access to medical care, and has limited access to his attorneys. If this can happen to Chief Gallagher, it can happen to anyone."

Bito donated a Half Face Blades hatchet to auction. The family started selling "Free Eddie" T-shirts. Soon the word was out and donations were pouring in. Andrea landed a sympathetic profile of Eddie in *Navy Times*, which focused on his glowing résumé and the harsh conditions in the brig.

Josh Vriens read the profile when it came out and chuckled to himself. He knew Eddie wasn't going to go down without a fight, and here it was. He was going to wage it through a proxy in the press. Smart. Unconventional. Very frogman. He sent a text to Warpinski with a link to the story, warning him that Eddie was "good at shadow campaigns" and saying, "Fox News will be next."

He was right. Andrea, working with Eddie's brother, Sean Gallagher, appeared on Fox News more than a dozen times between December 2018 and when Eddie went to trial in June 2019, sometimes twice in one day. While Eddie was compliantly awaiting trial in the brig, they were trying the case in the court of public opinion. And they hoped to win the support of the biggest Fox News viewer of them all, the one who had complete authority over the military and its courts: the president of the United States.

The strategy might have seemed crazy with any other commander in chief. For generations, presidents had avoided using their power to insert themselves in the low-level machinery of military order and discipline. And presidents generally only pardoned people after court cases and appeals were done. Donald Trump showed he was going to be different. He wielded the pardon like a partisan hatchet. In August 2018, just a few weeks before Eddie was arrested, Trump pardoned the longtime sheriff of Arizona's Maricopa County, Joe Arpaio, a proudly harsh targeter of illegal immigrants and a hero of conservative media who had branded himself "America's toughest sheriff." A month before the pardon, he'd been convicted of contempt of court for refusing to comply with a court order to stop racial profiling against Hispanics. In pardoning Arpaio, the president thanked him for "years of admirable service to our nation" and in a tweet called him "an American patriot," adding, "He kept Arizona safe!"

Perhaps the family realized that to the president's base—and maybe to the president—Joe Arpaio and Eddie were cut from the same cloth: two old-school lawmen not afraid to bend the rules a little to bring the fight to a foreign enemy and make America great again. Perhaps they realized the story of a blue-eyed combat veteran jailed by his own government would prove too much to resist. Eddie was a real-life version of Rambo made for the Trump era—an elite terrorist fighter in a battle against the deep state on home soil.

Andrea was a fan of the president and knew he watched *Fox & Friends* religiously, sometimes live-tweeting his reactions. Going on the show was the closest thing to a direct line to the White House.

The media blitz started when Eddie's brother, Sean, went on with Hegseth in November. Sean was in many ways the opposite of Eddie, a polished Washington lobbyist with a degree from Georgetown, but he was totally dedicated to his brother's cause. Even though he knew of Eddie's troubled past, he portrayed Eddie as a flawless hero and a humble civil servant who had been falsely accused. Sean always came off as sincere. And he may have been. Eddie was his only source of information for the case, and there was a good chance Sean believed what his big brother was telling him.

After Hegseth, Sean went on Fox News host Sean Hannity's radio show, then Hannity's Fox News cable show a few weeks later. The former New York City police commissioner and frequent Fox News contributor Bernard Kerik heard the family on the channel and had a phone conversation with Andrea. She told him all about the problems Eddie was having with young accusers in his platoon. Since 2001 Kerik had been a fierce antiterrorism hawk, and he was incensed that a SEAL was being charged for killing ISIS. He published an opinion piece on the conservative website *Newsmax* declaring that Eddie was the real victim. The SEALs who came forward, he wrote, have "engaged in a covert whining and whispering campaign in an attempt to discredit Gallagher, and divert focus away from them," and "have since been dubbed the 'mean girls,' and 'cowardly crew,' by the SEAL community."

For a conservative media world that often peddled racially charged grievance news to a mostly white, mostly male, mostly old audience, Eddie's story checked all the boxes. Here was a hardworking, traditional, Christian family man accused of killing a foreign, Muslim terrorist. The conservative media got around the conundrum that siding with Eddie meant throwing several other SEALs under the bus by framing it as a generation gap problem. The old-school SEAL was just trying to do what needed to be done when he was tattled on by pouty, politically correct millennials. Now a bunch of bureaucrats was trying to bring him down. The story touched the same resentments that had mobilized millions of people to vote for Donald Trump—the sense that in America, elites, lawyers, bureaucrats, brown people, and entitled youngsters were conspiring against real working Americans with traditional values. The conservative landscape was primed to embrace Eddie before he was ever arrested. All Andrea had to do was deliver the message.

She told the story of a conspiracy of millennials over and over. Hosts not only never challenged the family on the details of the case or bothered to seek other sources, they tacitly, and sometimes not so tacitly, suggested they didn't care if Eddie really did murder an ISIS prisoner. "Now I am going to admit my bias, I think your brother is a hero and frankly I think your brother should be given a medal," said a host on One America News Network when introducing Sean Gallagher. "Our special operators are out there to kill the enemy." In another interview a few weeks later, Brian Kilmeade of *Fox & Friends* asked Sean Gallagher incredulously, "It's the battlefield. Isn't the goal to kill ISIS?"

Military laws and professional standards, if mentioned at all, were generally dismissed with an eye roll, as if having rules in warfare was preposterously naïve.

When real journalists reported factual goings-on in the case, Andrea often attacked them. *The San Diego Union-Tribune* was one of the few news organizations that faithfully attended nearly every hearing. Andrea blasted the reporter—a former Navy chief—on Facebook and demanded an apology for printing "blatantly false fake news" and "salacious clickbait."

Fawning TV spots funneled thousands of people to Justicefor Eddie.com. Andrea started selling new T-shirts that read, "In a world full of *Mean Girls* be a Gallagher." The family soon raised more than $500,000.

Hegseth started bringing in other families with stories like Eddie's. Andrea appeared on *Fox & Friends* with the mother of Clint Lorance, an Army lieutenant turned in by his own men in 2012 for ordering the killing of three unarmed Afghan villagers. He was serving nineteen years at Fort Leavenworth. Also on the show was the wife of an Army Special Forces major named Mathew Golsteyn who was facing murder charges for killing an unarmed man he suspected was a Taliban bomb maker in Marjah, Afghanistan, in 2010.

"I'm not here to trash the Army," Hegseth told viewers with calculated outrage. "But why do our institutions work against our warfighters as opposed to giving them the benefit of the doubt?"

"I think there's a big difference between the actual warfighter and the people who are back here judging them in hindsight," Golsteyn's wife replied.

"Amen," Hegseth said.

No one on the screen realized it, but Golsteyn was the Special Forces officer in charge of the mission at the Thunderdome—the one who quietly removed the reckless SEAL sniper who had shot the farmer and endangered his whole mission.

Hegseth asked Andrea what she'd like to say to the president, if he was watching.

"We have to really look and wake up here as to what is going on in our country," she said. "These are atrocities being committed against our military service members, my children, my family, my husband. I would love to see the president take a good hard look at the systemic failure in all four branches of the military."

The Gallaghers were the perfect spokespeople for the brand—

always laser-focused on the message: The crime wasn't what happened to ISIS; it was what was happening to Eddie. He had provided medical care to an ISIS prisoner who had died of unrelated combat wounds. Disgruntled SEALs abetted by corrupt NCIS agents were building a fake case. A worthless commodore was too politically correct to stop it. They all were hoping to make a career off nailing an innocent chief.

"There is an overwhelming amount of evidence that clears my brother, that exonerates him from all of these charges," Sean told Fox News in January. Ironically, the family that was the main source of information on the case was prevented by gag order from seeing any of the evidence. In appearance after appearance, they were going largely off what Eddie and his lawyers had told them.

The family appealed directly to the president, arguing that Eddie's problem and the president's were one and the same. "Mr. President—you know more than most what it's like to be on this side of the system, to have your character maligned by lesser men, to see injustice unfold before your eyes, and be told to trust the process," Sean wrote in an opinion piece on the Fox News website in early February 2019. "The process is broken. We need your help to fix it."

CAPTAIN MATT ROSENBLOOM watched the Gallagher cable spots reach millions of people week after week and felt his blood boil. The commodore swore under his breath. He paced around his office calling Gallagher a liar and a psychopath and a hopeless narcissist. He had a few words for Eddie's wife, too. Rosenbloom had done twice as many tours as Eddie and seen twice as much action. Never heard of him? That was exactly the point. SEALs were supposed to be silent about their work. Now here was a middling chief whose family was pretending he was the greatest gift ever to the SEAL Teams.

Rosenbloom wanted to crush him like a cockroach. He wanted to show the Teams hundreds of pages of the investigation so everyone could know what he knew. He wanted to send a half dozen master chiefs in uniform to the Fox News studios to have them tell what a shitbag Eddie really was. He wanted to get up in front of every SEAL at Coronado and commend the men who came forward to shut Eddie down.

But the rules of the Uniform Code of Military Justice, which was the military's legal rulebook, had him shackled. Every time he wanted to correct the record, his staff warned that it would be unlawful command influence. He couldn't stick up for the guys in Alpha. That was unlawful command influence. He couldn't correct Andrea. That was unlawful command influence. If it had been a civilian jurisdiction, he could have refuted the family's claims on almost every point, trotting out text messages and poster-sized photos, noting that the witnesses who had come forward were some of the most respected operators in Team 7. Under the UCMJ, the Navy was afraid to say a word. Every time Rosenbloom suggested something, it was as if his staff lawyer had a shock collar on him. We can't do that, sir, undue command influence. Over and over and over. He felt like that was all he ever heard. *What about leadership?* he would fire back. What about the message our silence is sending? But every time, he grudgingly bit his tongue. The only thing the Navy ever said in response to the Gallagher family media blitz was "no comment."

ANDREA KEPT BUILDING ALLIANCES. There were plenty of people who wanted to use a Navy SEAL to question the credibility of the legal system. In January, with six months to go before the trial, Eddie's family joined forces with San Diego's representative in Congress, Republican Duncan Hunter. Hunter was a former Marine who had deployed to Iraq and Afghanistan as an artillery officer. Since getting elected in 2008, he had been the capital's most steadfast defender of combat troops. Like Eddie, he was facing multiple felony charges. In Hunter's case it was for covering up illegally spending $250,000 in campaign funds on personal expenses, including fancy dinners, clothes, private school, mistresses, and, famously, plane tickets for his pet rabbit. Whether Hunter saw Eddie's case as a just cause or a welcome distraction, he went all in. He visited Eddie in confinement and appeared multiple times on TV with Andrea to defend him. "Just an awesome Navy SEAL. Scary-looking guy, when you see him. He's the kind of guy we want out there killing people for us, killing bad guys," Hunter said on Fox News Radio after visiting Eddie. "He shouldn't be going to court at all for doing his job."

Hunter circulated a letter in Congress calling for the president to release Eddie pending trial. Soon forty members signed on. In March, Hunter stood beside Andrea in front of the Capitol, flanked by several members of Congress and a poster-sized photo of Eddie.

"We need to stick by the principles of our Constitution," Andrea announced to a small press conference. "We need to have due process. We need to have innocent until proven guilty, and I feel we have really seen the dark side I never knew existed." Andrea then spoke directly into the camera, hoping to reach the president. "Please, Mr. President, help my husband, help our family, and please just guide this process so that we do not get made just into another statistic of unlawful overreach by the government."

THE SECRETARY OF THE NAVY, Richard Spencer, was asleep in the early hours of the morning in a room at the former Hotel Del Monte on the California coast when the phone rang.

It was March 28, 2019. The old Mission-style hotel had grand halls, ornate tiles, and dazzlingly manicured gardens. Decades earlier, it had become part of the Naval Postgraduate School campus on the edge of Monterey Bay. The secretary had given a presentation on changes to the Navy's education program at the hotel the night before and planned to fly back to Washington in the morning. In the dark he fumbled for the phone and heard the words no top military official relishes hearing in the hours before dawn: "Please hold for the president."

Spencer had been a helicopter pilot in the Marine Corps in the late 1970s before becoming an investment banker who sat on the boards of several veteran charities. Unlike many Trump political appointees, he was a moderate—a silver-haired member of the East Coast establishment. For years during the Obama administration he served on a board to streamline some of the military bureaucracy. He was picked to be the civilian head of the Navy not by Trump but by Secretary of Defense Jim Mattis. He was not an old friend of the president; in fact, he had never spoken directly to Trump before.

"Richard," the president said as soon as he came on the line. "Get Eddie Gallagher out of solitary confinement."

The secretary had been following Eddie's case closely, but it took him half a second in the predawn darkness to remember who Eddie was. It was a nasty case, Spencer knew: allegations of murder, trophy photos, witness intimidation. But he saw the war crimes court-martial not as a sign of things going wrong in the Navy but of things going right. He knew about the concern in Navy Special Warfare circles of ethical drift in the ranks. Whether it stemmed from a pirate subculture or just a lack of discipline, it had to be dealt with before the SEALs went any further off course.

In the past few years, he knew, the SEALs had beefed up training in ethics and character development. Eddie was too old to receive most of the training, but the SEALs under his command were not. The fact that young SEALs had been willing to turn in a chief for doing wrong suggested that the training was working. It had to be allowed to continue to work. The court-martial needed to run its course. The SEALs had to see what happened to pirates. Now fully awake, he wondered why the president was asking to release Eddie.

"Mr. President, unless something changed in the last week, Gallagher's in general confinement, not solitary," Spencer said. "And it's for the safety of the witnesses."

"I don't really care where he is," the president cut in. "Have you been following Fox? They're raking us over the coals for this. These are my voters. Just get him out."

All winter Trump had been getting hammered in public by the investigation of his campaign's ties to Russia. Just a few days earlier, one of his closest allies, his lawyer and fixer Michael Cohen, had been sentenced to prison for making illegal payments to a porn star on Trump's behalf. There were lawsuits and probes. Approval ratings were stuck around forty percent. In the Navy SEAL chief, the president may have seen a bit of his own predicament. The president, too, was being hounded by the system. If he could do little about his own plight, at least he could help Eddie. By getting him out of the brig, he could show he was supporting the troops. He could deliver something decisive that didn't depend on approval from Congress. He could show how strong he was by standing up for a hardened warrior like Eddie. He told Spencer to make it happen.

Roger that, Spencer said. Intervening with the court-martial of an enlisted sailor was an unusual request that crossed the barrier traditionally kept between the White House and the military, but it seemed manageable. Spencer knew there were concerns about witness intimidation but figured the Navy could use GPS tracking and house arrest, or something similar, to protect witnesses while still making the president happy. And if it was a little unorthodox, President Trump was an unorthodox guy. That was why people had voted for him. On his flight back to the East Coast, Spencer tried several times to call the judge on the case, a Navy captain named Aaron Rugh, but couldn't reach him. Spencer went to sleep that night figuring he could take care of it in the morning.

The phone rang early again the next day, right after the Gallagher family had appeared on *Fox & Friends*. "I thought I told you to get Gallagher out," the president said. The tone of his voice had sharpened. Spencer started to explain that he was working on it.

"I don't give a shit, get him out of there," the president said. "Do I have to give you a direct order?"

Spencer said it wouldn't be necessary, he would take care of it right away.

"Okay, I want you to call over to Pete Hegseth at Fox and tell him what you're doing," the president said. He hung up. A White House operator came on and explained that she was connecting the secretary to Hegseth.

Spencer was annoyed at how the president had snapped at him. He was, of course, willing to carry out the president's wishes, but he wanted no part in whatever public relations campaign the president had cooked up with Fox News. He hung up.

Donald Trump had always been enamored of the military for the same reason he'd been enamored of the business world. He saw both as black or white, strength or weakness, winners or losers. Trump had spent his high school years at the New York Military Academy, a traditional military school with uniforms and lots of marching. He rose to the rank of captain his senior year. He inspected young cadets and issued orders. In the future president's senior portrait from the military academy, he wore a gray uniform covered in twelve medals marking years of good conduct and academic achievement. It had a gold braid distinguishing him as the student aide-de-camp. But the uniform wasn't his, nor were the medals. Both belonged to a friend. Trump had grabbed the friend's uniform so he could look more important in his portrait. If you couldn't be a winner, it was important to look like you were winning.

Trump graduated in 1964, just as the Vietnam War was ramping up, then got five deferments to avoid the military draft, including a letter from a family doctor that claimed the varsity athlete was unfit for service because of heel spurs. Vietnam was a loser war, Trump felt. Guys who got shipped over there were losers for not being clever enough to get out of it.

Vietnam became an important lesson for the future president: The country wouldn't win unless it was willing to do whatever it took to prevail. America had been strong when he was growing up in the 1950s, he told graduating students in a speech at Lehigh University in 1988. "It was a feeling of supremacy. It really was," he said. "I've known that since the Vietnam War and even a little bit before this country hasn't had the feeling of supremacy."

Trump initially backed the invasion of Iraq, but once it appeared to be a loser war, he abruptly changed his position. In 2006 he told Howard Stern it was "the biggest disaster ever," adding, "It's making Vietnam look like a good war." It was the same problem all over again. America had pulled punches. It didn't go in to win. On the campaign trail in 2016 Trump promised the American people he wouldn't make the same mistake.

"You have to fight fire with fire," he told a crowd in Ohio. America's current rules of warfare were weak and stupid. "We have to be so strong. We have to fight so viciously and violently because we're dealing with violent people." He didn't sugarcoat that he was ready to win by any means. When asked at another campaign stop whether he would approve waterboarding, he said, "I'd do much worse." Many in the audience laughed; some clapped. "Don't tell me it doesn't work, torture works," he said over their applause. "We have to be very strong, we have to be very vigilant, we have to be very tough. Waterboarding is fine but it's not nearly tough enough, okay?"

Eddie was an early believer in Trump. In May 2016 the candidate came to San Diego. As protesters clashed with police outside, Eddie stood in the crowd with his stepson and a few of his SEAL buddies holding a SEAL flag as Trump packed the stage with veterans in camouflage "Make America Great Again" hats. "We. Don't. Win. Anymore. As a country," Trump told the crowd, emphasizing each beat. His voice echoed through the city convention center. "We don't win with our military, with education, with trade, with anything! We don't win," he said. "We are going to start winning again, big league. We're going to win with our military. We're going to knock the hell out of ISIS!"

That promise resonated with Eddie. Almost every year since 2001 the military had grown more careful, more conservative, more restricted. Fighters on the ground had to deal with stricter and stricter rules of engagement. Increasingly, SEALs couldn't raid houses at night. On some missions they even had to knock at the door. The candidate was promising what Eddie likely had been waiting for, a chance to take the leash off. He was using a lot of the same words and promises as Demo Dick. It was a message that resonated across the SEALs. If you were going to win, you would have to be allowed to start killing the bad dudes that needed to die.

Three years after that San Diego rally, Eddie was facing murder charges and Trump was in the White House. When the president saw Eddie on *Fox & Friends*, there was the portrait of a SEAL chief who personified everything he had talked about on the campaign trail, everything he believed about Iraq and Vietnam. America could win if it wanted to win. If it wanted to win, it had to fight just as viciously as the enemy. And if it wanted to fight viciously, it needed men like Eddie.

By the end of the day, Secretary Spencer had worked out a deal for the president. The Navy would let Eddie out of the brig and confine him instead to the big Navy hospital in San Diego called Balboa. He would have a dorm-like room, as well as access to a gym, chow hall, and medical care, but would be miles away from the witnesses testifying against him and wouldn't be able to use phones or the internet. It seemed like a good solution. The next morning, March 30, 2019, the president announced the move in a tweet: "In honor of his past service to our Country, Navy Seal #EddieGallagher will soon be moved to less restrictive confinement while he awaits his day in court. Process should move quickly! @foxandfriends."

Eddie's family flew to meet him in California. Andrea soon posted photos to the "Free Eddie" page of her husband in camouflage uniform hugging his child. Before long, President Trump's sons picked up the photo and started sharing it with their followers. "Incredible picture of #NavySEAL #EddieGallagher being reunited with his son," Eric Trump wrote on Twitter. "After eight tours of duty and a lifetime of service in unthinkable places and circumstances, I believe Eddie deserves the benefit of the doubt . . . this story needs more attention."

Donald Trump Jr. replied, "I could not agree more!!!"

"Trump's Tweeting about Eddie," Dalton Tolbert texted to the rest of Alpha. The group text was a constant scroll of news, jokes, raw SEAL talk, and personal burns, often all rolled into one. But it was also how they kept up on news of the case. Dylan Dille read the president's announcement from his home in Colorado and shot a text back, "I thought for sure there'd be a #meangirls somewhere in that Tweet."

One by one, all over the country, the other guys picked up their phones and read the tweet. They had gone on to new assignments. Tolbert had made it through Green Team despite Eddie's interference and was now part of elite classified squadrons at DEVGRU in Virginia. T. C. Byrne had been cut in the last round and was teaching new medics in Mississippi. Craig Miller had been promoted to chief and was teaching BUD/S students to scuba dive in Coronado. Dille was out of the Navy and had moved back to the mountains to start a business making combat slings for assault rifles. Josh Vriens was teaching diving, too, but knew he was getting out of the Navy and had started to think about what would be next.

The guys knew in a few months they'd have to testify. Until then, all had decided to try to put it out of their minds. Most of them had young families. That plus work was enough to worry about without dwelling on what Andrea or some congressman was saying. But they had found the Gallagher family's Fox News campaign hard to ignore, especially the part about how the whole case was a bunch of lies made up by cowardly malcontents. That was so ridiculous it was funny. The part that wasn't funny was that tens of thousands of people, including the president, seemed to believe it.

Vriens followed the news obsessively. He had been a regular Fox News watcher for years and suddenly was confronted with stories on his favorite channel that he knew were false. He knew they were false because, unlike Andrea, he had actually been there. He wanted to go on *Fox & Friends,* pull off Pete Hegseth's little Army lapel pin, and tell him to shut the fuck up. But as an active-duty SEAL, he couldn't do or say anything. Like the rest of the Navy, he had to keep quiet. The other guys in Alpha were the only people he felt free to talk to.

"Welp there you have it. Civilians calling us cowards and pussies," Vriens texted the rest of Alpha after one of Sean Gallagher's appearances on Fox News. "At some point everyone will need to start speaking up as men because one day you will have to look your kid in the eyes and teach them about right and wrong."

Tolbert told him not to worry about it. "*Fox & Friends* has never been something I've concerned myself with," he texted. "Once it hits NPR and Joe Rogan's podcast and they call us pussies, maybe I'll care . . . but probably not."

Miller jumped in, too. Around the SEAL Teams, Fox News was the preferred news source. Everyone at Coronado had probably seen Andrea on TV. Online, SEAL veterans were threatening to track down members of Alpha and teach them a lesson. No one dared say anything to Miller's face, but he suspected SEALs were calling him a rat behind his back. At Coronado, the Sheriff could feel the stares as he walked across base. All of a sudden what he had always seen as a trusted brotherhood now seemed suspicious, even dangerous. Still, he was determined to keep the platoon united and on target. As for Sean and Andrea Gallagher, he texted the guys, "We don't have to worry about what these people say or think."

"Yeah," Vriens agreed. "Only about our own moral compass."

T. C. Byrne read the texts from his new assignment in Mississippi. He had been cut from Green Team in the last few days, and at first was consumed by whether it was due to Eddie's influence, but eventually he decided not to dwell on it since he'd never know the answer. Instead he was teaching a new generation of combat medics.

"Well said," he texted the group. "People can think what they want."

As Eddie sat in confinement, the guys in Alpha watched mesmerized as Andrea's campaign to make Eddie a saint drew in more and more people. Celebrity SEALs started joining, including one of the SEALs credited with shooting Osama bin Laden, Rob O'Neill. He appeared next to Hegseth on Fox News and trashed the guys in Alpha, even though he had never met them and had no idea what had gone on in Mosul. "I personally wouldn't testify against anybody I went into combat with, I mean it has to be something just outrageously illegal," he said. "To see someone else on the same team testify against someone in combat I think is absolutely disgusting."

The guys felt increasingly besieged. Many in the SEAL veteran community on Facebook were calling for their blood. The SEAL leaders were silent as stone and appeared to have abandoned them. And it felt like Andrea had convinced America that all the men in Alpha were despicable turds.

So far, no one in the media had leaked the names of the SEALs in Alpha, but the platoon suspected it was coming as the trial neared. That could mean the end of their careers and an escalation in the threats they were getting. "What a spectacle this has become. Circus," Tolbert texted the others. "Waiting for Tucker Carlson to say a news headline like 'Why do these Navy SEALs hate America?'"

———

CRAIG MILLER'S ALARM went off before the sun came up. He opened his eyes but didn't move. Lately he was having trouble getting out of bed. It was the first time that had ever happened. Since high school the SEALs had been everything to him—the shining light he was always sailing toward. It was not just a selfless way to give back, it was also cool as hell. He loved the training, he loved the guys he served with. He loved the intensity of the mission. There was nothing else he wanted to be.

But Eddie had changed it all. Suddenly everything was suspect. It seemed like the nation he had vowed to serve had turned against him. Miller had encouraged the other SEALs to step up and now wondered if he had steered them into the rocks. He was confused and disillusioned and, for the first time in his life, depressed. He wished there was some way he could make it all go away. He started to have dark thoughts about ending it. It wasn't a wish to die, really, just a wish not to have to deal with everything. He couldn't go back. He didn't want to go forward. There didn't seem to be any good way out. Part of him didn't want to be around anymore.

That morning Miller dressed in his instructor's uniform and got in his truck to go to work. The sun was coming up as he left San Diego and steered onto the Coronado Bridge connecting the city to the thumb of land on the far side of the bay that held the SEAL base. The bridge was two miles long and rose so high that the aircraft carriers could cruise underneath. It was a beautiful part of the drive, with sailboats cutting across the sparkling Pacific and the towers of downtown rising in the distance. But the bridge also had a sad history that every SEAL commuter knew. Over the years it had attracted a steady procession of suicidal jumpers who plunged to their deaths.

When Miller was near the peak of the bridge, traffic suddenly lurched to a crawl. He craned his neck to see what was happening. An old Lexus sedan was stopped in the outside lane. An accident, Miller thought. Cars put on their blinkers and merged left to go around. As Miller approached the Lexus he steered toward the center lane, but just as he did a woman got out of the car and headed for the edge. She was young, with shoulder-length dark hair. He could see she was crying.

Maybe because of Miller's own frame of mind that morning, he spotted what was about to happen. Within seconds he was out of his truck, jogging toward the woman. Other cars continued to pass. "Hey, are you all right?" he yelled above the traffic. She looked too upset to answer. She heaved the top of her body over the low concrete wall and was staring down at the two-hundred-foot plunge to the water, poised to go hurtling over. Miller sprinted forward, lunged, and grabbed her.

For a moment, Miller, too, was staring down into the dark waves far below. He saw the yawning space and in a flash pictured himself jumping to his death. He pictured the eternal silence that would follow: not being there to testify at Eddie's trial, not being there for the other guys in Alpha, not being there for his family. Instinctively, a thought shot through his mind: *That's not going to be me.* It immediately clarified everything for him. From that moment forward, he never had any thoughts about not being around. He was going to press on. However heavy the weight of Eddie's case was, he wasn't going to ring the bell.

He pulled the woman away from the ledge and held her tight. He hugged her as traffic sped by. She was still crying, still unable to speak. He held her there for a long time, until help arrived. As he did, he put his head down against hers and said, "I'm so glad you didn't jump."

After President Trump tweeted Eddie's release from the brig, Eddie had three months until trial. The family didn't slow its all-out media campaign for a second. They hit conservative radio shows, podcasts, blogs, and cable TV—anyone willing to telegraph the Gallagher story with little fact-checking. Andrea went on Fox News and erroneously said that the Navy was hiding video that clearly exonerated Eddie. A deep state conspiracy was afoot. She told the camera, "I just want to let the president know he is being lied to. There is corruption from the top down involved in this."

In mid-May, Navy lawyers in San Diego got a sign the campaign might be working. Word came down from the White House: Draw up the paperwork and send it over. Eddie Gallagher is going to be pardoned.

The request sent shockwaves from Coronado to the Pentagon. No one in the military questioned the constitutional pardon power of the president, but to use it before evidence had been presented at trial was alarming. Disagreeing with a verdict was one thing. This was disagreeing with the idea of due process. To drop a bomb like that on the military to protect a guy like Eddie—officers up and down the Navy ranks couldn't believe it.

As soon as Matt Rosenbloom heard about the request, he sprang into action. For months, the commodore had been pinned down by the specter of unlawful command influence and had bitten his tongue. Now the president seemed to be exerting the ultimate command influence. It made Rosenbloom sick, but there was one upside: If Eddie had his charges dropped, the commodore wouldn't have to worry about unlawful influence anymore. The court-martial would be done, and he'd be free to do what he wanted. He called his staff into his office, leaned on his desk, and told them, succinctly, "No fucking way Gallagher's getting out of this with his Trident."

Memorial Day was just a few days away. Rosenbloom knew President Trump planned to make a speech on the deck of a Navy ship in Japan that morning and had a reality-television penchant for pomp and spectacle. *He's probably going to spring the announcement on deck,* Rosenbloom thought. The Navy would have no choice but to comply. But Rosenbloom wasn't going to let Eddie walk away like a hero. He told his team to draw up a plan. The moment the words of the pardon were out of the president's mouth, Rosenbloom would sign the papers to pull Eddie's Trident and his security clearance and kick him out of the SEALs.

Rosenbloom expected to be fired for it, but he didn't care. It was in his authority as commander to decide who wore the Trident. Kicking Eddie out of the brotherhood was the only right thing to do. If it cost him his job, fine. He figured he was too rough-edged to be promoted to admiral anyway.

At the Pentagon, top Navy leaders were trying to discourage the president. The chief naval officer, Admiral John Richardson, asked Trump for a word. The justice process is important, Mr. President, he said. Let the Navy find the facts; let the process happen. Secretary Richard Spencer wrote a note to the president, marked "For your eyes only." "Mr. President, you've done some great things, do not let the Gallagher case be a stain on your record."

As the weekend neared, high-level military leaders and retired admirals and generals also pressed the president not to subvert the judicial process. Newspaper editorials across the country came out against it. On May 24, with the trial weeks away, the president dangled the possibility of a pardon as he left the White House to fly to Japan. "You know, we teach them how to be great fighters, and then when they fight, sometimes they get really treated very unfairly," he told the media gathered on the White House lawn. He had not made any decisions yet, he said, but was considering pardons for two or three men, adding, "It's a little bit controversial. It's very possible that I'll let the trials go on, and I'll make my decision after the trial."

IN SAN DIEGO, prosecutors made their final preparations with witnesses, knowing that at any moment the president could pull the rug out from under them. And that wasn't their only concern. Along with the president, conspiracy theories being spread by congressmen, intimidation of witnesses, Andrea's public smear campaign, and SEALs Fergusoning left and right, the Navy had another pressing problem in the case: leaks.

In the nine months between when Eddie was arrested and when he went to trial, confidential material from the case had repeatedly found its way into the media. Most of the leaked material went to *Navy Times*, but *The San Diego Union-Tribune* and *The New York Times* also got reams of sealed documents. The judge in the case put a gag order on all evidence, but details kept spilling out.

The Navy saw the leaks as a serious problem for three reasons: First, they were a violation of privacy for Eddie. Although the prosecutors thought evidence overwhelmingly showed Eddie was a murderer and a despicable human, both had been defense attorneys before becoming prosecutors, and both had an intrinsic respect for the rights of the accused. The leaks were undercutting that. Second, the leaks threatened to taint the already small Navy jury pool, which would make finding an impartial jury that much harder. Third, the leaks were putting pressure on the SEAL witnesses from the platoon, who were getting spooked by public exposure.

In March, *Navy Times* got hold of confidential material that showed NCIS had seized phones from SEALs at DEVGRU to look for evidence that Eddie was trying to retaliate against Dalton Tolbert and T. C. Byrne. That day the paper ran the headline "War Crimes Case Expands to SEAL Team 6." SEALs at DEVGRU started to look at Tolbert like a turd who had brought unwanted attention to their classified tribe. "It's getting worse," Tolbert texted Warpinski that day. "I know you're not media but this is getting very ugly for me." Tolbert implored the agent to do something.

Under pressure from the judge in the case, NCIS opened an investigation. Eddie's lawyers repeatedly said they thought the leaks were coming from the Navy—either from high-up SEALs eager to sink Eddie or prosecutors illegally trying to present the case outside the courtroom. Agents started by closing off access to the case files to almost all Navy personnel, leaving only a small crew of NCIS agents, prosecutors, and the defense. The leaks continued. NCIS agents quietly hunted through the email traffic of the Navy staff who still had access, looking for anyone who might be forwarding documents. They checked the prosecutors, Chris Czaplak and Brian John. They found nothing. The leaks continued.

NCIS ruled out anyone inside the Navy. They were almost certain the leaks were coming from the defense side. Eddie's lawyers had the material. So did Jake Portier's lawyers. Brian Ferguson had access to a lot of it, too.

NCIS wanted to track all of them, but agents couldn't monitor defense communications without a warrant. To get a warrant, they'd need some evidence. And they didn't have any.

In early May, with about a month to go until the trial, Czaplak was at his desk in the prosecutor's office. As usual he had on his white Navy uniform, and his white officer's cap rested on a stack of papers. The lead NCIS agent at Naval Base San Diego came in wearing plain clothes and asked to speak to him in private. It was not Warpinski, it was his boss, Assistant Special Agent in Charge Curtis Evans. Czaplak closed the door.

When they were alone, Evans said NCIS leadership in Washington was breathing down his neck about the leaks, and he had come up with a plan to find the leaker. NCIS would plant some bait and wait to see who took it, then use that information to get a warrant to search phones and computers. The plan was to attach a tiny bit of tracking code on one of the case documents protected by the gag order. It was simple, free software marketers put on emails all the time to gather data about customers. The lead agent wanted Czaplak to send an email with the bait to the defense. Then NCIS would wait and watch. The bit of code attached to the document would show up as a small image of the Navy Judge Advocate General's logo—an eagle spreading its wings over the scales of justice. The software would reveal who was looking at the document and give NCIS enough information to get a warrant. If they could find the leakers, they could charge them with contempt of court.

Czaplak was hesitant. As a former defense attorney he didn't want to get anywhere near violating Eddie's right to private, privileged communications with his attorneys.

Not to worry, the agent said. Czaplak would never see any of the data. Neither would Joe Warpinski or any of the agents involved in Eddie's case. NCIS would set up a separate group of agents, called a taint team. Attorneys from the Department of Justice would handle the rest. Top NCIS leaders in Washington were on board, the agent said. It was good to go.

Czaplak thought it over. The leaks weren't a big priority to him. Trial was less than a month away. Most of the big stuff—including nearly all of Warpinski's investigation—had already been leaked. There wasn't much to gain even if they caught the leaker. At the same time, the constant leaks and the contempt it showed to the legal process pissed him off. If people were breaking the rules, he wanted them called out. And if NCIS was itching to catch them, there was no reason to oppose it. Ethically he didn't see any immediate red flags as long as no one involved in the case would ever see the surveillance data. Just to be safe, though, he told the agent he wanted to talk it over with the judge overseeing Eddie's case.

A few days later, Evans and Czaplak went to Judge Aaron Rugh's chambers and explained the plan. Rugh listened and nodded. He said he wanted to see in writing how the taint team would work, but other than that, he expressed no reservations. Evans and Czaplak interpreted that as permission from the judge. On May 8, 2019, NCIS embedded the code in a humdrum document and email notifying the defense lawyers about an update. That afternoon Czaplak sent out the bait.

If things had gone as planned, Czaplak would have never heard about the tracking software again. He would have gone about preparing for trial. A separate NCIS team would have watched the tracker, and eventually someone might have been charged with violating the gag order. But things didn't go as planned.

At first, everything seemed to be working fine. The documents made their way to Brian Ferguson and to a reporter at *Navy Times*. But Ferguson had security settings on his Web browser that kept remotely stored images from loading. He immediately spotted that the logo was a potential tracker. He fired off an email warning Eddie's lawyers. He sent another telling Czaplak he had spotted the link back to the NCIS server. "Just in case this is a plot to track me," he said, "I went ahead and forwarded the logo to every reporter spy and malcontent and ne'er do well that I know."

Eddie's defense team went ballistic. Within hours, Ferguson and the defense attorneys in the case alerted every news organization that had been covering the case. The Navy intended the plan as a way to preserve the integrity of the judicial process. The defense said it was a corrupt conspiracy to subvert it. They claimed the government had tried to launch a "cyber-attack" against the SEAL and his defense team. Prosecutors were spying. They were using government "malware" to hack privileged, confidential communications. Eddie's lawyers called for the whole case to be thrown out for prosecutorial misconduct.

Chris Czaplak couldn't believe it. All he had done was press Send on an email. Now the defense was talking about trying to get him disbarred. Brian John had been completely in the dark about the plan until he saw it in the news. He was stunned. He suspected Chappy was trying to do the right thing, but the appearance was so bad. Now it was all crashing down on them on the eve of trial, and he wasn't sure if anyone would be left standing.

Soon Andrea appeared on Fox News. Fuming, she asked, "Now the question is who is going to start investigating these investigators and prosecutors for this criminal wrongdoing?"

The host asked whether Andrea expected President Trump to intervene.

Andrea observed that he had already stepped in once. Then she said, "We now know based on everything that took place that there will have to be further intervention because this entire system and process of the UCMJ is corrupt."

Trial was only a few days away. Judge Rugh held an emergency hearing to sort out what had happened and see if the case could go forward. In an unusual move, the judge took the stand in his own courtroom to answer defense questions about what he knew about the software plan. Later, the prosecutors watching could only surmise that the judge may have been confused about the whole plan. When asked if NCIS gave him accurate details about the plan to monitor lawyers, the permission they had to do so, and the full scope of the investigation, the judge repeatedly answered, "No, they did not."

"I hate to say this," Eddie's lawyer said, "but it sounds like they committed a felony."

He demanded the case be thrown out.

Czaplak was bewildered that blame was focusing on him. NCIS had come up with the plan. Top leadership had signed off on it. It had been briefed up to the level of the secretary of the Navy. NCIS had explained the plan to the judge. All Czaplak had done was press Send. Now the judge, the Department of Justice, and the higher-ups at NCIS were acting like it was a surprise. All the things Ferguson had warned that Navy lawyers would do to the platoon were now being done to the Navy's own lawyer. The upper ranks were denying everything and hanging Czaplak out to dry. He didn't know what was going to happen, but he knew it was about to get ugly.

Judge Rugh issued his ruling soon after. He said the government's action had tainted the entire criminal case and given the public the impression that Eddie would not get a fair trial. To try to fix things, he said, he was imposing several remedies. First, he took away the harshest sentence. Eddie would no longer be eligible for life without parole. Instead, the maximum he could face was life with the possibility of parole. Second, for the trial he gave the defense two extra chances to strike jurors without cause during jury selection, allowing them a better chance to stack the panel with people they thought would be sympathetic to Eddie. Third, the judge let Eddie leave the hospital grounds and go home with his family. And the judge had one last fix: The lead prosecutor was kicked off the case.

The judge found that his court did not have the authority to decide whether the lead prosecutor had acted unethically or unlawfully, but he ruled that because Czaplak was now an interested party in the leak investigation, it created a conflict of interest with the potential to undermine Eddie's constitutional right to a fair trial. Because of that, he was out.

Czaplak was in the middle of taking testimony from General Abbas al-Jubouri when the ruling came down. The Navy had flown the general in from Iraq for the trial, but the blow-up over the leaks had delayed things, so both sides had agreed to videotape the general's testimony and play it for a jury later. Eddie and one of his lawyers were in the room, waiting for their turn to question the general, when the ruling came out. Eddie's lawyer read the ruling on his phone and yelled, "Stop! You're done!"

Czaplak paused mid-examination and looked over. It took a few seconds for the news to sink in. The case was the most important one he had ever worked on. He had been focused on it for nine months. He had interviewed and re-interviewed witnesses, pored over documents, fought off defense efforts to get testimony and evidence barred from trial. He was ready. And now he was out.

It was as if someone had pushed a button and he had dropped

through a trapdoor. Brian John and the other junior prosecutors would have to muddle through alone. He felt like he had tried to make everything right, but instead he had let everybody down. He started to get angry that he was being blamed, but there was no point. There was no arguing, no second chances. A ruling was a ruling. The law was the law. Czaplak stood up, gave a half glance at the Iraqi general, who was visibly confused, and walked out of the interview, never to return. Later, in the office, he ran into John, who had already heard the news. The younger attorney looked at him and said, "I'm sorry."

Czaplak didn't have much more to say. He didn't want the betrayal he was feeling to poison the prosecution team right before the big event. He knew John needed to focus. He raised his eyebrows and flashed a "What are you gonna do?" smile. There were exactly two weeks until the largest, most complex murder trial the Navy had seen in a generation. Czaplak looked at the young lieutenant who had never tried a murder. "Looks like you're on your own."

CHAPTER 13

A JURY OF PEERS

Lieutenant Brian John stood up smartly in a crisp white uniform, walked alone into the center of the courtroom, and faced the jury.

A photo flashed up on the screen behind him: Eddie in his dusty combat uniform in Mosul gripping a knife in one hand and the hair of a dead Iraqi teenager in the other.

"I've got a cool story when I get back. I got my knife skills on," he said. His voice, like his face, seemed young—a bit too wholesome for such dark material.

John paused. He wanted to hit the jury with the worst facts first, show them the cold, premeditated brutality of the SEAL seated in dress uniform before them. He brought up a photo of Eddie and the corpse on the screen behind him.

"Good story behind this," John said, reading another text message. "Got him with my hunting knife."

Those were Chief Edward Gallagher's own words, the lieutenant told the jury. He sent them out shortly after killing a wounded captive in Iraq on May 3, 2017. He was proud of it. He thought it was cool. He wanted all of his friends to know what he had done.

"He celebrated that stabbing," John said. "He celebrated that murder."

It was June 18, 2019, the first day of Eddie's murder trial. Eddie arrived at the plain stucco courthouse on Naval Base San Diego like a movie star on the red carpet, pulling up in front of the court in a sleek, white Ford Mustang convertible with the top down. The courthouse had a back entrance where he could have slipped in unnoticed, but that wasn't his style—or the strategy his wife and legal team were going for. He walked up the front steps in inscrutable black Ray-Bans, past a phalanx of news cameras and supporters. He was buff and fit, impressively tan. Andrea was on his arm, meticulously done up and with a new hairdo, a fitted striped dress, and strappy high-heel sandals.

Inside, the small courtroom had none of the high ceilings or dramatic shadows of a Hollywood courtroom that would befit the grand moral struggle for the soul of the SEAL Teams. Instead, utilitarian office furniture sat under pallid fluorescent lighting reminiscent of a Department of Motor Vehicles branch. The judge, in black robes, sat behind a modest bench under a low ceiling. The jury sat to his left. A plain witness stand with a plastic swivel chair was on his right. Behind the small tables that held the prosecutors and the defense team stood six benches in the gallery with only enough room for about twenty-four people.

Eddie's mother sat down at the first bench, wearing a conservative floral dress covered by a cardigan; his father had the rumpled suit of a retired professor. Both of them had been conspicuous in their silence, never participating in the Fox News campaign on Eddie's behalf. Sean sat near them in a business suit, looking polished and professional. Andrea, next to them, sipped from a paper coffee cup. Next to her was Bernard Kerik, the former New York City police commissioner, who had become a personal friend. He put his hand on Andrea's shoulder and whispered a word of encouragement. The rest of the benches were filled with Navy officers and journalists.

Eddie sat at the defense table in a starched white uniform with gold chief's anchors on the collars, his Trident gleaming on his chest. His blue eyes and weather-lined face betrayed no emotion. Gazing straight ahead as Brian John gave his opening statement, Eddie looked like a recruiting poster for the SEALs, regal and tough, unmoving. His lawyers had instructed him not to react, even when the young prosecutor stood just a few feet away calling him a murderer.

"Chief Gallagher was the de facto leader of his platoon," John told the jury. "He's the one that they're looking to." But instead of being a role model, he said, the chief became so obsessed with killing that his own men took warning shots at ISIS in an attempt to keep him from killing civilians.

John declared the facts with confidence, but inside he was so shaken that he could hardly think. His senior counsel had been pulled with no time to get someone else up to speed. Even under normal circumstances, that would have been hard to manage, and John had not had a normal week. Seven days before opening statements, John was going through the evidence when his phone rang. His father had been riding his bike when he suffered a catastrophic heart attack and died. They had been close. John's father had served in Vietnam and was one reason his son left teaching civics to join the Navy. His death was a complete shock. John raced home to Northern California. He now had to try to run a complex trial without his partner while also helping his mother deal with the sudden death, all while trudging through his own grief. On the plane home, John switched between writing the eulogy for his father and the opening statement for trial.

After Czaplak was removed, the Navy had scrambled to find another senior trial lawyer for the case. Given that there were only two weeks to prepare and the president had publicly hinted that he might reverse the verdict, no one volunteered. The Judge Advocate General's Corps assigned a replacement from the East Coast, a veteran of both defense and prosecution cases named Commander Jeffrey Pietrzyk. In thirteen years as a Navy lawyer, Pietrzyk had worked in Afghanistan, Guantanamo Bay, and Japan as well as Navy courtrooms on both coasts. In the courtroom, he was almost indistinguishable from Czaplak—both were respected senior trial attorneys, both were completely bald with Polish surnames that judges struggled to pronounce. It was as if the Navy had ordered a stunt double. But there was an important distinction. Czaplak had studied the case for months. When Pietrzyk took over, he had about a week.

Because of the time limitations, Pietrzyk couldn't truly act as the lead attorney. He would be there as an advisor and an expert on the law, but the young lieutenant, Brian John, would be the expert on the case. After the death of his father, John was not sure he could handle it. When wildfires destroyed his entire community, one of the few things that remained in the ashes was family. Now that was in ruins. John worried his mother was too fragile to leave alone. He called Pietrzyk at the office. I can't do the trial, he said. My head isn't clear. I wouldn't be effective. I can't be in court. I'm needed here.

Sorry, there's no choice, Pietrzyk said. The stakes are too high. "This is your case. You can grieve later, but right now we need you here." Pietrzyk said others would try to shoulder most of the load, but no one knew the case as well as John. Do the first day, the opening statement and the witness right after, he said, then pick one other witness, the most important one in your mind, and focus on him. Pietrzyk said he could pull in other lawyers to help handle the rest.

John agreed. For his witness, he picked Corey Scott. The medic was the key to everything. He had been just inches from Gallagher when he pulled out his knife. He saw it all clearly. He watched the captive die. NCIS and the prosecutors had interviewed him a half dozen times and knew every detail. He was the strongest witness and the key to putting Eddie away. John didn't want to chance leaving Scott to anyone else.

As John prepared for trial, he was calling home several times a day. His mind was in so many places he walked around as if it were a blur. Now the first day of trial had arrived and he was giving the opening argument, trying to project confidence that he was far from feeling.

He led the jury through the crucial morning of the case. The platoon was fighting ISIS on the outskirts of Mosul. A wounded prisoner was brought to them, and in front of multiple witnesses, Eddie killed him, then held an enlistment ceremony over the body. On the big screen, John put up the photo of platoon members gathered around the body with Eddie.

When SEALs tried to speak out, Eddie threatened to kill them and worked to ruin their careers, John said. You will hear from those

SEALs, he said. "At the end of this case, it will be clear that Chief Gallagher stabbed a wounded ISIS prisoner under his care, that he celebrated it with photographs, that he shot at civilians, and that he systematically tried to intimidate those who had the courage to report him."

In the plain jury box, just a few feet in front of the young prosecutor, seven men in military uniforms sat in two rows listening silently. It was a jury like none of the Navy lawyers had seen before because there was hardly anyone on it from the Navy. Of the seven, only two wore white Navy uniforms—one was a surface warfare commander, the other was a SEAL senior chief. The rest wore the khaki of the United States Marine Corps. All of them were either enlisted Marines or prior-enlisted warrant officers. On their chests, the vast majority wore the same service ribbons as Eddie: the Iraq Campaign Ribbon, the Afghanistan Campaign Ribbon, and the distinctive Combat Action Ribbon, which signified that they had personally engaged with the enemy. A few had on aluminum bracelets in memory of comrades killed in battle. They were, overwhelmingly, a group of ground-pounding, battle-hardened grunts just like Eddie.

The combat-heavy jury represented an early victory by the defense. Eddie's lawyers had asked the judge to select a jury from a pool of troops with combat experience, arguing it wouldn't be fair for anyone else to judge him. The Navy had enough confidence in the evidence to agree. They didn't want Eddie to be able to blame a conviction on being unfairly judged by a bunch of rear-echelon desk pilots. Any hint of an unjust conviction would invite the interference of the president, which the Navy was eager to avoid. So the admiral overseeing the court-martial granted the request.

The concession carried significant risk. There was a good chance that combat veterans would never convict a fellow grunt for the death of an enemy, no matter what the evidence showed, and might vote to acquit out of loyalty. The Navy hoped, though, that they would do the opposite, that their experience would allow them to judge Eddie without getting swept up by rhetoric about heroes, split-second decisions, and the fog of war. Senior enlisted grunts with combat experience understood the Law of Armed Conflict and the need for leaders to set an example. They knew the importance of discipline and order in a chaotic war zone. The SEAL on the jury would know the SEAL ethos. He'd be able to see clearly that Eddie had betrayed it. There was a decent chance that a combat-heavy jury would be the least likely to let Eddie off the hook.

The defense team maneuvered to increase the proportion of grunts when it was time for jury selection. They had been given extra chances to strike jurors after the email tracking fiasco. Right away, they got rid of three officers, including the only woman in the pool. By the end of jury selection, the seven men seated were so heavy with enlisted combat experience that even one of the jurors sitting in the group was struck by it. He wondered if it was possible to have a fair trial. A jury of peers is one thing, he found himself thinking, "but you would never get a jury of all police for the trial of another police officer."

Eddie had another advantage when it came to the jury, one that he knew about but the prosecutors did not. He was personally acquainted with the lone SEAL on the panel. When prosecutors had asked the SEAL if he knew the defendant, he said not really. Coronado was a small community, so he knew who Eddie was, and maybe had seen him at the gym a few times. "I've said hi to him before," he said. "That's about it." In fact, the SEAL had been to Eddie's house five times, including for Bible study, and he was such a believer in Eddie's innocence that he told other SEALs he had donated a thousand dollars to the "Free Eddie" campaign after Eddie was arrested.

Eddie perked up when he heard the SEAL lie. Obviously Eddie wasn't about to tell the prosecutors, but at a recess he sure as hell told his attorneys. "That guy's fucking lying, I know him," Eddie said. Okay, his legal team acknowledged, but is he lying so he can hurt you, or lying so he can help you? Eddie said he wasn't sure. After a lot of discussion, the team decided to keep it all quiet and leave the SEAL on the jury.

LIEUTENANT JOHN FINISHED the Navy's opening statement and sat down. Eddie's lawyer stood up and strode into the middle of the court. In the room full of Navy men in plain uniforms, he was a pea-cock. He was big and tall and broad with a thatch of blond hair swept stiffly to the side. He was forty but looked older. His volumi-nous neck drooped over the stiff white collar of a striped shirt paired with a mesmerizingly colorful necktie. Silently but theatrically, he picked up the podium and moved it so he was standing directly in front of the jury like a pastor about to deliver a sermon, then smiled and introduced himself as Timothy Parlatore.

"My negros," he announced in a loud voice. "Craig's done some good work making progress with handling the diablo situation, how-ever, this will only work if we're all on the same page. If guys want we can meet at my house tomorrow afternoon and talk about it."

He paused, letting the confusion of his opening statement sink in. Then he explained that it was a text message to the platoon by one of its snipers, Josh Vriens. Some malcontents in the platoon had a secret group text they had used to conspire to spread lies against Eddie, Parlatore said. They called the secret group "the Sewing Cir-cle." Vriens's text was part of the proof that the Sewing Circle hated their chief so much that they called him "El Diablo" and had gotten together to cook up a lie that would take him down.

"This case is not about a murder," Parlatore said, looking at each of the members of the jury. "It's about a mutiny."

Parlatore wore a fat ring with a blue stone on his left hand to show that he was a graduate of the Naval Academy. He also had a pin on his lapel for the missile cruiser he had served on as a junior officer years before. But the garish ties and brash shirts he liked to wear in court showed a different influence. Parlatore had never worked as a lawyer in the Navy, and as a civilian he did not specialize in Navy cases. His practice was in Manhattan, far from any bases, and though his clientele varied widely, if he could be said to have had a specialty, it was the Mafia.

Parlatore graduated from the Naval Academy in 2002 under his birth name, Timothy Payne. His short Navy career was distinguished largely by a written reprimand for disobeying an order and being absent without leave in 2005. That same year he was convicted of reckless driving near his base, and he left active duty before his five-year Naval Academy commitment was up. He legally changed his name soon after to his mother's maiden name, then got his law degree from Brooklyn Law School in New York and began several years of understudy with some of the city's most prominent mob lawyers.

Parlatore cut his teeth working for lawyers like Eric Franz, whose clientele included a number of old-school capos with nicknames like "Mikey Scars." Then he went to work with a theatrical, sharp-dressed lawyer named Bruce Cutler, who for years had represented Gambino crime boss John Gotti. In the 1980s, Cutler's often combative style had produced three acquittals for Gotti and earned the mob boss the tabloid nickname "the Teflon Don." At one point he famously argued that Gotti couldn't be head of a Mafia family because there was no such thing as the Mafia. FBI wiretaps suggested that while Cutler was representing Gotti, he advised the don on criminal activity. A federal judge in 1991 ruled that Cutler could no longer represent Gotti because he appeared to have become "in house counsel" for the mob.

Under Cutler, Parlatore started taking on his own Mafia clients, but by then it was 2012 and the grand old days of Mafia prosecutions were long gone. One of his few mob clients was a woman on the reality show *Mob Wives,* and Parlatore readily admitted to the Associated Press in 2016 that "the existence of *Mob Wives* proves organized crime is dead."

Eventually Parlatore went out on his own, representing a broader array of clients. He defended three men who illegally jumped with parachutes from the rebuilt World Trade Center and a lawyer accused of sexually assaulting a woman on a fold-out office bed. (In that case he argued that the assault couldn't have taken place because the woman was too fat for the bed to support her. His client was found guilty.) He also took work that brought him into the conservative news sphere and eventually connected him to Eddie. In 2014, Parlatore started representing Bernard Kerik, who wanted to sue one of his former lawyers for cooperating with the feds in a case that sent Kerik to prison on fraud charges. Four years later, Parlatore represented none other than Fox News host and family-values champion

Pete Hegseth, who was going through a second divorce after cheating on his second wife and having a child with a Fox News producer.

At the time, the Gallagher family was already represented by two experienced and established civilian lawyers who specialized in military law, Colby Vokey and Phillip Stackhouse. But Eddie and his wife didn't like how the lawyers were operating. Andrea voiced her frustrations to Kerik, who recommended his own lawyer.

Parlatore was brash, bombastic, and, just like his mentor, proudly combative in court. He seemed to realize that a jury trial was not necessarily about who presented the most compelling legal argument but who told the best story. It was local theater without the makeup. And he knew in the Gallagher case that his audience stretched beyond the courtroom.

"This case is about battle," he told the jury. Some of the witnesses against Eddie had never fired a shot before. They got dropped into combat in Mosul and were terrified. Eddie refused to coddle them. He called them out for the cowards they were. So, Parlatore said, "they banded together and made a plan to take Eddie Gallagher out of the fight permanently. That's why we have this case. It's not because of a murder but because of a mutiny. What they failed to think about at the time is that Eddie Gallagher was never out of the fight."

Parlatore strode across the court, stood next to Eddie, and asked him to stand. He listed Eddie's past accomplishments: eight combat deployments, two Bronze Stars for valor, number one lead petty officer, number one chief, sailor of the year. And, Parlatore said, smiling, Chief Eddie did the impossible for a SEAL. He married his high school sweetheart and they stayed together.

People in the courtroom chuckled.

Eddie stood absolutely still. Parlatore walked back to the jury and leaned close, as if to let them in on some juicy gossip. They weren't going to see much evidence in the case, he said. No body. No autopsy. No forensics of the crime scene, no science, no physical evidence, he said, "because there was no murder."

The young SEALs in the platoon had helmet cams and videoed everything on deployment, but they didn't bother to record the murder that was so important to them or the alleged ceremony after, he said, because it never happened. An enemy had died of wounds from the battlefield. Now Eddie was being condemned for trying to do his job.

As Kerik listened to his lawyer from the gallery he leaned over and whispered to Andrea. After introducing the Gallagher family to Parlatore, he had signed on to the case as an investigator and consigliere. The family called him "the Godfather." Kerik was a longtime friend of former New York City mayor Rudy Giuliani, who had become one of President Trump's lawyers and close advisors. The family already had a direct line to President Trump through Pete Hegseth and *Fox & Friends*. With Kerik, they also had a potentially powerful back channel.

Kerik also brought to Eddie's team one of the president's personal lawyers, Marc Mukasey, who had represented various Trump businesses and the Trump Foundation. Mukasey was a powerhouse boutique litigator and former federal prosecutor, accustomed to big cases with complex strategies. He was rail-thin and dour; journalists in the gallery during the trial compared him to Mr. Burns, the vulture-like billionaire from *The Simpsons*. Both Mukasey and Parlatore were bankrolled by the thousands of donations Andrea had collected online. Mukasey agreed to take a back seat to Parlatore and only do the most technical legal arguments, but every night he was there to steer strategy—a director for Parlatore's theatrics.

The defense strategy that they chose was a full-frontal assault on the charges, one that would have been familiar to Parlatore's mob-lawyer mentors. They weren't going to offer mitigating circumstances. They weren't going to argue that Eddie had acted in self-defense or that Eddie had a PTSD flashback that triggered the attack. The plan was to argue that nothing ever happened, and anyone who said something had happened was a liar. It was an all-or-nothing, scorched-earth tactic demanding not only that they show the evidence couldn't be trusted and that the government couldn't be trusted but also that they destroy the credibility of every SEAL who took the stand.

Parlatore plowed through the charges against Eddie. The alleged sniper shots at the old man and the girl? No evidence there. No photos, no video, no bodies. There weren't even dates when some of the supposed crimes took place. They were so weak, he told the jury, that the prosecution should be embarrassed for even filing them. "That is a theme you're going to see throughout all of these charges," he told the jury. "No body, no forensics, no science, no evidence, no case. Because there was no murder."

He got right up to the rail of the jury box and said he would show how a small group in the platoon had conspired to take Eddie down and how NCIS agents who wanted to make careers by nailing a SEAL went along for the ride. They ignored evidence. They raided the chief's house, and dragged his children out at gunpoint in their underwear. They stuck a decorated SEAL behind bars and threatened him with life in prison.

Parlatore looked at each of the men sitting there in uniform, most of them with multiple deployments to war zones, all of them about Eddie's age, all of them predisposed to be sympathetic. "This was a sham investigation," he said, "and should be terrifying, terrifying to all of you, terrifying to all of us, terrifying to anybody that has to go down range and then have their actions questioned by investigators like this."

TOM MACNEIL RAISED his right hand and swore to tell the truth, the whole truth, and nothing but the truth. Opening statements had concluded, and the prosecution now planned to march through a series of eyewitnesses that they hoped would leave no doubt as to what Eddie had done. With minimal physical evidence, the accounts of the platoon were crucial. Alpha's junior-grade lieutenant was the first witness taking the stand because MacNeil could take the jury through the whole day of the stabbing from premeditation to confession.

The young officer sat down in the witness chair without glancing at Eddie. He was dressed in the same starched whites but wore a totally different demeanor. If Eddie was grizzled and statuesque, MacNeil seemed nervous and uncertain. He had always been a reluctant participant in the criminal investigation. Though he had no love for Eddie, he had not pushed to go to NCIS like Corey Scott or Craig Miller. As an officer, even a very junior one, he could be on the hook for not turning Eddie in.

When agent Joe Warpinski had MacNeil in an interrogation room a year before, the junior officer mumbled for nearly an hour about Eddie's "performance issues" and a "decline in professionalism," never mentioning the stabbing or the shootings. Warpinski eventually had to stop him and tell him to cut the crap. "Can I be completely honest with you, man?" Warpinski told him. "I can see you in every one of your answers being extremely careful about every single word you say. I get what's going on here. And I told you before we came in here that I've talked to most of the platoon. I know these stories. I know what happened. I know these details and I think you might be trying to cover for yourself." Over time, MacNeil had grudgingly come around. He ended up giving a detailed written statement to NCIS about the day of the murder and a long list of other misconduct. On the stand that day, MacNeil was cooperative but tense, as if waiting for someone to sucker punch him.

Brian John took him back to the morning of May 3. MacNeil told the jury he was with Eddie near the front lines near Mosul. They were in gun trucks on the flank of the Iraqi soldiers attacking a village when word came over the radio that an injured ISIS fighter was being brought to the compound. MacNeil heard Eddie say on the radio, "Lay off him, he's mine." Eddie then drove back to the compound, forcing MacNeil's truck to leave its position on the battlefield and follow. Mentally John checked off a box: There was the premeditation.

At the compound, Eddie began providing medical care to a dirty, nameless teenage fighter, MacNeil told the court. After watching for a minute, MacNeil wandered off to do other things, then passed back by the scene just in time to see Eddie above the captive holding his custom hunting knife. John checked another box: the murder weapon.

John stopped MacNeil. He put up on the screen a photo of Eddie wearing the knife in a black sheath across the back of his belt. He asked if it was the same one. Yes, MacNeil said. He had seen that knife every day in a room they shared, hanging on the nail where Eddie hung his pants.

When MacNeil saw Eddie holding the knife over the captive, he thought little of it and walked past to talk to General al-Jubouri in the building, he said. But when MacNeil came back outside, the captive was dead. There was blood splattered on his neck and on the ground. Then Jake Portier reenlisted Eddie next to the body.

The jury sat silently riveted. Most of them were taking notes.

John put up a photo on the big screen: a dozen SEALs arranged in two rows like a high school soccer team, Eddie in the captain's spot taking a knee in the center, the nameless victim splayed in the dirt with his hair gripped in Eddie's hand. Is this photo from that day? he asked.

Yes, MacNeil said. He identified the victim and Gallagher, then himself in the back row, standing with his rifle dangling in his right hand. In the photo, a few SEALs were smiling. MacNeil wore a concerned glare. John checked another box: evidence of a dead body and the accused murderer holding his head. Now he needed one more: Eddie admitting to the crime.

John asked about the evening of the stabbing. There was an argument between Eddie and some of the guys over what had happened, MacNeil said. MacNeil had not been there, but when Eddie came back to their room, Portier asked how the confrontation went. Gallagher said the guys were upset. I don't care, think about what would have happened if they had one of us, Portier said. Eddie responded, "Yeah, exactly." John checked a box: acknowledging the killing.

John thanked MacNeil and said he had no further questions. MacNeil had set the scene, identified the murder weapon, introduced the photos from the compound, and said Eddie had essentially admitted to the killing. The ground was laid for the eyewitnesses. It was a promising start.

Parlatore stood up for the cross-examination. He was about to give a preview of what he planned to do to every SEAL in Alpha who took the stand. The public had placed a halo of heroism on all SEALs, and he planned to knock that halo off. The case, he knew, would come down to whether the witnesses could be believed. He was determined to dredge up every piece of dirt he could and smear it all over them, until each one was discredited. He hit MacNeil hard right at the start.

"You were arrested for assault and battery, public intoxication?" he said.

MacNeil cleared his throat and said yes. It was early in his career, before he went to BUD/S. "I was intoxicated, and I got into a fight, and I defended myself."

Is drinking permitted in Iraq? Parlatore asked.

"No, sir."

"Were you drinking in Iraq?"

The prosecutors tried to object, but the judge overruled them.

Which members of the platoon were you drinking with in Iraq? Parlatore asked.

"I mean, I drank on the rooftop of the safe house with most if not all the enlisted SEALs that were at my outstation," MacNeil said uncomfortably.

Parlatore put up a photo of MacNeil. It was night on the rooftop and he was playing DJ. MacNeil smiled nervously.

That's the first time I've seen that photo, he said. He protested that the photo was from the end of deployment, after the battle in Mosul was over. No one had been drinking during operations.

Parlatore kept punching. Did the platoon take other photos of other dead bodies? he asked.

Yes.

Would you be surprised to find out other SEALs had taken photos posing with the body of the stabbing victim?

No, MacNeil said.

Parlatore hammered at why it took so long for MacNeil to come forward about Eddie. He was an officer. If he had a problem with Eddie taking the photo with the dead body, why didn't he stop him? If he suspected a murder, why didn't he say anything or do anything? Why didn't he report it?

MacNeil stuttered that he reported it to Portier that night. He said he also had tried to get Eddie to confess in front of Brian Alazzawi in Iraq. With Alazzawi right there, he had told Eddie to tell Alazzawi about the situation with the stabbing. But Eddie smoothed it over. Nothing was done.

One of the Marines watching from the jury box was stunned at what he was hearing. SEAL officers were on a first-name basis, drinking beers with their men in a war zone? Total lack of discipline. If Navy SEALs had a time-honored tradition of working around rules and regulations, the Marines were the opposite. Every detail of military life had to be followed to the letter, from the roll of the uniform sleeves to the laces of the boots. Enforce the small stuff and you have to worry less about the big stuff. These officers weren't doing their job, the juror thought, and Eddie seemed to be just as bad. How could these screwballs have risen up through the ranks to leadership positions? The juror had always thought the SEALs were the elite of the elite, but the details coming out made them seem more like a bunch of drunk frat boys with guns. He couldn't wait to hear from Portier. The lieutenant seemed to be right in the thick of things, and he clearly had to answer for it.

DYLAN DILLE COULD feel the tension growing as soon as he arrived back in San Diego for the trial. He'd moved back to the Rockies a year before and had tried to put Eddie behind him. It wasn't easy. It seemed like Fox News was talking about the case every day, and never in a way that made the guys look good. On Facebook, SEALs who referred to themselves as "the real brotherhood" were calling him a coward and traitor. He was now only checking the SEALs' private 5326 page to monitor threats against his safety. Every time the case came up, Dille would get showered in hate. None of the SEALs on Facebook seemed to care that a chief had targeted civilians. They were just mad that guys in Alpha had said anything about it. One SEAL who had served in Vietnam and gone on to write several books about the SEAL Teams posted about Dille, "I wonder if he wants to hear about the time I dropped a high explosive round into a hooch we were taking fire from and four little kids got killed!

FUCK THAT ASSHOLE." Dille went for long runs with his dog to clear his head. He grew a thick beard and never wore clothes that suggested he was a veteran. He went hunting with his father deep in the mountains. Slowly, he was starting to move on.

As his plane touched down in San Diego, he could feel his heart speeding up. He was slated to appear near the beginning of the trial and hardly slept the night before it started. The first day, he sat all day in a small witness waiting room, then was dismissed. He came back the second day. Again he sat, waiting. He listened to a meditation app on his phone, trying to clear his head. He had been warned by the prosecutors that the defense attorney would try to tear him apart. That's what they do for a living, they said. Anything you've done wrong, they are going to bring up.

But the defense wasn't what had Dille on edge. His conscience was clean about Iraq—he had refused to get in any of Eddie's photos, he had never taken a sniper shot that he wouldn't stand behind, he didn't do drugs or get involved in pirate shit. When Portier refused to do anything about Eddie, Dille had tried to save people by firing warning shots. *Let them try to tear me apart,* Dille thought, *I have nothing to hide.*

Something else was bothering him. He was starting to suspect that something sinister was unfolding in the platoon, something that seemed to be covered in Eddie's fingerprints. It had started on the first day of the trial. Dille had gone to the courthouse, expecting to go up on the stand. Going through the metal detector at the front door just ahead of him were Eddie's mother and father. Dille put his head down. He felt bad that they had to go through this. He knew he was going to say hurtful things about their son in front of them. No parent deserved that. As they were getting their bags searched by a security guard, Corey Scott came in. He nodded at Dille, whom he hadn't seen in months, then turned to the parents. "Hey, are you the Gallaghers?" Scott said. "I don't think I've met you, I'm Corey Scott."

Dille snapped to attention. What was going on? His patient sniper's instinct to watch for patterns couldn't make sense of it. Scott detested Eddie. Despite his reputation as the Ghost, he was the one who encouraged everyone to turn him in. As an eyewitness to the stabbing, he had the most damning testimony of anyone in the whole platoon. It was going to fry Eddie. And now he was getting chatty with the parents?

Scott made small talk with Eddie's parents as they shuffled through the metal detector. Dille followed, feeling as confused as he had on the day of the stabbing. Both Dille and Scott went to the witness waiting room where Dille sat warily, hesitant to say anything. The youngest SEAL from Alpha, Ivan Villanueva, walked in. As Eddie's gopher, he was the other guy who had been right there at the body when Eddie stabbed the prisoner.

Scott and Villanueva immediately started catching up like they were kicking back on the couches in the high bay. Villanueva said he was with Alpha for another workup. They were headed to Guam again. Scott was an instructor at BUD/S but was about to get out of the Navy. They talked about family and about other guys in Alpha. Dille volunteered little. Eventually, conversation turned to the trial. Villanueva said he had gone to see Eddie the other day, and they had hung out a little bit.

Dille's head involuntarily ticked to one side. *Did I hear that right? Why would anyone be hanging out with Eddie?*

Oh nice, Scott said, I went to visit Eddie, too.

Dille *had* heard right.

What the hell is going on? he thought. A year ago these guys hated Eddie. Villanueva was pissed that Eddie had made him get his mom to buy drugs. Scott had encouraged others not to let Mosul drop. He had asked them how they could live with themselves if Eddie ever led SEALs again. Now they were *hanging out?*

You seem quiet, Dylan. What's going on? Scott asked.

Dille shook his head. "I've just got a lot on my mind," he said.

As the other SEALs continued to chat, Dille felt a creeping dread, like dark water was slowly filling the room. He knew when Eddie had told MacNeil he had "shit on all of you" there was some truth to it. Eddie had ordered guys to fire rockets and Javelins at bad targets, and guys had done it—especially the younger guys. Eddie had encouraged bad sniper shots. Guys might have done things they regretted, maybe even things that could get them arrested. But who was on that list? Dille didn't know.

Then there was the massive fuckup with the Switchblade. Dille knew guys in Squad 2 were worried it would come out. Was that enough to scare guys into working with Eddie? Who else was in? He knew Dalton Tolbert was solid, but what about T. C. Byrne and Josh Vriens?

Dille shook his head and told himself he was being paranoid, but he couldn't stop thinking about it. This was how the pirates survived and how they spread. They had shit on everyone. It was easy to get tangled up in it. In fact, at first, it seemed like a favor. Pirates like Eddie let junior SEALs get away with things or smoothed things over. Maybe it was drugs or a drunken arrest, maybe it was a bad shot on deployment. But what seemed like a favor was, in fact, insurance. Once the pirates had helped a guy cover something up, they owned him. He could no longer speak out because there was collateral. It was mutually assured destruction. Forced loyalty. It ensured silence. And by staying silent, even a SEAL who hated the pirates effectively became one.

As Dille crossed the courtroom to the witness stand on day two in a civilian suit, he looked directly at Eddie. He wanted to send a message that whatever pirate plan was in the works, it could not touch him. He was clean. He wanted him to know that now that the chief had no power over him, he would finally get to say the things he couldn't say in Iraq. He held his gaze for a second longer, hoping to meet eyes. Eddie did not look up.

Commander Jeff Pietrzyk, the prosecutor who had just come to the case, swore in Dille, and the sniper sat down. Dille tried to put his concerns about the other guys in the platoon out of his mind. He couldn't control how anyone else would testify. Eddie might have shit on some guys. He didn't have shit on Dille.

Pietrzyk took Dille through the stabbing and the meeting afterward where Eddie acknowledged it, then turned to the Towers. It was the first time the jury was hearing about Eddie's shots on civilians. It was what Dille was most eager to get off his chest. He went on for several minutes talking about how the chief shot at groups of civilians and women by the river. He mentioned that he saw Eddie shoot at an unarmed boy, adding, "He missed on that one."

"Objection!" Timothy Parlatore said standing up. "This is wildly vague and wildly prejudicial."

The judge allowed Dille to continue, but he urged the prosecutor to keep things specific.

Pietrzyk steered Dille to June 18, 2017. It was Father's Day, Dille said. He saw two elderly men standing on a corner. He heard a shot ring out from Eddie's position and saw a vapor trail as a bullet cut the hot air. A spot of blood appeared in the small of one man's back. He fell to the ground, struggled to get up, fell again, lurched to his feet, and stumbled out of Dille's view.

"I don't know what happened to him after that," he said. Then Eddie came over the radio and made a comment about the shot. Dille said the chief "thought he had missed."

Pietrzyk checked several boxes: attempted murder and Eddie taking credit for the shot on the old man. No further questions, he said.

Parlatore stood up to cross-examine the sniper. For day two of the trial, he had on a pink striped shirt and a dazzling pink-and-purple tie. Dille thought he looked slimy but high-dollar. He caught himself looking over at the Navy lawyers to see if they were outgunned. They seemed quiet compared to Parlatore. Maybe even timid.

"You never personally watched Eddie Gallagher pull the trigger, did you?" Parlatore said.

"Correct," Dille said.

The stories about seeing vapor trails and hearing Eddie say he missed on the radio, those were all new, weren't they? You hadn't told investigators about those in the year leading up to the trial.

That's true, Dille said.

Parlatore read a text message Dille had sent to the rest of the Sewing Circle a few weeks after returning from Iraq, when they were discussing who they could trust in reporting Eddie to the authorities. Alpha's texts were the uncensored, full-throttle talk of a bunch of young gunfighters, and they were full of dick jokes and filthy language. Parlatore seemed to relish each chance he got to read them in court and juxtapose the dressed-up, polished SEALs on the stand with their locker room talk.

"'Our shit is watertight,'" Parlatore recited with a half grin. "'And if people take Eddie's side, they are going to have a dick on their forehead when this is all done.'"

He looked at Dille. "What do you mean, 'Our shit is watertight'?" he asked.

If the question was meant to rattle Dille, it didn't.

"The truth is watertight, Mr. Parlatore," he said firmly.

Parlatore barreled forward, unfazed. He wanted to show the jury that the platoon had never mentioned the murders until months after the deployment. It had started out with petty gripes about cookie butter and had grown into a story about war crimes only when their gripes were not enough to sink Eddie's career.

When the platoon met after deployment in the high bay to complain about Eddie, Parlatore said, Dille only mentioned Eddie stealing his cookie butter. You never confronted Eddie about the stabbing or the shootings, did you? he asked.

Dille admitted he had not.

If Dille was so worried about civilians, Parlatore asked, why didn't he report Eddie in Iraq or tell the platoon so it didn't happen again?

"We did that," Dille said, a little upset. "I did that." He looked around, as if waiting for a ref to blow a whistle. He had told Portier multiple times. So had Miller. NCIS knew that. Dille didn't understand why Parlatore was saying he didn't. He glanced over at the prosecutors, hoping they would object or something. They were silent.

"And, again, there's no proof or anything that you actually did that. That's just what you're telling us here, right?" Parlatore said.

Dille was deflated. "Yes," he said.

Dille wanted to explain that he had reported the shooting to his lieutenant, and he had seen Dalton Tolbert do the same, but Parlatore turned and walked back to the defense table. "No further questions," he said.

Dille left the courtroom physically drained. His joints hurt, and his muscles were trembling with fatigue. His father had come to San

Diego to be with him. The two drove off the naval base, past the ranks of gray warships, to San Diego's Balboa Park, where the sniper lay down in the grass in the shade for a long time and stared up at the sky. He knew that even if Eddie was convicted, he'd have to testify all over again at Jake Portier's trial. The end of a career he had loved would be spent revisiting the worst moments over and over in detail as roomfuls of people stared. It was all too exhausting and sad to think about.

CRAIG MILLER PULLED on his white uniform and checked that his Trident and chief's anchors were positioned just right, hoping that the polish and precision could camouflage his roiling thoughts. He was dying to get the trial over with but dreaded his part. For two years he had kept the platoon in line as Eddie went off the rails. The Sheriff had led the effort to investigate the chief. In many ways, he was the moral center of Alpha, a man who truly tried to live what he believed. The SEAL ethos was the closest thing he had to a religion. He knew all he had to do was tell the truth. Still, he felt unprepared. He was a professional gunfighter but didn't know anything about courtrooms. The SEALs practiced everything over and over until he knew exactly how to rush the door, sweep through the house, and take down the target. The Navy legal team seemed more thrown together. They barely met with him as trial neared. He was used to working with Chris Czaplak, but Czaplak was gone. He had no idea what to expect from Eddie's lawyers. He worried that he would say the wrong thing. It was not how the Sheriff liked to run things, but it was out of his jurisdiction.

Miller took the stand in dress whites, tall and fit, with new chief's anchors on his collar. His eagle gaze swept the room and focused on Eddie's legal team. The chubby lawyer with the dazzling tie looked to him like a mobster. Behind him, the bald investigator with the furrowed brow next to Andrea looked like his hired goon. *Where did Eddie find these guys?* he wondered. Then Miller looked at the prosecutors' table. It was a few young guys who barely filled out their uniforms. It didn't inspire confidence.

Like Dille, Miller was worried that Eddie somehow had worked out a backroom pirate deal to worm his way out of trouble. Miller had run into Corey Scott in the waiting room that morning. They sat down together and tried to make small talk, but it was awkward. They weren't allowed to talk about the trial, and of course that was the one thing consuming both of them. Scott said the whole thing had been really stressful. He seemed like he was about to cry. Scott told Miller, "I hope when this is all over, we can still have a beer together."

"Of course we will," Miller replied. But Scott sounded truly worried. And that made Miller worry, too. He found himself thinking, *Why wouldn't we?*

Miller was called to the stand still thinking about Scott's words. There was a brand-new prosecutor there, not Brian John or Jeff Pietrzyk, but a new lieutenant named Scott McDonald who had been pulled in to help. Miller couldn't believe they were going into this having never practiced together. You would never do that in the Teams.

Miller began to give an account of the stabbing that was in step with the testimony of Dille and MacNeil. The platoon was on the edge of Mosul on May 3 helping Iraqi soldiers clear a village when there was a commotion and the Iraqis arrived at the compound with a wounded ISIS fighter.

Eddie came back from the front lines without explanation, he said. "I saw him arrive at the scene. It was just him. And, yeah, that was surprising, because I didn't hear anything over the radio."

From the prosecutors' table, Pietrzyk noticed the mention of the radio and waited for the young prosecutor to ask for an explanation. Why had Miller not heard Eddie tell the platoon "He's mine" when the other witnesses had? It was a small detail, but telling. Pietrzyk had joined the case only about two weeks before, but knew the Gallagher family was on a public campaign accusing Miller and the other witnesses of lying. Pietrzyk had almost no time to learn the case, but he did have one advantage: He was fresh. He had no investment in the investigation that could bias him and he hadn't come in dead set on trusting the witnesses.

Miller had changed that. Pietrzyk had interviewed him before trial and specifically asked if he had heard Eddie come over the radio and say, "No one touch him, he's mine." Miller said he had not. The battery in his radio had been loose that morning, he explained. It had been going in and out without him noticing. If Eddie had said anything about the ISIS prisoner, Miller hadn't heard it. For Pietrzyk, this was huge. If the platoon truly had been lying to try to frame Eddie, they would have cooked up a consistent story. They would have all said they witnessed the same litany of damning details. But Miller had not. That told Pietrzyk that this SEAL was completely trustworthy. The others probably were, too. It gave Pietrzyk confidence in the whole case. He hoped that McDonald would ask that question. He didn't.

Instead the new lieutenant wandered through questions in a way Miller had never encountered. On the stand, Miller was struggling. The man who had been the backbone of Alpha seemed to teeter on a tightrope of worry. With no preparation, he didn't know what was expected of him. He wanted to avoid answering in the wrong way. He paused. He stammered. He equivocated. He had not had a chance to review what he said to NCIS more than a year before, and he was unsure about simple details. He testified that he saw the Iraqi Humvee bring in the captive and that he watched Eddie start to give medical care. But he couldn't remember who else was working on the captive. He couldn't explain exactly why he left the scene. All of Miller's take-charge confidence seemed to have evaporated, as if the courtroom was his kryptonite.

The new prosecutor stumbled through questions on how Miller returned to the yard and spotted Eddie kneeling over the kid with his hunting knife.

Corey Scott was there, Miller said. "There was another SEAL that was there as well on the other side. And there was somebody also behind, but I can't see like their faces."

Miller was visibly nervous as he tried to picture it. Eddie, he said, "was on both of his knees and he was kind of like leaning forward a little bit, his shoulders were forward. I kept walking and I saw his— I saw him stab the prisoner in the neck, on the side of the neck."

The new prosecutor asked Miller to describe the blood flowing out of the wound.

"It just came out," Miller said. His wife had just had their second son, and he reached for a familiar image. "It looked similar to a baby throwing up."

Miller gestured with his hand to show where the knife entered.

The new prosecutor was about to move on, but the judge intervened to tell him how to do his job. The official court record wouldn't be able to see Miller's hand, he said.

"Thank you, Your Honor. And for the record, Chief Miller gestured. He had his hand on the right side of his neck. I'm not an anatomist." He pointed to the left side of his neck.

"Other side," Miller said grimly.

"I apologize," the prosecutor said.

Miller was not inspired by the leadership he was getting, but he pressed on. He testified that after the stabbing he immediately went to find the officer in charge. He told Jake Portier what happened and said they should leave. Instead the officer conducted a reenlistment ceremony and pulled everyone together for a photo.

It hurt Miller to say it, but he admitted he was in the photo. He didn't agree with it at the time, but he had done it anyway. "It's just unprofessional," he told the jury. "There's no reason for it."

The evening of the stabbing, Miller said, Eddie had confronted him about the killing. "He said, 'Who's not good with this?' And I paused and said, 'I'm not good with this. I'm not good with it.'" Miller said. "And he sighed. And then he told me that he was going to get another one."

The prosecutor then pivoted unexpectedly. He asked Miller if on that deployment, Eddie ever said he killed four women. The judge cocked his head in surprise. As Miller started to say yes, Parlatore shot up from his seat and yelled, "Objection!"

The judge shot a disappointed look at the young lawyer representing the Navy. To the jury he said, "Members, I apologize." He asked them to leave the court.

With the jury gone, the judge did not try to hide his annoyance. "Come on, guys," he said to the prosecution. "You just can't launch in here with talking about killing four women and there's nothing like that on the charge sheet." He glared at the new prosecutor. "You owe me better than that."

The prosecutor, clearly realizing he had just screwed up, said, "I apologize, Your Honor."

Eddie watched the testimony from the defense table with no sign of malice, even though he considered Miller the leader of the effort to turn him in and the worst kind of traitor. On Facebook his wife, Andrea, had been taunting Miller with the same style of insulting nickname the president often used, making fun of the supposedly sealed evidence in his taped NCIS interview, calling him "Cryin' Craig Miller." But in the courtroom, Eddie didn't bat an eyelash as Miller laid out the bloody details. At recess, before Parlatore got to question Miller, Eddie stood up and leaned casually against the bar. Andrea came over and kissed him. They talked low, faces close, and he smiled. They didn't seem worried at all. They knew what was coming for Miller.

Miller knew little about courtrooms and didn't really know what a cross-examination was. He watched almost no TV, so he had missed the courtroom dramas where lawyers angrily confront witnesses. He just thought he had to tell the truth. No one in the prosecutor's office had warned him that it was Parlatore's job to try to shred his credibility.

"How many times did you meet with NCIS and the prosecutors?" Parlatore asked at the start of cross-examination. Miller said he wasn't sure, but it was several.

Yet you refused to meet with the defense, he said. You hate Eddie Gallagher, don't you?

"I think I don't trust Eddie Gallagher," Miller said.

You told NCIS you thought he was evil, Parlatore said.

Yes, Miller said. He looked around the room. He didn't know where this was going.

Parlatore planned to show that Miller was the leader of the Sewing Circle conspiracy, driven by hatred and a bald-faced liar. He'd been privately telling people for weeks that when Miller broke down in tears at the NCIS office a year before, they were clearly fake tears squeezed out to manipulate the investigators, and he couldn't wait to get Cryin' Craig Miller on the stand.

You set up the Sewing Circle, Parlatore said. You sent a text to the other guys about "getting together to get their stories straight."

Miller said he didn't remember that text. He shifted in his chair a bit uncomfortably. The Navy prep had been so minimal that no one told him it would include Alpha's private text messages. How had Eddie's lawyer even gotten those?

Parlatore smiled at him. How about the text where you said, "I spoke with Al and he's good with the deal," the lawyer said. What deal did the Sewing Circle have worked out?

Miller stammered. He couldn't believe he was getting attacked when he had worked so hard to try to do the right thing. He stumbled, caught off guard. "The deal was for us to hold off going to talk to the master chief and the commodore while they I guess tried to get Eddie out of state or continue on with their investigation—I don't know," he said, exasperated.

Parlatore switched to the day of the stabbing, asking rapid-fire detailed questions that left Miller flustered. What was the age of the fighter? Miller said he didn't know. When you first talked to NCIS about the stabbing, you didn't say you saw any blood, did you? Miller said he didn't remember. In the photo with the dead fighter, is there any blood on Eddie Gallagher? Miller said he didn't know. Who are the SEALs in the platoon who wore helmet cams? Miller said he wasn't sure. What did Miller say to Portier when he reported the stabbing? Miller said he couldn't remember, specifically. "But I remember telling him we should leave because we were combat-ineffective and stuff was going down that was not good," he said.

Then what did you do? Parlatore asked.

Miller said he didn't remember.

You don't remember? Parlatore raised his voice, as if to clue in the jury that they should be suspicious. Hasn't NCIS and the prosecution asked you this question before?

"Sir," Miller said, clearly growing frustrated. "This process has been a very long process, I don't remember every conversation I've had. I don't know!"

He looked around the room, as if searching for help. None of the guys from Alpha were there. The prosecutors had their heads down, taking notes. He was alone.

Where was the body put afterward? Parlatore demanded. Miller said he wasn't sure. Was the body still there the next day? "I think it was," Miller said.

Parlatore raised his voice again. "You're trying to report your chief for stabbing this terrorist. Did anybody think to go take a picture of the body, take a picture of the stab wound, if one exists?"

Miller stammered. No, he said.

Then Parlatore switched gears again. "You ever lived in New Mexico?" he asked.

Miller paused. He said no. He was confused. What did New Mexico have to do with this? He looked over at the prosecutors for help.

Then how come you were a volunteer police officer there? Parlatore asked.

A tiny town in New Mexico for a few years had issued police badges to nearly any volunteer deputy who paid four hundred dollars. They didn't have to do anything but sign a check. The volunteers were almost all from out of state. Scores of SEALs had gotten in on the deal because it gave them the ability to get around concealed weapons laws in California. It was a classic frogman workaround for a group of guys raised to believe the rules didn't apply. The guy who claimed to have killed Osama bin Laden had done it. So had Eddie's knife-making buddy Andrew Arrabito and the SEAL sitting on the jury. Eventually authorities caught wind of the scheme and shut it down. But Parlatore had learned that Miller had gotten in on the deal, too.

I volunteered for them, Miller said sheepishly. I never worked there.

No, it was a scam, Parlatore said. You were part of a scam that would allow you to get a badge and carry a concealed weapon in all fifty states. Did you ever get permission from the Navy to volunteer off duty? Did you ever do any patrols for them?

The Sheriff looked downcast. He realized, maybe for the first time, that he was just as vulnerable to the dark side of the frogman subculture as every other SEAL. He said no.

One of the Marines in the jury watched Miller, convinced that he was hiding something. After seeing the photos and texts from the stabbing on the first day, the juror had been ready to convict. Now he wasn't sure. Something messed up was definitely going on in Alpha platoon. But what? He wasn't sure he could trust the chief or the men.

Miller left the courtroom feeling hollowed out. He had watched his chief commit murder. He had kept pushing forward even though no one seemed to care, including the president. He kept getting knocked down, but he refused to ring the bell. He had sworn to serve and protect the rule of law, and now finally, he thought the battle had come. He wanted to tell the world what he had seen. He wanted it heard. He wanted justice. But he got on the stand and it seemed like a struggle for the prosecutor to even ask questions. Then Parlatore hit him with so many things that had nothing to do with the murder, and the Navy never seemed to object. He wondered if, amid the fusillade from the defense attorney, anyone had heard what he said about Eddie.

Miller checked the news later that day to see how he had done on the stand, and his fears were confirmed. One news outlet ran an article that began, "The main thing to remember about Navy SEAL Chief Craig Miller's testimony on Wednesday is that he didn't seem to remember a lot."

A CRUSH OF news crews jockeyed for the right shot in the parking lot at the end of the day. Cameras were barred from the courthouse, but appetite for news of the trial was ravenous. Timothy Parlatore stepped out of the courthouse and greeted the throng with a smug grin for the first of what would become sometimes twice-daily public briefings by the defense.

It appeared to be a key part of Parlatore's strategy. Inside the court there were rules of conduct, of evidence, of cross-examination, a chance for a response on the record. But not out in the parking lot.

Parlatore could give the daily defense spin on everything that happened, knowing that the Navy's lawyers and leadership would not respond. Even the civilian Navy spokesman whose job was to speak to the press just stood by with his arms crossed.

Parlatore called the prosecution embarrassingly inept. Witnesses were traitors colluding in a conspiracy. NCIS was corrupt. And Miller? "Craig Miller is an absolute liar," he proclaimed. "When you're not telling the truth you can't remember anything," he said. That, he told the media, is what everyone saw in the courtroom that day.

Parlatore knew the seven jurors couldn't necessarily hear what he was saying. Another lawyer might not have bothered with the cameras because those millions of viewers didn't get a vote. But Fox News was in the crowd of cameras, and Parlatore knew that the president, who was mulling a pardon, would be watching. Even if the seven jurors couldn't hear him, the all-important eighth juror in the White House would hear just fine.

A reporter asked how Eddie was holding up. Parlatore's tone became dour. "This entire process for him has been difficult. People he thought were his brothers, who he went to combat with, then turned on him."

Eddie left the courtroom out the front door and passed the cameras feeling good. He had enjoyed watching his lawyer pick Miller apart piece by piece. Parlatore had gotten Miller so frustrated that Eddie later joked he saw him almost cry. From Eddie's point of view, it couldn't have gone better. As the cameras crowded around and reporters shouted questions, he and Andrea got into their convertible and drove off.

CHAPTER 14

THE WOODSHED

THE NEXT MORNING, Eddie arrived outside the courtroom with Andrea on his arm, just as he had every morning. As usual, she was wearing a body-hugging dress and dark sunglasses and carrying a coffee cup. As usual, they breezed through the front door and were followed by a line of defense lawyers and investigators and Eddie's brother and parents. But something had changed. For the first time Eddie brought along his teenage stepdaughter and stepson.

The reporters watching the family file into the courtroom did a double take. Medic Corey Scott was slated to testify that morning. For prosecutors he was the key witness that everything rested on. He had been the closest to the body and was the one who saw the stabbing most clearly. He was also the guy with the medical expertise who could describe the seriousness of the wounds, and he had stayed at the victim's side as his blood pumped out into the dirt. Everyone following the case expected it to be a pretty gruesome morning for Eddie. Not one you would want to have the kids watch.

An aide for Congressman Duncan Hunter was also in the court-room for the first time, monitoring the proceedings so he could report back to his boss. The reporters filing into the press seats in the back row of the gallery noted the new faces and began whispering to one another behind their notebooks. The reporters now had the same suspicion as Dylan Dille: Something was definitely up.

A few minutes later Brian John called Scott to the stand. After this witness John planned to go back to be with his family. He had spent almost every free minute outside of court dealing with his father's sudden death and trying to console his mother. He was tired and flustered but determined to do his best.

Scott walked in looking like he had just stepped off a Cracker Jack box. He wore the classic Navy enlisted dress uniform, wide-legged white trousers and a white tunic with blue stripes on the collar. His head was shaved, and around his thick neck he had a neatly knotted dark neckerchief.

Before Scott began his testimony, he had arranged for the judge to go over his immunity deal on the record. His lawyer, Brian Ferguson, was in the gallery, wearing a suit instead of his customary faded blue polo. Ferguson looked around the courtroom with a nervous grin. He had been working for months to orchestrate this moment.

Before trial, Ferguson told the prosecutors Scott would refuse to cooperate any further unless he had two kinds of immunity. The first was testimonial immunity, which would bar the Navy from using any of Scott's testimony on the stand against him. He also insisted on transactional immunity, which prevented the Navy from prosecuting Scott for any crime he admitted to, even if investigators later tracked down evidence independent of Scott's testimony. Ferguson then went a step further and got an immunity agreement not only from the Navy but from the U.S. Department of Justice. The government gave in grudgingly, believing it had no choice.

"This is the golden ticket," Ferguson told his client after working out the deal. As long as Scott didn't lie on the stand, he could say anything and not get in trouble. He was completely bulletproof. By that time Scott had a young child and a second on the way. It was important for him to know he wouldn't get in trouble.

That morning, the judge advised Scott of the two different layers of immunity he had with the Navy, then asked him if he would agree to testify. Scott looked over at Ferguson, who nodded vigorously from the gallery. Scott looked back at the judge and said, "Yes, Your Honor."

Brian John had watched over several months as Scott had slowly changed from a willing whistleblower to a reluctant witness protected by a lawyer, but he felt the case was safe. He knew Scott was working with Ferguson, but the immunity arrangement the Navy had worked out would still lock Scott into his previous statements. Those statements included all the key points about the stabbing. John knew what the medic was going to say on the stand. All that was left to do was have him say it.

John stood up after the jury was seated. He had the Ghost raise his right hand and swear to tell the truth. Then he began. He knew this witness was critical. The first three witnesses had not gone great. MacNeil had not witnessed key moments of the crimes. Dille laid out what he had seen powerfully, and with conviction, but the evidence for the shootings was weak. And while Craig Miller had witnessed the stabbing, his testimony had foundered under disjointed questioning and legal missteps. The Navy needed Scott to save the case. John was determined to give this key witness all he had.

He asked the medic a few establishing questions about his role in the platoon and where Alpha was deployed, then said, "I'm going to direct you to the incident with the prisoner. Do you recall the incident?"

"Yes, I do," said Scott. He was slouched down in the plastic witness chair, swiveling slightly like a kid in the back row of the class.

John had to walk Scott through a series of simple questions about that morning, starting with Eddie coming over the radio and saying, "No one touch him, he's mine," and work up to the stabbing and the reenlistment. They had gone through it all several times before in the office.

"What do you first recall about that day?" John asked.

Scott replied with all the emotion of a reptile.

"I was in a vehicle and there was some sort of commotion. I don't remember if it was some sort of radio traffic or watching people convene to the other side of the building. For whatever reason I went over there. While I was on my way over there someone asked me to grab my med bag. I went back, got my med bag, went over to where the ISIS fighter was."

"You heard something over the radio, do you remember what that was?" John asked.

"No, I don't," Scott said without hesitation. He didn't explain more.

John paused and looked directly at Scott. He needed Scott to say he'd heard Eddie say something like "No one touch him, he's mine." That detail would help establish Eddie's intent: Eddie heard there was an ISIS captive, he said the captive was "mine," he went and killed the captive. Clear premeditation. John was sure Scott had said it before. His failure to say it here was confusing. The pause grew uncomfortably long as John shuffled through papers, looking for something.

"Okay . . ." he said, distracted. "You said after you had heard something over the radio—sorry, would anything help you refresh your recollection about what you had heard over the radio chatter? Would your previous statement to NCIS refresh your memory?"

It was a standard move in criminal court: Show the witness the transcript where he said those words, forcing him to admit them.

"It's possible," Scott said.

John handed Scott a stack of paper. "Does that refresh your recollection about what you heard over the radio chatter?" he asked.

Scott glanced at it briefly and looked right at the prosecutor.

"No, it does not," he said.

John was incredulous. "You still don't remember?" he asked curtly. This was supposed to be an easy question.

"No," Scott said. He sounded bored, as if going through some ceremony he had long ago lost interest in.

"Okay," John said, shuffling through his notes again, trying to regain his footing. "So after you heard whatever you heard over the radio chatter, what, uh, what did you do next?"

"I don't remember if it was radio chatter or some other commotion, I want that to be clear," Scott said.

John was confused. The Navy needed Eddie's statement over the radio and for some reason Scott wouldn't give it to him. It was a tiny fact, but huge for Eddie. Without premeditation, a life sentence was off the table. Maybe Scott knew that, maybe not, but either way, it didn't look like he was going to give it to the prosecution.

John pressed on with questions leading to the murder. Scott described going over to the captive and seeing Eddie and the other medic, T. C. Byrne, providing treatment.

"What treatments did you witness when you walked up there?" the prosecutor asked.

"I don't remember," Scott said.

There was another awkward pause. John looked at Scott. Of course Scott remembered the treatments. He had described them all multiple times before. Now, suddenly, Scott's memory was getting fuzzy? John muttered under his breath as he shuffled through his papers again, unable to find what he needed. "Just a moment, please, Your Honor," he said.

Scott poured himself a glass of ice water. The jingle of ice cubes was clear in the silent room. Eddie's children watched from the gallery. His wife leaned over and whispered to Bernard Kerik. The jury members' eyes shuttled from the witness to the prosecutor. Finally, John found what he was looking for. "Would looking at a transcript of your interview with NCIS help refresh your recollection?"

"It's possible," Scott said, sounding even more bored than he had earlier. Scott took a leisurely glance over the paper and sniffed, then looked up.

"Does that refresh your recollection of the treatments that have been done?" John asked.

"Not really," Scott said.

John slapped his stack of papers down on the prosecution table. He had never had a witness resist like this. Suddenly it hit him what was happening. The witness appeared to be deliberately sabotaging the prosecution. Even though Scott had been called to testify by the Navy, it appeared he had become a witness for the defense.

Trial attorneys can spend years learning how to draw details out of reluctant or combative witnesses. If they know the statements they want to elicit, they can build questions like traps that lead only to one simple answer. In the quiet world of Navy law, John had never needed to perfect that skill. Now he was off-balance and didn't know how to move forward. He could have asked for a recess so he could have time to confer with the senior attorney. But he decided to push ahead with his original plan.

John went back to the murder. Scott seemed to relent. He described how he had knelt down next to the fighter and pressed two fingers against the side of the neck to feel his pulse. It was normal. There were no injuries to the neck. He felt the breath coming out of the tube inserted in the kid's throat. It was normal, too. Then he sat there, monitoring the patient. All of it was consistent with his interviews with NCIS.

"What happened next, if anything?" the prosecutor asked, knowing that Scott had been interviewed by NCIS and the prosecution at least six times and each time he said next Eddie stabbed the prisoner. But there was tension in John's voice that made it clear he had no idea what Scott would say this time.

Next, T. C. Byrne left the scene, Scott said. "And then at some point Chief Gallagher pulled out his knife and . . ."

Scott paused. Four seconds went by. It was a brief time by most measures but an eternity in the middle of an eyewitness statement about a murder. Eddie's family and the reporters packed in the gallery barely took a breath.

In those four long, drawn-out seconds, the images of the chief kneeling over the body in the sun-bleached gravel almost certainly flashed before Scott's eyes. But there was also time for flashes of the conversations with Ferguson and with Eddie. There was time to consider what Scott planned to say, what he practiced saying, what he was advised to say. And there was time to hesitate and to think about how everything would play out among pirates and among SEALs. Even though it was just four seconds, there was time to remember that for months he had been thinking about Alpha and the different possible meanings of the word *loyalty*.

If nothing else, the four-second pause showed hesitation. Whatever Scott's plan was going in, he had come to a key moment, and he seemed to waver.

What happened next, if anything?

"Chief Gallagher pulled out his knife and . . ." *One. Two. Three. Four.* Scott made his decision and pushed forward, ". . . stabbed the ISIS fighter right underneath the collarbone."

There it was.

The eyewitness had seen the stabbing. And he had said it on the stand. The biggest box on the prosecutors' list had been checked. John relaxed just a bit. He was over the hump. Whatever Scott had been planning, it looked like he had stepped back from the brink.

"And how many times did he stab the ISIS fighter?" John immediately asked, relieved that the most important fact had now come out.

"I don't remember," Scott said.

John sighed. Scott was back to his original tactic.

John leafed angrily through his notes. The first time Scott talked to NCIS he said he had seen Eddie stab the victim "two or three times" and "a few times," pushing the knife from the base of the neck "down into the neck, lungs." The second time he told NCIS that Eddie had "stabbed the ISIS fighter two or three times in the neck and then went around him and stabbed him again in the chest." John shuffled through the prosecution's stacks of documents furiously, looking for the third and fourth time Scott had described the stabbings. Every time Scott was interviewed, he was asked to read over his past statements and make additions or corrections. He never made any big changes.

John marched up to the witness stand with papers in hand. He had Scott review the notes from one interview, then a second. Whatever calculation Scott was making mystified John. If the witness was trying to help Eddie, why would he say he saw the stabbing but then balk at the number of stabs? It had John rattled all over again. He asked if any of the notes had refreshed his recollection.

"No, it has not," Scott said calmly.

After several seconds of searching and trying to find yet more interview notes, John gave up and pressed on. He started to ask about Eddie leaving the scene, but then realized he had lost his bearings and skipped a couple of questions. He apologized and brought Scott back to the stabbing. "After he stabbed the prisoner," John said, "can you please show the members the direction of the knife and how and where he stabbed him?"

"Behind the collarbone, parallel with the head, down right here," Scott said, showing how the knife stabbed down through the base of the neck toward the lungs. Eddie's wife and stepchildren watched without moving.

"What was your reaction to this?" John asked.

"I was startled and I froze up for a little bit," Scott said.

"What did you do next?"

"I stayed at the scene until the ISIS fighter asphyxiated," Scott said.

John pushed on to the enlistment ceremony and the confrontation the platoon had with Eddie where Eddie threatened to kill guys for talking. Again, Scott resisted. He downplayed the threat Eddie made, said he couldn't remember key details.

John sat down frustrated after forty-one minutes of questioning, not realizing that the worst was yet to come. In the midst of his testimony, Scott had set a trap—a trap that the defense attorney, Timothy Parlatore, was ready to spring. When Scott had uttered the word "asphyxiated," Parlatore punched Eddie in the leg under the defense table and whispered to him, "We got 'em!"

PARLATORE STOOD UP SMILING, wearing a particularly busy blue-and-orange paisley tie. He walked up to the podium and looked at the medic.

"You didn't think Chief Gallagher was serious about killing members of the platoon, did you?" he said with confidence.

"No," Scott said politely. He clearly wasn't nervous about facing Parlatore.

"How long you been in the Navy?" Parlatore asked.

"Ten years now," Scott said.

"You ever met a chief that didn't threaten to kill members of his platoon in jest?" he asked. Chuckles rippled through the courtroom. Members of the jury smiled.

"No," Scott said, grinning and shaking his head.

"If you had thought that was a serious threat you would have reported it, right?" Parlatore asked.

"Yes," Scott said.

It was a textbook cross-examination. Ask several simple questions building to a larger point. Never ask one you don't know the answer to. Hit the punch line and move on. John and Pietrzyk sat at the prosecutors' table, unsure where Parlatore was going.

Parlatore asked several questions that suggested to the jury that the platoon had little combat experience before Mosul and that several of the men, including Scott, didn't like Craig Miller. It was the first time he had ever made a statement like that. Unlike Scott's testimony with Brian John, there was no hemming or hawing. There was no not remembering. He answered like a willing ally.

Now Parlatore turned to the stabbing. He appeared to already know the answers to all of his questions. "You said you saw chief Gallagher stab this individual. You never saw any blood, did you?"

"No."

"There wasn't any blood on his knife, was there?"

"No."

He asked a few more questions about the stabbing and Scott's medical training, then paused for dramatic effect. He turned toward the jury and raised his voice just slightly. "You used an interesting word. You said you watched him until he 'asphyxiated.' Asphyxiated as a combat medic, that means someone who is deprived of oxygen, doesn't it?"

"Yes."

"Why'd you use that word?" Parlatore asked. He thought he knew the answer. It had all been choreographed beforehand.

"That was . . . what killed him," Scott said.

"You didn't say that Chief Gallagher suffocated him, did you?" Parlatore said.

"No."

"Craig Miller suffocate him?" Parlatore asked, raising his voice.

"No."

"Did *you* suffocate him?" he said accusingly. It was time to spring the trap.

"Yes."

Scott didn't bat an eye. He didn't stammer. There was no regret or worry, no pause of four seconds. He took credit for the killing with a confidence that almost sounded like relief. The courtroom was silent, absolutely frozen except for the reporters scribbling madly in the back row. The jury was locked on Scott. Everyone, even the prosecutors, seemed breathless waiting for what would come next.

Parlatore let out a quick breath—a kind of half laugh. Huh. After a brief pause, he said, simply, "How?"

Scott continued with his reptilian delivery even though he was about to shatter the whole case, and he knew it.

"After Chief Gallagher left the scene, I was left there monitoring him. I thought he would die, but he was continuing to breathe normally as he had before, so I held my thumb over his E.T. tube until he stopped breathing," Scott said, referring to the plastic endotracheal tube protruding from the victim's throat.

Parlatore pointed over at the prosecution and said, "Have you told *them* that he asphyxiated?"

Parlatore was going to pile it on. Another SEAL had just taken the rap for the murder. Now Parlatore wanted to make it clear to the jury that the Navy was at fault for not figuring it out before throwing Eddie in the brig. It wasn't enough to create doubt that his client murdered someone, he wanted to make the prosecutors and agents look guilty in the process.

Scott explained that he had told the prosecutors and investigators multiple times that the kid had asphyxiated, but no one had ever asked him *how* he asphyxiated.

"Nobody ever asked you a single follow-up question on that?" Parlatore asked.

"No," Scott said.

Parlatore didn't act shocked because he wasn't. Before the trial, Ferguson and Scott sat down at least twice with Eddie's legal team to go through his story. Scott answered questions right up to when Eddie walked away after stabbing the prisoner. How did he die? asked Eddie's team. It was the same kind of question NCIS and Navy prosecutors had asked. But with Eddie's lawyers, Scott gave a very different response. He said he couldn't answer without incriminating himself. He couldn't say what happened, but Eddie hadn't killed the guy. Eddie's lawyers later claimed they didn't know exactly what Scott would say, but began preparing for something shocking and exculpatory to be revealed in court. Andrea brought the kids to come watch.

Now it was time to exonerate Eddie. Parlatore asked why the medic decided to kill the nameless prisoner.

"I knew he was going to die anyways. And I wanted to save him from waking up to whatever was going to happen next to him," Scott said calmly.

"What does that mean?" Parlatore said. It was an absolutely vital clarification. Parlatore needed to make sure that Scott didn't give the jury the idea that the victim was going to die from the stab wounds, and out of mercy the medic had decided to put him quickly out of his misery. That would leave Eddie on the hook for murder. To protect Eddie, Scott had to make it completely clear the kid wasn't going to die from Eddie's knife. "You stated before that he was going to die anyway, there was no medevac coming for this guy, was there?" Parlatore asked.

"No," Scott said.

He was going to be turned over to the Iraqis? Parlatore said.

"Yes."

And have you ever seen how the Iraqis treat prisoners in the past? Parlatore asked.

"Yes."

"Have you ever seen them detain, treat, and then release a prisoner?"

"No."

"Have you seen them torture, rape, and murder prisoners?"

"Yes."

"Is *this* why you asphyxiated the ISIS fighter?"

"Yes."

"You weren't concerned that the ISIS fighter may die because of anything Chief Gallagher may have done, were you?"

"No."

"You were only worried about him being tortured and killed by the ERD?"

"Yes."

"No further questions," Parlatore said. He walked back to the defense table with a broad smile.

LIEUTENANT BRIAN JOHN shot up from his seat before Parlatore sat down. He had been betrayed by a witness who was on the stand trying to burn down the most important case John would probably ever work on. The fact that the medic was trying to cover his lies by insisting that the Navy had done a half-assed job was gas on the fire.

"Multiple times you were asked what happened next after the stabbing," John demanded. His voice was loud and accusing. "And you never mentioned that you had covered the tube in any way. Did you?"

"No," Scott said, still deadpan.

John read some of the medic's past statements to the court: "I kind of, like, stayed with the dude's head and then like for a few minutes until he died," and I "stayed next to the prisoner until he stopped breathing," and I "monitored the patient's vital signs until he stopped breathing." He said Scott had been given a chance to review and correct those statements.

"So when you told Mr. Parlatore that no one had ever asked you any follow-up questions with regard to how he stopped breathing, that's not entirely accurate, is it?" John said.

"I think it's accurate," Scott said, unmoved.

And now you have immunity that will protect you, John said. "So you can stand up there and you can lie—"

"Objection! Argumentative," Parlatore shouted. The judge overruled him.

In fact, lying was the one thing Scott's immunity did not protect. Later that day the Navy would start a separate perjury investigation against Scott, suspecting it could get Scott to flip and implicate Brian Ferguson and Eddie's lawyers in a conspiracy to commit the crime. But that would have to wait. In the moment, John had to focus on trying to pull the murder trial out of a nosedive. And to do that, he had to make it clear to the jury that his own key witness could not be trusted.

"You don't want Chief Gallagher to go to jail, do you?" he said.

"I don't want him to go to jail," Scott said.

This is a completely new story, John said. You have never told anyone you stopped the captive's breathing until today.

Scott said he had never told a soul except his lawyer.

"Did you tell the rest of your teammates, the ones who you knew would actually have to come up here and testify in this case?" John said. The anger was clear in his face. "Did you tell them, 'No, Chief Gallagher didn't actually kill him, I'm the one who killed the prisoner'?"

"If I'm going to be frank," Scott said, "that would be really stupid."

"Because the only time you ever said that to anyone that matters, to any official, is now when you are testifying under a grant of testimonial immunity, correct?" John demanded.

"Yes," Scott said as he swiveled listlessly in the chair, showing no contrition for what he had just done.

Scott had conned his friends in Alpha. He had pushed for a criminal investigation. In part because of him, the guys spent a year working with special agents and Navy lawyers, and went through a gauntlet of hate and harassment. It wasn't just dozens of agents and lawyers and the platoon who were counting on him, it was Captain Rosenbloom who had been biting his tongue for months, trying to preserve the fairness of the trial. It was all the SEALs who saw the Teams drifting off course and needed someone to right it. Scott had led them all on, and at the last possible moment, he grabbed the case and slit its throat.

"I have no further questions, sir," John said.

It was Parlatore's chance for a victory lap. He didn't care if the case was dead. In fact, that was the whole point. He got up and began firing off questions to reinforce the notion that while Scott had been hiding that he killed the ISIS fighter when he talked to investigators, he was telling the whole truth now.

"Did you think it was a good idea to tell NCIS, 'Hey, I did it,' without immunity?" Parlatore asked.

"No."

"Now you have the immunity, now you are able to tell the truth," Parlatore said.

"Yes."

For months, while Scott had grown increasingly reluctant with prosecutors, he had been working out a plan with Ferguson. Early on, Scott told him that he had suffocated the prisoner after Eddie walked away. True or not, Ferguson believed him and right away urged his client to tell the truth on the stand. You don't want to send another SEAL to prison because you didn't speak out, he said. How are you going to feel when your kids are graduating from high school and he's still behind bars? With guilt like that you'll end up an alcoholic, living under a bridge. Don't worry, Ferguson said, I'll get you out of this. He started building the immunity strategy. Now they had pulled it off. Scott could admit to murder and not be touched.

Parlatore pushed ahead with his victory lap. He seemed to be enjoying himself.

"You say you don't want Chief Gallagher to go to jail," Parlatore said. "Is that because you don't want an innocent man to go to jail?"

Scott, who had not hesitated to answer a single one of the dozens of questions Parlatore asked, including the one where he confessed to murder, suddenly paused. It seemed as if putting the phrases "innocent man" and "Chief Gallagher" in the same thought had tripped him up. He had, after all, testified that the chief had stabbed the prisoner in the neck. But he was going along with Parlatore now, so he didn't argue.

"Thaaaaat . . ." he acknowledged, drawing out his response as he figured out what to say, "and I believe I have always got along with Chief Gallagher. He's got a wife and a family. I don't believe he should be spending his life in prison."

It was the answer that said perhaps more about his motivations than any other. After the trial, Corey Scott always insisted that he really did suffocate that captive. He said he was telling the truth. And while other guys who testified were shocked, when it came down to it, they didn't find it too hard to believe parts of Scott's testimony. In Mosul, Scott had been left alone with the kid as blood pumped out of his neck onto the dirt. Scott had told NCIS he might have tried to put a bandage on the wounds, but as he later told Warpinski, "There was really nothing I could put a bandage on." The kid was going to die. What was a guy supposed to do? What was the humane thing to do?

Eddie had shoved the knife into a part of the neck full of major veins and arteries. Maybe Scott expected the kid to die within a few minutes, which is how long he originally told investigators he stayed with the patient before he died. But maybe staying for that long was harder than it sounded. The kid could have been struggling as blood gurgled in his lungs. His breaths could have grown frantic and agonal as he inched closer to death. The senior guys in Alpha couldn't believe what Scott had done in the courtroom, but found it at least possible to believe that Scott covered the breathing tube as an act of mercy.

The prosecutors did not. To them, Scott's testimony sounded not so much like a confession as a strategy. Yes, it made sense. But it made *too much* sense. To their trained ears, it seemed specifically crafted by legal minds not only to protect Scott but to get Eddie off.

Pietrzyk listened from the prosecutors' table, knowing that, legally, Scott couldn't take the fall for Eddie just by saying, "Eddie didn't kill that guy—I did." That would still leave Eddie on the hook for murder because of an aspect of criminal law known as *proximate cause*. Under the law, someone couldn't fatally wound another person but then not be responsible if the victim died of something else. A man who shot someone in the chest during an argument, for example, still committed murder even if the victim then staggered into the street and was hit by a car, because the shooting was the *proximate cause* of death.

Pietrzyk doubted a medic like Scott understood the legal subtleties of proximate cause, yet he watched the Ghost nimbly navigate it on the stand. It convinced him that someone had taken Scott aside and made him rehearse specific false testimony—a practice lawyers often call "woodshedding." The term implied that someone with an understanding of the law had taken the witness out to the woodshed and coached him. Going through truthful testimony was standard. Advising a witness on ways to safely lie was unethical and illegal. But also reliably effective.

On the stand, at crucial points, Scott had carefully amended his story. He never changed it enough to contradict his previous statements and potentially open himself up to perjury charges. Instead, in crucial places where his story was vague enough to leave gaps, new details emerged. It was as if someone had studied his statements to NCIS looking for places to insert material that would help Eddie while protecting Scott. In this new testimony, Eddie still stabbed the victim, but Scott saw Eddie stab the victim only once, not multiple times. This time there was no blood. Scott was careful to say he didn't think the wounds were fatal. He said the victim continued to breathe normally and appeared stable. And Scott was very clear on why he covered the tube. He didn't do it because he was concerned the boy was going to die from the stab wounds. That would mean the proximate cause of the murder was still Eddie. Instead, he killed the boy because he feared what the Iraqis would do. If the stabbing wasn't lethal—if it was a nonfatal wound with no blood—then there could be no murder, no attempted murder, no life sentence. The most Eddie could be convicted of was aggravated assault with five years in prison and a dishonorable discharge. The testimony threaded all the legal needles perfectly. It meant, if the jury believed Scott, Eddie couldn't be convicted of murder. And thanks to Ferguson's immunity deal, neither could Scott.

Pietrzyk didn't know if Ferguson or Eddie's team or some pirate he had never met had concocted the scheme, but given the strategic legal navigation evident in Scott's words, it sure looked like someone had taken the medic to the woodshed.

PARLATORE GOT UP in front of a crowd of reporters in the parking lot, grinning in his stripes and paisley. He said he was as surprised as anyone else with the medic's confession. With Eddie standing silently beside him in whites, he proclaimed that the shocking testimony proved that the case should be dismissed.

"Between all of the missteps up until now," Parlatore continued. "Between the spying operation, between the prosecutorial misconduct, between never bothering to ask their witnesses the cause of death, how much more embarrassment is the Navy going to take before they say enough?" Scott's witness stand confession was the kind of courtroom drama that typically only happened in scripted primetime dramas, and here it was playing out in real life. The Navy, as usual, said nothing.

Fox News ran the headline "Navy Won't Drop Murder Charges Against SEAL Edward Gallagher Despite Bombshell Testimony." Andrea posted an update to her tens of thousands of Facebook followers: "Big Day for our team! Gallagher's & The God Father @bernardkerik who has been a Godsend to our family and helped us to assemble our INCREDIBLE Legal Team #TEAMGALLA-GHER #TRUTH."

Craig Miller read the headlines and shook his head. After all this time, Eddie somehow had figured out a way to divide Alpha. Miller felt anger building toward Scott, as if he had just caught the SEAL abandoning his post. Then he realized it was much bigger than just the cowardice of one man. It wasn't Scott so much as the culture, the toxic loyalty that had for generations defined the SEALs.

Matt Rosenbloom read the news in his office. The commodore was just a mile across San Diego Bay but felt like he was seeing news from another planet. Parlatore was saying the Navy should dismiss the case? Was he insane? Did everyone miss the part where Corey Scott said he saw his chief stab a sedated captive in the neck? Were they not tracking that Scott was the *second* SEAL to say that in two days? No one outside the courtroom had seen the photos of Eddie posing with the corpse. They hadn't seen his racist texts or the stuff about buying drugs that Rosenbloom had seen. Part of him marveled at how masterful the Gallaghers were at unconventional warfare. The Navy was shackled by a traditional legal strategy. The Gallaghers had flanked them and were out in the bush, sniping with Fox News, Facebook, and tweets from the White House.

There was no one from the Navy to point out to the public that Scott's story had changed in critical ways. There was no one to say that, in spite of Scott, the jury could still find Eddie guilty of murder. There was just Parlatore at the microphone with Bernard Kerik behind him, and Eddie standing silent as a Ken doll to the side, beating up on the Navy for trying to give Edward Gallagher the very thing that he never gave the captive—a chance at a fair trial.

Maybe it would have been different if the victim had been presented as a real person. Maybe if the Navy had been able to find out his identity and give him a name, it would have changed how everyone viewed the killing. Maybe they could have made him a son, a brother, a human. His parents could have been seated in the courtroom right alongside Eddie's family. Maybe his father could have told the family's story of surviving years of war. Maybe if any of that had happened, the victim would have been more than just a nameless jihadi. Maybe Fox News commentators wearing red, white, and blue wouldn't have been able to turn him into a faceless caricature of all the nation's fears, just as they had turned SEALs like Eddie into a caricature of the nation's hopes.

But NCIS investigators never learned the victim's name. They never even called him "John Doe" to suggest he had a name. Throughout the whole investigation and trial he was only known as "the kid," "the victim," "the ISIS guy," "the patient," "the prisoner," "the fighter," "the terrorist," "the dirtbag."

CHAPTER 15

THE FIGHTER

HIS NAME WAS Moataz.

Before he was killed, he had run away from a father and a mother and four brothers and sisters who waited and hoped for his safe return after the war. They searched for him in hospitals and prisons and combed the rubble of bombed-out neighborhoods. For more than a year they looked and prayed. Then when Eddie was charged, news of the court-martial reached Iraq, and they finally learned what had happened to him.

Moataz Mohamed Abdullah was seventeen years old the day he was killed. He had been born in western Mosul in 2000, just a few years before the United States invaded, and grown up a Sunni Muslim in a city dominated by Sunnis. His parents were not particularly religious, nor were they part of the connected political class of Sunnis that had enjoyed preferential treatment under the dictatorship of Saddam Hussein. His father sold used cars for a living. They were simple people. Moataz went to the public schools. He worshiped at a small neighborhood mosque. He liked to play soccer in the street and swim in the Tigris. Up to the day he ran away, his parents still called him by a nickname he had been given as a baby, Azooz.

His father, Mohamed Salim, had also been born in Mosul. Before the Americans came, there was Saddam. Mohamed didn't love Saddam or hate him. He just lived with him. Saddam was far from perfect, but at least during the time of Saddam the city was safe. Sunni and Shia Muslims, Christians and Yazidis all lived together. And people bought cars. On days off, Mohamed liked to go down to the Tigris to fish in the slow green water.

By the time the United States invaded in 2003, Mohamed was married and had two sons. Moataz was the second. Mohamed tried to keep going with his old life as foreign troops surged into the city and the streets slowly fell into chaos. Saddam's ruling party was driven out of power, and there was no one to make the city run. Looting and blackouts followed. Garbage piled up in the streets. The resentment toward the American soldiers fed an armed insurgency that became increasingly bloody. Bombs targeted police stations and hospitals. Shootings and sectarian revenge killings became part of life. Suicide bombers would hit the Americans at their checkpoints. In response the Americans would sweep in at night, making scores of arrests in search of terrorist cells. A lot of people died for no reason. The raids stoked resentment, which led to more bombings. The Americans erected concrete blast walls to divide up neighborhoods. Long lines at checkpoints and harsh curfews became the norm. Residents sometimes felt like they were treated like enemies in their own city.

Mohamed tried to raise his family peacefully amid the violence, but people weren't driving as much, and his business suffered. The family sometimes barely scraped by. He and his wife kept going about their simple daily efforts to provide, hoping that with patience things would get better. Mohamed's biggest worry was that one of his loved ones might get killed in the crossfire.

When the Americans left in 2011, the Iraqi government that replaced them wasn't a big improvement. The government and military were mostly Shia Muslims and took a harsh stance toward overwhelmingly Sunni Mosul. The Iraqi soldiers stationed in the city often viewed the locals as terrorists and treated people even worse than the Americans had. Blast walls and checkpoints kept the city in lockdown. Nighttime raids still took young men from their homes.

Life in Mosul was a far cry from what it had been before more than a decade of war, but Mohamed's son, Moataz, had never known anything different. Despite the violence and uncertainty, he appeared to be growing up to be a fine young man. He did well in school and was kind to his parents. His face would light up when his mother made Mosul's famous dolmas with stuffed eggplant and spicy peppers. He shared a bedroom with his older brother and covered his half with posters of pop stars and soccer players. Soccer was his passion. When he wasn't kicking a ball, he was watching matches on TV or searching for stats about his favorite strikers.

Moataz had a natural charisma. He knew how to talk to people. He would sometimes help his father close deals on cars. Though the family business traditionally went to the oldest son, his father thought Moataz would be a better fit. He had a head for numbers and a durable charm. He was just about to start high school when the Islamic State invaded.

ISIS appeared from the west, arriving in swarms of commandeered pickups and stolen Humvees. When the fighters swept into the city, some of the family's neighbors fled. With five children and no obvious place to go, Mohamed decided to wait it out. He had seen militants attack parts of the city before, only to be driven out in a few hours. The Iraqi Army had tanks, helicopters, and thousands of troops. Taking back Mosul from what amounted to a street gang with a few Toyotas wouldn't take long. He kept the family inside and waited. But the Iraqi counterattack didn't come that day or that month, or even that year. The family found themselves living in the largest city of the Islamic State's self-described caliphate.

At first, ISIS didn't seem any worse than the city's previous occupiers. Yes, they tore down posters and billboards that displayed women in Western dress and other images forbidden by their harsh brand of Islam. They banned cigarettes, alcohol, and Western music. They shut down Moataz's school. But they also dismantled many of the blast walls and checkpoints, giving a long-lost sense of freedom and dignity to many of the locals. Sunnis were allowed to be Sunnis again, without fear or shame. There were no more curfews. No more arrests. For Sunni families, ISIS didn't behave like occupiers but rather like liberators. At least at first.

Then the fighters started taxing locals heavily. They clamped down with rules that started out strict and became draconian. They forced locals to work for ISIS, often with little or no pay. Anyone caught resisting could be killed. It wasn't long before they were beheading people in the park.

As ISIS tightened its grip on the city, Moataz was growing old enough to start venturing out on his own. He gravitated toward the soccer field in his neighborhood. Soon he was going every day and joined a local team. Mohamed was encouraged to see his son developing a passion. They still went fishing together at the river sometimes, but he allowed Moataz to spend time playing soccer with his friends—it was one of the few pleasures still available under the occupation.

One morning, Mohamed realized he had made a grave mistake. He discovered it the way parents often stumble upon the vices of their teenagers: by going through his son's phone. Moataz had left the phone out in the house. His father found videos of radical imams with long beards preaching violent jihad. There were photos of the black banner flown by ISIS. Along with the music of Western pop stars, there were ballads of jihadis singing about the glorious martyrs in the battles to come. Of all the things Mohamed could have found on his son's phone, the ISIS propaganda seemed the most dangerous, because it was a clear sign his son was being radicalized. And if his son joined ISIS, he was as good as dead.

Mohamed tried to remain calm. When Moataz came into the kitchen he confronted him and told him what he had found. He warned that those men in the streets with the big beards and guns were not true Islam. The men preaching violence were not true Islam. He had seen enough of war. He told his son to stay away. And if any of his friends were preaching that nonsense, he should stay away from them, too. Moataz promised he would. But there was a look in his eyes, almost like he was hypnotized.

Moataz kept going to the soccer field to practice with friends. ISIS guys also hung out at the field, and Moataz would sometimes scrimmage with them. They were older but not nearly as old as his father. A lot of them had good moves with the ball. They were confident and cool. They were funny. The ISIS guys started taking some of the kids under their wing. They would offer tips on ball handling. They bought new shoes and jerseys and gave them to the boys. Moataz may not have known it, but he was being recruited.

ISIS had a program called "Cubs of the Caliphate" that recruited boys as young as nine. By the end of the battle in Mosul it was a forced conscription program that sent boys in suicide belts to their death. But in the beginning, it was more subtle. ISIS knew the battle was coming and it would need young, fit bodies to fight. The soccer field was the perfect place to find them.

ISIS put up posters around the field that celebrated their righteous stand against evil and played songs that celebrated the brave men who would defend the city. The ISIS guys would often talk about what it meant to be a good Muslim. Moataz considered himself pious, but the ISIS guys insisted it wasn't enough to just pray each day. The Shias and the Americans were coming to take back the city. They would kill all of the Sunnis in Mosul. True Muslims had to stand up and fight not just for their religion but to protect their families. The enemies would kill their parents, rape their sisters. Men of God had to be willing to stand up and stop them.

One afternoon Mohamed went down to the soccer field to find his son and heard the songs and saw the posters. He saw the men giving out new shoes and filling kids' heads with lies. He realized they were grooming his boy to become a fighter. He dragged Moataz away by the arm. He slapped him and told him to think.

"You are too young to get into this. Promise me you will stop," Mohamed told him. "I need you to stay with me. We all need you with us. If you want to defend us then stay with us and help us through these difficult times."

Moataz promised he would stay. But the soccer field, the draw of his friends, the draw of being able to do something and be someone important and heroic, was too much. It didn't take long before he ran away to the soccer field again.

By 2017, the honeymoon of the ISIS occupation was long gone. The fighters increasingly clamped down on the people of Mosul. They kept demanding taxes even though the economy had collapsed. Mohamed's car business had dried up. Electricity, water, and food were increasingly scarce. Mohamed realized he had made a mistake by not fleeing in the first days of the occupation, but it was too late. Anyone who tried to escape the city at that point was shot.

When Moataz ran away, Mohamed marched down to the soccer field and forced him to go back home. It was a risk. If ISIS saw he was interfering with recruiting, he could be beaten, even killed. But he was determined. If he couldn't escape the city, at least he could try to keep his family together and alive until the fighting was over. He forbade his son again to go out and play soccer. And again, when his father wasn't watching, Moataz ran away.

By that point it was the spring of 2017. The Iraqi Army had come to the edges of the city. The final battle was underway. Everywhere ISIS was preparing for the assault, digging trenches, welding suicide cars, and recruiting any young men they could find. The American fighter jets were screaming over the city. Acrid black smoke billowed from huge piles of burning tires. It was going to be a bloodbath. At seventeen, Moataz considered himself a man, but he didn't really know how to take care of himself. He had never been out on his own. At the start of the year, he'd been injured in a bomb blast. Shrapnel just missed his head, clipping off the bottom piece of his right ear. If Moataz went into the trenches with ISIS, Mohamed had no doubt, he would soon end up dead.

Mohamed went out into the streets and found his son hanging out with his gang of soccer friends who had been tricked into thinking they were soldiers. He brought him home a third time. He was desperate to keep Moataz safe, so he chained him up in the house. But Moataz's mind was made up. The more his father told him no, the more he was determined to fight. When no one was looking, Moataz used a kitchen knife to break the chain and slipped away. His family never saw him again.

The night he ran away for good was right around when the battle for western Mosul started in earnest. Helicopters and fighter jets circled above at all times, raining down bombs. Plumes of smoke wrapped the city in a black haze. The Iraqi Army launched unguided rockets into the neighborhoods that exploded at random. There was no escape. One morning a coalition bomb hit an electrical substation near the family house. The explosion blew in all the windows, showering the family with glass. They cowered in a corner, bleeding from the cuts, not knowing when the bombing would end. Around that time, Mohamed's brother got caught in the crossfire between ISIS and Iraqi forces and was shot. Moataz was missing, but it was too dangerous to go out and look for him.

A few weeks after Moataz disappeared, two of his soccer friends came to Mohamed. They had seen him try to keep Moataz away from the field and considered him a traitor and an infidel. That day they didn't try to hide their disgust. "Moataz is missing," one of them said. "We think he was martyred during the battles." The other scowled at Mohamed and said, "He died as a brave man, not as a coward." Without saying more, they walked away.

Mohamed did not want to believe that his son had been killed, but he grudgingly accepted that it was almost inescapable. Death and destruction were all around. The city was in flames. People were getting killed every day, even while hiding in their houses. What chance did a seventeen-year-old have on the front lines?

Weeks went by with no word from Moataz. The fighting drew closer and closer to Mohamed's home. The family stayed hidden inside. Then in May 2017, the front line of the fighting passed right down the family's block. ISIS was beaten back, and Mohamed found his family suddenly liberated. For the first time in months they were able to go out and get food and clean water. They were also able to watch the news on TV, which had been forbidden under ISIS. Mohamed switched on Iraq's most popular news channel, Al Iraqiya. He couldn't believe what he saw. There on the screen, with a blue foam Al Iraqiya microphone pressed up to his face, was Moataz.

Mohamed leaned forward, listening closely. Moataz was laid out in the dirt on a street somewhere in Mosul. It was definitely him, right down to the injured right ear. One of Al Iraqiya's combat correspondents was questioning him. It was the same video footage later sent to NCIS. Mohamed could tell by the way his son mumbled and struggled for breath that he was hurt, but at least he was alive. He listened to his son say that his father had beaten him and had told him not to go with ISIS, but he went anyway so they could tell him, "Good job." He listened as the reporter then turned to the camera: "Dear viewers, here is a young man, about seventeen years old. ISIS fooled him into joining them and this is the result, he got injured during the battles. He was brought here by the heroes in ERD. They will take him to be hospitalized and then question him."

Praise God, my son is alive! Mohamed thought. He could not contain his relief. In all the death and destruction, his son somehow had been spared. He would have to go to prison for what he had done. But one day he would get out and come home. He could live his life. He could have a family. Mohamed went to tell his wife. He was overjoyed.

The Battle of Mosul ended about eight weeks later. Mohamed kept searching the city for his son. He went to the hospitals and the Iraqi Army. He went to prisons and refugee camps. He never found him. Piece by piece Mosul started to rise from the rubble. Bulldozers cleared the roads and filled in craters. Shops began to reopen, and people came back to try to piece together their neighborhoods. Many of Moataz's friends eventually went back to school. They got jobs. Some got married. Mohamed kept hoping that Moataz would one day appear at his door.

More than two years after Moataz disappeared, Mohamed read a local Iraqi news story about the trial in San Diego of the American who was accused of a number of killings in Mosul. They showed a photo of the boy the SEAL was accused of stabbing—a still from the Al Iraqiya video interview. It was Moataz.

Mohamed felt the world suddenly fall in on his chest. He had suspected for a long time that his son had been killed in the fighting. At times he had accepted it. He had tried to move on. But there was always some sliver of hope that Moataz was still alive. Learning he had been killed by an American after he had been taken captive tore a new wound in Mohamed's heart. Why would anyone do that to a child? Certainly these Americans had children, they had to know what raising them is like. Mohamed expected that kind of brutality from ISIS and maybe even from some Iraqi forces. But he had always seen the Americans as more professional, more humane. They were supposed to be the good guys. Maybe, despite all their talk about democracy and rule of law, he thought, the Americans weren't different from anyone else.

LEADING UP TO the trial, Fox News and other media often portrayed Eddie and the unnamed fighter he'd killed as polar opposites. It was us versus them, the SEALs versus the terrorists, order versus chaos, good versus evil. And in such a black-and-white fight, some commentators questioned the wisdom of even trying to follow battlefield rules that showed mercy to the enemy.

In fact, Eddie and Moataz weren't so different at all. It was their circumstances at key moments that seemed to make all the difference. Like Moataz, Eddie had also been a passionate soccer player in his teens. They both grew up in close families but chafed under their fathers' rules as they got older. They both snuck around behind their fathers' backs and got into trouble. They both were confronted by caring parents who warned them, scolded them, begged them to change their paths. And in both cases, the sons ignored the warnings. When both continued to get in trouble, their parents took desperate measures. That is where vast differences in resources and in geography offered the boys starkly different paths. Mohamed felt his only recourse was to chain his son in the house in a war-torn city; the Gallaghers sent Eddie to prep school in Connecticut.

Both efforts failed. Eddie was kicked out of prep school for fighting. Moataz broke his chain and escaped. Eddie went back to his hometown in Indiana and started hanging with a wild crowd. Moataz ran out into his neighborhood in western Mosul and joined up with the other young Sunnis who wanted to fight. Both were looking for a way out, a way to forge their manhood and prove their worth. Both thought the honorable way was through war. Both craved acceptance. They wanted to be told, "Good job." Both chose combat. And in choosing combat, their paths diverged again: Eddie became a U.S. Navy SEAL, trained and mentored in the laws of armed conflict, schooled in the expectations of maximum lethality with minimum collateral damage to noncombatants, theoretically beholden to the

Constitution. Moataz was taken in by violent radicals and got little if any training, only the assurance that God would help him against the Infidels. Two very different societies with very different expectations, but two men with a lot in common.

In the end what separated the two also brought them together—both were in Mosul fighting for what they saw as right, both felt their society and values were under attack, both were bent on destroying the other side. Of course the SEALs would bristle at the comparison. ISIS was nothing but a band of criminal marauders with no respect for individual rights. They didn't abide by the Geneva Conventions or agree to the humane treatment of captives. They were savages. The United States had discipline, rules, and laws. Though the SEALs dealt in lethal force, just like ISIS, they did it on the side of order and decency. They were professionals with standards. They were the good guys.

But when Moataz was laid out wounded in the sun-bleached gravel, helpless, underage, gasping for breath, and Eddie pushed a knife into his neck, he threw away all that order and decency. He threw away discipline and standards. He threw away the ideals and aspirations that made the United States the United States. When he did that, Eddie was no longer really a SEAL. He had turned into a pirate who was no different from the ISIS fighters he despised.

CHAPTER 16

THE VERDICT

Aᴄᴛᴇʀ Cᴏʀᴇʏ Sᴄᴏᴛᴛ testified, the trial was all but over. The Navy still had five key witnesses: T. C. Byrne, the other medic who had worked on the captive right before Eddie stabbed him; Ivan Villanueva, who had seen the stabbing from a foot away; Dalton Tolbert, who had seen the old man shot; Josh Vriens, who had watched a girl get shot down by the river; and Joe Arrington, who Vriens said could confirm the killing. The troop's leadership, Brian Alazzawi and Robert Breisch, were also on deck.

But Scott's bombshell revelation had introduced so much doubt and confusion that the prosecutors thought at best they might get an aggravated assault conviction, and even that was iffy.

In the afternoon after Scott's testimony, Byrne took the jury through how he, as lead medic, had treated the patient with Eddie. He explained the chest tubes and cricothyrotomy clearly visible in the photos, told them about how the patient was stable and then he had gone to get his gear and returned to find the patient inexplicably dead with blood pooled by his shoulder and a bandage on his neck.

"Then a lot of weird things started happening," he said. He described the photos and the enlistment ceremony. He said there had been videos, but Eddie and Portier had later told the platoon to erase everything.

Parlatore, fresh off his victory with Scott, came out and in a cross-examination tried to portray Byrne as a cowboy who was inserting chest tubes and pushing drugs into the captive for no reason, abusing him like a guinea pig so that he and other SEALs could practice medical procedures. He accused Byrne of faking his shock at the situation and showed footage of Byrne flying a small drone around the yard after the killing. Parlatore neglected to show the footage of the drone dive-bombing the captive's body with Eddie at the controls.

Byrne left the stand angry. He wasn't sure he'd been able to help the case at all, and Parlatore ended up making him look defensive, even guilty, as if by administering medical care, he was the one who had something to hide.

Dalton Tolbert and Josh Vriens took the stand the next day to testify that they saw Eddie shoot an old man and a girl from his sniper hide in the Towers. But neither of them had the kind of testimony that could counter Scott. The snipers had no dates, no names for the victims, no physical evidence to back up their stories. Parlatore demanded to know if they actually saw Eddie pull the trigger on the so-called shootings. Both admitted they had not. He turned toward the jury and asked if the snipers had thought to document the killings in any way. Both said no.

Parlatore read more embarrassing text messages and implied that both Vriens and Tolbert were part of the larger Sewing Circle conspiracy. He seemed especially tickled by quoting texts that Tolbert sent to Alpha not long before trial. For years in Alpha, Tolbert had loved to get the platoon riled up and laughing. He often acted outrageous in group texts. The trial had been delayed repeatedly by legal jockeying, setbacks, leaks, and screwups, and everyone in Alpha was growing irritated. At one point the Navy flew Tolbert to California for Eddie's trial, only to put him back on a plane with instructions to return in a few weeks. He let Alpha know just how he felt about it.

"I'm going to burn this motherfucking courthouse to the ground," Parlatore recited to the jury in a loud voice, reading from one of Tolbert's texts from that time. "If the motherfucking court burned down, I did it. What a fucking joke. Somebody fire this pussy ass fucking judge. Who's fucking courtroom is this? Time to man the fuck up fags."

After Parlatore finished, he looked at the judge, then at the jury, then at Tolbert. He wanted to show that SEALs said all sorts of stuff in texts. It wasn't just Eddie. And a lot of it was just dark humor that meant nothing. He asked if Tolbert was aware the judge was a Navy captain. Tolbert cleared his throat and said yes.

No further questions, Parlatore said.

BEHIND THE SCENES, the Navy was moving to charge Corey Scott with perjury. The top legal officer at Naval Base San Diego sent Scott a letter notifying him that he was under investigation and provided him with a Navy lawyer independent of Brian Ferguson. That was important, because the Navy wanted to learn from Scott what Ferguson had done to prepare Scott for his testimony, and whether he had ever conspired with Timothy Parlatore, Bernard Kerik, or anyone else on Eddie's legal team to come up with the carefully crafted testimony. The Navy was hoping Scott would turn on the others to save himself. He had, after all, already apparently done it once.

As they worked quietly behind the scenes, Josh Vriens took the stand. By then Vriens had heard about what Scott had done in court. It had left him feeling hollow. The one part of the SEALs he thought he could still rely on was the guys in Alpha. Apparently he was wrong. Maybe, Vriens thought, the remaining guys could still pull off a win. There was still so much evidence against Eddie.

Vriens testified that in the evening after the stabbing he had been looking at photos of the body on a computer. Eddie walked by and said, "Oh, this is the guy. I stabbed him in the side, grabbed his hair and looked him in the eyes and I stabbed him in the neck." It was, he thought, a clear and unmistakable confession that bolstered the case.

Vriens described the day when he was looking through his sniper scope and saw the girl in the flowered hijab get shot by the river. He recalled how he had assumed that ISIS had shot her, but then at the end of the day another SEAL, Joe Arrington, said Eddie claimed to have shot her. The evidence was thin, but Vriens knew Arrington would be able to back him up once he took the stand.

When asked by the prosecutor if the girl might have been a legitimate target, Vriens was unequivocal. "The girl had nothing in her hands. I wouldn't dream of her as a threat."

Then Parlatore got up. Given how intense Vriens had been in Mosul, how single-minded he had sometimes seemed in his desire to confront and kill ISIS, it was especially ironic that Parlatore's theory of the case was that Vriens was a disgruntled coward who was angry that his chief had exposed him to enemy fire. He challenged his knowledge as a sniper and fired off a number of questions that made it sound like Vriens was unlawfully colluding with NCIS. Then Parlatore got Vriens to say what could not be denied: He had not actually seen Eddie pull the trigger.

"You didn't see where the bullet came from, did you?" Parlatore demanded.

"No, sir, I did not," Vriens admitted.

"All you saw was the little girl get shot in a manner more consistent with a small-caliber bullet, is that correct?"

"That is what I saw, sir." The sniper was trying to be honest. As soon as the words left his mouth, he knew they would give the wrong impression, but the questions seemed to offer no other avenue.

"You told Lieutenant Portier, 'ISIS is shooting civilians,' correct?"

"Yes, sir."

Then Parlatore brought up the one thing Vriens dreaded most. He wasn't afraid to testify in front of Eddie. He wasn't ashamed of testifying against another SEAL, but it pained him to talk about the Switchblade strike. Parlatore seemed to know asking about the strike would push Vriens off balance. He fired questions at the sniper in a way designed to suggest Vriens was a liar, because if he wanted to report Eddie to authorities, he knew exactly how to do it, because it had been done to him.

"You know what happens if you see civilians get killed, right?" the lawyer asked.

"Unfortunately, I do, sir," Vriens said.

Andrea Gallagher seemed to enjoy watching the suffering after what the platoon had put Eddie through. In the gallery she put her arm around Bernard Kerik.

"You know how to report?" Parlatore said theatrically. "Because you were, in fact, investigated for the death of civilians, weren't you?"

"Yes, sir, I was," Vriens said. His head was bowed. He could see the last images sent from the Switchblade even as he said it.

The Navy prosecutors did little to object to Parlatore's withering cross. They seemed to be back against the ropes, unsure how to proceed. Brian John had gotten on a plane right after the Scott testimony and flown to Northern California to be with his mother. Other lawyers filled in. One was so inexperienced that when he tried to show the jury Eddie's custom hunting knife, he didn't know how to pull on the gloves used to handle evidence, and he had to try to hold the knife with most of his fingers stuck like flippers in the palms.

After testifying, Vriens walked out to his car in the parking lot, sat in the driver's seat, and had a breakdown. He covered his face and wept. The tears poured out unchecked. He had tried to do the right thing. He had resisted the warnings to keep quiet. He had stood up and told the truth. And Parlatore had made him out to be the bad guy. This trial was supposed to be when Alpha could finally stand together and be honest and be recognized for doing the right thing. Instead Vriens was punished. Rage, regret, disgust, and even relief poured out in a storm of emotion.

Eventually, the sniper wiped his eyes and looked up. The Ghost was standing outside his window, his pronounced brow looking down.

"You all right, man?" Scott said. He seemed genuinely concerned.

Vriens wiped his face, embarrassed. He now considered Scott one of Eddie's boys, and he didn't want to have anything to do with him. He certainly didn't want to cry in front of him. He looked away.

"Well . . . hey man, if you need anything, just call me," Scott said. "Or . . . I guess you don't want to talk to me, so . . . maybe call Craig."

He walked away.

THE PROSECUTORS' CASE was so wounded that they shifted into damage control. They had already been broadsided by Corey Scott. They didn't want to take more hits, so they pulled the next two witnesses.

Ivan Villanueva was supposed to be the third SEAL to testify that he saw the stabbing, but Jeff Pietrzyk no longer trusted him. Villanueva was represented by Brian Ferguson, and during the lead-up to the trial his story had subtly shifted much like Scott's. At first Villanueva had told NCIS that he saw Eddie stab the prisoner. He was looking away and might not have caught all of it, but there had been movement, and when he looked over Eddie stabbed the guy in the rib. After Villanueva got an immunity deal, he wanted to add amendments to his account. Yes, Eddie stabbed the prisoner, he told NCIS, but when he did, the prisoner was already dead. It was a change that he had never mentioned to senior members of the platoon or anyone in NCIS. And it had big consequences. Stabbing a dead body wasn't murder, it was a crime called "desecration of a corpse," and under military rules carried a maximum seven years in prison. Just like Scott's change, it would get Eddie out of a life sentence.

Villanueva was a key witness but also another potential bombshell, so the prosecutors never called him to testify.

It was the same with Joe Arrington. At first, the JTAC told NCIS that he had heard Eddie fire a shot from the Towers, then spotted an old man with a water jug bleeding on the ground. But after Arrington retained Ferguson, he clarified that he wouldn't necessarily describe the man as "old" and was not so sure how much time had really elapsed between when he heard Eddie shoot and when he saw the wounded man. It might have been several minutes, maybe more. Pietrzyk decided that he, too, wasn't worth the risk.

In a case where witnesses had always been the strong point, the prosecution was suddenly running short, and that was not entirely the fault of Brian Ferguson. There were other witnesses who could have bolstered the SEALs' accounts, but not only were they never called, they were never even interviewed. NCIS never put more than a handful of agents on the case and had kept the investigation focused only on Alpha platoon. NCIS never spoke to the psychologists in Germany who interviewed Alpha right after the deployment. NCIS never interviewed members of the platoon's families who learned of the killings while the SEALs were still in Iraq. NCIS never interviewed Golf platoon. There were SEALs in Golf platoon who would have told agents that they had heard Eddie brag about shooting the girl and other crimes. Agents not only never interviewed those SEALs, it was not even clear they had done enough work to realize there was another platoon living next door in Mosul.

The Navy also had evidence in its possession that it wasn't allowed to use. Before the trial started, the court barred prosecutors from presenting their most compelling physical evidence: the DNA on the knife. Analysis had found Eddie's DNA and the DNA of an unknown male from the region around Mosul. There was too little residue to tell if what was on the knife was blood of the victim or from the touch of some unrelated Iraqi. Because the Navy had never figured out the identity of the victim, it had never been able to collect family DNA for a match. All the Navy knew was that it had generic Middle Eastern male DNA.

DNA is so persuasive as evidence that the defense argued it threatened to unfairly lead the jury to conclude a stabbing took place, even though the Middle Eastern DNA could have come from millions of unrelated people, including SEALs at Coronado. The judge ruled that any mention of DNA had the potential to bias jurors more than it had the potential to reveal anything, and ordered that the DNA on the knife could not be mentioned to the jury.

After what happened with Corey Scott, the prosecutors wanted the jurors to see the visitor logs showing that Scott and other potential witnesses had gone to see Eddie in the brig. The judge wouldn't allow it. Prosecutors also couldn't mention Eddie's drug use. It was a crime, but it had not been charged, so it was off-limits. And, most frustrating of all for the Navy, the prosecution could not mention Eddie's character. All the lying and stealing, made-up kills, racist slurs, and false claims for medals were blocked because evidence of a bad character was not evidence of a crime. Just because Eddie was a turd didn't mean he was a murderer. It was human nature to draw conclusions, but because of that, over the years courts had ruled that character evidence carried so much weight that prosecutors could use it only in certain circumstances. If, for example, a defense witness testified that Eddie was a fantastic chief, prosecutors were then free to object and present evidence to the contrary. During the trial, Parlatore had been careless. He talked about Eddie's character multiple times, saying he was a good chief, and let a witness do the same on the stand. But one of the young prosecutors brought in last-minute had failed to object. Later in the trial the lead prosecutor, Commander Jeff Pietrzyk, tried to fix their mistake by asking to call Tom MacNeil back to the stand, arguing to the judge that MacNeil would tell the jury "that Chief Gallagher multiple times was a leadership problem, that he would turn GPS off and go beyond areas that the Commanding Officer authorized."

The judge cut him off. "All right," the judge said. "I'm not going to allow any of that testimony."

"Sir, there's more," Pietrzyk said, almost pleading.

"I'm not allowing you to wander into that on the record," the judge fired back. It was too late. They had missed their chance. All the jury ever heard was Parlatore telling them what a good SEAL Eddie was.

Maybe most compelling, the jury was not allowed to hear key testimony from Master Chief Brian Alazzawi. More than a year before trial, Alazzawi had confronted Eddie about the captive, and Eddie admitted that the guy had gone for his gun, so "I fucked him up." But Alazzawi had solicited the statement without first reading Eddie his rights, which the judge had ruled he was required to do under military law, so Parlatore had gotten the confession thrown out.

Of course, the jury never heard what it wasn't told. They didn't notice the witnesses that were pulled. They never knew about the Middle Eastern DNA on the knife. At one point Parlatore told the jurors there was "nothing found on the knife." The prosecution couldn't correct him.

The prosecutors called experts to testify about the stab wounds and the cause of death, but with no body and no autopsy, it wasn't very convincing. On cross-examination, the Navy's medical expert admitted to Parlatore he could not determine the cause of death—something Parlatore played up in his daily parking lot briefings.

Short on physical evidence, with two key witnesses pulled and two key prosecutors either barred from the case or waylaid by personal circumstances, the Navy's case slowly fell apart. Only six days after opening statements, the prosecution in the Navy's most complex murder case in years rested.

Pietrzyk was downcast. It was a decent case that had been dealt a bad hand. With Chris Czaplak pulled, Ferguson working behind the scenes, and a jury full of combat grunts, he wasn't sure there was much of a chance to get a conviction even before Corey Scott. But maybe it didn't matter. Even if they were able to pull off a win, the president was indicating he would reverse it anyway.

PARLATORE STOOD UP the next day in front of the jury in a striped dark blue shirt with a white collar to present the defense. He would not be calling Eddie to testify on his own behalf. There would be no shocking Hollywood-style "you can't handle the truth" admission about the cruel realities of war. Eddie, in his starched white uniform, stayed silent behind the defense table, as he had throughout the trial. Instead Parlatore began calling one witness after another to undermine the Navy's witnesses.

He called Josh Graffam, the new guy in the platoon who years before had won the paint round and pistol game. In Mosul, he had often acted as Eddie's spotter. Like many of the guys in Alpha, he was a Ferguson client, and he was testifying under immunity. Parlatore asked Graffam about a man he had seen Eddie shoot from the Towers. Months before, Dylan Dille had told investigators that Graffam had been spotting for Eddie on Father's Day in June 2017 when the old man was shot in the back, and Graffam had told Dille he had seen the shot. Parlatore asked if Graffam had seen Eddie shoot anyone on Father's Day, 2017. Graffam said yes. But it wasn't an old man. It was "two shitheads moving from one side of the road to the other."

"When you say shitheads, you mean an ISIS terrorist?" Parlatore asked.

Yes, Graffam said.

Did Eddie ever take any bad shots? Parlatore asked.

"Based on what I saw, no," Graffam said.

Parlatore asked if Graffam would deploy again with Eddie Gallagher.

Graffam didn't hesitate. He said he would.

"What about with Craig Miller?" Parlatore asked.

Graffam paused. He had always been close to the senior guys in the platoon. They had stood up for him to Eddie. But something had changed. He stammered. Serving with Miller? "I don't feel as confident about it," he said quietly.

Next the jury heard taped testimony from General Abbas al-Jubouri, who swore he had stayed with the captive until he died, and that Eddie had never stabbed anyone. "I would stop him if he did any mistake with this kid. I would be very upset," al-Jubouri said in the video.

Then the defense called the command team of the troop, Lieutenant Commander Robert Breisch and Master Chief Brian Alazzawi. If the jury was confused before, the command team only added to it by contradicting each other. Breisch insisted he had only heard about the crimes shortly before he reported them to the Team 7 commander in April 2018. Alazzawi said both men knew at least six months before that. He said Miller had come to him upset in October and told him everything.

Barred from saying anything about the confession, Alazzawi instead talked about seeing the photos that the platoon took with the body. Parlatore asked if anything about the photos surprised him. "I was surprised to see certain individuals smiling considering how distraught over the situation they were later," he said in an apparent reference to Miller.

The contradictions in the testimony appeared designed not to tell a clear story but to obliterate one. If several SEALs had told a relatively consistent story about the day of the stabbing, the long delays in reporting to their superiors telegraphed to the jury that something was fishy.

By that point a number of jury members were hoping the next witness would be Jake Portier. He more than anyone could connect the dots. He could say who knew what when. He could either side with Eddie or side with the guys. But he never appeared.

Instead the jury heard from Staff Sergeant Gio Kirylo, the signals intelligence Marine. On deployment Kirylo had exuded Eddie levels of bravado, even though he often did little more than monitor computer equipment in an armored truck. He had seemed hungry for acceptance, eager to show he was a badass operator. Kirylo and Eddie had kept in touch after deployment. Like Eddie, he was a rabid Trump supporter. He'd even brought a Trump flag to Iraq. Not long after Eddie's house was raided, they had a thirteen-minute-long phone conversation. Kirylo began to fear what NCIS might do to him if he got involved in the case. He refused to talk with investigators. When they called him, he said he did not see anything and would not be much help. He left out that he had been standing by the body as Eddie and Byrne worked. Before trial, Kirylo visited Eddie in the brig and met with Eddie's lawyers multiple times.

Kirylo came into the courtroom wearing the same khaki Marine uniform as most of the jury. He had a cast on his hand because he had recently accidentally shot off one of his fingers. With only nine fingers, he was on his way out of the Marines on a medical retirement. He grinned like a pageant contestant almost the whole time he was on the stand. Kirylo described Alpha as cocky, especially considering that they were green troops with little combat experience. Parlatore then asked what kind of guy Eddie was.

"The chief was old school," Kirylo said. "Strong leadership style, very gruff, kind of exactly what I had been used to in the Marine Corps."

The prosecutors sat silently, listening to the Marine discuss Eddie's character.

The Marine talked about watching the captive being brought in and worked on. He readily admitted that he saw nothing wrong with taking a photo with the dead body. "I chose to take a cool-guy trophy photo with my dead ISIS fighter," he told the jury. "This is the fruits of my labor on the ground.

"This was our unofficial war trophy just like some of our grandfathers took in fighting Japanese in World War II, just like some of our dads took in Vietnam," he said. Lots of other guys took pictures, too, he said: T. C. Byrne, Joe Arrington, even Craig Miller. Miller had never taken a photo, but Parlatore let that slide.

Kirylo said he moved the body to take the photo with "his head on my boot like he was a dead deer." During the move, he claimed, the bandage on the neck had come loose and he had seen the neck.

How many stab wounds were there? Parlatore asked.

"Not a single one," he said, smiling.

The next day, the defense rested.

THE JURY OF COMBAT VETERANS filed out of the courtroom and into a small space set aside for deliberation. It was July 1, 2019—almost the Fourth of July. The jury had been listening silently for nearly two weeks, and now it was time to make a decision. As Bernard Kerik walked out of the courtroom with Andrea, he said, "We'll have a verdict by noon and celebrate the holiday right."

The jury room was bare except for a table and seven chairs, a whiteboard, a TV, and a coffee machine. The only decoration was the rows and rows of service ribbons on the men's chests. It was 3:45 P.M. They put their hats on the table and sat down. Each had listened attentively without showing emotion to the prosecution's case for six days and the defense's case for two. They had heard the closing arguments. They had taken notes. There was almost no physical evidence, so they started sorting through the SEALs' testimony one by one.

In one way, Eddie faced a disadvantage in military court. A civilian court required a unanimous jury for a guilty verdict. Even one holdout would mean a hung jury and a mistrial. The Uniform Code of Military Justice did things differently. It required that only two-thirds of the jury vote guilty to get a conviction. In Eddie's case, that meant five of seven jurors. There could be two holdouts, and he could still go to prison. But rules of the UCMJ also worked in his favor. Jurors didn't have to be unanimous to reach a verdict of not guilty, either. In fact, the majority could vote guilty, but if they didn't reach the two-thirds threshold, if only three men voted not guilty, Eddie would walk free.

Some of the jury members felt deeply conflicted. They knew something awful had happened but didn't know what. They had heard from only half of the platoon. Some of them had studied Eddie throughout the trial, looking for some kind of tell. Other than a clear look of contempt for some of the witnesses, there was nothing.

Civilian juries often begin deliberation by taking a straw poll to see how each member will vote. As they discuss the case, they may take several more polls before reaching a unanimous verdict. It is not uncommon to have juries start out favoring one outcome, then end up voting for another. Military juries are allowed to vote only once. The members go into the vote not knowing what the outcome will be. Because no one knows if the jury is leaning to convict or acquit, there is far less chance for the jury to debate and persuade. The members go through the evidence, then vote. They either reach two thirds or don't. Military verdicts often come surprisingly quickly.

Halfway through the second day of deliberation, the jury asked to listen again to a recording of Tom MacNeil's testimony. They wanted to hear his description of seeing Eddie holding his knife over the prisoner. To the prosecution, that was a promising sign. The panel seemed to be focused on every tidbit of the murder.

Noon came and went without Kerik's prediction of a quick verdict coming true. But the jury was moving fast. By the end of the second day, they had gone through everything they thought they needed. No one had any more questions. No one wanted to review any more recordings of testimony. No one wanted to discuss. They were ready to vote. The foreman suggested they sleep on it. No need to rush a big decision. They could come back and vote in the morning.

As they waited, the different factions all tried to guess the outcome.

Matt Rosenbloom paced in the commodore's office across the

bay. He knew that more hinged on the verdict than the fate of one chief. There was nothing particularly special about Eddie Gallagher. Despite his family's pronouncements, he had a fairly average résumé. And the SEALs would see many more guys like him. Guys captivated by violence would always gravitate to the Teams. There were just some guys whose goal in life was to kill people. The issue was how the Teams responded. What culture would the Navy build to mold its elite warriors? Would they be SEALs or pirates?

The outcome had the power to influence platoons deploying all over the globe for years to come. If Eddie walked, pirates would feel free to do things they thought they could get away with. Their influence would spread as they became senior chiefs and master chiefs and ran platoons in ways that created new ranks of pirates. Rank-and-file SEALs who witnessed crimes would think twice about speaking out. After all, what was the point? Eddie's case would have shown them that after all the time and effort Alpha went through, all they had to show for it was reputations as rats. On the other hand, if Eddie was convicted, it would put all the guys carrying hatchets and canoeing people on notice. It would let the Craig Millers and Dylan Dilles of the world know they—not the guys calling them traitors— were the real brotherhood. It would show that the Navy's response to a virus like Eddie was robust enough to keep the SEALs healthy.

Either way, Rosenbloom was eager to have the verdict. Then the court-martial would be over, and he would no longer be muzzled by unlawful command influence. He could tell the Teams what he really thought of Eddie. And he could call the chief into his office and take the Trident off his chest.

The prosecutors waited in their office off the courtroom, knowing they were now looking at a long shot. Brian John was worried he had screwed everything up by not spotting Corey Scott's deception before he was on the stand. Pietrzyk tried to console him. Look, he said, you did what you could, the case was probably decided the day that a jury dominated by combat vets was seated.

Craig Miller watched with worry. Had he been wrong? Had he led his platoon into a massacre? He needed to try to get his mind off it. That evening, he walked up a flight of stairs in a trendy neighborhood of San Diego called Pacific Beach. The stairs opened up to a rooftop with an ocean view as the sun was setting over the water. The trial was over. The shooting had stopped. It was time for a debrief. On the roof he saw Josh Vriens digging a beer out of a cooler. T. C. Byrne was kicked back in a patio chair, talking to Dylan Dille and Dalton Tolbert. They all looked over and saw the Sheriff. It was the first time they had been together since Iraq. There were hugs all around.

A mutual friend had offered his patio, a stack of pizzas, and an icy cooler of beer so the guys in Alpha could have an evening to decompress. No family. No lawyers. Just the guys. It was something they never got a chance to do when they got home from Iraq because of all the shit with Eddie. Once the investigation started, the Navy had cautioned them not to talk to one another about the case. Now it was done, and they could finally meet as friends. It had been a dark few years, and they needed it.

Out under the sky surrounded by good dudes, Miller could let his guard down and finally relax. He was just happy to finally see the boys again. It felt so good that he started laughing out loud.

Dille came up and gave him a beer.

"Dude, did you guys see what Graffam said? Oh my god!" Dille said, clapping his hands. "We were so nice to the new guys, we stuck up for Graffam when Eddie tried to bench him. Like, what happened?"

"I guess Craig was too hard on him," Vriens said with a broad smile.

"Well, if he likes Eddie so much, he can go serve with him again then," Miller said, cracking a grin.

"Yeah. So can the 'real brotherhood,'" Dille said, referring to the army of keyboard commandos and former SEALs who had been blasting the platoon on Facebook. Dille had been alone at home for months, way too focused on them. It felt great to be back with his friends. "With a crack squad like that, Eddie could defeat ISIS in no time."

Tolbert shook his head and gave a dramatic wave of his hand. "Nah, old El Diablo doesn't need any help. It'd just be a bunch of pussies holding him back. Just send him back to Iraq alone. Middle East? Never heard of her."

Everyone cracked up.

"Bro, what was up with Eddie's lawyer's suits!" Vriens said. Back among friends he felt his whole body relax. It was as if the platoon had just done a big, dangerous op and was now back at base. "It's like he's trying to dress like a mobster but doesn't quite have the budget to pull it off."

"I thought the mobster was that bald dude in the gallery," Dille said, referring to Kerik.

"No, man, that guy's like a chief of police of New York," Vriens said, laughing.

Well, they looked better than the Navy lawyers, Miller said. Some of those guys looked like they were about twenty-five years old. And Parlatore still managed to do a pretty good job making us look like idiots.

True, true, Tolbert said, grinning. "I'm pretty sure I'm getting fucking fired when I get home."

Vriens stood up tall and looked at the faces arranged around him on the roof. He felt energized. They'd gone into the fight outgunned. Now that the smoke had cleared, he was proud to see that the guys still standing were the guys he most admired from the platoon. He got the sense that no matter what, they would always have his back. A real brotherhood. "Man," he said out loud. "I freakin' love you guys!"

The SEALs stayed on the roof late into the night. Notably absent were all of the guys who had signed on with Ferguson. The fallout would linger long after the trial. Some guys vowed it would be permanent. To hell with those guys, Vriens thought. The mourning for the end of Alpha would come later. That night they would celebrate the brotherhood that still remained.

In the morning, the jury came in ready to vote. The foreman in his white Navy officer uniform asked if there were any more questions. In the ranks of enlisted khaki, no one spoke up. The SEAL who knew Eddie stayed silent, never mentioning his relationship to any of them. They were going to vote on one charge at a time, starting with the relatively minor charges. Conduct of a nature to bring discredit upon the armed forces—the charge related to taking a photo with the corpse. The foreman took off his officer's cap and passed it around the table. Each man dropped in a scrap of paper with a G or N. The foreman counted the paper scraps. Almost all Gs. Guilty for the photo. Then obstruction of justice. The foreman passed the hat again and counted. This time it was almost all Ns. Not guilty for intimidating witnesses. Then attempted murder, for the sniper shootings. Again, not guilty.

Eventually it was time for the big charge: first-degree murder. The foreman passed the hat and the men scribbled on their scraps. Each of the men had weighed all they had heard from the SEALs. They knew they had not heard from all of the platoon, including the lieutenant. They weighed that too. They weighed all the physical evidence they had seen and all the evidence that was clearly missing. When the hat came back the foreman counted. There were a few Gs, but not enough. Eddie Gallagher was found not guilty of murder.

The jury took a vote on the lesser charge of aggravated assault for the stabbing. Again they found him not guilty. One of the members who voted to convict on the murder couldn't believe it. The trial had been a fair process, and the jury had done its job and considered all the evidence, he thought. But the outcome was striking. Eddie Gallagher, who texted he *wanted* to bury a knife in someone, whom witnesses *watched* bury a knife in someone, and who *bragged* to friends afterward about burying a knife in someone, was somehow going to walk.

The jury announced their verdict just before lunch. Not guilty on all counts except the one no one could deny: appearing in a photo with a dead body. It was a minor crime, but the jury decided to sentence Eddie to the maximum punishment—a message that they found the behavior despicable, especially by a man of his rank. There was a mix of shock and celebration in the courtroom. Eddie looked at his lawyers, then turned back and looked at his wife with a broad grin.

Eddie stood for the reading of the sentence. The jury gave him four months' confinement, two months of docked pay, and reduction in rank one step from chief to special operator first class. Since Eddie had already served more time in the brig awaiting trial than he was sentenced to serve, he was a free man.

When Eddie heard that all he was losing was some money and his rank, he turned to Andrea, moved his hands to his collar as if plucking off his chief's anchors, smiled, and shrugged. He had just dodged a life sentence.

President Trump had been following the case closely. After the verdict he tweeted in celebration, saying, "Congratulations to Navy Seal Eddie Gallagher, his wonderful wife Andrea, and his entire family. You have been through much together. Glad I could help!"

Dylan Dille had a feeling the verdict was coming that day and went for a long run to try to avoid it. When he got back to his pickup, a text was waiting on his phone. He felt a void, as if he were falling. He wondered if Eddie was just going to walk free. And if so, what would happen if they met face-to-face again?

Craig Miller and Josh Vriens heard the news at work, while they were training new SEALs to dive. They looked at each other for a long time without speaking. On the rooftop, everyone expected Eddie to go down at least on assault and go to prison. Now neither knew what to say. They had worked so hard, risked so much, and come out the other side worse than if they had just buried everything in Iraq. The case had been one disappointment after another. The leaders had tried to sink it, the lawyers had screwed it up, the jury had believed Eddie over Miller. After so many letdowns, Miller felt like a beat dog. He couldn't get much lower.

He looked at Vriens and shrugged, trying to hide the hollowing sorrow.

"I'm going home," Vriens said, and he walked away.

THE GALLAGHER FAMILY campaign for Eddie ended where it began, on *Fox & Friends*. Pete Hegseth, wearing his signature red, white, and blue ensemble, announced Eddie's exclusive first public interview on July 3. After talking a bit about the victory, Hegseth asked Eddie if he had any words for future Navy SEALs.

Eddie paused to think. He could have said a lot of things. Instead, he gave probably the most pirate answer he could, echoing what Demo Dick had said almost four decades earlier when he created SEAL Team 6: Young SEALs should concentrate on loyalty.

"Loyalty is a trait that seems to be lost, and I would say bring that back," he said. "You are part of a brotherhood, you know, you are there to watch your brother's back, he's there to watch your back. Just stay loyal."

ACROSS THE BAY from the courthouse, in the Alpha platoon high bay, the Bad Karma Chick on the back wall stared down at a new group of young SEALs, her red devil tail pointed in the air. SEALs in her high bay had enlisted and sworn an oath to the Constitution, believing in some abstract way that they were the agents of the cosmic struggle between good and evil. Their job was to do bad things to bad people. Karma was a bitch. You could stay ahead of it for only so long. Eventually it would catch up. Few of the new guys likely realized that the devil's rules applied to the SEAL Teams themselves.

Some SEALs outside Alpha who had been in the Teams for decades saw Eddie as karma being visited on the entire Teams. After all, Eddie hadn't come out of nowhere. He was the product of decades of experiences and decisions. He was the offspring of the green-faced frogmen who learned to fight dirtier than the Viet Cong and the mafia of "motivated dirtbags" Demo Dick brought together in the 1970s and 1980s. Their lessons had been passed down, their actions echoed through time as one generation learned from another until they became culture. Sheltered by secrecy, armored by public adoration, they built a tradition that celebrated brotherhood, rule-breaking, and blood. It morphed into a pirate culture that revered knife kills and canoe shots, where men were more loyal to the tribe than to the nation they served. The culture hid under the halo of public goodwill the SEALs had created. By the time Eddie was acquitted, pirates had reached nearly every rank.

Eddie was karma even for the SEALs who weren't pirates. Low-ranking SEALs stood by silently when they saw some platoons go down dark paths. High-ranking SEALs stood by silently while SEALs sold books and made movies that created a shining white mythology of the Teams, even though they knew that darker things scurried around in the bilge.

And Eddie was karma for the endless wars of his generation, for the admirals and generals who ordered men like him over and over to Iraq and Afghanistan expecting them to keep coming back whole. Officers who gave sunny appraisals of the wars and tried to downplay the growing influence of pirates amid the frenetic need for operators, who promised year after year that the wars had turned a corner, that victory was near. Officers who despite uncounted dead in foreign lands would never have to answer for anything like Eddie had.

Brian Ferguson, the lawyer who considered himself a champion of the little guy, was left ambivalent about Eddie. When Eddie and Andrea celebrated with their family in front of the cameras before getting into their white Mustang and driving off, Ferguson had little reaction. Despite what many thought, he insisted he had never been working to protect Eddie. He'd been working to protect guys like Corey Scott who got sucked in. For him it was always about trying to keep real people from getting crushed by the machine. If the machine didn't like it, he was hardly surprised. Eddie was probably guilty, Ferguson said. But who wasn't guilty in this whole Iraq mess? The stray cruise missiles of the invasion, the torture at Abu Ghraib, the countless sectarian killings, the near obliteration of Mosul by air strikes. Maybe Eddie was guilty. Eddie served nine months in confinement. Ferguson shrugged and said, "That's nine months longer than any of the generals or politicians who started these wars."

CHAPTER 17

FRAG RADIUS

"WHAT THE HELL are we going to do about Eddie Gallagher?"

The secretary of the Navy, Richard Spencer, shot the question across a long glossy table to the chief of the Navy, Admiral Michael M. Gilday. They were in the chief's office on the top floor of the Pentagon—a room festooned with paintings of smoke-obscured battleships and tall frigates in the ocean wind.

Gilday, in a khaki uniform covered in medals and stars, looked back without immediately answering.

Spencer, in a dark civilian suit, waited to see if the speakerphone on the table would offer anything. On the line from San Diego was the commander of Naval Special Warfare, in charge of all Navy SEALs, Rear Admiral Collin Green. It was early November 2019, four months after Eddie had walked out of court a free man. There was silence. No one had any good ideas.

Most people who had narrowly escaped a murder conviction might have slinked away quietly. Not Eddie. He wore his acquittal and President Trump's congratulations like a medal, knowing the president's support offered not only fame but total protection from military repercussions. The Navy had banned Eddie from the SEAL base at Coronado to keep him away from the witnesses, but after the trial he held court at various SEAL bars outside the gate, regaling

SEALs with the *Fox & Friends* version of his case. On Facebook and Instagram, Eddie and Andrea bashed the men who testified by name, calling them liars, cowards, and #meangirls. They insulted Commodore Matt Rosenbloom and Admiral Green, telling them in a post, "You are a bunch of morons!!!" Eddie put the hunting knife he carried in Iraq on a table of honor in his workout room, surrounded by his other awards and plaques, and went around wearing a hoodie that read "Canoeing Club." He had his friend Bito craft custom bowie knives for his legal team with FREE EDDIE etched on the blades, and posed in photos holding the knives with Bito and Gio Kirylo in an Instagram post that, using the Iraqi name of ISIS, Daesh, was tagged #Loyalty #Honor #Brotherhood #WeDontHaveAnEthics-Problem #NoOneCriesOverSpilledDaesh. Eddie had managed to pull off one of the most pirate feats of all: He had not only gotten a knife kill on an ISIS fighter, he had also stuck it to the Navy brass and the military justice system that were always pursuing and harassing the pirate subculture. And then the president had congratulated him for it.

The Navy's top leadership knew it had to stop. They had to show the rest of the SEALs that the laws and regulations still applied. But what could they do?

After the trial, Eddie had put on his uniform and returned to his job at the Navy. He was back in the system, still technically a sailor under control by the chain of command, and yet, the command all knew they had no control over him. They couldn't do anything to Eddie because President Trump had his back. He was untouchable.

That became clear just a week after the verdict. The Navy's local legal office in San Diego held a small ceremony for the prosecution team. The captain in charge of legal services gave out four letters of commendation and Navy Commendation Medals, praising the team for their hard work, noting that the junior attorneys had stepped into senior roles, and Lieutenant Brian John had pressed on despite the death of his father. It was standard consolation. The military can't give bonuses or pay overtime, so it often gives out medals to recognize hard work and sacrifice, even if there isn't a win. "No matter the result, we were right to prosecute him," the captain told the team.

When President Trump heard about it, he went ballistic. He was ready to smash anything that looked like insubordination when it came to Eddie. After news of the ceremony hit conservative media, Trump sent out a barrage of angry tweets. He immediately had the medals rescinded. A few days later, the captain who gave out the awards was pushed out of her command early under a cloud. It was a clear shot across the Navy's bow: Anyone who tries to mess with Eddie will suffer the president's wrath.

Eddie seemed to realize he had top cover from a fellow pirate in the White House. He went on Fox News without clearance from his command—a serious breach for a special operator expected to be anonymous. Then he went to Nashville for a banquet called the Patriot Awards, where he was honored along with Bernard Kerik and Michael Flynn, the former Army lieutenant general who had pleaded guilty for lying to the FBI during the investigation of Russian collusion with the Trump campaign. Eddie didn't bother to clear that with his command, either. He knew he didn't have to.

Eddie and his crew had the Navy in retreat. After Trump publicly pulled the prosecution's medals, the Navy's legal branch realized that pursuing cases even tangentially related to Eddie would invite trouble. So the Navy quietly dropped the charges against Jake Portier for failing to report Eddie. It ended its criminal inquiry into whether Robert Breisch had covered up the crime. And there was more. The Navy also dropped charges against a good friend of Eddie's, Chief David Swarts, and three other SEALs who were facing charges in the 2012 beating death of a detainee in Afghanistan. The Navy did nothing to punish the band of senior enlisted SEALs that Eddie's texts revealed were illegally abusing drugs with him. All were allowed to continue on as if nothing had happened. And law enforcement quietly dropped the conspiracy to commit perjury investigation into Corey Scott.

SEAL officers started to refer to the wrench Eddie's case had thrown into the whole disciplinary system as "the Gallagher effect." Eddie and Andrea caught wind of the term and started selling "Gallagher Effect" T-shirts.

Of course, Rosenbloom still wanted to crush Eddie like a cockroach. He had managed to hold his fire for more than a year, but with the court-martial over, he wanted to publicly pull Eddie's Trident and kick him out of the SEALs so everyone in the Teams could see what a turd he was. He thought there were more than enough grounds to fire Eddie. There was the stolen equipment found at his house, the toxic leadership, the lying, the fraudulent attempts to get medals, and, of course, getting his youngest SEAL's mom to buy drugs.

The commodore believed flushing Eddie out of the SEALs would send a critical message that pirates had no place in the brotherhood. The courts had had their say, and in Rosenbloom's mind, they had completely fucked up. Now it was on the frogmen to try to fix it. If Trump didn't like it, Rosenbloom didn't really care. Some fights were worth fighting even if you knew you were going to lose. Eddie could be his Alamo. "Just let me kick him out of the SEALs, it will be on me," he kept telling the admirals. "I don't give a shit if the president fires me. At this point, it would be an honor."

The guys in Alpha agreed with Rosenbloom, not that anyone was asking them. The courts and the SEAL Teams were different worlds. A conviction or an acquittal didn't mean much to guys in the Teams. But the Trident meant everything. Anyone could hire fancy lawyers and beat a charge. It was another thing to be held accountable by fellow frogmen.

The admirals urged caution. They were in dangerous waters with the White House. Since the beginning of the republic, the military and its civilian commander had maintained an unwritten courtesy. The president set policy and made the political decisions, and the military leaders got to execute those orders as they saw fit. The president stayed out of rank-and-file operations, and the military stayed out of politics. But Trump had upended the long-held agreement. He had not only reached down into the rank and file, he had intentionally made the rank and file political. Eddie had become a partisan icon. Now authority over the Trident, which was squarely in Rosenbloom's court, was also political. If the pin was pulled, it could be seen as the Navy defying the civilian commander in chief. It wasn't exactly an insurrection, but it was a step in that direction. And if the president saw his authority challenged, it wouldn't end well.

That was the problem Secretary Spencer laid out to the chief naval officer as Admiral Green listened in. What do we do? If you don't pull the Trident, you set a bad example. If you pull the Trident, you are openly picking a fight with the president.

Plus, it's unlikely it will do any good, Gilday added. Pull the Trident, and after firing us all, the president will just give it back.

It was a standoff, and by November it had just grown even more caustic.

Throughout the fall, Eddie and his family had pushed for the president to intervene again and reinstate his rank to chief. The jury had knocked him down from E-7 to E-6. That not only cost him his chief's anchors, but it also cost him a step in retirement pay that over the next several decades could add up to more than $200,000. Eddie's allies on Fox News and in Congress were demanding a fix.

In early November, just days before the top Navy leaders met, Pete Hegseth appeared on *Fox & Friends* and gleefully announced he had spoken directly to Trump, and the president was going to use his executive power to reinstate the chief. Hegseth was so excited he started talking with both hands. "This president recognizes the injustice of this," he said. "You train someone to go fight and kill the enemy. Then they go kill the enemy the way someone doesn't like and we put them in jail or throw the book at them."

Meanwhile, Trump was sliding from a rough summer into an even worse autumn. In every direction he was blocked and embattled. The border wall he had promised to chanting crowds in 2016 had added less than ten miles of new barriers in his three years in office. The trade war he had started with China to boost the economy was instead squeezing farmers in states critical to his reelection. He wanted tanks at his Fourth of July parade in Washington, but he couldn't get tanks. And Democrats in Congress were holding hearings to impeach him. There weren't many things the president had total authority over, but Eddie Gallagher was one of them. Intervening for a guy like Eddie would be a way to put on the uniform of a decisive and effective leader and rally his base, who didn't necessarily care if ISIS had been killed in a way that was legal.

The Navy, as usual, did not comment.

The instinct of the Navy leaders was to attempt an impossible task: stop the president from interfering with the military without making it appear that the military was interfering with the president. They knew it had to be done, they just didn't see a clear way to do it.

So what the hell are we going to do about Eddie Gallagher? Spencer asked again. The problem had once rested only on a few young, low-ranking enlisted SEALs in a platoon in Mosul. Now it was occupying the top leaders in the Navy. And just like the guys in Alpha, the officers at the top saw only bad options. The question lingered in the secretary's office as the top officers silently calculated the possible moves.

"It's a shitty situation," Spencer observed.

Admiral Gilday wondered if it was better to do nothing. All naval ships were built of independent compartments with waterproof hatches that could be sealed if enemy fire breached the hull. The Navy had obviously suffered a hit. But Eddie had put in his retirement papers. It was November. He would reach twenty years in a month, and they could have him out the door that day. Maybe they could just seal the hatches and wait. Let Eddie and Andrea go on Fox News and talk trash, let them troll officers on Instagram. A few insults were better than getting into a dispute with the White House that could lead to a crisis.

Admiral Green, on the phone from California, disagreed. The collateral damage to the credibility of the SEALs would be too great. SEALs couldn't walk around thinking Eddie got away with everything because he had important friends. What would stop the next SEAL who got in trouble from hiring Timothy Parlatore and Bernard Kerik and running to the White House? There had to be some accountability, Green said. He didn't feel strongly about whether the president should restore Eddie's rank, but he wanted to be able to pull Eddie's Trident. Let's let the president do what he wants with the rank, he said, then we pull his bird.

If you do, the president will just order you to pin it back on, Gilday countered.

Or worse, pin it on Eddie himself, Spencer said. That leaves us right back where we started, but worse off.

Spencer was determined to try to protect the Navy's authority to handle its own personnel and preserve the centuries-old arrangement between the White House and the military. "What about this?" he said. "We restore Eddie's rank, rather than have the president do it. That way he doesn't turn this into something political. Then, at the same time, the Navy holds a Trident review board of his peers—other SEALs. They look at what he's done, and they decide how to handle him."

Guarantee they'll pull his bird, Green said.

Right, Spencer agreed. And they probably should. It will send a message to the SEALs that Eddie Gallagher is bad news. But then I'll reverse the decision and give Eddie back his Trident, he said.

Admiral Gilday looked puzzled.

Look, Spencer said, everyone in the SEALs will know what happened. Everyone will know the Teams decided to kick him out. If I give the Trident back, Eddie will be walking around with it, the president will be appeased, but the SEALs will know it doesn't mean shit. The process gets a chance to work, the SEALs have a chance to be heard. The Navy sends a message. But when I reverse it, it will keep the president from getting involved. Everyone can just blame it all on me, the secretary said. I don't mind taking the fall for this.

Spencer saw the job of secretary of the Navy as being the circuit breaker between the White House and the Navy. Civilian rule of the military was a delicate thing. It required respect, deference, and a mutual understanding. Sometimes things got too hot and a fuse needed to blow. If it meant losing his job, it was worth it to preserve the peace. Since Spencer's first day as secretary, he had kept a typed resignation letter in his desk drawer. It was advice given to him by a former secretary of the Navy. If you have the letter, the secretary told him, it will make your decisions much clearer. Now that he had to deal with the Gallagher case, he was glad he had that letter.

Spencer looked at Gilday. He was not met with immediate and vigorous enthusiasm.

"I know it's not perfect," said Spencer, "but in a shitty situation, sometimes you just have to do the best you can."

Grudgingly, the men agreed that it was worth a try.

———

"Dear Mr. President, I believe I have a path forward for us for Gallagher that would not need your interdiction," the secretary wrote in a note on his personal stationery. It was a few days after Veterans Day, on November 14, and Spencer was on a flight back from a meeting with top defense officials in Norway. "If I could ask you to postpone any action regarding Gallagher until we've had a chance to discuss the outcome I'd be greatly appreciative. I'm landing at Andrews at 1500."

That afternoon Spencer got a call from the White House counsel, Pat Cipollone, who said the president wanted to know more. Spencer explained his plan to Cipollone, trying to sell it as a win-win: The SEALs would get their say on the Trident, the White House would get the outcome it wanted for the chief, and the president would not have to get involved. A few hours later, Cipollone called back. The president had said no way. Trump was not interested in avoiding the case, he said. To the contrary, he was going to send a personal, handwritten order the next morning telling the Navy to promote Eddie.

Spencer had tried to design a way to keep the president from getting publicly involved, but after talking to Cipollone, he realized that, for the president, getting publicly involved was the whole point.

The next day was a Friday. Eddie's phone rang and when he picked it up, a voice on the other end said, "Please hold for the president of the United States." President Trump came on a moment later. He was jovial, almost chatty. He talked about how horrible it was that the prosecution had spied on Eddie's lawyers. Try that stuff in New York and you'd get arrested, he said. Then he told Eddie he was reinstating his rank. Everything would be totally expunged. It would be like nothing ever happened. The president said he wanted to instill confidence back in the warfighters. He didn't want them second-guessing themselves. He wanted them to know they had a president who had their back.

The president hung up and made a few more calls. That afternoon, the White House announced the president was not just reinstating Eddie's rank but was also pardoning two Army officers, First Lieutenant Clint Lorance and Special Forces Major Matt Golsteyn.

All three were accused of murder in a war zone, and all three had been championed by Pete Hegseth and *Fox & Friends*. That's where the similarities ended. Lorance had been convicted of murder. Eddie had been acquitted of murder. And Golsteyn was still awaiting trial.

It never came out publicly that Golsteyn was the Special Forces officer who had been the commander on the ground in Marjah, Afghanistan, when an unidentified SEAL had killed an unarmed farmer. But it appeared that Eddie and Golsteyn remembered each other, because they kept their distance. Both were interviewed on the same *Fox & Friends* set after the clemency, but never at the same time. And neither ever even mentioned the other's name.

In many ways Golsteyn was the opposite of Eddie. His record was stellar. His men respected him; some downright loved him. They never turned him in. He had killed an unarmed man in Afghanistan because he had believed the man was a bomb maker who would kill locals and American soldiers if he went free. Golsteyn was charged with murder because he transparently admitted to the killing during a job interview with the CIA.

Golsteyn and Lorance appeared onstage together with Trump at a Republican fundraiser a few weeks later in Florida. Even though Eddie lived in the same state, he wasn't on the stage. Rumors started spreading after the pardons that Eddie and Golsteyn might campaign for Trump together. Eddie's lawyer, Timothy Parlatore, quickly shot that idea down. He said Eddie said he would never appear with Golsteyn. When asked why, he didn't mention Afghanistan or a farmer, he said, simply, "Because Golsteyn's a war criminal and Eddie's not."

EDDIE HAD SPECIFICALLY *not* been given a full pardon. The president could have struck down the chief's conviction, but he had only ordered the Navy to restore his rank. There was no directive from the White House on what to do with Eddie after he was a chief again.

Admiral Green saw it as a sign that maybe the president wasn't as supportive of Eddie as *Fox & Friends* thought.

Captain Rosenbloom was still pounding the table, demanding that Eddie should lose his Trident. He pressed Green to move ahead with the plan and put Eddie through a Trident review board of his peers. He relished the idea of letting a bunch of senior frogmen look at the evidence from NCIS without lawyers in the way. Green took the idea to Spencer and Gilday. After some discussion, the secretary and chief naval officer agreed; if the SEALs really wanted to do it, he said, they'd give him top cover with the White House.

President Trump had restored Eddie's rank on a Friday. Over the weekend, Green called in his advisors. Like Rosenbloom, Green had spent his whole career in the SEALs and had made it part of his mission when he took command in 2018 to try to steer the SEAL culture back on course. He told his staff he was considering pulling Eddie's bird, and he wanted to hear their thoughts.

"Sir, this could be perceived as you bucking the president, thumbing your nose at his orders," one officer said. Another warned that if Trump saw the admiral as disloyal, he would immediately fire him.

Green said he wasn't worried about getting fired. He was worried about doing right by the SEALs. The Trident was the symbol of the SEAL ethos, he said, and he knew the ethos by heart. With his staff there, he recited a line from their creed: "I serve with honor on and off the battlefield. The ability to control my emotions and my actions, regardless of circumstance, sets me apart from other men. Uncompromising integrity is my standard. My character and honor are steadfast."

"How do I look a young SEAL in the eye and say we are living the ethos if we let this guy go?" Green asked.

Green had his staff draw up the paperwork to convene a review board for Eddie. He also had them draw up paperwork for Lieutenant Jake Portier, Lieutenant Commander Robert Breisch, and Lieutenant Tom MacNeil. MacNeil had testified against Eddie, but he had also kept silent all through deployment and for months after. He had left it to the lower-ranking SEALs to report the chief. Green wasn't sure if he deserved to be fired, but he wanted the board to take a hard look. He wanted everyone to know that he wouldn't stand for any kind of pirate cover-up.

Once the papers were ready, Green left them unsigned on his desk. He wanted to make sure it would fly in Washington. On Monday, three days after the pardon, he reached out repeatedly to the Pentagon and the White House. No one was responding, but no one was telling him to stop. Green took it as a sign to go. On Tuesday, he signed the papers starting the Trident review boards.

Fox News exploded. "The arrogance of the Navy knows no bounds. Knew this coming. Lots of anti-Trumpers at the top," Pete Hegseth wrote on Twitter on Tuesday afternoon after news broke. "Think they can flick-off POTUS. Have a feeling I know how this will end . . ."

The next morning *Fox & Friends* interviewed Timothy Parlatore. The host kicked off the conversation by asking the lawyer, "So, you think this is personal, don't you?"

"Absolutely," Parlatore said. He wanted to make it clear that this was not just about Eddie. It was about the deep state working against its own president. Green could have taken Eddie's Trident at any time, Parlatore said, but the admiral had specifically decided to do it right after the president had restored Eddie's rank. "What he's doing here is just an effort to publicly humiliate Chief Gallagher and stick it right in the president's eye."

Parlatore—who had been an undistinguished officer and had left the Navy before fulfilling his five-year obligation—then called Admiral Green—who had served in Iraq and Afghanistan, had been repeatedly decorated, and had a Bronze Star—the worst thing you could call a SEAL: He said he was "a coward."

President Trump was watching. Parlatore must have known he would enrage the president by saying that one of the few parts of the federal government the president could actually command was trying to buck the White House. Trump was holed up with advisors that morning, waiting to watch some of the most damaging testimony of his own impeachment hearing. A former aide planned to describe the "drug deal" a top presidential aide had worked out with the leader of Ukraine to sway the election. But at 8:30 A.M., before the hearings started, Trump tweeted: "The Navy will NOT be taking away Warfighter and Navy Seal Eddie Gallagher's Trident Pin. This case was handled very badly from the beginning. Get back to business!"

It didn't take long for the tweet to reach the Navy leadership, but they didn't know what to do with it. For security reasons, military orders from the president must follow a specific chain of command. An order by tweet cannot be followed because the military has no way of knowing if the thumbs typing a presidential tweet are really the president's. Accounts are vulnerable to hacking. A prankster or an enemy actor could easily take over.

The Navy waited for a formal order to stop the review board. In the meantime, Secretary Spencer still hoped he could deploy his circuit breaker plan: Let the Trident boards go forward, which would probably result in a vote to pull Eddie's Trident. Then, as secretary, Spencer would give it back. The president would get what he wanted. The Navy could blame the secretary, and the Teams would know that Eddie was a turd.

Spencer briefed the plan to the White House chief of staff, Mick Mulvaney. That night the president made a flight to Dover Air Force Base, about eighty miles east of the White House on the Delaware coast, to greet the remains of service members coming home. On the short flight, his top military advisor, the chairman of the Joint Chiefs of Staff, Army General Mark A. Milley, spoke directly to the president about the plan. Sir, the SEALs have their own community, their own way of doing things, he said. You do not want to get involved in this tribal stuff.

The next morning, still with no written order from the president, Spencer left for an international security forum in Halifax, Nova Scotia. When he arrived, the military press was on him, asking if he was going to obey the tweet to stop the Trident review board or if he was going to defy the president. Spencer tried to steer between both rocky shores. He still hoped the president would see the plan could work.

Because Spencer had been not only a Marine but a Marine helicopter pilot, he fundamentally believed in the small regulations and tasks that made grand endeavors possible. Yes, there was room for big ideas and leadership, but you also needed the process. If you didn't follow the process—if you didn't do things like carefully inspect the helicopter and go through a checklist before flight—things could quickly fall apart. Orders shouldn't come through tweets. Officers shouldn't defy the president. And the president shouldn't screw with rank-and-file SEAL decisions. Of course, things had gotten way past where they should be, but he still hoped he could land it all gently.

"I believe the process matters for good order and discipline," he told a Reuters reporter in Nova Scotia. The president could order him to stop, and he would obey, but until then, he would press on, he said. "I think we have a process in place, which we're going forward with, and that's my job."

What he didn't yet see was that to Trump, it wasn't process that mattered, it was appearance. Eddie's supporters were yelling that Spencer was openly defying the president. It was something Trump couldn't appear to tolerate. On Saturday, more reporters pressed Spencer at a panel discussion, asking whether he had threatened to resign. "Contrary to popular belief, I am still here. I did not threaten to resign. But let us just say we are here to talk about external threats, and Eddie Gallagher is not one of them."

By Sunday, Spencer was home in Washington. *The New York Times* and *The Washington Post* both ran stories of the standoff between top Navy leadership and the White House over Eddie. There were reports that admirals Green and Gilday might both resign in protest. It was everything Spencer had hoped to avoid. As he was driving through the city that morning, he got a call from Defense Secretary Mark Esper. They had known each other for years.

Esper told Spencer he was fired.

Publicly, Esper said he fired Spencer because the Navy secretary had gone behind his back and tried to make a deal on the Trident with the White House. Privately Spencer knew it was because he had appeared to defy the president. It was, he knew, just politics. Even at the highest level, Eddie Gallagher had friends. He was untouchable. The guys in Alpha couldn't believe it: A perennial screwup enlisted SEAL named Eddie Gallagher had managed to get the secretary of the Navy fired. What was next?

Spencer left the Pentagon the next day with a paper shopping bag packed with a few things from his office. He had a long coat and scarf to guard against the November cold. Everything he had tried to do to preserve order and discipline had backfired. He had wanted to avoid a standoff over a Navy chief defying his officers, and instead he had created a spectacle. On the stairs leading out of the Pentagon, Spencer was caught by David Martin, the venerable national security correspondent for CBS News. The reporter, who had served as an officer on a Navy destroyer during the Vietnam War, asked the secretary what he thought the ramifications were.

"What message does that send to the troops?" Spencer asked, his brow furrowed, his breath showing in the cold. "We have to have good order and discipline. It's the backbone of what we do." Spencer then gave a blunt assessment of the president. "I don't think he understands what it is to be a warfighter," he said. His voice stung with anger. "A warfighter is a profession of arms. And a profession of arms has standards that we hold them to and that they hold themselves to."

The camera followed Spencer as he walked down the stairs. His Department of Defense black car and driver had disappeared with his job. Instead, someone was waiting in a Ford C-Max. It was a stunning departure. A well-connected Washington insider and advisor to the president had been undone by an enlisted sailor and a host on *Fox & Friends*. That day the president tweeted, "Eddie will retire peacefully with all the honors he has earned."

Eddie was given back his chief's anchors. All of the Trident boards were canceled. Jake Portier, Tom MacNeil, and Robert Breisch never had to answer for their leadership. A few hours after Spencer was fired, Eddie and Andrea posted a photo of a dumpster fire on their Instagram. They added the caption: "the current state of Navy leadership."

CHAPTER 18

FROGMEN

O N A D ECEMBER evening in Palm Beach, a month after the secretary of the Navy left the Pentagon with his things in a paper bag, Eddie stood up from his seat at dinner and pulled his wife in close. He was wearing a black suit and tie. Andrea was in a black sleeveless dress with the same jagged gold necklace she had worn when she first appeared on Fox News to battle for Eddie. Donald Trump Jr. was chatting with someone just across the table. He smiled and urged everyone to crowd in for a photo, just as Jake Portier had two years before. Eddie had been invited to Mar-a-Lago, President Trump's ritzy private club in Palm Beach. He and Andrea navigated around a table scattered with fresh flowers, tall, delicate glasses of red wine, and martinis sweating in the Atlantic air. They pressed in for a photo. Trump's lawyer Rudy Giuliani was there. He stood up from the table and leaned in next to Don Jr. and his wife. Eddie put his arm around Andrea's waist and held her close. Everyone smiled.

The president had arrived at the resort that day to spend two weeks for Christmas. Fresh off being impeached and determined to fight, he planned to surround himself over the vacation with his legal team to form a defense. That night, though, was a chance for him to hobnob with some of the conservative talking heads who had been loyal through the whole impeachment ordeal.

Eddie had been a fan of Trump since the first days of the 2016 campaign. He still had photos on his Facebook page from the San Diego rally he attended. He had literally flown a Trump flag in Mosul. He had even gotten to speak to the president a few times by phone about his court-martial. But he never dreamed when he was a platoon leader in dirty cammies in Iraq that he would be rubbing elbows at the Trump resort.

Eddie had retired honorably from the Navy in December 2019 with a chief's pension. He went back to his new house with its big front porch in the Florida panhandle, where he kept his hunting knife on his trophy table. He gave podcast interviews to other retired SEALs and starred in a sympathetic lifestyle piece on *60 Minutes*. He showed no remorse for the saga that had torn his platoon apart and left a cloud over the entire SEAL organization. Instead, when he told his story, he focused on Eddie. Eddie being jailed, Eddie being spied on by the prosecution, Eddie fighting admirals trying to take his Trident. In his mind the whole thing seemed to boil down to another war story, one against a domestic enemy. As usual he was at the center. He saw his acquittal as divine intervention. God had stepped in on the side of Eddie Gallagher.

With newfound free time, Eddie started teaching a few freelance gigs on urban combat techniques to civilians, showing them how to sweep rooms with a rifle and toss grenades around corners. He took his local congressman to the shooting range. He went on a healing retreat to Mexico, where he took hallucinogens and went through guided therapy, writing down the things that were burdening him and throwing them into a fire, then taking ibogaine and having a ten-hour-long vision. He told people he came out of the trip feeling completely at peace. Slowly, he began to admit in interviews that he had, in fact, pulled out his knife and stuck that kid, but just to check that he was already dead.

Eddie also tried to cash in on being Eddie Gallagher. He started writing a book with the subtitle "From Fighting ISIS to Fighting for My Freedom." During the court-martial and the battle over the pardon, Eddie and Andrea had amassed nearly a hundred thousand social media followers. They wasted little time trying to capitalize on his newfound fame. He started doing product posts for diet supplements and CBD oil. He created his own pirate-themed line of customized brass knuckles and shirts with skulls and blades.

Others also used Eddie's win as an opportunity. Two of the men who had stuck by Eddie through the court-martial, Congressman Duncan Hunter and Bernard Kerik, were pardoned by the president, who wiped away their felony convictions. Eddie's lawyer, Timothy Parlatore, started getting hired by other SEALs. By the time Eddie retired, Parlatore was representing another SEAL Team 7 chief. This one had been charged with sexual assault after his platoon was drinking in Iraq on the Fourth of July to celebrate Eddie's acquittal.

The invitation to Mar-a-Lago had come as a surprise. Eddie's court-martial had turned him into a conservative darling who had taken on ISIS and the deep state and vanquished both. He had been invited to something called the Turning Point Student Action Summit, which featured thousands of high school and college kids packing the Palm Beach convention center to hear conservative speakers like Rush Limbaugh and Sean Hannity. President Trump was speaking, too. After the convention, Eddie found himself invited to Mar-a-Lago. And not to just any part, he was at the tables roped off for VIPs, sitting with Don Junior and Rudy. It was too much. As they sat down for dinner, word came that the president, himself, wanted to meet Eddie.

Eddie and Andrea were led into a hallway off the dining area. There stood the president with his signature long tie flapping below his belt and the First Lady on his arm in a sleek black dress. Eddie and Trump talked just briefly, standing in one of the resort's decorative corridors. Trump did almost all the talking, gesturing the whole time. Melania stood silently by his side looking down at Eddie. Eddie kept his hands in his pockets. Andrea was beaming. She leaned in and put her hand on the president's arm and thanked him for everything.

It wasn't hard to see what the president saw in Eddie. Trump had promised his screaming crowds that he would knock the hell out of ISIS, bomb the shit out of 'em. Waterboarding wasn't good enough. Killing them wasn't nearly enough. You had to take out their families. You had to be worse than they were. You had to show strength. Eddie was a real American who had actually done it. Forget being loyal to the rule of law, he had been loyal to Trump, and Trump had been loyal to him. That was what it was all about.

Eddie pulled a small black item from his pocket and told the president he had a gift for him. It was something he had brought back from the rubble of Mosul that he knew the president would appreciate: a small black flag with white Arabic writing—a captured flag of ISIS. For a president who often framed things in stark terms of winning and losing, a captured flag was exactly the right gift. And without realizing it, Eddie fulfilled an ISIS boast that one day their flag would be in the White House.

ALMOST A YEAR LATER, Josh Vriens was dropping off his son at preschool when he got a text. It was from Corey Scott. The medic wanted to meet up.

Right after the trial Vriens had left the Navy and moved far from San Diego. Alpha's onetime most aggressive SEAL found a quiet house in a quiet neighborhood and got a quiet, boring desk job that was about as far as he could get from being a SEAL sniper. He tried to keep a low profile. He needed a break from the past. Now the part he wanted to remember least had found him. The Ghost was in town.

It wasn't the first time Scott had reached out to guys in Alpha trying to patch things up. He had texted Craig Miller a few months before, asking to meet. Miller texted back that he didn't trust Scott and had nothing to say. Scott had called Dylan Dille. By that time Dille had gone back to school for a master's degree in strategic leadership. He was ready to move on and was open to the idea of reconciling, but only if they could have a truly honest exchange about what happened. On the phone, Dille demanded to know about the trial. Scott refused to say. Maybe if we're alone on a mountain sometime, with no phones anywhere, I'll tell you, Scott said. Dille hung up. No point in talking to that guy.

A few of the other guys had texted Vriens, too—guys like Christian Mullan, the Switchblade pilot, who had Fergusoned immediately and stayed silent. Vriens wasn't interested. What was the purpose of patching things up with anyone who had rung the bell when it really mattered? Cowards, he thought. He had no use for them.

But Vriens was curious about Scott. He had always liked the medic and wanted to know what the hell had happened on the witness stand. He texted Scott back. Okay, let's meet, but in public. He told him to meet outside a swanky grocery near where Vriens now lived.

When Vriens arrived, Scott looked the same, if slightly older. Same shaved head, same brow. He was out of the Navy, but looked like he was still working out. He had on a T-shirt and jeans and was looking at his phone when Vriens walked up. Vriens went to shake Scott's hand; Scott hugged him.

Vriens embraced the medic with guarded tenderness. Scott was both a longtime friend and a man who had betrayed him. He wasn't sure if he wanted to forgive him or punch him, and he tried to keep himself open to either. Scott on the other hand seemed to want to act as if nothing had happened. He started making small talk. He moved to Virginia to start a job with a company that built coffee drive-thrus. His wife and kids were doing okay.

"You talk to any of the other guys much?" Vriens asked.

Joe Arrington and Ivan Villanueva, Scott said.

Only guys who had Fergusoned, Vriens thought. He knew Ferguson's guys had been calling around, trying to patch things up. Josh Graffam and Arrington had both reached out to Miller. Both clearly wanted to bury the hatchet, but instead of apologizing, they had just made excuses. Miller had politely pushed them away. Now that he was a chief in charge of making new SEALs and enforcing standards, he simply didn't believe that guys who bailed on Alpha belonged in the Teams.

Scott dug his hands in his pockets. "I texted you in July, but you never answered," he said.

"Yeah, well, I was in a rough spot," Vriens said.

"How you doing now?" Scott asked. The conversation had started cordial, but it turned on that question. The rough spot Vriens had been struggling through had been due in large part to Scott. What Eddie had done in Mosul was bad, but it didn't bother Vriens half as much as the feeling that other guys in Alpha had betrayed him. Scott had encouraged Vriens to stand up and speak, then had ducked out. Part of Vriens wanted to hurt Scott as much as Scott had hurt him. Maybe break his nose.

Shoppers passed by on the street, oblivious to the tension between the two men.

"Let's get to the elephant in the room, Corey," Vriens said. His voice turned sharp. "When this all started, *you* were the one who said we should report Eddie. *You* asked how we could look ourselves in the mirror if someone's kid was killed because of Eddie. And then *you* helped him. So *you* tell me. How are *you* doing now? What the fuck happened, bro?"

Scott sounded deadpan and rehearsed, just as he had on the witness stand.

"You know family is the most important thing to me," he said. "I had to put them first."

"What's that got to do with anything?" Vriens said.

"Well, if we could live in a world where no one went to jail and Eddie was out of the Navy, and everyone could just move on, wouldn't you want that?" Scott asked. "Think about it. That's what happened. And the only dude who really got hurt was an ISIS fighter."

The words filled Vriens with so much pain and rage that he felt like he was watching a girl get shot in Mosul all over again. As time passed, he had started to get over the disappointment of the trial. At first everyone he knew—his family, his friends, and guys he knew in the SEALs—tiptoed around him, not mentioning the trial, as if he was too fragile. Then people started constantly trying to comfort him. Even William McRaven, the officer who had tangled with Demo Dick in the 1980s and had gone on to oversee the raid on Osama bin Laden, had called to console him. But after a while, he got tired of being treated like a victim. He wasn't a victim. He had been tested—tested like few people ever are—and he had made the right choice. He didn't see that as a tragedy; he saw it as a triumph. He was free and clear. He could live the rest of his life without regret.

Now Scott was here telling him he hadn't even been tested at all, that the whole thing was a sweet deal that had worked out great for everyone.

That morning Vriens had been half-ready to forgive Scott. But Scott hadn't come asking for forgiveness. Instead, the former would-be avocado rancher was trying to convince him that the scheme had been great, and didn't seem to realize it was actually a disaster. Vriens started to boil inside.

"No, man, you fucked us," Vriens said. "You got up there and lied for Eddie."

Scott cut in, insisting he didn't lie. He said he really did cover the kid's breathing tube and was ninety-nine percent sure no one had seen it, so he kept his mouth shut, and he was glad he did because he could have gotten in real trouble.

"Yeah, but you had immunity for months," said Vriens. "Why didn't you tell anyone? Why didn't you tell your friends? Why did you lie?"

Scott insisted again that he didn't lie.

"What about the knife, then? You said you didn't see any blood?"

"There wasn't any blood," Scott said, folding his arms.

What about all the blood in the photos? asked Vriens.

Scott smiled and said, "That was after the fighter died."

Vriens had seen the photos and the spatter from when the blood spurted out of the neck. That hadn't happened after the kid's heart stopped. Scott was lying all over again, this time to a fellow SEAL. Vriens could feel the muscles in his neck get tight. As they stood on the street, inches from each other, he spread his shoulders and made himself larger.

"Look, Corey, I told NCIS everything. Everything. The Switch-blade thing. Every bad thing I ever did. I didn't care. We agreed to take it on the chin," Vriens said. "I know Ferguson told you to do it that way, but that guy is messed up. I'm pretty sure he was working with Eddie and his lawyer. Just tell me this, at what point did Gallagher's team pitch you?"

Scott said he wasn't working with them. He just visited Eddie a couple times. Eddie's lawyer just knew what questions to ask.

Scott was shaking his head to imply Vriens was being stupid. Then he smiled and said, "It's not my fault he's smarter than NCIS."

Vriens was ready to knock the smug look off the medic's face. Did Scott really think he'd won? Did the deal still seem that sweet? Look at the fallout. He was having lunch with Brian Ferguson because his old friends wouldn't return his calls. He had traded his integrity and the brotherhood for a short-term win, or worse, for Eddie. It was just another raw deal, another dead-end avocado farm.

"Corey, you always think you're so smart," Vriens shouted. "You got caught up in some lawyer games. They used you! You think you're the puppet master, but really you were just a fucking puppet!"

Scott started to yell back. Both men were on the verge of a fight. Then Scott took a breath, appeared to remember he had come to make peace, and tried to be conciliatory. "That's just water under the bridge now," he said. He said he wanted to put the past behind and be friends.

"You serious?" Vriens clenched his jaw. "Water under the bridge? Do you have any idea what we went through? Eddie was outside my house, bro. I fucking moved my family across the country. It's not just water under the bridge. How 'bout if I banged your wife and came back a year later and said it was water under the bridge? It doesn't work that way."

People on the street were now staring. Vriens still wanted to hit Scott but figured the truth would hurt more. He narrowed his eyes and looked right at the medic. "How do you look at your kids? How do you teach them how to be good to their friends? How do you lay down at night and say, 'You know what, I'm a good father'? How do you live the rest of your life knowing what you did?"

Scott paused. "I just thought we could put water under the bridge," he said.

"Fuck you, Corey," Vriens said, and he walked off.

AT NAVAL BASE CORONADO, the dawn breaking over the beach revealed the silhouettes of BUD/S students running along the sand in twin lines. They passed the Alpha high bay, wet, sore, exhausted, each one hoping to have the grit to make it through to earn the SEAL Trident and join the elite brotherhood. The bell hung on its post on the Grinder, offering comfort and rest for anyone who could live with the willingness to accept it.

Craig Miller drove past in his old Jeep. He had on his blue instructor shirt and a frogman Rolex Sub. It was a new one. After Mosul he had set his original watch aside and started wearing another because he and his wife now had two young sons. He wanted eventually to pass a watch down to each.

Eddie was thousands of miles away, selling pirate T-shirts, posting about his preferred protein powders, and giving interviews about how he used to be a SEAL chief. Miller was actually doing the job. He was coming through the gate at Coronado each morning to teach the next generation of SEALs. His task was to take the students who made it through Hell Week and put them through an underwater crash course until they knew their equipment so well that he could rip it away from them underwater in the dark, tie it up in knots, and know they would be able to fix it. That night, he was taking students on a night dive in the murky water of the bay.

The experience in Mosul made Miller harder than he might have been on students, but also made him realize that aggression and grit were not enough. The Navy would always be able to find guys who wouldn't quit no matter how much you beat them. You could train them until they were the best small teams of killers in the world. But those teams also needed something else that was harder to instill. The advantage of the SEALs, Miller realized, wasn't lethality. After all, the Navy had missile cruisers and fighter jets that could deliver far more firepower than a SEAL platoon. The true value was that even in this technologically advanced age, SEALs were still human. Some missions required a group of commandos who could think, react, and sort through the shifting complexities of war. The commandos had to be loyal and tough, of course, but because SEALs were always going to do the up-close, face-to-face fighting, they would also need an extremely durable sense of humanity. SEALs had to have a killer instinct but also empathy, restraint, the ability to stay on course in the stormy morality of combat. It had to be more than just skill in fighting. SEALs had to have the clarity and courage to remember what they were fighting for.

Miller decided to stay in the SEALs for that very reason. He could have rung the bell. He could have gotten out, maybe moved back to Texas, probably made more money and had more time with his family. But he had spent two years realizing that there were pirate friends of Eddie in the SEAL Teams who didn't want guys like Miller around, and because of that, he had to stay. It might end up being a fight. But he had joined the SEALs to fight, and no fight was worth waging more than the fight for the SEALs.

Miller suspected there would always be Eddie Gallaghers who made it through BUD/S. When they did, he was determined to be there to either mold them into SEALs with character or flush them out of the force. After all, Eddie was both a guy who had found trouble his whole life and a product of the culture at Coronado. Pirates had made him who he was. They had taken a fundamentally insecure screwup who had been seeking approval and raised him in a subculture where status came through killing. Miller had come to believe the biggest reason that Eddie had killed the prisoner was actually a really small one: that he thought it would make him cool. If Eddie had been raised by better chiefs, everything might have been different.

If Miller could make good SEALs, they would become good chiefs, who would make more good SEALs. It would have to start with guys like him. He knew it wasn't only on him—there were plenty of good dudes in the SEAL Teams. Even so, if he retreated, there'd be one fewer in the fight. He planned to stay as long as the Navy would have him.

Other SEALs from Alpha were also determined to stick it out. As Miller went to his operator's cage to get his gear ready for the day, T. C. Byrne was stepping in front of a classroom of combat medics in Mississippi to instruct the next generation who would deploy with platoons. When he would hear students whispering that he had been in that platoon in the news, he'd readily admit it. Here is what happened, he'd say. Here are the lessons from it. As medics, you better be prepared to deal with way more than just someone getting shot. Dalton Tolbert was on a classified mission with DEVGRU. Despite Eddie's efforts, Tolbert had been accepted into the elite tribe. Of course, guys asked him about Eddie. Tolbert was more than happy to tell them.

Tom MacNeil had finished a stint at the Naval Postgraduate School and was taking over command of a platoon on the East Coast. He had managed to keep his officer's commission despite what had happened. Officers up the chain figured that the SEALs could use a guy who had been through a deployment like Mosul. It was one thing to send lieutenants to courses on leadership. It was another to have them learn the hard way. MacNeil had come out of the court-martial determined to never be a Jake Portier or a Robert Breisch.

That core group of guys from Alpha had gone up against Eddie. The common perception, both in the civilian world and in the SEAL Teams, was that they had lost. They had broken the unwritten rules of loyalty by turning in a fellow frogman. They had taken a beating on Fox News. They had poisoned their own brotherhood by testifying. And Eddie had not only dodged nearly every criminal charge, he had walked away a hero of the conservative media and a personal champion of the president.

But when it was all said and done, the truth was that the guys in Alpha had achieved the mission they had set in the beginning: Eddie was out of the Navy. He would never lead SEALs again. They had taken casualties. Nothing had gone as planned, but they were still standing. None of them thought Eddie got what he deserved, but at least he'd never be behind one of the Navy's sniper rifles again or in front of one of its platoons.

Captain Matt Rosenbloom sometimes imagined what it would be like to call Eddie out of retirement for one day, have him put on a uniform and report to Coronado so the commodore could ceremoniously take his Trident. But it was just a passing fancy. More than anything he wanted to help the SEALs move on. If civilian wannabes chose to worship Eddie online and buy his T-shirts and protein powders, that was their problem. Rosenbloom wanted to ensure that in the SEALs everyone knew he was a turd.

Late in 2019, when Eddie was pushing for the president to reverse his sentence, Rosenbloom's two-year command spot as the commodore at Coronado ended. At that point, no one in the Navy leadership had spoken out against Eddie. Politically, he was still too hot. Even the admirals who were willing to lose their jobs over condemning Eddie—and there were a few—ultimately thought the corrosive effect of having a showdown between high-ranking officers and the White House would do more harm than good. As it had during the whole court-martial, the Navy stayed silent.

But Rosenbloom was determined to get a covert message to the ranks—especially to the guys in Alpha. At his change of command ceremony, a crowd of SEALs gathered in a small memorial park on the water at Coronado that looked out over San Diego Bay. Rosenbloom stepped up to the podium in a white uniform. In his time as commodore, he said, he had the privilege to see a lot of battlefield heroics, but he also had the rare chance to see true moral courage. Without calling them out by name, he told the story of Alpha through the analogy of a historic World War II naval battle.

It was the height of the fight for control of the Pacific in 1944. The Allies were making a crucial ground invasion in the Philippines when a Japanese decoy fleet drew the U.S. fleet's battleships away, leaving only a tiny guard of lightly armored destroyers with the radio call-sign "Taffy 3." At dawn the next morning, the entire Japanese strike force swept down from the north with Taffy 3 in their sights.

"You could say their chain of command let them down," Rosenbloom said, sweeping his eyes across the SEALs gathered at the park to look for men from Alpha. The Americans had only eleven small ships protecting a hundred thousand troops packed on supply ships. The Japanese had the largest battleship in the Pacific.

"Knowing that they were alone, abandoned by their chain of command, would face an enormous assault from all directions and no doubt take heavy losses, the sailors had a choice to make," Rosenbloom said. "They could make a run for it, decide not to engage, and they probably could have gotten away with no damage, and maybe no one would have known the difference. The problem was, they were all that stood between the Japanese main battle force and the almost completely undefended ships of the invasion fleet. So, in this moment of extreme adversity, they made a courageous decision. They would go into the attack."

The tiny defense fleet motored full-speed into the Japanese armada and unleashed everything they had: guns, torpedoes, fighter planes, and dive bombers. One pilot, after running out of ammunition, even emptied his .38 revolver out of his cockpit window. Taffy 3 took heavy damage. Four of the seven destroyers were sunk by the Japanese. A number of men who abandoned ship died in the water from shark attacks. "You could say they lost the battle. But a funny thing happened," Rosenbloom said. "They had fought so hard that it was the Japanese who retreated. They limped back to their ports and would have no further influence on the war."

Rosenbloom pointed across the bay to San Diego. By the water there was a bronze memorial to the men of Taffy 3. "It acknowledges them for the heroes that they are," Rosenbloom said. "There is no memorial to the Japanese task force, and they have been completely forgotten, as if they never existed."

The Navy had taken repeated fire during the Gallagher case. Not everyone had survived. Some of the SEALs from Alpha left the service disheartened. Commander Chris Czaplak was forced to retire after the email scandal. But others pressed on. Joe Warpinski kept working cases for NCIS. Brian John got quietly promoted and assigned to the Navy legal division that shapes all policy on criminal matters.

After Rosenbloom left command as commodore, his next assignment was to head up the teaching of ethics and leadership in the SEALs. It was supposed to be a cushy job to give the officer a bit of a break after two years as commodore. He didn't see it that way. If there was ethical drift in the force, he was taking over right at the rudder. Careful moves in early ethics training—moves that would fly below the radar of the Pentagon and the president—would years later steer the SEALs to a much different place.

When the guys in Alpha were coming up through the SEALs, ethics was a footnote—an hour-long talk by some retired frogman that many young SEALs soon forgot. In the wake of Eddie's court-martial, Rosenbloom and Green decided to build ethics courses into every step of leadership. When officers took command of platoons or troops or teams, they would learn to think through the ethical traps of being a SEAL—how their culture of pushing boundaries and breaking rules was both a huge advantage and a potential pitfall, how their celebrity in the civilian world was both well-earned and toxic. They would look at how the demand for loyalty was vital in such a high-stakes profession but also a liability. And, Rosenbloom decided, they would work through those lessons by looking specifically at the story of Alpha platoon.

It was a plan that Big Navy would never approve. The Pentagon feared another confrontation with the president. It wanted to pretend Eddie's court-martial never happened. Any mention of him in the Navy was unofficially forbidden. But when did the frogmen ever pay much attention to what the Navy approved? Rosenbloom knew he had to make the mission small, covert, and deniable. He would hit where his tiny force could have the most impact. It was classic frogman tactics. When a frontal assault would be suicide, when the brass had your hands bound in red tape or the standard approach wouldn't work, you had to get creative. Find another way to attack the problem.

Rosenbloom decided the right spot to hit was the training for all new lead petty officers. It was the first step enlisted SEALs took to being leaders. It was where he could have the most influence on the most SEALs in platoons actually deploying and fighting. He would make sure every LPO knew the story of Eddie Gallagher. The real story. To connect with those first-time leaders, though, he needed the right wingman. As a captain with graying hair, Rosenbloom knew he'd have a hard time connecting with the junior SEALs he needed to reach. It would be too easy for guys in their twenties to view him as a fossil. He needed someone to make it real, and of course there was only one man. He tracked down the Sheriff.

The only way this is going to work, Rosenbloom told Craig Miller, is to tell the whole story. I'm giving you clearance to tell it however you want as long as you tell it how it really happened—no bullshit. Will you help us set this right?

A few weeks later Miller walked into a classroom just off the beach in Coronado where about a dozen SEALs were on the cusp of becoming lead petty officers. It was the first time of many.

Standing together, Rosenbloom and Miller started briefing the case. It was, Rosenbloom told the class, a perfect storm: A narcissistic sociopath comes of age in the SEALs when civilian culture has made the force out to be angels and a bunch of pirates are busy building a dark culture obscured by the halo. Over a few deployments the SEAL is taught not only how to put the culture into practice but also how to get away with it. The SEAL Teams are too enthralled in their own mythology to take a hard look at the subculture spreading in their ranks. A warped idea of loyalty causes guys to give a turd like Eddie too many second chances. He is put in charge of a small unit with almost no oversight. The trust and leeway the Navy sees as the advantage of the SEALs becomes the downfall. The chief goes completely off the rails.

Rosenbloom made sure students knew about all the stuff that never made it to the news: Eddie's pointless missions that endangered SEALs' lives, his lying and stealing, his absurd and selfish write-ups for medals, and the numerous times Alpha was told by superiors to just drop it.

Then Miller walked to the center of the room to deliver the real take from the lead petty officer who'd actually been through it. The Sheriff crossed his arms. He was just as tall and imposing as he had been in Alpha, but he had changed a lot since those days. He had started out as one of Eddie's biggest backers. He wanted to see the chief succeed. He knew it was the door to his own success. Miller told the class he felt a duty to be loyal to his chief, he felt he needed to be loyal to his commanders, he felt he needed to be loyal to the guys in the platoon. It had been drilled into him since the first day he showed up at BUD/S. But he never really understood what loyalty meant. He doubted anyone in the platoon did.

"You need to understand what we're really talking about when we say 'loyalty,'" Miller said to the group of younger SEALs. "It should be loyalty to the Constitution first, to our values, then the Navy, then your buddy, then, last, yourself.

"Most of the time there's no problem there, you can be loyal to your buddy and to the Constitution with no conflict. But if that gets out of whack and you put your buddy first, it goes against everything we stand for—the whole reason the SEALs exist. Without it, what the hell are we even doing in the military?"

Sometimes while telling his story in classes, Miller thought about the guys in Alpha he no longer spoke to. He knew they would probably never describe themselves as disloyal. But the fight had come and they had not stood up. They had abandoned their brothers—not just Alpha, but every SEAL in the Teams.

Miller figured the guys in the classroom all knew about Eddie's court-martial. They'd probably seen Andrea on Fox News and maybe heard gossip around Coronado. Maybe a few even had "Free Eddie" shirts hanging in their closets. He wanted to set them straight. He wanted to explain how it had started slow, with a chief they all liked leading them in a direction they wanted to go. It seemed at first like he was doing them a favor. First the SEALs were turning trackers off; then Eddie was telling them to fire suspect shots or launch rockets. They wanted it; it was exciting. They kept following. Eddie was conditioning them. Step by step, things got darker until they were watching the cold-blooded murder of a skinny, wounded kid and the platoon commander was taking photos like it was cool.

Miller didn't want the story of Eddie's knife kill to become legend. The SEALs needed the truth—not just the men in the room but everyone. Over the years the SEALs had been too ready to congratulate themselves, too quick to cover up fuckups by awarding medals, and too willing to think that nothing like Eddie Gallagher could ever happen. They had to be willing to study what happened and understand. They had to take a hard look at the dark truth: Eddie was not an outlier of the SEALs but a product.

When he was done talking, Miller folded his arms and stared at all the young SEALs looking back at him. The light caught on his Rolex Sub. "All right, ask me anything," he said. "What do you want to know?"

ACKNOWLEDGMENTS

*A*LPHA would not be possible without the trust and cooperation of scores of people. Many of them are active-duty military personnel and can't be acknowledged by name. Thank you for your bravery and commitment in telling this story.

The New York Times provided the financial backing and fellowship for this project as well as the inspiration of generations of ink-stained reporters who have come before. My gratitude and admiration to this feisty institution runs deep. This book would be nothing without the day-to-day beat reporting that laid the foundation, which the *Times* supported from Day One. Thank you to Pat Lyons, who edited all of the articles about the Gallagher court-martial, and Marc Lacey, who made sure those stories got noticed. Thanks also to Sam Dolnick, who realized that the story wasn't over when the court case ended. And thanks to the legal team assembled by the *Times* to fight for the First Amendment right to tell this story.

Special thanks to *Times* correspondent and former Baghdad bureau chief Tim Arango, who had the clarity to ask, "Does anyone know who the victim is?" and the reporting chops to then find the identity. Thanks to Yasir Ghazi, the intrepid Iraqi reporter who tracked down and interviewed the family of Moataz.

Thanks to Kevin Doughten at Crown, who saw the dramatic potential in the story of Alpha and persuaded me to write another book not long after I had sworn off book writing for good. Thanks to Ethan Bassoff, a tireless agent and a good friend. Thanks to peripatetic advisors Ben Schultz and Chad Holderbaum, whose daily discussions helped *Alpha* grow from a few ideas into a final work. Thanks to Peggy, the best freelance copy editor west of the Mississippi. Thanks to Whitman, who provided the first edit and offered just the right advice, and Frost, who was always there when I needed a break. The last thanks, as always, to my smart and lovely partner, Amanda.

Notes on Sources

Foreword

The quotes by Tim O'Brien are taken from the piece "How to Tell a True War Story," included in his book *The Things They Carried* (Boston: Houghton Mifflin, 1990).

Prologue: Chief Gallagher

Details of Edward Gallagher's activities at the Intrepid Center come from medical records from the center, which were included in the Navy's criminal investigation files. Details about Gallagher's wife encouraging him to go to the Intrepid Center come from notes taken at an intake interview at the center that were included in his medical records. The description of Alpha's mascot, the Bad Karma Chick, comes from interviews with Alpha members and with Chuck Pfarrer, the SEAL who originated the SEAL concept of "Bad Karma" in the 1980s. Gallagher's recollections of joining the Navy and of being arrested and processed into the brig are from two lengthy interviews he gave to the podcasts *Cleared Hot*, published January 27, 2020, and *Mike Drop*, published February 13, 2020. In those interviews, he also described joining the Navy and becoming a corpsman, despite not knowing what a corpsman was. Gallagher's decision to join the military "to go to war" comes from Navy medical records included in his criminal investigation file. The statistics of the platoon's accomplishments in Mosul come from performance evaluations of SEALs in Alpha. The estimates that Eddie had killed more than a hundred people with his sniper rifle come from statements he made to other

SEALs in Mosul that were relayed to the Naval Criminal Investigative Service. Additional details about Gallagher's family life, his return home from Mosul, and what he told people about the rumors being spread by malcontents come from author interviews with his wife, Andrea Gallagher, and brother, Sean Gallagher, in 2018.

CHAPTER 1: ALPHA PLATOON

The description of Alpha's general attitude toward Gallagher when he took over the platoon and his reputation is from interviews NCIS agents conducted in 2018 with the following SEALs: Craig Miller, Dylan Dille, Josh Vriens, Dalton Tolbert, Joe Arrington, Ivan Villanueva, Corey Scott, T. C. Byrne, David Shaw, and Tom MacNeil. Descriptions of the new-guy games at La Posta as well as the accounts of Gallagher's safety violations are from author interviews with seven SEALs who were present. The description of the story of shooting the little girl in Afghanistan is from NCIS interviews with Lieutenant Commander Robert Breisch, Josh Vriens, and Dylan Dille as well as author interviews with three other SEALs. The characterization of the guys in Alpha as nerds comes from Gallagher's description on the podcast *Mike Drop*. Gallagher's characterization of Jake Portier is taken from NCIS interviews of Alpha SEALs as well as author interviews with SEALs from Alpha. The description of Gallagher presenting Portier as "like an enlisted guy" is from author interviews with three SEALs. The characterization of Portier's friendly relationship with Gallagher and their lax approach toward fraternization comes from interviews with SEALs and text messages that suggest they regularly went drinking together. Text messages sent by Gallagher included in this chapter are from NCIS reports summarizing text messages from his seized cellphones. Gallagher skipping drug screenings comes from a signed proffer submitted to the Navy by Lieutenant Tom MacNeil. Details of Gallagher skipping training to go to Mexico come from Gallagher's texts, which detail the trip and how leaders later discovered his unauthorized absence, and interviews with five SEALs who discussed the event. Descriptions of Gallagher as a BUD/S instructor are from author interviews with SEALs who had him as an instructor.

CHAPTER 2: MOSUL

Descriptions of the conversation between Craig Miller, Dalton Tolbert, and Dylan Dille in the truck are from author interviews with multiple SEALs familiar with the conversation. Gallagher's preoccupation with SEALs getting wounded and Purple Hearts is from NCIS interviews with Craig Miller, T. C. Byrne, and Josh Vriens. The general description of Alpha platoon's advise and assist mission in Iraq is from NCIS interviews with Craig Miller, Dylan Dille, Josh Vriens, Dalton Tolbert, Joe Arrington, Ivan Villanueva, Corey Scott, T. C. Byrne, David Shaw, and Tom MacNeil. Additional details are from author interviews with SEALs. Gallagher's comments about having to get creative about getting close to the action come from an interview on the podcast *Mike Drop*.

Details of the first combat operation and the altercation afterward come from author interviews with four SEALs.

CHAPTER 3: AMERICAN SNIPER

The pattern of daily operations in Mosul and Gallagher's unwillingness to act as tactical lead are from NCIS interviews with ten SEALs from Alpha. Gallagher's habit of turning off trackers and giving false locations comes from author interviews with six SEALs. Descriptions of Dalton Tolbert's childhood come from an author interview with Tolbert's mother. Descriptions of Gallagher's account of shooting at a sniper on the first combat mission come from three SEALs who heard the account given by Gallagher and Joe Arrington. Descriptions of Tolbert's time with Gallagher in sniper hides come from conversations Tolbert had with Dylan Dille that Tolbert shared with the author. The description of the shot Gallagher took comes from an account created by Tolbert at the time that was provided to the author.

Descriptions of the relationship between Gallagher and Jake Portier come from NCIS interviews and author interviews with seven SEALs who described Gallagher as dismissive and disrespectful toward the officer. Portier did not speak to investigators and did not respond to requests to be interviewed for this book. Gallagher's relationship with Golf platoon is based on text messages sent by Gallagher that were on a phone seized by NCIS and on interviews with former Golf platoon and Alpha platoon members. Descriptions of the mustard attack come from interviews with SEALs and from Gallagher's texts seized by NCIS. Gallagher's description of his affinity for the Javelin missile is from the podcast *Cleared Hot*. The descriptions of Gallagher seemingly shooting at nothing or inventing kills are from NCIS and author interviews with several SEALs, including an NCIS interview with Brian Alazzawi. Descriptions of the final battle in the chapter are from eyewitness accounts of several SEALs who were there and photos that show the damage the Javelin missile caused to the mosque. Descriptions of differences between the platoon's two medics come from interviews with SEALs in Alpha platoon and other platoons that worked with the SEALs. Descriptions of Corey Scott's failed side businesses and reputation for not exceeding expectations come from author interviews with four SEALs. Additional descriptions of the battle come from official Navy citations for multiple medals awarded to platoon members for actions that day. The description of firing forty-millimeter grenades into the city comes from two SEALs who observed the incident.

Chapter 4: Pirates

The quotation about David and Goliath comes from Chuck Pfarrer's book *Warrior Soul: The Memoir of a Navy Seal* (New York: Random House, 2003), p. 75. The quotation that begins "They considered all of us as crazy" comes from Edward Higgins, printed in Dick Couch and William Doyle, *Navy SEALs: Their Untold Story* (New York: William Morrow, 2015), p. 42. The story that ends, "Yes, sir, but they got the job done," comes from Edwin R. Ashby, quoted in Kevin

Dockery, *Navy SEALs: A Complete History from World War II to the Present* (New York: Berkley, 2002), p. 44.

Admiral Bill McRaven's quote about SEALs being creative comes from an interview with the *The Dallas Morning News,* December 24, 2011. The description of the Phoenix Program in Vietnam comes from Michael J. Walsh, *SEAL! From Vietnam's Phoenix Program to Central America's Drug Wars* (New York: Pocket Books, 1994); Bill Fawcett, ed., *Hunters and Shooters: An Oral History of Vietnam* (New York: William Morrow, 1995); and Dockery, *Navy SEALs.* The characterization of SEALs as "assassins" comes from Couch and Doyle, *Navy SEALs*, p. 91. Roy Boehm's quote about fighting dirty comes from Dockery, *Navy SEALs*. Mike Beanan's description of his platoon stealing and killing in Vietnam was published under the pseudonym "Mike Beamon" in Al Santoli, *Everything We Had* (New York: Ballantine, 1981). Details of Bob Kerrey's mission in Vietnam come from Amy Waldman, "Bob Kerrey Reveals His Role in Deaths of Vietnam Civilians," *The New York Times,* April 25, 2001. All descriptions and quotes from Richard "Demo Dick" Marcinko are from his book *Rogue Warrior* (Pocket Books, 1993), with the exception of the quote that begins, "There's something to be said about the purity of a small war," which is from Dockery, *Navy SEALs.* Marcinko's description of William McRaven is from Barton Gellman, "William McRaven: The Admiral," *Time,* December 14, 2011. Descriptions of SEALs leaving Vietnam in 1971 fearing war crime prosecution are from the article "Navy 'SEALs,' Super Secret Commandos Are Quitting Vietnam," *The New York Times,* November 29, 1971. Descriptions of SEALs being taught to use knives and garrotes by superiors are from Pfarrer, *Warrior Soul,* p. 40. The description of the covert SEAL mission in Libya comes from "Papers Say U.S. Troops Landed in Libya in '86," Associated Press, September 17, 1987. Descriptions of SEAL Team 6 and the use of hatchets and "canoeing" are from Matthew Cole, "The Crimes of SEAL Team 6," *The Intercept,* January 10, 2017, and Mark Mazzetti, Nicholas Kulish, Christopher Drew, Serge F. Kovaleski, Sean D. Naylor, and John Ismay, "SEAL Team 6: A Secret History of Quiet Killings and Blurred

Lines," *The New York Times*, June 7, 2015. Descriptions of ethical drift and lack of discipline in the most hectic period of the war in Iraq come from author interviews with current and former SEAL officers. Quotes from Chris Kyle and descriptions of Kyle using the Punisher emblem are from his memoir, *American Sniper: The Autobiography of the Most Lethal Sniper in U.S. Military History* (New York: William Morrow, 2012).

CHAPTER 5: THE CAPTIVE

The details of Gallagher's views on killing and on seeing the village on May 3, 2017, come from a 2020 interview with the podcast *The Shawn Ryan Show*. The characterization of the relationship between Gallagher and Tom MacNeil comes from statements Gallagher made about MacNeil to three SEALs interviewed by the author, and from statements MacNeil made in a proffer to Navy prosecutors. Accounts of the May 3 stabbing, the events leading up to it, and the aftermath come from interviews with NCIS agents conducted in 2018 with the following SEALs: Craig Miller, Dylan Dille, Josh Vriens, Dalton Tolbert, Joe Arrington, Ivan Villanueva, Corey Scott, T. C. Byrne, David Shaw, Tom MacNeil, Air Force Technical Sergeant Ryan Rynkowski, and General Abbas al-Jubouri, as well as court testimony from Marine Staff Sergeant Gio Kirylo, Miller, Byrne, MacNeil, Tolbert, and Dille. Scott's description comes from NCIS interviews. He provided additional descriptions of his actions that day in trial testimony, which are detailed in Chapter 14, but declined to be interviewed for this book. Descriptions of Jake Portier organizing a group photo come from statements to NCIS from Dylan Dille and Craig Miller, as well as author interviews with multiple SEALs who witnessed the event. Details of Gallagher's previous reenlistment with the Good Old Boys come from a video of the ceremony seized by NCIS. The account of Gallagher seeing the photo of the dead captive and telling Josh Vriens he had stabbed him comes from testimony Vriens gave at Gallagher's trial. NCIS's attention to this one day was meticulous for obvious reasons. Additional details come from video and photos from that day. Background of

Terence Charles Byrne II comes from congressional testimony by Representative Henry Gonzalez, January 21, 1993, and from Tim Kelsey, "How the UK Fed a War Machine: A European Network of Firms Secretly Supplied Ammunition to Both Sides of the Iran/Iraq Conflict, Often with Government Complicity," *The Independent,* August 29, 1992. Gallagher's text messages are from an NCIS report on his seized cellphone. Background on Andrew Arrabito comes from numerous third-party interviews Arrabito has given, including a 2020 interview with the publication *Skillset*. Details of Ivan Villanueva's arrest come from a Coronado Police Department arrest record, as well as text messages between Gallagher, Portier, and Villanueva.

CHAPTER 6: MAN DOWN

Descriptions of the pink house come from photos and videos taken on-site by the platoon. The descriptions of the rat holes and the IEDs they contained come from author interviews with three SEALs who went through those holes. The description of Dragon getting shot and the response comes from helmet cam video. The description of Jake Portier not calling in a medevac immediately comes from four SEALs who witnessed the event and the proffer Tom MacNeil submitted to the Navy. The description of Gallagher directing the evacuation and carrying St. John Mondragon-Knapp on his shoulder comes from author interviews with three SEALs who witnessed the event. The description of Gallagher receiving a hatchet and knife from Andrew Arrabito comes from Gallagher's texts and author interviews with three SEALs. The story of Gallagher cutting himself with the hatchet and trying to claim a combat injury comes from NCIS interviews with Byrne as well as author interviews with two SEALs who directly witnessed the injury and Gallagher's attempt to file Purple Heart paperwork. The account of Gallagher deciding to carry a hatchet comes from author interviews with six SEALs and the MacNeil proffer. The description of Dragon's injuries comes from three SEALs who were present as well as helmet cam footage of medics treating Dragon. The description of the interaction with the second captive comes from the MacNeil proffer as well as author interviews with three SEALs who were present. The descriptions of Gallagher's childhood, decision to join the Navy, and problems in the military come from interviews he gave to the *Mike Drop* and *Cleared Hot* podcasts as well as military records, including medical records seized when he was arrested. Gallagher's failure to complete special operations combat medic training the first time comes from Navy records. Gallagher's use of racist, transphobic, and homophobic comments comes from interviews with five SEALs and text messages on Gallagher's phones, which were seized by NCIS. Descriptions of Josh Vriens's perception that Gallagher purposefully exposed him to fire come from Vriens's interview with NCIS and author interviews with three SEALs. Descriptions of Gallagher getting in trouble as a BUD/S instructor come from author interviews with two SEALs and statements by Robert Breisch to NCIS. Reports that Gallagher went back repeatedly to the pink house come from interviews with four SEALs and photos provided by those SEALs. The confrontation between Dalton Tolbert and Gallagher comes from an author interview with two SEALs. Details of Gallagher and Portier telling the Special Operations Task Force commander that "friendly fire" had hit St. John Mondragon-Knapp come from the proffer by MacNeil, who witnessed the exchange.

CHAPTER 7: THE TOWERS

Details of repeated trips to the Towers come from interviews by NCIS agents conducted in 2018 with the following: Craig Miller, Dylan Dille, Josh Vriens, Dalton Tolbert, Brian Alazzawi, Joe Arrington, Ivan Villanueva, Corey Scott, T. C. Byrne, David Shaw, Tom MacNeil, and General Abbas al-Jubouri, as well as court testimony from Miller, Scott, Byrne, MacNeil, Tolbert, and Dille. Additional details come from author interviews with six SEALs. The physical description of the Towers comes from photos taken by the platoon and by NCIS. Details of Dille's journal were included in the NCIS investigation files. The description of Gallagher's lack of formal sniper training comes from his Navy records and from an NCIS interview with a Marine official. Details of Gallagher's drug use come from medical records showing years of prescriptions and texts between Gallagher and several other SEALs that were seized by NCIS. The platoon's observations of possible drug use come from NCIS interviews with Vriens, Dille, Arrington, and Miller as well as author interviews with SEALs. In addition, Gallagher's wife seemed to acknowledge his drug use in at least one text message she sent to him in July 2018. Gallagher's belief that Dalton Tolbert and Dylan Dille were starting a mutiny comes from Gallagher's statement on the *Mike Drop* podcast. Reports of petty theft by Gallagher come from several SEALs' accounts to NCIS, author interviews with four SEALs, and trial testimony by Dylan Dille. The account that Gallagher got Ivan Villanueva to ask his mom to buy him tramadol in Mexico comes from author interviews with three SEALs, as well as the text conversations between the two men. Evidence of Gallagher's use of Provigil comes from author interviews with three SEALs. Evidence of Gallagher's testosterone use comes from a text saying he can't get "vitamin x" and is wasting away, as well as author interviews with four SEALs, and photos showing the testosterone Gallagher asked interpreters to buy for him in Iraq. The accounts of his abuse of tramadol come from author interviews with four SEALs. The account of Josh Vriens seeing a girl shot, then hearing from Joe Arrington that Gallagher had shot the girl, comes from Vriens's interview with NCIS and his trial testimony. Joe Arrington did not mention the death of the girl in NCIS interviews and did not testify at Gallagher's trial. Gallagher denied killing the girl by pleading not guilty, and in multiple public statements after the trial has said he did not shoot any civilians in Iraq, including the old man Dille and Tolbert claimed they saw killed and the girl Vriens claimed he saw killed.

CHAPTER 8: BAD TARGETS

Accounts of Gallagher growing increasingly erratic, going on "gun runs," and ordering junior SEALs to fire rockets into neighborhoods come from NCIS interviews with Craig Miller and Dylan Dille, author interviews with three SEALs, and Tom MacNeil's proffer to the Navy. Details of the confrontation between Joe Arrington and Gallagher come from interviews conducted by NCIS agents in 2018 with the following SEALs: Craig Miller, Dylan Dille, Dalton Tolbert, Joe Arrington, and Tom MacNeil. Additional details come from author interviews with SEALs. The timing of the incident was determined by text messages sent by Gallagher that were on his phone when it was seized by NCIS. Details of the Switchblade incident that killed several civilians come from an NCIS interview with Josh Vriens. Additional details of both episodes come from author interviews with two SEALs who were there. Details of Gallagher's attempts to leave the deployment early come from interviews with SEALs, the MacNeil proffer, and text messages sent by Gallagher during that time, which were later found by NCIS on his phone.

CHAPTER 9: LOYALTY

Gallagher's conversations with Master Chief Brian Alazzawi come from interviews NCIS agents conducted in 2018 and author interviews. Gallagher's statement to Christian Mullan about breaking someone's nose comes from text messages seized by NCIS and interviews with SEALs who spoke to Mullan. Gallagher's account of the meeting in the high bay and his statements come from an interview on the *Mike Drop* podcast. Other details of the meeting are from author and NCIS interviews. Gallagher's statement "I have shit on all of you . . . if you take me down, I will take all of you down" comes from trial testimony by Craig Miller and Tom MacNeil, who witnessed the statement. Details of the meeting between Miller, Alazzawi, and Portier after Miller told Alazzawi about the stabbing come from author interviews with two SEALs. Details of Gallagher's activities after deployment in the fall of 2017 are based on records and text messages obtained by NCIS. Descriptions of Gallagher seeking treatment that fall for traumatic brain injury come from his text messages and medical records. Those records include his summary of the blast he said may have caused the injury. Author interviews with three SEALs suggested that Gallagher had not mentioned the blast during deployment. Descriptions and photos of the Alpha plaque and its mistakes come from Sewing Circle texts included in NCIS investigative files. The description of the January meeting between Robert Breisch and Miller comes from NCIS interviews of both men and additional reporting by the author. Breisch confirmed to NCIS that he met with SEALs from Alpha more than once before formally reporting Gallagher to NCIS but said they did not discuss criminal misconduct. Breisch did not respond to requests to be interviewed for this book. He was never charged with any misconduct. Gallagher's admission to Brian Alazzawi that the captive had reached for his gun and Gallagher had "fucked him up" comes from Alazzawi's statement to NCIS. The description of the meeting in the Donnell Classroom comes from NCIS interviews with Alazzawi, Breisch, Miller, Dille, Scott, and Vriens. Regarding Robert Breisch's apparent failure to report Gallagher, Breisch told NCIS he first heard about SEALs taking photos with the dead captive shortly after they were taken in May 2017 but was unaware of any other criminal activity until April 2018. However, Craig Miller and Brian Alazzawi both testified that they told him about Gallagher's other crimes in the fall of 2017. Several other SEALs told NCIS that Breisch was also informed of the killings during a meeting in March 2018. The description of the meeting where Breisch failed to report the crime comes from an NCIS interview with Brian Alazzawi, the MacNeil proffer, and interviews with two SEALs. The date and wording of the email sent by Breisch to report the crime come from the original email, included in NCIS files. Details on the horrifying My Lai episode come from Joseph Goldstein, Burke Marshall, and Jack Schwartz, *The My Lai Massacre and Its Cover-Up: Beyond the*

Reach of Law? (New York: Free Press, 1976), and "G.I.'s, in Pincer Move, Kill 128 in a Daylong Battle," *The New York Times*, March 17, 1968. The description of Miller's conversation with Brian Ferguson comes from NCIS notes and author interviews.

CHAPTER 10: SPECIAL AGENTS

The details of conversations SEALs had with NCIS Special Agent Joe Warpinski come from videos of those interviews produced by NCIS. The description of Gallagher believing he could beat the accusations unless there was hard evidence comes from statements Dylan Dille made to NCIS agents in 2018. Descriptions of NCIS views of the development of the case come from interviews with Navy personnel. Details on how and when Gallagher learned about the case come from text messages recovered from his cellphone seized by NCIS. Gallagher's possession of Brian Ferguson's contact information comes from text messages recovered from his cellphone, later seized by NCIS. Background on Brian Ferguson comes from articles by the University of Texas *Daily Texan* as well as interviews with people familiar with him. The description that Ferguson reached out to most of the platoon and warned them about the risks of talking to NCIS comes from author interviews with four SEALs, a review of text messages sent to them by Ferguson, and the list of SEALs Ferguson eventually represented. Descriptions of Gallagher walking past Vriens's house come from NCIS reports and interviews with SEALs. Gallagher's statements about the SEALs at Green Team come from text messages recovered from his cellphone, later seized by NCIS. The account of the investigation of the crime scenes in Mosul comes from an Army Criminal Investigative Division report included in the NCIS files. The account of the search of Gallagher's house comes from photos and a report generated by NCIS. The account of Warpinski questioning a young sailor about stolen grenades comes from a court brief from *United States v. Aaron A. Booker*. The description of the search of Gallagher's operator box comes from several photos taken by NCIS. Descriptions of the texts

Gallagher sent taking credit for the killing of the prisoner come from NCIS reports on the contents of his seized cellphone. The assertion that Gallagher and Portier told SEALs to delete the photos from May 3, 2017, comes from the testimony of T. C. Byrne at trial, author interviews with three SEALs, and a proffer Tom MacNeil submitted to the Navy. In an interview with *The Shawn Ryan Show* in December 2020, Gallagher acknowledged that he told SEALs to delete the photos. Descriptions of Andrew Arrabito come from the Half Face Blades website and Arrabito's Instagram account. Arrabito's text conversations with Gallagher were included in Gallagher's phone, later seized by NCIS. The description of the meeting between Vice Admiral Tim Symanski, Rear Admiral Collin Green, and Captain Matt Rosenbloom comes from interviews with two SEAL sources.

CHAPTER 11: IMMUNITY

Information on Joe Warpinski's conversations with prosecutors comes from NCIS reports and interviews with Navy personnel. The translation of the Al Iraqiya video is by *The New York Times*.

Abbas al-Jubouri's interview comes from a summary in NCIS files. Details of the DNA evidence come from NCIS reports and reports by an outside lab hired by the Navy. The account of the Navy SEAL shooting a farmer in Marjah district, Helmand Province, Afghanistan, in February 2010 comes from three sources: the NCIS summary of the FBI interview with John Rindt and author interviews with two soldiers from 3rd Special Forces Operational Detachment Alpha 3121 and Advanced Operational Base 1220. The news article reporting Gallagher was under investigation for the killing is Andrew Dyer, "Navy SEAL Charged with Iraq War Crimes Also Under Investigation in Death of Afghan Civilian in 2010," *The San Diego Union-Tribune*, April 23, 2018. Evidence of Gallagher's presence in the Marjah district during the same time comes from his Navy performance evaluation, written a short time later by Robert Breisch, which was included in the NCIS files. Details on Brian Ferguson representing more SEALs come from letters of representation contained in the NCIS files. Details of Ferguson's texts with Miller are in the NCIS files, as is an account of Ferguson's phone conversation with Josh Vriens. Criminal charges against Jake Portier and a letter notifying Robert Breisch he was under criminal investigation were publicly reported by *Navy Times*.

CHAPTER 12: ANDREA'S WAR

Details of what Andrea Gallagher was wearing and what she said during her initial television interview are based on videos of that interview, which aired on *Fox & Friends*, December 22, 2018. Andrea Gallagher's background as a photographer and brand consultant comes from her personal business websites. The warning to Warpinski by Josh Vriens of a "shadow campaign" was included in NCIS files. Bernard Kerik's description of Alpha as "mean girls" comes from his article "The Persecution of Navy Special Warfare Operator Edward Gallagher," *Newsmax*, December 3, 2018. Statements about giving Gallagher a medal for killing ISIS were made on the One American News Network on January 30, 2019. Descriptions of the murder charge against Army Special Forces Major Matt Golsteyn come from Helene Cooper, Michael Tackett, and Taimoor Shah, "Twist in Green Beret's Extraordinary Story: Trump's Intervention After Murder Charges," *The New York Times*, December 16, 2018. Fox host Brian Kilmeade interviewed Sean Gallagher and said, "Isn't the goal to kill ISIS?" on *Fox & Friends* on February 8, 2019. Andrea called reporting by *The San Diego Union-Tribune*'s Andrew Dyer "salacious clickbait" on her Facebook page on January 30, 2019. The amount of money the Gallagher family earned from donations was publicly reported by the family. Andrea Gallagher appeared with the Lorance and Golsteyn families on *Fox & Friends*, December 22, 2018. Sean Gallagher appealed directly to the president in an op-ed article, "Plea from a Navy SEAL's Brother: Mr. President, the System Is Broken and We Need Your Help to Fix It," Foxnews.com, February 7, 2019. Duncan Hunter described meeting with Gallagher on *The Brian Kilmeade Show*, Fox News Radio, April 3, 2019. The account of Navy Secretary Richard Spencer's conversations with the president and Navy leaders about Edward Gallagher comes from interviews with Navy officials familiar with the exchanges. The account of Donald Trump wearing a high school uniform that did not belong to him comes from a 2016 author interview with the owner of that uniform, Mike Scadron. Trump told crowds that waterboarding wasn't good enough at a rally at Ohio University, Eastern, June 29, 2016. Trump vowed to "knock the hell out of ISIS" at a rally in South Carolina, February 17, 2016. Trump tweeted about Gallagher's release from the brig March 30, 2019. Eric Trump and Donald Trump Jr. tweeted about Gallagher's release April 3, 2019. Former SEAL Rob O'Neill criticized Alpha platoon in an appearance on *Fox Nation Deep Dive,* February 26, 2019. Craig Miller was given a medal for saving a suicidal woman on the Coronado Bridge. The account of the rescue comes from that citation and author interviews. Accounts of Trump considering a pardon for Edward Gallagher were first reported by the author in *The New York Times,* May 18, 2019. Efforts by Navy officials to dissuade the president come from author interviews with people who were present. The account of leaks in the Gallagher case and the investigation that followed comes from court proceedings, author interviews with Navy officials, and a time line created by Commander Chris Czaplak that was obtained by the author.

CHAPTER 13: A JURY OF PEERS

Accounts of the trial come from the observations of the author, who was present, and from transcripts of the trial. Background on Brian John comes from interviews with people familiar with him. Background on Timothy Parlatore comes from a review of Navy records conducted by NCIS as well as from work histories Parlatore posted online. Parlatore's statement that the mob is dead comes from the article "Mob's Bloody Heyday Is Gone, but Violence Is Not," Associated Press, August 16, 2016. Parlatore's connection to Pete Hegseth and Bernard Kerik comes from author communication with Parlatore. The details of Hegseth's marriages come from Tom Scheck, "Words and Deeds Out of Alignment for Potential Cabinet Appointment and Fox News Personality," *American Public Media*, March 27, 2018. The views of the jury come from author interviews with two jury members. The revelation that one of the jurors gave a thousand dollars to Gallagher's defense fund comes from statements that juror made to several SEALs during a training. Details of the juror's relationship with Gallagher and Gallagher's discussion of them with his legal team come from statements Gallagher made on *The Shawn Ryan Show*, December 2020. The account of Bruce Cutler being "in-house counsel" for the mob comes from Arnold H. Lubasch, "Judge Disqualifies Gotti's Lawyer from Representing Him at Trial," *The New York Times*, July 27, 1991.

CHAPTER 14: THE WOODSHED

Accounts of Corey Scott's testimony come from audio and transcripts of the trial. Details of Gallagher's legal team meeting with Scott before trial and Parlatore telling Gallagher "We got 'em!" come from an interview Timothy Parlatore gave that was published in Yaron Steinbuch, "Navy SEAL Acquitted of ISIS Murder Says Media Tried to Frame Him," *New York Post*, July 3, 2019, as well as other public statements by Parlatore and Marc Mukasey acknowledging the meetings. Jeff Pietrzyk's assumption that Scott had been woodshedded comes from interviews with Navy lawyers familiar with Pietrzyk's thinking. Scott declined multiple requests to be interviewed for this book.

CHAPTER 15: THE FIGHTER

The identity of Moataz Mohamed Abdullah was found through careful reporting by the Iraqi news staff of *The New York Times*, and while his family is convinced he was the victim in the case against Gallagher, it is not absolutely certain. There is a competing claim by another family. Moataz was identified by a reporter hired by *The New York Times* who in the fall of 2019 canvassed the neighborhood of Mosul where the fighter was from. The staff was able to find Mohamed Salim and interviewed him on multiple occasions. He had identified his son independently as the victim before the *Times* contacted him. Mr. Salim provided information on the age of the victim, when he joined ISIS, where he was from, and how his family reacted when he joined ISIS. Mohamed provided more than a dozen photos of his son that were then compared to the photos of the stabbing victim. In addition to a general resemblance, the photos show a specific detail that Moataz and the victim had in common: A few months before joining ISIS, Moataz was injured in a blast and his right earlobe was taken off by shrapnel. Photos of both the victim and Moataz show this injury. In the fall of 2020, based on a name provided by an unnamed Iraqi security official, National Public Radio identified the victim as a different teenager, Khaled Jamal Abdullah, from a town thirty miles south of Mosul. Photo analysis of both men did not provide a conclusive match. The Navy did not respond to requests to share DNA evidence that might have provided a definitive answer.

CHAPTER 16: THE VERDICT

Accounts of testimony in court come from author observations and court transcripts. Accounts of decisions by the prosecution not to call witnesses come from author interviews with Navy officials and civilian lawyers familiar with the discussions. Details of Gio Kirylo's communications with Gallagher before trial and his fear of talking to NCIS come from NCIS notes on the communications, based on Gallagher's phone records. Details about Kirylo visiting Gallagher before trial come from Kirylo's testimony and NCIS records. The list of evidence barred from trial, including Brian Alazzawi's claim that Gallagher confessed that he had killed the captive, comes from official Navy court transcripts of the hearings where that evidence was discussed. Accounts of the inside of the jury room come from author interviews with two jurors. The description of the rooftop meeting by members of Alpha comes from author interviews with multiple SEALs.

CHAPTER 17: FRAG RADIUS

Deliberations among top Navy officials about their response to Gallagher come from author interviews with some of the officials involved. Gallagher's post-conviction activities, including his insults of Navy officials, come from posts on his Instagram account and author interviews with SEALs. The decision to close several criminal cases in response to the Gallagher case comes from author interviews with Navy legal personnel. The tally of the lost pension payouts Gallagher faced through a demotion comes from a filing by his legal team. Pete Hegseth announced "imminent action" on Gallagher's case on *Fox & Friends*, November 17, 2019. The appearance at a closed-door fundraiser of two pardoned soldiers, Clint Lorance and Matt Golsteyn, was first reported in the *Miami Herald*, December 9, 2019. Timothy Parlatore appeared on *Fox & Friends* to rebuke the Navy's decision to take Gallagher's Trident on November 21, 2019. Golsteyn's identity as the officer in charge of the Special Forces team that witnessed a Navy SEAL sniper kill a farmer in Afghanistan in 2010 comes from author interviews with two soldiers in the team. Trump tweeted that the Navy would not take Gallagher's Trident on November 21, 2019. Navy Secretary Richard Spencer was removed from his job November 24, 2019.

CHAPTER 18: FROGMEN

The description of Gallagher attending a dinner at Mar-a-Lago on December 22, 2019, comes from his Instagram account and the public posts of other guests who were there. The detail that Gallagher had flown a Trump flag on operations in Mosul comes from interviews with two SEALs. Details of Gallagher's life after retirement come from posts on his Instagram account. His belief that his acquittal was the result of divine intervention and details about ibogaine therapy giving him a feeling of peace come from statements he made on *The Shawn Ryan Show*. The account of the meeting between Josh Vriens and Corey Scott comes from an author interview with Vriens. The details of the SEALs represented by Brian Ferguson who tried to contact other SEALs come from author interviews with Dille, Vriens, and other SEALs. The details of the case study presentations the Navy SEALs began presenting on the Gallagher court-martial to all lead petty officers come from author interviews with Navy SEALs.

INDEX

About the Author

David Philipps is a national correspondent for *The New York Times*, where he has sought to write about military and veterans from the ground up. His first job was delivering the *Colorado Springs Gazette Telegraph* by bicycle, and he has been in the news business ever since. His articles have appeared in the *Los Angeles Times*, the *Chicago Tribune*, *The Philadelphia Inquirer*, and *The Seattle Times*, among other publications. His military coverage won the Pulitzer Prize for national reporting, and he was twice named a Pulitzer finalist, for local reporting and for breaking news. He lives in Colorado Springs, Colorado, with his family.

Twitter: @David_Philipps

About the Type

This book was set in Caslon, a typeface first designed in 1722 by William Caslon (1692–1766). Its widespread use by most English printers in the early eighteenth century soon supplanted the Dutch typefaces that had formerly prevailed. The roman is considered a "workhorse" typeface due to its pleasant, open appearance, while the italic is exceedingly decorative.